RINGO

RINGO

A FAB LIFE

Tom Doyle

new modern

new modern

First published in the UK in 2025 by New Modern
An imprint of Putman Publishing
Mermaid House, Puddle Dock, Blackfriars, London, EC4V 3DB

@newmodernbooks
@newmodernbooks

Hardback ISBN: 978-1-917923-13-2
eBook ISBN: 978-1-917923-14-9

A CIP catalogue record for this book is available in the British Library.

Publishing and editorial: Pete Selby and James Lilford
Typesetting: Marie Doherty

1 3 5 7 9 10 8 6 4 2

New Modern is an imprint of Putman Publishing
www.newmodernbooks.co.uk
www.putmanpublishing.co.uk

MIX
Paper | Supporting
responsible forestry
FSC
www.fsc.org   FSC® C018072

Printed and bound in Great Britain by Clays Ltd, Elcograf S.p.A.

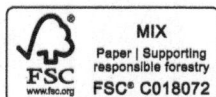

To the memory of Derek Hood,
drummer extraordinaire, who was always handy
with, as he put it, 'a big, flappy Ringo roll'

CONTENTS

CONTENTS

CONTENTS

1

SCREEN TO SCREEN, FACE TO FACE

Conversations with Ringo, 2024 and 2010

The video call flashed into life and there he was.

'Morning, Tom!'

I don't know quite why I did it. But probably through some weird mixture of nerves and anticipation, I greeted him with an involuntary and very Scottish, 'r's-rolling cry of 'Rrrrrrrringo! How you doing, man?'

'I'm grrrrrrreat!' he echoed back with a laugh, sounding like Tony the Tiger with an exaggerated Scouse burr.

It was Tuesday, 12 November 2024, 6 p.m. in my loft room in north London (where I'd kicked the mess into the corners and out of shot ahead of the call), 10 a.m. in Los Angeles where Ringo Starr sat in his Roccabella West home studio. He looked trim and dapper: gold-rimmed, gradient-lensed shades, dark brown-dyed beard and side-parted hair; black Teddy Boy-styled jacket with a rocker-popped, white-trimmed collar and a purple camo T-shirt matched with a silver peace symbol pendant.

On the wall behind his head were two of his self-created art pieces: a large, psychedelically spin-painted star and one of his digital doodles that he enjoyed messing around with on his laptop while on tour. This one, which he'd created in 2005 and titled *OOO Man Two*, was a cartoonish pop-art close-up of a bespectacled and moon-eyed bloke whose expression appeared to be frozen somewhere between surprise and terror.

On either side of Ringo hung assorted items of memorabilia from his long and head-spinning career. A vintage black Gibson SG electric guitar adorned with silver stars. A circular clock featuring the image of himself and his fellow Fabs as seen on the cover of 2013 Beatles compilation *On Air – Live at the BBC Volume 2*. One highly significant frame contained an original ticket for his first official gig in 'The Fabulous Beatles Band': Saturday, 18 August 1962, at an 'After Show Dance' on the Wirral, held by the Port Sunlight Horticultural Society.

It may have been bright and early on his side of the world, but his demeanour was chipper. At the age of 84, at least on today's evidence, he remained irrepressibly jovial. It was also noticeable that, unlike some other longtime British rock star residents of LA, there was very little Californian corruption of his seemingly indelible Liverpool accent, other than the word 'and' twanged to 'end'.

We were talking via Zoom for a *MOJO* magazine feature mainly celebrating the fact that, a mere five-and-half decades after his Nashville-recorded, second post-Beatles solo album, *Beaucoups of Blues*, Ringo was set to release a quickly recorded, surprise follow-up country album. His last full album had been 2019's *What's My Name* (no question mark) and since then he'd committed to only releasing a series of EPs.

Look Up, produced and largely written by T Bone Burnett, who'd known Starr since the '70s, had rapidly expanded from another planned EP into a full album. In fact, the record's swift realisation had taken Starr aback too.

'Oh, it was an absolute surprise to me,' he marvelled, explaining that he'd recorded his drum and vocal contributions to the album at home in a mere handful of takes. 'I just went into that room right there,' he said, gesturing to the left towards his studio live room, 'and played drums. In an hour, we'd done seven songs.'

'I sat about five feet from him,' Burnett told me the week before. 'He would do two takes and then, "Next song!".' The producer, a Beatles fan since his youth, was thrilled during the session to learn that Starr was playing the same pair of hi-hat cymbals he'd used on the Beatles' earth-quaking appearance on *The Ed Sullivan Show* in 1964. Burnett had since re-watched that and other early Beatle performances and been struck by the poetic thought that 'those girls screaming were harmonising with his hi-hat. Ringo put the electricity into them. He was that wild energy that set everybody off.'

~

It was clear that, even as an octogenarian, Ringo still liked to do everything at pace. Especially his interviews. Similar to my experiences of talking to Paul McCartney, Starr was not *entirely* jaded by the notion of talking to a writer. But there were strict (and rigorously adhered to) time limits placed on interview lengths by both. Paul's was half an hour. Ringo's was twenty minutes.

Knowing this, I'd worked for two whole days on my notes for our chat. Then, once we got going, the challenge was to get through as many topics as possible before, as with a contestant on a game show, the buzzer sounded. Throughout, Starr's amiable US publicist Elizabeth Freund silently listened in on our conversation. Thankfully, in these constrained circumstances, Ringo's responses tended to be short, honest and to the point, and entirely free of minutes-devouring digressions or waffle.

I asked him about the lifelong appeal of country music for him, which ran from his childhood idolisation of singing cowboy Gene Autry, through many of his vocal and song contributions to the Beatles, and now, on into his eighties. It's heavily emotional music, I pointed out...

'Well, yeah, I'm an emotional guy,' he said, before turning strangely self-conscious. 'I can't wait for those headlines,' he boomed with laughter. 'But I am in a way...'

'I think, y'know, maybe, it suits his personality,' McCartney reckoned of Starr's love for – and compatibility with – country. 'He's a very sincere, straightforward guy and I think that's the sort of theme behind a lot of country music.'

Perhaps for that reason, *Look Up* was Ringo's best album in years, not least because Burnett had tastefully matched his vocal performances with simpatico modern country foils (Larkin Poe, Molly Tuttle, Billy Strings) and, lyrically, aimed to get inside Starr's head.

'I was trying to write in his voice and into his aesthetic,' Burnett said. 'I just wanted to do something that was true to him.' The producer, previously responsible for a series of top-quality late-career records by Roy Orbison,

Robert Plant/Alison Krauss and Elton John/Leon Russell, felt that Starr still had a solid, credible album left in him.

'He was always doing light-hearted things,' he gently noted. 'He never did, like, serious music, really. With this record, I wanted to take him as seriously as I thought he should be taken. As a musician, as a singer, as an artist.'

Ahead of the project, Burnett was inspired by a chance hearing, on Sirius XM Radio's The Beatles Channel, of Ringo's crooning rendition of Harry Nilsson's 'Easy for Me', from Starr's 1974's *Goodnight Vienna* LP. 'I thought, *Man, this cat…*' he sighed. 'Nobody has talked about what a beautiful singer he is.'

Starr, meanwhile, praised Burnett's attention to detail in terms of finding the right keys for his vocals, while pointing out that often people sent him prospective songs that were way beyond his natural range.

'They're in F demented,' he quipped, Ringoishly. 'Y'know, I'd have to lose my legs to reach that high. But these are all, like, the right key. They're really great.'

He admitted, however, that, in his advanced years, maintaining a functioning singing voice on tour with his All-Starr Band could sometimes be a challenge.

'Well, it gets worn out very fast. I mean, I can get through the show. I have a singing tape that a guy gave me in 1989 and I still have it. I put that on.' He sang up and down a scale to demonstrate: 'No, no, no, no!' Then, he hit a high note. '*Weeeee!*'

In *Look Up*'s closing track, 'Thankful', Starr's sole writing contribution to the album (with collaborator Bruce Sugar), Ringo had produced what T Bone Burnett reckoned to be 'the most personal song he's ever done'. In its lyrics, he referred to troubled times in the past when he'd lost sight of what mattered in his life, before declaring that love for his wife of forty-three years, former model/film star Barbara Bach, had made him a better man. He even happily reported that it was a beautiful day in California as he wrote the song's words.

A longtime habitué of Los Angeles, having lived in the city on and off since 1973, Starr became a permanent resident there in 2014 after selling up his last home in England – Rydinghurst in Surrey. For someone who'd grown up in wartime and post-war Liverpool, California must have seemed like paradise to him. But when the Beatles first came to the US in 1964, he'd initially fancied living in New York.

'Then we went on tours around,' he explained, 'and we'd come to LA. And so it was like, New York? Yeah. (*Having second thoughts*). Uh, maybe LA… New York! Maybe LA. (*Decisively*) L… A! I just loved the atmosphere. I loved the light. I loved the heat.'

Not that Ringo ever felt the urge to grab a surfboard and become a beach boy.

'It took me seven years to go to the ocean,' he beamed. 'A limo took me down to the Pacific Coast Highway. I got out the car, walked across the beach, put my feet in the water, turned around, walked back to the car and went for lunch.'

It was a funny yarn that was at the same time indicative of his generally breezy approach to life. 'I love that there's no big plans. It's just like you go with the flow, and the flow is good, y'know.'

By the time we were nearing the crucial twenty-minute cut-off point, we'd managed to zip through everything from his early influences – from Gene Vincent to Marvin Gaye to Lightnin' Hopkins (whose music had inspired him to consider emigrating to Texas in his early twenties) – to his 'Starr Time' singing turns with his late-'50s/early-'60s band Rory Storm and the Hurricanes, and the fateful day when Brian Epstein knocked on his front door, asking him to join the Beatles for a lunchtime session at the Cavern. We moved through his writing of songs such as 'Don't Pass Me By' and 'Octopus's Garden', on to his first solo albums, *Sentimental Journey* and *Beaucoups of Blues*. Then, we circled back to his sickly boyhood – stuck in hospital for two years in total, after bouts of peritonitis and tuberculosis – and to the first time, as a left-hander, he sat down at a right-handed drum kit, serendipitously informing his unique playing style.

Finally, we projected forwards into the future with his upcoming touring plans. As we sailed over our allotted time, Starr was caught up in an anecdote about when, post his (and Bach's) 1988 rehab treatment in Arizona, he had, the following year, put together the first line-up of his All-Starr Band and returned to touring with a group of friends that included his close drumming buddy Jim Keltner (John Lennon, Bob Dylan), Joe Walsh of the then-defunct Eagles, and

Rick Danko and Levon Helm of the Band. Ringo remembered being genuinely surprised when everyone he called up instantly accepted the gig.

'I just went through my phone book,' he said. 'Oh, Joe Walsh. "Yeah." Levon. "Yeah." Rick. "Yeah." Y'know... Dr John. Well, it was a bit interesting with him. I was in Monte Carlo and I called him, and we had a friend helping us, and after the phone call, I said, "I don't think he wants to be in the band."'

The go-between later told Starr he'd received a call from Dr John, who was equally convinced that, by the end of their conversation, Ringo didn't want him involved. The problem, it transpired, had been a miscommunication, due to the pair's clashing Liverpool/New Orleans accents.

'He was difficult sometimes to understand,' Ringo laughed, as we broke into our twenty-second minute. Of course, I cheekily pushed for another question before Elizabeth Freund politely cut me off: 'I'm so sorry, but we're over time.'

Bzzzzzzzzzz.

'OK, no worries,' I said.

'Anyway, brother,' said Ringo. 'Great talking to you. And ... remember ... peace and love.'

His enthusiasm was infectious. It was impossible not to flash the peace and love sign back at him. Both hands.

~

I'd met Ringo once before, face to face.

The date was 12 April 2010, a Monday. It was just after 4 p.m., in the ground-floor boardroom of the Apple Records headquarters, situated in a townhouse discreetly tucked away in Ovington Square, Knightsbridge. As a black-and-white image of Starr and his three former Beatles bandmates, in their last fully functional year of 1969, stared down from the wall behind him, the real, modern-day Ringo sat opposite me across the table, sipped bottled water and turned to my recorder.

Dressed down but well-groomed (in black T-shirt, suit jacket and jeans), diminutive (5 foot 6) and impressively svelte for his then-sixty-nine years, he was in London to talk about his sixteenth solo album in four decades.

6

He'd named it *Y Not*, in flippant response to anticipated queries as to why – what with all his money and fame – he had even bothered making another record.

Similarly, I was there to chat to him for *MOJO*, in an encounter that lasted all of seventeen highly entertaining minutes, again overseen by Elizabeth Freund, her eye on the clock. (The arrangement had been for us to speak for the usual twenty minutes, but there was an air of urgency, as he was running behind schedule.)

At this point, Starr had earned something of a reputation as a curmudgeon, not least because of his October 2008 video announcement on his website that he was henceforth refusing to respond to any further fan mail, including requests for autographs. But on this day, he was upbeat, mischievous and frank.

Even in this short space of time, I caught flashes of various Ringos. Cheeky chappie. Comedy grump. Characterful and inventive musician with a deep understanding of his drumming craft. Surprisingly dogged love-and-peacenik. Devoted practitioner of Transcendental Meditation. Happily still-touring bandleader (even then past typical retirement age).

During that conversation, he became even more animated when you veered off the expected topical paths, away from well-worn lines of enquiry. Despite his Californian lifestyle, salty, working-class Richy Starkey from the Dingle was still very much in evidence behind the ever-present sunglasses and tanned exterior – particularly when, around our sixteenth minute, I asked him to tell me something he'd never told an interviewer before.

'Fuck off!' he mock-snapped, grinning.

'What?' I said. 'You've never told an interviewer to fuck off before?'

'I have, actually,' he laughed. 'But I'm not gonna tell you nothing … and if I've got something really special to tell someone, I'm gonna tell *you*.'

This front of playful argumentativeness sometimes gave way to glimpses of the self-doubt that had apparently plagued him on and off down the years. Like McCartney, Ringo remained a working musician to his bones. But, before this album, he'd never been a producer of his own records.

'I didn't have the courage, maybe, to, like *produce*,' he confessed.

As to his decision to now oversee his recording process, Starr shrugged. 'It's just how it was. There was no big masterplan: "I'm waiting". The solo records

I started with George Martin and then Richard Perry and Don Was. I just left it in their hands actually. This one I just started, and it was going well, and I knew what I wanted, and I had a lot of good friends coming over … musicians to play and help out. Then I thought, *Well, I'm going to just finish this and, finally, put my stamp on it.*

'For me, listening to my record,' he added with a wry chuckle, as he briefly pondered what Ringo's 'stamp' represented, 'there's a lot of space and there's not a lot of harmony.' It was true. Starr's first self-production, reflecting his unfussy nature, was characterised by a stripped-back rock sound and no extraneous layers of backing vocals.

Still, as a former Beatle, he was a magnet for fellow musos, as evidenced by the procession of different players through his home studio during the making of *Y Not*: the likes of his good pal (and, since 2008, with his marriage to Marjorie Bach) brother-in-law Joe Walsh, former Tom Petty and the Heartbreakers keyboard player Benmont Tench, one-time Eurythmic Dave Stewart... Beatles nuts all.

I wondered whether being the Fab in the room was ever noticeably off-putting for these former teenage fans-turned-seasoned players. Ringo reckoned it wasn't, stressing that his approach to directing the sessions was altogether laid back, spontaneous and old-school. 'I didn't do charts or anything. "Well, you can play, can't you? *Bom bom bom.* Get on with it." So, that's how it worked out. I mean, the joke is, if you were passing our house in LA, you're on the record.'

Often, it seemed, from Los Angeles, Starr's thoughts tended to wander back in the direction of his hometown in north-west England. This latest album featured the second instalment of his intended autobiography-in-song, begun in 2008 with the title track of his previous album, *Liverpool 8* (referring to L8, the postcode district containing his childhood haunts of Toxteth and the Dingle), wherein he'd given a bluff, if misty-eyed and hopefully anthemic account of the years 1956 to 1965. The second part was the altogether darker 'The Other Side of Liverpool', depicting a dank, grey 1950s Merseyside involving factory work, public baths and playing skiffle gigs in return for warm ale.

Ringo wasn't sure if growing older was making him more nostalgic.

'I don't know ... I think the song just came naturally because of "Liverpool 8". That was from, y'know, "I was in a factory and then I was at Shea Stadium." In a song, in two lines, you can say eight paragraphs.'

The Beatles had, of course, helped to romanticise Liverpool as a place. In 'The Other Side of Liverpool', it sounded as if Ringo was trying to puncture that myth.

'Well, I was born there and, yeah, the holidays went on forever and it was always sunny ... and the streets in Liverpool 8 were all *avenues*. But I've been back since and they're really not. There was another side of Liverpool that I lived in and that's what I tried to express.'

Interestingly, unlike many of his rock star peers who'd penned their memoirs (or had them ghosted), he insisted he'd never write an actual autobiography.

'No, that's the point of these songs. I was asked to write an autobiography. I don't really want to write a book because you only want to hear about 1962 to 1970. You're not really interested in my growing up. I don't believe that. So I can put it in a song a lot easier – and it's a lot less painful, I think.'

In his mind, his autobiography would be a forbiddingly hefty proposition.

'There'd be nine volumes before I got to the Beatles,' he smiled, 'and fifteen after. So it would go on forever.'

One highly notable guest on *Y Not* was Paul McCartney. It was the first time since 1997, and Ringo's fair-to-middling 1998-released *Vertical Man* LP, that McCartney had stepped back into the studio to play on one of Starr's solo records.

Back in 1970, their friendship had suffered a severe dent in the grim days of the Beatles' breakup, especially after Starr turned up on McCartney's doorstep in St John's Wood at the end of March that year. He had been sent by the others as the affable emissary to deliver a letter informing Paul they'd all instructed EMI to delay the release of his *McCartney* solo album to give the upcoming *Let It Be* some retail breathing space.

McCartney angrily refused to compromise, threw Starr out of his house and ended up releasing his own record in the middle of April, forcing *Let It*

Be's release to be pushed back to May. But even after the gnarly Beatles court battle of 1971, where McCartney successfully won the right to have a receiver brought in to oversee the band's financial affairs, his and Ringo's friendship had been repaired quickly. The drummer initially remained closer to Harrison and Lennon during the early '70s, in the three's misguided alliance with their appointed manager, the McCartney-hated Allen Klein. But Paul had then performed on two tracks – and co-written one (with Linda), the regretful, if scarf-waving pop of 'Six O'Clock' – on Ringo's standout, self-titled album of 1973. It had, in fact, featured all four Beatles together on vinyl for the first time since their split, although, tantalisingly, not all on the same tracks.

Now, there was a certain poignancy to hearing the two surviving Beatles harmonising together, their voices audibly aged, on 'Walk with You' from *Y Not*, a song that was evidently about friendship. In terms of his relationship with Paul, Ringo insisted, surprisingly, that it was in better shape than when they'd worked together intensively in the '60s.

'Well, the friendship has grown over the years because *we* have. Y'know, we're not living with each other, and he has his life, and I have mine. But if we're in the same country and hopefully the same town, we say, "Hi".' I went to see him here [at the O2 in London] in December [2009]. It was great. It was like a family affair.'

McCartney's long-time touring drummer, Abe Laboriel Jr, is a powerful and impressively adaptable player. But did Ringo ever watch him performing old Beatles songs and think to himself, *He's not getting that pattern right?*

'No, I never do,' he grinned. 'Abe does really good. I played with them in New York. We did a TM show [a Transcendental Meditation benefit for the David Lynch Foundation at Radio City Music Hall in April '09] and I got up and I sang "…Little Help…" with Paul's band. So, it's not like we won't play together. It's just that, y'know, I'm not going on tour with him.'

I pointed out that Paul had a slightly odd habit of referring to the Beatles in the third person – for instance, 'They were the greatest little rock band going' – as if to divorce himself from the phenomenon and maintain his sanity. Ringo could relate.

'Well, I think we've put it in its place now … *they* … y'know … *the Beatles* were fab,' he laughed.

When it came to the ongoing reissue programme of the Beatles' records, Ringo was a fan of the remastering – and remixing, care of Giles Martin – process that, in the manner of painstaking art restoration, revealed more of the details of their recordings as time passed.

'What I like,' he pointed out, brightly, 'from the *Love* [2006 'mashup' remix] album on, really, is they've actually now found a way to bring the drums up. You can really hear the drums! And people are saying, "Ooh God, he *can* play."'

Everyone could now clearly hear how he drove that band and those songs on…

'And that was what was happening. But they didn't have the capacity to put it on the record in those days. You never heard a bass drum.

'You heard *doof-doof-doof-doof…*' he added, thumping out a muffled 4/4 beat on the Apple boardroom table. 'Then, with stereo, we got a bit better. And, now, the way they can clean up the tracks is incredible. And I don't think it detracts at all. Y'know, there's some aficionados out there [*affects a plummy tone*] "Oh, I like the mono". Well, that's good. I like the stereo. We can all like whatever. We're still talking about twelve records here.'

In the 1980s, even after the horrific murder of John Lennon, the Beatles' standing, and influence, had waned. Only in the mid-'90s, with the *Anthology* outtakes albums and TV documentary series, had a new appreciation of the band begun to grow.

'I think it gave people another point of view,' Ringo offered. 'It gave us a human aspect to that madness. We were here and we had gone through it. We could sit together and we had a laugh. So I think it was a good thing.

'What was incredible, the one thing that blew my mind, was that the guy who was interviewing us … which was Jools Holland … he says, "The second time you played Shea…" I said, "What? We played it twice?" 'Cos it was so big the one time. And then they went and interviewed George, who didn't know what I'd said. [Holland] said, "George, the second time you played Shea…" and he said, "What? We played it twice?"

'So, we all had brain damage. And we all had brain alignment.'

If, ultimately, the Beatles' lasting message had essentially been one of love, dovetailing in 1969 with John Lennon's determination to use his fame to promote world peace, it was Starr who'd taken it onwards into the twenty-first century. 'Peace and love' had become a Ringo catchphrase. Did he feel he was carrying the torch for John?

'No, I'm not carrying it for John,' he averred. 'I'm carrying it for me and the universe. Peace and love. Y'know, John was instrumental at… he is a huge image of that. But you see Paul, he's on his live show, "peace and love". You see people around the world … I don't care as long as you're doing that [*flashes peace sign*]. 'Cos, for one second, you've thought, *Peace and love.*'

While the popular perception for a long time was that Starr was the least spiritual of the Beatles, particularly after he'd left the ashram at Rishikesh in the spring of 1968 after only two weeks, one particular teaching by the Maharishi Mahesh Yogi had resonated in Ringo's mind down the decades.

'I learned from the Maharishi,' he recalled in his 2019 annotated photo book, *Another Day in the Life*, 'that if you do something good, then two other people will do something good, then three, then five and then a thousand. The whole planet will support you. You're always loved. I live in that world.'

Any lingering suspicion that 'peace and love' was merely a snappy, vaguely hopeful slogan for Ringo was countered by his deeper explanation, and understanding, highlighted on page 75 of the same book. Under a photograph he'd taken of a white statue of ancient Indian spiritual teacher Mahavira, he explained his ongoing attraction to Jainism.

'I love it,' he wrote, 'because it teaches you that the way to enlightenment is through absolute focus on peace and love and non-violence towards all living things.'

Elsewhere, he admitted that he practised meditation mainly to alleviate symptoms that might be recognised by those who've suffered complex trauma. There's an argument that, post-split, all four of the Beatles suffered from different forms of PTSD and were all learning to cope with it in their own (sometimes unhealthy) ways until 1980, when Starr, Harrison and McCartney were further thrown into deep shock with Lennon's killing.

'Sometimes I feel like there are fifty people in my brain and they all have something to say,' Ringo confessed. 'There's always an argument going on in there. Meditation brings it down to five people in my brain, and that's the improvement.'

At the same time, some of his photographs – daft faces he could see in stones or electrical plug sockets, artful pictures of his own shadow – revealed a thoughtful, whimsical and still in some ways childlike soul.

There were clearly many unseen layers to him. Only a fool, it seemed, would take Ringo Starr at face value.

~

In June 2022, Starr stood on the stage at the esteemed Berklee College of Music in Boston, Massachusetts, wearing a graduation gown and tasselled hat, to receive an honorary doctorate. Looking back over his life, he said, 'it's like some strange fairy tale'.

Ringo's assertion that it might take dozens of autobiographical volumes to tell his story only serves to highlight the fact that his life has been extraordinarily eventful. It's a tale involving an ordinary guy, with a standout talent, who stepped from his drab and troubled early life into an unimaginably colourful world and set off on a grand adventure, which, as he stressed, is 'still unfolding'.

'I just think sometimes I make the right moves,' he told me in 2024, with modest understatement, before offering up one of his famous Ringoisms. 'Y'know, I make more right moves than left moves.'

2

LAZARUS

The Bounceback Kid, 1940–1955

The sick teenager felt the urge to drum, but he didn't have any sticks. So instead he picked up a pair of long weaving spindles he'd found somewhere and began beating out a rhythm on the cabinet beside his hospital bed.

It was the second time that Richy Starkey had been forced to spend an extended period cooped up in convalescence. Seven years before, he'd been a patient – a child at death's door with peritonitis – for more than twelve months at the Royal Liverpool Children's Hospital in Myrtle Street. This time he'd been transferred from there after ten weeks to its rural sanatorium out in Heswall on the Wirral peninsula, where it was hoped the cleaner air would aid his slow recovery, along with all of the other kids suffering from tuberculosis.

At least here, every fortnight, a music teacher visited the young in-patients and tried to fire their synapses with rudimentary band sessions. She'd hand each of them a simple percussion instrument and then point at coloured notes on a board indicating when they had to play: yellow for triangle, green for tambourine, red for drum. Richy always wanted a drum, or else he wouldn't join in.

When the teacher left, he didn't want to stop drumming. And so he began determinedly hammering on the nearest available surface with his makeshift mallets, likely driving his wardmates mad.

Doof-doof-doof-doof.

The unlikely sound of his future calling.

~

Richard Starkey's young life was hellishly rough.

By the time he was three, his parents, Richard Sr and Elsie, had split. The pair met while working together in a bakery and confectioners, bonded over drinking and dancing, and married in 1936, moving into the former's parents' home at 59 Madryn Street, half an hour's walk from the Mersey in the Dingle's warren of terraced housing. Elsie fell pregnant within weeks of the start of the war in the grim autumn of 1939 – Richard avoiding conscription due to bakers being deemed key workers – and the couple relocated down the street to number 9, where Richard Jr was born in an upstairs bedroom just after midnight on 7 July 1940.

But it became clear that Richy's father wasn't cut out for domestic family life and, in 1943, he walked out on his wife and son. He was to become an almost spectral presence in the latter's life, a figure half-formed from a few sketchy memories. 'I only saw him probably five times after he left,' Ringo later said.

Unable to afford the rent on the six-roomed house at 9 Madryn Street, Elsie – juggling jobs as a cleaner, a barmaid and a shop assistant – was forced to look elsewhere. Number 9 was far too big for two of them anyway, and since they'd effectively slipped from being working class to lower working class after Richard had scarpered, they needed somewhere far cheaper.

A decade earlier, 10 Admiral Grove – a two-up, two-down with its toilet in the yard – had been condemned. But it was only a couple of minutes' walk from 9 Madryn Street, so when they moved their belongings in a van, the drive was ridiculously short. Five-year-old Richy sat in the back, feeling glum, resistant to living anywhere new.

In the August of 1945, he started school, enrolled at St Silas Church of England Primary, only half a dozen streets away, yet a distant, alien and unsettling environment for him. 'About a million kids in the playground and me,' he recalled. 'I was pretty fearful.'

While Richy grew up in a single-parent household, Elsie remained close to her errant husband's parents and so he was also cared for by the colourful characters that were his grandad and granny. Johnny Starkey, to his grandson's eyes, was a 'little guy', while Annie was a 'big woman': a cartoonish combination. She would raise her fists at her husband when he was drunk and threaten to thump him.

Annie Starkey would later be described by her grandson as 'the voodoo queen of Liverpool'. Discovering that Richy was naturally left-handed, she deemed it to be the result of some kind of demonic possession and attempted to exorcise this malevolent spirit by forcing him to use his right hand. More prosaically, she was always ready with a homemade bread poultice or hot toddy to treat various ailments. But, still, she couldn't save the boy from perilously ill health.

At the age of six, Richy was in a coma. In the early summer of 1947, a few weeks shy of his seventh birthday, he was struck down with agonising stomach pain at home in Admiral Grove. A doctor was summoned and the kid was quickly stretchered and sped in an ambulance to hospital, before being rushed into surgery with a suspected burst appendix. En route to theatre, where he was met by what he later evocatively referred to as 'the smell of ether and quiet oblivion', he asked a nurse for a cup of tea. She told him he could have one when he came around after the operation. It would be another ten weeks before Richy tasted tea again.

When the surgeon opened him up, it was found that Starkey had peritonitis, caused by infection from his burst appendix. The procedure to remove the affected area was a serious and dangerous one, especially in the 1940s. While Richy was out cold for weeks on end, doctors three times informed his mother that he might die. Even after he finally resurfaced, he faded in and out of consciousness for another four months.

By the start of 1948, however, Richy was miraculously mended and almost ready to be sent home. Placed in a high-sided cot bed to keep him out of mischief, he one day leaned out to show another kid his prized toy bus, fell out and ripped his stitches open, resulting in another six months in hospital. On his return to Admiral Grove, he seemed to his mother to be altogether quieter but, perhaps due to his traumatic recent experience, even more of a strangely wise old soul. Since he was a baby, with his enormous blue eyes alert to everything happening around him, Elsie believed he'd 'been here before'.

Now, having effectively risen from the dead, Richy earned himself a new nickname: 'Lazarus'.

~

Already woefully behind his classmates in his learning, Richy Starkey lost all interest in school and, from the age of eight, began to bunk off. Instead, he gained himself a streetwise education in the chaotic urban terrain of the Dingle, which he remembered as being filled with 'gangs and fights and madness and robberies'. He felt 'closed in' by the inner-city and hankered for space and greenery. Often, he was drawn to the nearby Prince's and Sefton parks, away from the choking air of his neighbourhood where, street after street, chimney after chimney belched out coal smoke.

It wasn't until he was nine that Richy learned to read – and only then due to the devoted home schooling of a babysitter-turned-effective-big sister, Marie Maguire, four years older and the daughter of Elsie's friend, Annie. Marie patiently sat Richy at the kitchen table in Admiral Grove and took him word by word, line by line, through Chambers' primary-age reader books and some others detailing the adventures of Dobbin the Horse.

Marie was also great fun and up for messing around. She took Richy roller-skating along nearby High Park Street, to children's matinee screenings at local cinemas, and back home to bash away on the piano and lead him in noisy singalongs involving 'You Are My Sunshine' or 'Bobby Shafto's Gone to Sea'. One day, he took off his shirt and she painted his back in primitive shapes, underlining the fact that she was still a kid herself. 'He was just so happy and easy-going,' she reflected.

Thanks to Marie's sterling efforts, Richy was catching up on his education, but it wasn't enough to prevent him being placed in 'C' stream, the second from bottom, when he started at Dingle Vale Secondary Modern in 1951. As a result, his truanting intensified. He and his friends had a cunning strategy that seemed to work. They'd 'hang around outside before school 'til the final bell went,' Elsie remembered, 'and they just wouldn't go in, [then claiming] they'd been locked out. They would go and spend the afternoon playing in Sefton Park.'

When not whiling away time in green spaces, Richy and his pals could be found scrambling around a bombsite. He had no memories whatsoever of Hitler's wartime pounding of Liverpool, but he could obviously see the pits and scars on the city. Yawning gaps where houses had stood became arenas of adventure for semi-feral kids. Richy's closest two buddies at the time were

Davy Patterson and Brian Briscoe. The trio would run wild, indulging their detective or cowboy fantasies, before they grew older and dabbled in smoking (lung-busting Woodbines), drinking (a bottle of whisky half-guzzled at the age of twelve) and petty thievery (pilfering random items from Woolworths).

'Dave and Brian were my childhood friends from five,' he recalled. 'We were the Three Musketeers. We did all that growing up together.'

Even if Richy didn't attend school half the time, one report card from 1952 described him as being 'quiet' and 'thoughtful', and someone who did well in drama, the only subject in which he scored an 'A'.

Then, in the summer before his fourteenth birthday, his health failed him spectacularly once again. Likely due to his immune system being generally battered and weakened by his earlier sickness, when he caught flu, it then caused pleurisy in his lungs. Back in Liverpool at the Myrtle Street hospital, in the period before he was sent to the Wirral, it developed into TB.

'I had my seventh birthday in hospital, I had my fourteenth birthday in hospital,' he later reflected, though not with an enormous amount of self-pity.

There were some upsides to being a long-term in-patient once again. As a hormonal fourteen-year-old, Richy flirted with the younger nurses, most of whom were still in their late teens. 'Will you kiss me goodnight, nurse?' he'd cheekily enquire of them. Otherwise, he'd sneak into the girls' ward to try to engage in a spot of fumbling with someone of his own age, although with little luck.

'I'd stand there for hours trying to get a touch of tit,' he colourfully noted.

It was a dreary existence for the most part and, by the time he was sent home in late 1955, he'd spent another entire year hospitalised.

Music had always been on the fringes of his life, what with Annie and Johnny playing mandolin or banjo or ukulele at family gatherings. But now music became the centre of it.

Richy was eight when he was first entranced by a song. At the pictures, watching Gene Autry singing his pining 1939 cowboy ballad 'South of the Border' in the film of the same name, he was haunted by the keening 'ai-ai-ai-ai' refrain that closed the tune. Later, he cited it as being 'my first musical influence … he sent shivers down my spine. It was a magical moment.' Autry provided a gateway into a lifelong love of Americana. Richy's ear was then drawn to other country singers down the years, among them Hank Williams and Hank Snow.

His other key musical epiphany arrived when he was thirteen, between his extended hospital stays, on one of the rare days he attended Dingle Vale. Walking to school via Park Road, he stopped outside a music shop, Park Music & Radio, his eye caught by the sight of a tom-tom in the window. At £26, it was frighteningly expensive and, of course, way out of the reach of a poor Dingle teenager. Yet, he was compelled to return to the pavement outside the shop again and again, just to look at it.

Soon, everyone became aware of Richy Starkey's growing obsession. Marie Maguire brought him a present during his second period in hospital: a 10-inch 78rpm shellac record of English drummer Eric Delaney's big band jazzy 'Delaney's Delight', much of which was a clatteringly loud and elaborate drum solo. On the flipside was a swinging version of the folksong 'Oranges and Lemons', replete with boomy, tone-bending timpani.

It was the perfect gift for a lad stuck in hospital animatedly playing rhythms on his bedside cabinet.

'Drumming,' he said, 'was all I thought about.'

From this point on, the only thing that was important to him – apart from girls – was this internal beat, this rapidly developing *doof-doof-doof-doof* that he felt the need to express.

3

DRUMS

The Beat Goes On (and On),
1951–2015

Harry Graves had suffered a death in the family and so he was forced to travel back down south to Romford, his Essex hometown that had been absorbed into East London back in the 1930s. For the past ten years, since 1946, he'd been living up in Liverpool, renting a house on Jacob Street in the Dingle. Through the Maguires, and via various boozy singalong house parties he'd been invited to, he'd met the Starkeys and taken a shine to Elsie.

Richy was eleven when Harry wandered into his life. As a painter and decorator for Liverpool Corporation, Graves was a hard grafter and a funny, likeable soul. Working for a time at Burtonwood, the US air force base fifteen miles outside Liverpool near Warrington, he'd return with exotic gifts of American chewing gum and DC comics for the lad. Harry and Elsie married in 1954, and Graves brought an air of good humour to Admiral Grove – Richy jokily referred to him as his 'stepladder' – and also filled it with music. His tastes tended toward big band jazz or the smouldering voices of Dinah Shore and Sarah Vaughan. As he played his records, he'd repeatedly ask Richy, 'Have you heard this? Have you heard *this*?'

In a Scouse working-class environment that was characteristically rough and mouthy, Graves was a kind and laid-back presence who greatly affected the boy's upbringing. 'I learned gentleness from Harry,' Starkey would later reflect. 'He was a really sweet guy.'

Following the fifteen-year-old's second extended hospital stay, Graves also encouraged him to play. Richy's compulsion to drum had driven him to create ad hoc percussive set-ups: a biscuit tin filled with nuts and bolts to mimic a snare, a huge 50-inch single-headed bass drum that he'd either kick or bash with lengths of wood that were supposed to go on the fire. He became a singing/drumming turn at the Starkey parties, performing Hank Snow's orphan lament 'Nobody's Child' (comically directed at Elsie) or simply keeping a beat to accompany the others, particularly Harry when he crooned his way through 'Stardust' or 'That Old Black Magic'.

Returning from his trip to Romford at the tail end of 1956, Graves brought Richy back another gift that was to be a life-changing one: his first real drum kit, lugged all the way home by Harry on the train from Euston to Lime Street, and given to the beaming lad at Christmas. Although it cost £12 (a week-and-a-half's worth of the average UK wage at the time), it was second-hand and not much to look at: a pre-war jazz kit with a big marching band-style bass drum (albeit one with a foot pedal), an actual snare drum, a small tom-tom, a hi-hat and a top cymbal.

But with this thrilling acquisition came a renewed sense of purpose. Richy took three lessons from 'a little man who played drums', who taught him paradiddle exercises and showed him how to write out patterns on manuscript paper. Way too boring, the student decided. He quit. He wanted to play by feel alone.

At the same time, despite Annie Starkey's efforts to expel the southpaw demon from him, Richy led with his left hand when he played, giving his rolls an unusual character.

Only twice did he attempt to play the kit at home in his back bedroom. An almighty racket inevitably ensued and the result was the same both times: complaints from the neighbours and shouts upstairs from Elsie to keep the noise down. It quickly became clear that the only way he could practise was to join a band.

⌒

For the time being, he had to get on with the dreary business of employment.

Having effectively left Dingle Vale Secondary Modern at the age of thirteen, Richy returned there two years later to collect his 'sign-off papers' that would allow him to go looking for work or to collect unemployment benefit. At first, the school could find no record of him and only a deep search of the files unearthed the proof that Richard Starkey had ever been a pupil there.

The first job he landed at fifteen, in 1955, was as a messenger boy for British Railways, delivering notices to factories to let them know that their orders had arrived at Lime Street station. One of the added attractions was the prospect of a nice, warm uniform but, disappointingly, he was only given a hat. Five weeks in, he belatedly underwent a medical and, still weakened by his health scares, failed it. He was forced to sign on the dole.

There was plenty of work around, however, and his next paid gig was as a bar waiter on the SS *St Tudno*, a pleasure excursion paddle steamer sailing daily from Liverpool to Llandudno in north Wales, then along the Menai Strait and around the island of Anglesey, leaving at ten in the morning and returning at eight at night. Like many Liverpudlian youths, Richy was attracted to the notion of a life at sea. The merchant seamen he saw around town were always 'the best dressed' and attracted the girls. His plan was to work on this boat for three months and gain enough experience to get a union card and possibly a job on one of the 'big liners'. That was until, little more than a month after he'd started, he turned up hungover, had an argument with his gaffer and was immediately given the sack.

It was no great loss. He'd been growing worried that having some experience at sea also left him exposed to being drafted into the Royal Navy to serve his compulsory year-and-a-half of National Service when he turned seventeen. As it was, peacetime conscription in Britain was abolished in the spring of 1957 for those, like him, born after October 1939. Also, by that time, Richy was already working as an apprentice engineer – a profession that qualified for exemption – at H. Hunt & Son, a company manufacturing gym equipment.

In 1957, up and down Britain, skiffle was all the rage, mainly due to its turbo-charged, beat-driven mix of folk, blues and country being accessible to a generation of aspiring musicians with cheap guitars, washboards and home-made upright tea chest basses. At the same time, Richy was gripped by the crackling medium-wave sound of rock 'n' roll records emanating from Radio Luxembourg, spun by 'the American rock 'n' roll king', DJ Alan Freed.

The year before, while on holiday in the Isle of Man with his grandparents,

Richy witnessed first-hand the frenzying power of this new music. Taken to see the Freed-starring film, *Rock Around the Clock* – essentially a big-screen vehicle for Bill Haley and His Comets – he'd been thrilled to be surrounded by feral teens ripping out the cinema's seats with vandalistic abandon, an infectious act of riotous destruction instigated by Teddy Boys at London screenings of the movie at the Trocadero cinema.

'I didn't join in because I was a sickly child,' he remembered, although Annie and Johnny surely wouldn't have allowed him to. 'I was just so excited that they were doing it for me.'

Richy was soon sweeping his hair up in the protruding Teddy Boy quiff style. Mooching around the fair at Sefton Park one evening, he bumped into Roy Trafford, another Ted and a fellow apprentice at H. Hunt & Son. From that night on, the two became firm pals, through their shared interests of rock 'n' roll, drinking and girls. 'We became more like brothers,' said Trafford. 'I was the nearest thing he ever had to one.' Together one day, they were fitted for bespoke drape suits – Richy's in black, Roy's in blue. They'd hang out at the Cavern on Mathew Street, watching skiffle bands and nipping back and forth to the pub for underage beers.

In the June of '57, when the fair returned to Sefton Park, Richy and Roy even lost their virginity at the same time, after coaxing two girls to a quiet spot on a grass verge. Starkey would always remember hearing the shivering tones of Frankie Laine singing '(Ghost) Riders in the Sky' floating on the breeze from the speakers on the waltzers.

Mainly for protective reasons, the two were soon part of a gang in the Dingle. The threat of violence lurked on every street and Richy filed the metal buckle on his belt to blade-like sharpness to use as a weapon. He saw other lads get beaten up with hammers, stabbed, one losing an eye. Luckily, by this stage he was no longer such a weakened specimen and had turned into a good runner.

'My sickliness left me when I was about sixteen,' he later reckoned.

During breaks at the factory, Richy would restlessly beat out rhythms on biscuit tins and coconut shells. When another guitar-playing apprentice (and the Starkeys' next-door neighbour at Admiral Grove), Eddie Myles, decided to start a band, Trafford fell in on tea-chest bass and Richy was the natural fit for the drummer. Thus the Eddie Clayton Skiffle Group, adopting Myles's fancified performing name, were born.

'Our first gigs were for the men in the basement at dinnertime,' their drummer recalled. 'I had a snare and brushes, that's all I had. But Eddie Myles was a brilliant musician. He was one of those guys, he could play anything. Give him a trumpet, he'd get something out of it. And Roy played guitar and upright bass, and we started as lads.'

From knocking out 'Rock Island Line' in the cellar for their sandwich-chewing co-workers, the band picked up other members and ventured further afield, from skiffle contests at St Luke's Hall to the Labour Club in Peel Street, the Wilson Hall in Garston and then the Cavern, where they were admired by other teenage skiffle-heads, including John Lennon, the gobby singer with the Quarrymen. A younger guitarist named George Harrison remembering seeing them perform and thinking, *Hey, these are good.*

By early 1958, the Eddie Clayton Skiffle Group were playing weddings and making decent money, often kitting themselves out in matching-coloured shirts and bootlace ties. Then, Richy's individual dress style turned ever snappier, with sharper tailored suits and even a gold lamé waistcoat.

All of this stage experience was, of course, invaluable. Rapidly transforming from an ill or jobless little-hoper to factory worker-cum-stylish and talented drummer, as he turned from seventeen to eighteen, Richy was well on his way to becoming an experienced semi-pro musician.

Fashions changed and, by 1959, the skiffle craze began to fade, as rawer, electrified rock 'n' roll became the dominant teenage musical force. The Eddie Clayton Skiffle Group ran out of steam when their leader got engaged. Richy Starkey moved on to other bands.

At eighteen, he even tried forming his own group. They comprised Roy Trafford on guitar and a tea-chest bass-player, along with, as Starkey recalled, 'a clarinet player who could only play in B-flat, a pianist who could only play in C ... and a trumpeter who could only play "When The Saints Go Marching In".' They were a comically disparate troupe that lasted all of two rehearsals before packing it in.

But, before long, Richy was back onstage, spending four months playing in the Darktown Skiffle Group, a six-piece, female-fronted outfit who were also much admired by John Lennon. Starkey's name was getting around on the scene and he was invited to try out for Al Caldwell's Texans (soon to be the rocked-up Raving Texans), fronted by a stylish and charismatic blond guy who stuttered when he spoke but not when he sang. Uncharacteristically, Richy turned up to the audition looking a tad rumpled in his old black Teddy Boy drape jacket, but played well, kicking the band up a notch with his beats. He was told he could have the job if he spruced himself up. The fact that he had his own drums sealed the deal.

All the while, naturally, Richy had wanted a better kit. On 23 April 1958, he went to Frank Hessy's music shop on Stanley Street in town and put down £11, with monthly payments of £16 towards a total of £68, on an Ajax budget-range Edgware 'Elegance' kit with pigskin heads and black shells pearled with golden threading. Harry signed the HP agreement, witnessed by Elsie. Then Richy changed his mind, convincing his grandad Johnny to lend him £46, effectively a month's wages, to make up the £57 cash price.

~

Five years later, and by now famous, in the spring of 1963, Starkey was standing on the pavement outside Drum City on Shaftesbury Avenue in London when he spotted in the shop's window an instantly alluring four-piece Ludwig Downbeat kit, with a mesmerising black oyster pearl design. 'Oh great! Look at this kit!' he enthused to Beatles manager Brian Epstein, who was accompanying him on the shopping trip.

The Mahogany Duroplastic four-piece Premier kit he'd ended up buying in 1962 and battering to death for the past year was worn out and sorely in need of replacement now that the band were in the big time.

Epstein cut a deal with the store's owner, Ivor Arbiter, and enquired as to whether it would be possible to have the group's name featured on the front head of the bass drum. Arbiter sketched out a logo on the back of a cigarette packet featuring a stylish 'Drop T' lettering highlight in 'Beatles' and then paid a sign-writer, Eddie Stokes, a fiver to paint it on the skin.

Ringo was to own four different black oyster pearl Ludwig kits during the

'60s, playing this first set on *With the Beatles* and *A Hard Day's Night*, and at the band's Beatlemania-sparking appearance on *Sunday Night at the London Palladium* in the October of '63.

After 9 February 1964, when he appeared on a circular drum riser on *The Ed Sullivan Show*, rattling through 'All My Loving' and 'She Loves You' with both the Ludwig and Arbiter's Beatles logos visible to more than 73 million American viewers, the drum manufacturer's sales doubled. Starkey's name was to be forever linked with the Ludwig company (who were to be forever thankful).

Then, in 2015, fifty-nine years after Harry Graves had humped that first shonky jazz kit on the train to Liverpool, Starkey's original Ludwig set sold for $2.1 million at Julien's Auctions in Beverly Hills. It remains the most highly valued drum kit on Earth.

4

STARR TIME

Reborn at Butlin's, 1960–1962

Six foot two, with an added few inches of golden quiff, the singer leaped from the lid of the piano, over the drummer's head, and landed on the stage in front of the bass drum that featured the crudely inked legend 'Ringo Starr'.

Rory Storm and the Hurricanes were fast becoming the big wow rock 'n' roll turn at the Butlin's holiday camp in Pwllheli, north-west Wales, in the summer season of 1960. Stammering Al Caldwell had successfully reinvented himself as the gymnastic rebel rocker Rory Storm. Having caught his high-kicking act back in Liverpool, John Lennon comically exclaimed, 'He does legs!'

Photographs taken at the time captured Storm in full flight, as if his high-kinetic moves had been caught by the flashing light of a stroboscope: wearing a black leather jacket, finger pointed to the sky, leaning back in a Gene Vincent pose, or dropping to one knee, with his mic stand hoisted aloft, or using it to mock-stab his bandmate Johnny Guitar, who was playing his electric six-string behind his head with mad abandon. At other points in their set, the frontman lifted his long leg onto the guitarist's back and the two would convulse wildly, as if shot through with 500 volts. The next minute, he'd pull up a chair and coolly comb his hair while eyeing the girls in the crowd.

Then there were their stage get-ups: Rory in a pink suit, or in aquamarine with a gold lamé shirt, the rest flanking him in fluorescent crimson. Richy, growing more flamboyant by the day, went even further, acquiring a new nickname and future identity. Having been given a cygnet ring for his sixteenth birthday by Elsie and Harry, he'd more recently acquired a second ring, a gold wedding band belonging to grandad Johnny, who'd died aged sixty-nine in October 1959, devastating Richy, who swore to always wear it.

A third addition was even more significant: an engagement ring. Richy had been going out with the petite brunette Geraldine McGovern – Gerry – since turning eighteen (she was a year older) and things were getting serious. A plan was hatched for a wedding sometime in 1961. 'I did love her,' he later said, 'and she loved me. We'd got our bottom drawer started and made all the preparations that go into marriage.'

Three jewellery-adorned fingers on a young man in Liverpool in 1960 caught the eye. He attracted cries of 'Poof!' from lairy blokes, but also admiring looks from girls. Soon, people were calling him 'Rings'.

When they first hit Butlin's in the June of 1960, the Hurricanes all adopted vaguely American-sounding stage names, like characters in a Western. Plain old Wally Eymond, bassist and occasional vocalist, became Lu Walters. Guitarist Charles O'Brien became Ty O'Brien and Richy 'Rings' Starkey became Ringo Starr.

At first, as he later recalled, 'I became Ringo Starkey. But that didn't really work so I just took the "key" off and called myself Ringo Starr. I cut the name in half and added an "r".'

~

Six months earlier, Rory Storm and the Hurricanes – previously Al Storm and His Hurricanes, then Jett Storm and the Hurricanes – had earned their notoriety onstage at the Cavern. Rock 'n' roll was banned in the Mathew Street cellar venue, but skiffle reluctantly permitted.

Invited onto a bill there on 17 January 1960 as the token skiffle band – alongside Micky Ashman's Jazz Band, as part of the Liverpool Jazz Festival – they opened their set with the relatively safe, driving folk of Lonnie Donegan's 'Cumberland Gap'. Then, when they brazenly broke into Jerry Lee Lewis's rib-rattler 'Whole Lotta Shakin' Goin' On', the affronted jazz purists began to collectively fling a shower of coins in the direction of the stage. The Hurricanes defiantly carried on but battled against a chorus of boos. The result was that they were fined six shillings by furious Cavern owner Ray McFall. Some compensation for the group members came from sweeping up the coins left on the stage floor.

'Johnny Guitar brought a big radio down and plugged his guitar into it,' their drummer remembered. 'We got thrown off, but we didn't care. We could do what we liked. "We're gonna play rock!"'

Often Rory and the Hurricanes sounded like a messy pre-echo of punk rock, not always quite in sync or tune, but absolutely throwing themselves into every performance. After a show, their singer sometimes burned off his unspent energy by running all the way home.

Starkey was a frequent post-gig visitor to Storm/Caldwell's home, where he lived with his mum, Vi, who noted that her effusive son seemed to have quite an influence on the younger drummer. 'They used to sit there chatting for hours,' she recalled. 'But I seem to remember that it was Rory who did most of the talking while Ringo did most of the listening.'

At first, Al's powers of persuasion didn't quite extend to convincing Richy to leave Liverpool to join the Hurricanes at Butlin's for a three-month stint. Not only would it involve quitting his apprenticeship at H. Hunt & Son a year before he was due to become a qualified engineer, but it also meant saying goodbye to Gerry McGovern for most of the summer, at a time when his fiancée was already beginning to moan about the amount of time he spent out in the clubs, playing drums.

Elsie and Harry weren't too enamoured of the idea, either. 'There was a little consternation at home,' he remembered. 'They said, "It's alright as a hobby, son". But I said, "No, this is what I'm going to do", because I just loved to play.' Even the foreman at Hunt's warned him, 'You'll be back and brushing the floor because you'll have lost your job as an engineer.'

All of the stress might have turned his hair grey, if it hadn't gone that way already, a prematurely silver patch having appeared on the right side of his head when he was eighteen. Richy believed it to be a strange by-product of his childhood illnesses and was acutely self-conscious about it. The one upside was that girls seemed to like it.

While now cutting an unusual and exotic figure with his grey streak and multiple rings, Starkey initially baulked at Al Caldwell's suggestion that the band wear make-up onstage.

'Ringo refused point blank and said he wouldn't "put that muck on my face",' recalled Al's sister, Iris. 'He gave in, in the end, only smearing a thin layer over his face.'

~

By Rory Storm and the Hurricanes' second season performing at the strangely named Rock 'N Calypso Ballroom at Pwllheli in the summer of 1961, Ringo Starr had fully adapted to his new persona. If asked to sign his autograph for Butlin's holidaymakers, he'd prefix his name with the cocky, showbizzy words, 'The Sensational...' and add a scribbled star.

Off duty and on the dancefloor, meanwhile, he stood out, cutting elastic-limbed rock 'n' roll shapes. Each and every Saturday, busloads of girls left and busloads of girls arrived. Unsurprisingly, Ringo's prolonged absences and holiday camp rock star status put unbearable pressure on his and Gerry McGovern's relationship. They called off their engagement and agreed to break up.

'Rich's drums were his most precious possession,' she told a reporter in 1964. 'His music always came first.'

'She started to put the pressure on: it was her or the drums,' said Ringo. 'That was a very poignant moment in my life. I left her one night and I got on the bus and thought, *Well, what happens if I don't go back?* And I never went back. I just wanted to play. It was more important to me.'

Free of his relationship, he grew restless. Having been unable to satisfy his wanderlust as a teenage sailor, he began to make enquiries into the possibility of emigrating to the US, specifically Texas, the home state of one of his heroes, country blues singer-guitarist Lightnin' Hopkins. Following his second season at Butlin's in 1961, he and a friend went as far as picking up immigration forms from the US consulate in Liverpool and writing to the Houston Chamber of Commerce, looking for available factory jobs. In the end, they were frustrated by having to fill out the seemingly endless paperwork.

'They gave us a list of factories we could apply to,' he recalled. 'And then we went back to say, "We've done these forms". And they gave us *more* forms. We ripped them up and got on with our lives.'

By the next summer of 1962, he was back playing at Butlin's: this time at their camp in Skegness, 180 miles from Liverpool on the east coast of

England. There, the highlight of the Hurricanes' week was their appearance at the rock 'n' roll show at the Butlin's Theatre, the fervour of the crowds cooled by the fact that, as it boasted over its proscenium arch, it was 'Europe's first air-conditioned theatre'.

Ringo was now a star of the show, positioned at the back of the stage on a drum riser above the others, his bass drum emblazoned with a star and the letters 'RS'. His act had developed to involve him frenziedly shaking his head as he hammered away at his kit.

The highpoint of the Hurricanes' Butlin's sets in the summer of '62, the number that 'really got the place jumping', according to one eyewitness, was a rowdy, oddly non-gender-flipped version of the Shirelles' 'Boys', sung by Ringo from behind his kit. Before taking a break from the stage, Storm would introduce the drummer's spot-lit appearance with the words, 'Ladies and gentlemen, Ringo's Starr Time'.

But, as exuberant and eye-catching a performer as Rory Storm was, no agent or manager who came to see him and the Hurricanes would agree to take them on and help further their career. They were slowly going nowhere.

At the same time, the reborn Ringo Starr was suddenly much in demand. Near the end of the stint at Skegness, he received a letter from Ted 'Kingsize' Taylor, the leader of rival rock 'n' roll band the Dominoes, offering him twenty quid a week to join. Starr said yes.

Not long after that, though, he changed his mind. He'd had a better offer. He'd been asked to join the Beatles.

5

LIVERPOOL-HAMBURG, HAMBURG-LIVERPOOL

Becoming a Beatle, 1960–1962

I t all happened slowly. Over the space of more than two years, Ringo Starr found himself orbiting around and around the Beatles, before being pulled entirely into their world.

The first time he set eyes on them was at the Jacaranda, the hip coffee bar and live venue on Slater Street owned by Allan Williams, a businessman and rock 'n' roll aficionado. Recently turned thirty, he'd started to branch out as a promoter of the young bands on the circuit. Not long before Storm and the Hurricanes set off for Butlin's in June 1960, Rory, Johnny and Richy wandered into 'the Jac' and heard some guys playing guitars in the basement. Intrigued, or simply nosy, they descended the stairs to find Paul McCartney and John Lennon there, teaching their pal Stuart Sutcliffe his basslines.

Immediately, in Starkey's mind, there was a hierarchy. The Hurricanes were sharp-dressed aces, booked for an upcoming summer season. By comparison, the group calling themselves the Silver Beatles, or sometimes simply the Beatles – their line-up also featuring seventeen-year-old guitarist George Harrison, absent that day – seemed to Richy like kids messing around.

'We were the professionals,' he reckoned, 'and they were the boys, the struggling artists. They meant nothing in those days. They were just a bunch of scruffs.'

Over the summer, in the holiday camp where Richy became Ringo, he thought little more of the other Liverpool band, until Rory and the Hurricanes landed in Hamburg that October.

The route taking Merseyside groups to perform in the West German port city had opened up almost by chance. At the beginning of 1960, Williams travelled there to check out the nightclub scene, instigating a meeting with Bruno Koschmider, the war-wounded owner of the Kaiserkeller, a subterranean music venue positioned on the corner of Grosse Freiheit and Schmuckstrasse amid the seedy bars and strip clubs of the St Pauli district. In an attempt to promote Liverpudlian rock 'n' roll bands, Williams pulled out a reel-to-reel demo to play to Koschmider. A few seconds of hiss were followed by wonky noise: the tape had somehow been damaged in transit and the meeting ended there.

Six months later, in July, Williams drove to London and the 2i's Coffee Bar on Old Compton Street in Soho, the British rock and skiffle nexus where the likes of Tommy Steele, Cliff Richard and Adam Faith had all made their names, and itself the inspiration for the Liverpool entrepreneur's opening of the Jacaranda. In tow with him were Derry and the Seniors, a Merseyside band who felt that Williams owed them a big favour after his short-lived association with Larry Parnes had ended in a fall-out, losing them their summer booking at Parnes's 'Idols on Parade' theatre revue in Blackpool.

'Allan came up with a suggestion,' remembered the Seniors' saxophonist, Howie Casey. 'He rang me up, and said, "Look, we can go down to the 2i's cafe and we can see what we can do there." There were two cars and we all piled in and got there early afternoon. Downstairs at the 2i's was where the music was. They had this all-day thing going on. They fitted us in and we started playing.'

In a stroke of serendipity, Bruno Koschmider was in the audience that day. He and Williams instantly reconnected, with the German club owner, impressed by Derry and the Seniors, booking them for a residency at the Kaiserkeller. 'We were the first Liverpool band to go out there,' Casey noted with some pride.

Fewer than two weeks into their stay, the sax player received a letter from Williams, informing him that the group who'd now definitively changed their name to the Beatles were coming over to perform at the Indra, a small club a minute's walk from the Kaiserkeller on Grosse Freiheit. Casey had previously seen them play at an audition for Parnes back in Liverpool and been unimpressed.

'That's when I wrote my infamous letter back,' he bashfully recalled. '"Don't send that bum band over here. Why don't you send the Big Three or Rory Storm and the Hurricanes?" When they did arrive, we went to see them and they'd improved, obviously. They'd worked and they'd got their drummer, Pete Best. They were talented.'

Once in Hamburg, clocking up more than 200 hours of stage time across forty-eight shows at the Indra between 17 August and 3 October, the Beatles – more through perspiration than inspiration – took giant steps in their development. So much so that when Derry and the Seniors returned to England in early October, at the same time that complaints about the rock 'n' roll racket emanating from the Indra became impossible for Koschmider to ignore, the quintet – Lennon, McCartney, Harrison, Sutcliffe and Best – were asked to fill the slot at the Kaiserkeller. Alternating 60-to-90-minute sets with them, providing non-stop live music at the venue for twelve hours a day, were Rory Storm and the Hurricanes.

The Beatles had been shocked by the living conditions that Koschmider had inflicted upon them, packing them like itinerant workers into a single bare-walled room behind the screen at the Bambi Kino cinema. While they'd travelled over crammed in a van, the Hurricanes flew to Hamburg and, given their comparatively lofty status, refused to bed down in the similarly skanky accommodation the German promoter provided.

Ringo remembered it being 'a 10-foot room with old settees that had been puked on and pissed on, and old rags to keep us warm. We said, "Hey, we're not going to sleep here, we have suits!" That was our excuse. So we all went into the Seamen's Mission: the five of us in one room. It was luxury compared to where they tried to put us.'

At the Kaiserkeller, swapping onstage shifts, the Beatles and the Hurricanes naturally tried to outdo one another. The Beatles, flying on booze and 'Prellies' (their nickname for the powerful, pill-form methamphetamine Preludin) were utterly feral. Starr was struck by how good the other band were: 'They were great in Hamburg … great rock. That's when the battle started.'

The two groups even bet on which of them would be the first to demolish the Kaiserkeller's shonky stage, a precarious arrangement of wooden planks laid over beer crates. Persistent nightly stomping by both bands produced a tantalising crack, before Storm's acrobatic leap from the piano to the stage, over Ringo's head, provided the winning moment of destruction.

Offstage, the musicians intermingled, although the Beatles were initially wary of Starkey's character. To them, he seemed too brash, possibly dodgy. George Harrison remembered them talking among themselves about the other band's drummer and deciding he looked like trouble. 'With that big grey streak in his hair and half a grey eyebrow and a big nose, he looked like a real tough guy. But it probably only took half an hour to realise it was actually… Ringo!'

The quiet, semi-detached figure of Pete Best typically chose not to hang out with the others and often disappeared into the city on his own. The Beatles began to enjoy having Starkey around. Still, he seemed prone to moodiness and more than once came in to the Kaiserkeller while the Beatles were playing, sat on his own near the front of the stage, got slowly drunk and requested they play sentimental, wee small hours slowies such as jazz standard 'Moonglow' and Duane Eddy's bleary, tear-in-the-beer shuffler 'Three-30-Blues'.

On 15 October 1960, a part-amalgam of the Beatles and the Hurricanes entered the tiny Akustik Studio for a recording session. Allan Williams enjoyed the parts of the latter band's set when bassist Lu Walters stepped into the spotlight to take a vocal turn, and believed he had the makings of a popular ballad crooner.

Lennon, McCartney and Harrison were roped in to back Walters, partly due to their playing skills but mainly for their vocal harmonies. Starr, not Best, was chosen as the drummer, making it the first time the future Fab Four appeared together on record, performing George Gershwin's Porgy and Bess aria, 'Summertime', Peggy Lee's super-slinky 1958 hit 'Fever', and Kurt Weill's mournful, reflective 'September Song'.

Between five and seven 78rpm acetate copies were made. Memories differed; looking back, no one could quite agree on whether all three of the songs, excepting 'Summertime' on the A-side, were actually cut to disc. Still, none of the records were considered important enough to preserve and were forever lost. Or, in the case of Allan Williams's copy, left in a London pub.

~

Back home in Liverpool, by the end of the following year and with their local reputation fast growing, the Beatles ended 1961 at the Cavern on 27 December headlining their 'Christmas Party', topping the bill above Gerry and the Pacemakers and Kingsize Taylor and the Dominoes.

As was becoming a more regular occurrence, Pete Best phoned in sick, sealing his ultimate fate. The Beatles asked Ringo to step in for him at the last minute. It was a revelatory moment. George, in particular, felt that the band were far better when their songs were being driven by Starr's intense and insistent beats. 'It seemed like,' Harrison later said, '"This is it".'

Three days later, however, Ringo returned to Hamburg, having accepted a gig drumming at the Top Ten club in the amorphous backing band of Norwich-born singer-guitarist Tony Sheridan, who'd been resident in the city since first performing there in the summer of 1960. Starkey was lured back there by the prospect of a flat, a car and a fat wage packet. Within weeks, though, he realised he'd made a mistake. The bandleader was an erratic presence, frequently chopping and changing songs in the middle of the set without telling the band.

Worse, Sheridan had recently had a son, Richard, with his girlfriend, Kaiserkeller barmaid Rosi Heitmann, and was notably, and very aggressively, the jealous type. 'If anybody talked to his girlfriend, Rosi,' Ringo recalled, 'he'd put his guitar down, run off the stage, jump into the audience and fight the guy. So we would just carry on playing. We'd be jamming away and he'd be punching and fighting, and then he'd come back on stage like nothing happened.' That was if Sheridan won the fight. Ringo remembered him more than once clambering back to the microphone 'covered in blood if he'd lost'.

By March, Starkey was back in Liverpool. Around noon on the 26th at Admiral Grove, Elsie knocked on Richy's bedroom door to let him know that the Beatles' manager Brian Epstein was outside. Pete Best was sick again.

'Would you play the lunchtime session at the Cavern for us?' Epstein asked Starkey.

'Give's a minute to get a cup of tea and get me trousers on and I'll come on down,' the drummer replied.

In fact, the Beatles had two gigs booked for that day: the lunchtime session at the Cavern and a night-time show at the Kingsway Club in Southport. At both shows, the quartet's musical chemistry was once again apparent to all. In between that day's performances, the four hung out together again, drinking and joking and enjoying an easy camaraderie. Harrison made overtures to Starkey about joining the band permanently.

'Yeah, I'd love to,' he responded, 'but you've got a drummer…'

George began to push the idea further with John and Paul, saying, 'Why don't we get Ringo in the band?'

Instead, a couple of days later, less through loyalty and more due to their lack of courage to sack their current drummer, Pete Best returned.

But the others' doubts about Best continued to grow. On 1 January in London, when the Beatles fluffed their Decca audition through collective nerves, Best's performance was conspicuously ropey, playing behind the beat on the band's cover of the Coasters' 'Searchin'' and stiffly on Lennon-McCartney originals 'Like Dreamers Do' and 'Hello Little Girl'. Pushing and dragging, dragging and pushing.

Then, on 6 June, at EMI Studios on Abbey Road, Best's drumming on a clippety-cloppety 'Love Me Do' was lumbering. In the middle eight, when he moved from rimshot cracks to snare drum beats, he suddenly *slowwwwwwwed* in tempo in a way that was unacceptable in a professional environment. The Beatles sounded like a clockwork toy with an unwinding spring. Parlophone A&R man/producer George Martin was forced to have a word with Brian Epstein.

'I said, "Look, I think the weak link in this band is the drums",' he remembered. '"Next time you come along, I will provide a professional drummer. No one need know." I didn't realise that I was touching a sore point and the other boys said, "OK, let's get rid of him."'

Still, it took another ten weeks before Best was called to a meeting at Epstein's office on 16 August, the day after his final lunchtime and evening shows at the Cavern. The Beatles knew they were being cowards by not breaking the news to their drummer themselves.

'We weren't very good at telling Pete he had to go,' Harrison confessed. 'But when it comes down to it, how do you tell somebody?'

By this point, having heard that Ringo had taken a job with Kingsize Taylor and the Dominoes, John and Paul motored over to Butlin's in Skegness, arriving by 10 a.m. at the caravan that Starkey was sharing with the Hurricanes' Johnny Guitar. The latter opened the door, surprised to see the pair. Paul told him, 'We've come to ask Ringo to join us.' Storm was duly roused and a proposal was offered. 'Mr Epstein would like Pete Best to come and play with you,' said McCartney.

Starkey accepted the offer to join the Beatles on the spot. 'I loved playing with them,' he simply reasoned. The job came with the condition that he shave off the chinstrap beard he'd grown that summer, snip his quiff and comb his hair into a fringe.

Best, even after Storm dashed back to Liverpool to try to convince him, turned down the job with the Hurricanes, too upset by his sacking from the Beatles. Storm and the Hurricanes were set to go through drummer after drummer. In January 1964, Liverpool music paper *Mersey Beat* ran a story on the struggling band with an evocative headline: 'The Ghost of Ringo Haunts This Group'.

~

Under the coved ceiling of the Victorian-built Hulme Hall in the vividly named village of Port Sunlight on the Wirral peninsula, on the evening of 18 August 1962, the definitive Beatles line-up played together for the first time as an official unit. Musically, with Ringo, they had more pace and *snap*. Offstage, they shared quick and slightly surreal banter.

The occasion was the annual dance held by the Port Sunlight Horticultural Society and so the hall was festooned with blooms. There, John, Paul, George and Ringo played songs of love love love together, surrounded by flowers. It was as if a portal had opened up into a possible future.

6

REPERCUSSIONS

Ringo and Pete, 1961–2022

ight months before the Port Sunlight show, there was a black-and-white photograph, taken on 8 December 1961 by *Mersey Beat* snapper Dick Matthews, that seemed of no great importance at the time.

It showed the band changeover interval at the Tower Ballroom in New Brighton, the seaside suburb of Wallasey on the tip of the Wirral. Topping the bill were the Beatles. Second on the bill were Rory Storm and the Hurricanes. Between sets, moving their gear on and off the stage, left to right were George Harrison, uncoiling a guitar lead while grinning and chatting to John Lennon, then Ringo Starr carrying a cymbal off the platform and saying something to Pete Best, waiting to lift his kit up, as Paul McCartney stood to his left absorbed by something on the floor.

It was for many years believed to be the only shot of the Beatles with both of their drummers, and certainly the only one of Pete and Ringo together. The significance of the handover, dramatically reversed within a year, was later lost on no one.

Subsequently, another picture appeared, thought to have been taken the following week at the same venue: a bird's-eye view of the Beatles, with Ringo watching on, sitting just offstage.

'Ringo and I were very good friends,' Best later stated, although there was never any real evidence to support this. Even any casual association between the two, whether it be in Liverpool or Hamburg, ended in the middle of August 1962. Being sacked from the Beatles privately hit Pete Best hard, although he attempted to maintain a sanguine attitude and dignified public face. In reality, as he later confessed, 'I felt like putting a stone 'round my neck and jumping off the Pier Head.'

Twice in 1963, after Best began playing drums with another group, Lee Curtis and the All-Stars, he endured the ignominy of supporting his former band: once at the Cavern, and then at the Majestic Ballroom in Birkenhead.

'It meant that as we were coming offstage, the Beatles were going on stage,' he told David Letterman in the July of 1982, a month shy of the twentieth anniversary of him being kicked out of the group. 'Nothing was ever mentioned,' he added. 'There was no acknowledgement. Just stony silence.'

The hapless drummer's appearance on the US talk show was seen by more than 1.5 million viewers. It was an awkward encounter. Best came across as a shy, normal bloke, visibly nervous in the spotlight. Letterman tried to bring an air of light comedy and sympathetic pathos to a conversation that was frequently toe-curling. Best's anecdotes tended to peter out uneventfully and the audience began to titter.

He tried to go with it. Letterman enquired about the sacking and wondered, 'What does that do to a person?'

Best mock-grimaced, before admitting that being rejected by his former bandmates 'caused me a lot of hardship, grief, financial embarrassment. But I persevered with my own lifestyle and I was strong enough in character to turn around and say, "OK, no matter what happened in the past, let's forget about it."'

Talking about his post-Beatles music career (with the Pete Best Four and then the US-based Pete Best Combo), he pointed out that he'd enjoyed 'mediocre success', when he probably meant to say 'middling'. A woman off-screen hooted with laughter. Perhaps the outburst was genuine and she thought he'd meant to say 'mediocre'. The studio audience might have expected a Beatle, even a former one, to be quick-witted and slightly surreal.

All the while, behind Pete Best's every forced grin, there seemed to be underlying pain.

~

There was clearly, and understandably, no love lost between Best and Starr. Down the years, in interviews, the latter was pragmatic, though perhaps not gracious in victory.

In 1992, in an acutely tetchy encounter with *Q* magazine, writer Tom Hibbert asked Ringo if he ever felt sorry for Pete.

'No. Why should I?' he argued. 'I was a better player than him. That's how I got the job. It wasn't on no personality. It was that I was a better drummer.'

Three years on, interviewed for the Beatles' authorised *Anthology* project, Starr hadn't softened his stance.

'I never felt sorry for Pete Best,' he said. 'I was not involved [in his sacking]. Besides, I felt I was a much better drummer than he was.'

Still, *Anthology* was to provide Pete Best with the surprise windfall that he was perhaps owed, having been forced to live for decades in the long, black shadows far from the stellar light of Beatles' success. *Anthology 1*, the first of three double CD compilations of the band's outtakes and works-in-progress – and released in 1995 to coincide with the TV series *The Beatles Anthology* – contained no less than ten of his studio performances with the band, no matter how heavy-handed and tempo-erratic they remained.

In a tie-in promotional piece for the *Sun*, he said, 'for me, the poignant tracks are those that I was involved in. Frankly, I'm bloody proud and believe they really stand the test of time.'

Coaxed in 2020 by Irish TV host Ryan Tubridy to reveal how much he'd earned in *Anthology* royalties, Best smiled coyly. 'Somewhere between one and six notes', presumably meaning million.

Rarely did he show any public resentment in regard to Starr.

Rarely.

In 2022, appearing on the breakfast TV show *Ireland AM*, he was asked by presenter Anton Savage, 'Did you rate Ringo?'

'As what?' Best shot back.

Savage burst out laughing. His co-host, Elaine Crowley, exclaimed, 'Woah!'

'Ringo has his own style, put it that way,' Best casually offered. 'Whether people like it or not is a difference of opinion. So I let the audience judge that.'

7

THE HATED BEATLE

Commotion in the Cavern, 1962

'**W**e want Pete!'

The first shout rose up from the crowd, all too appropriately, just as the band kicked into 'Some Other Guy'. A male voice was quickly echoed by a female one.

'We want Pete!'

Four days after Ringo's first official gig as the Beatles' drummer in Port Sunlight, at the lunchtime Cavern show on Wednesday 22 August 1962, there was loud, angry dissent among the group's fans about his replacing of Best.

On the scratchy recording made that day by Granada TV soundman Gordon Butler, a counter cry from another girl fan was audible.

'We want Ringo!'

Capturing the drama on film was the crew from Granada's *Know the North* show, drawn to Liverpool and the Mathew Street basement after receiving umpteen letters from Beatles devotees keen to spread the word. A single 16mm camera was pointed at the stage, recording the proceedings in black and white, while a sole microphone cracked into distortion due to the sheer volume.

The Beatles were being professionally filmed for the first time and this low-lit, grainy footage would forever serve to prove that they were a fully formed act by the summer of '62. But, as they finished the song, their souped-up cover of Philadelphia singer Richie Barrett's R&B groover, the voice of the same bloke in the audience could be heard again, louder this time, and more insistent.

'We want *Pete!*'

'There was a lot of fighting and shouting,' Ringo remembered, more than three decades later. 'Half of them hated me, half of them loved me.'

That afternoon, whether boldly or defiantly, Pete Best slipped into the Cavern to catch the gig and witnessed the furore. 'It was a nice feeling to realise that I had true loyal supporters,' he would reflect. 'There was a hell of a fan reaction.'

During the Beatles' set, in the crowd, their spurned drummer was spotted by Jim McCartney, Paul's dad. 'Great, isn't it?' Best remembered McCartney Sr saying to him, in a moment of excitement yet clear insensitivity. 'They're on TV!'

Two days later, at the next lunchtime Cavern show, the fan protest had gained momentum, and gained two new chants.

'Pete is best!'

'Ringo never! Pete Best forever!'

George took the haranguing personally, perhaps because he'd been the one who'd lobbied hard for the change of drummer. Half an hour into the set, the guitarist started hurling abuse back at the disgruntled fans. Then, later, when he emerged from the Cavern's poky dressing room, 'some guy nodded me one, giving me a black eye'.

Some of those present later argued that the headbutt had nothing to do with Pete Best's sacking. McCartney believed the attacker to be a jealous boy-friend, angered by the starry-eyed attention his girlfriend was giving Harrison. *Mersey Beat* named the perpetrator as someone else entirely: 'Bruno, a Best fan'. Others there claimed that it was simply an act of random violence by a well-known Scouse 'hardcase', Denny Flynn.

In any event, it only strengthened the bond between Harrison and Starr. 'George got a black eye,' Ringo would point out, with barely disguised, brotherly pride.

The conflicting accounts were symptomatic of the mood of paranoia in the Beatles camp in the weeks after Best's sacking. Many fans unfairly blamed Brian Epstein and someone tipped paint stripper over his Ford Zodiac. When the Beatles played an evening show at the Cavern the following Sunday (26 August), the club's owner Ray McFall was forced to have bouncer-turned-bodyguard Paddy Delaney stationed by the manager's side.

Worse, Epstein was initially ambivalent about the line-up change that caused all this hassle. 'They all liked Ringo, although I thought he was rather loud,' he admitted, before allowing that Starr 'did seem to complete a visual pattern with the Beatles. I didn't want him but … I trusted the boys' instincts.'

As far as Ringo was concerned, even the Beatles' roadie Neil Aspinall seemed to hate him and appeared to go on strike, refusing to set up his drum kit. Complicating matters, in a slightly odd pairing, the twenty-year-old Aspinall was in a relationship with Pete Best's mother, Mona, thirty-eight at the time. Their partnership had produced a son, Vincent, born only the month before. It seemed clear where Aspinall's loyalties lay.

'He was a little miffed,' Ringo said. 'This lasted for a few weeks, but he got over it.'

In his defence, Aspinall claimed he simply hadn't known how to set up a drum kit since Best had always done it himself. 'He thought I was thinking, *Fuck you*,' he said. In the months and years that followed, Aspinall sensed that Starr never quite forgot the rebuff.

Meanwhile, Granada considered the murky footage shot in the Cavern that day to be too poor quality to screen. Inevitably, by the following year, it was considered to be of far higher value, being the first celluloid frames of a cultural explosion. On 6 November 1963, the station proudly featured it on their teatime magazine programme, *Scene at 6.30*.

By this time, of course, the cries of 'We want Pete!' had long faded away and been drowned out by the white noise screams of Beatlemania.

8

TWELVE MONTHS OF MADNESS

The View from Behind the Kit, 1963

From his position at the back of the stage, in the gaps between John, Paul and George's arses, Ringo looked down at a small audience 'all wearing wellies ... farmers and country people'. Worse, they appeared to be *laughing at* – as they were named on the bill – 'The "Love Me Do" Boys', these cocky, long-haired, out-of-town rockers stomping their way through 'Roll Over Beethoven' and 'Whole Lotta Shakin' Goin' On'.

The venue was the Two Red Shoes ballroom in the small town of Elgin, forty miles north-east of Inverness in the Scottish Highlands. The date was 3 January 1963, a Thursday. The show – the Beatles headlining over the swinging sounds of the Alex Sutherland Sextet – was being promoted by the Elgin Folk Club, who'd also generously laid on night buses for the punters to return to 'Buckie, Forres, Lossiemouth, etc'.

The first-floor dancehall was shaped like a dog's leg, with the stage located in the 'paw', meaning that more than half the audience couldn't actually see the Beatles. Not that it mattered much at first anyway, since there was virtually no one there to see them.

Arthur McKerron, a local rugby player, who'd just finished a meal at the café downstairs, wandered up at around 9 p.m. to have a look and found a 'deserted' ballroom. 'There was just these four boys on the platform,' he remembered. 'One couple were just walking or jiving around the hall and three or four couples were at a wee higher level where they had seating and tables. The place was dead.'

Later reports suggested that anything up to 200 people eventually turned up, but that may have only been because the pubs closed at nine-thirty, and

45

there was nowhere else for the welly-wearing country folk to go apart from the Two Red Shoes, with its soft drinks bar and sailors from the port of Lossiemouth peddling their cheap 'blue liner' Royal Navy issue cigarettes.

It was a rough crowd – and one the Beatles didn't win over, being openly mocked. Ringo remembered it as 'one of the strangest gigs we played'.

Adeline Reid, a trainee nurse who lived in a boarding house nearby, hadn't been able to afford tickets for the dance, but heard that the band 'did not go down too well'. The next day she was walking to work, wearing her 'hideous outdoor nurse's uniform', and passed various Beatles hanging out of the window of their guest house, being 'cheeky and outrageous'. John shouted over to her, wondering if she fancied taking his pulse, and her face turned scarlet.

The worst thing about Elgin being such a shit gig was what a schlep it had been to get there. The new year began with a flight from Hamburg to London, after two hated weeks in December playing at the 'converted gas chamber' (Lennon's words) that was the Star-Club. On 2 January, the four were supposed to fly from London to Edinburgh, but bad weather forced a diversion to Aberdeen. They landed in Scotland during what was to be long remembered as the Big Freeze of '63, one of the coldest winters on record.

Virtually all of the Scottish roads were clogged with snow or coated with sheets of ice. The first gig at Longmore Hall in the Highlands town of Keith on the 2nd was cancelled when the band simply couldn't get there through the impassable routes. Ringo later remembered 'freezing your balls off, fighting for the seats … sliding all over Scotland'.

Being a touring Beatle in the early weeks of 1963 took some nerve and dedication: endless drives in a Bedford van, in body-numbing cold and freezing fog, often slowed to one mile an hour. Neil Aspinall was driving, with the luckiest or fastest Beatle in the passenger seat. The three others lay horizontally piled in the back, sharing a bottle of whisky and rotating their positions when whoever was on top began complaining that, as Starr put it, they were 'so cold that hypothermia was setting in'. Paul likened them to 'a Beatles sandwich … so non glam'.

The night after Elgin, they played to nineteen people in the town hall in Dingwall. The following evening, they managed to fill the Museum Hall in Bridge of Allan with 100 punters – 'ninety-six drunk young farmers and four women' as promoter Andi Lothian recalled – who were clearly up for a rowdy Saturday. Pennies were thrown at the stage, one chipping Paul's bass. A chandelier above the dancefloor was 'almost wrecked' by flying debris.

The weather conditions didn't improve when the Beatles got back down south. On Tuesday 22 January, they recorded a radio session for the BBC in London. The following day, as they were driving home to Liverpool, a rock flew up from the road and cracked their van's windscreen. Assistant roadie Mal Evans, a hulking gentle giant, manfully punched out the remaining glass and drove on in sub-zero temperatures as the Beatles once again sandwiched for warmth in the back.

It wasn't the most auspicious of beginnings to what would be the most monumental year of their lives.

~

Five days later, Paul McCartney heard himself on the radio for the first time, as he motored out of Liverpool to hook up with the other Beatles for a gig at the Three Coins club in Manchester. Even though it was nearly a month after 'Love Me Do' had reached number seventeen in the charts, he hadn't yet caught the record floating out over the airwaves.

'I'm down by the ballrooms that we used to play ... the Locarno and the Grafton,' he recalled many years later, still so thrilled by the memory that he could pinpoint the exact location as West Derby Road. 'I was driving right there and it came on the radio, y'know. I remember just wanting to lean out the window and scream at everyone, "That's me! Listen to this! This is me!"'

Their reputation rising, though not quickly, in February the Beatles moved up from the halls and clubs to their first theatre tour, although they were plonked at the bottom of a six-act package bill. The headliner was sixteen-year-old London wunderkind Helen Shapiro, the youngest artist ever to top the British charts, at fourteen in 1961, with pining weepie 'You Don't Know'.

Still, the gigs remained a slog and, from his drum riser, Starr watched the band playing to largely disinterested audiences. Nightly, though, they increasingly began to capture the crowds' attentions.

On the road, the Beatles shared twin rooms: John with George, Paul with Ringo. Harrison, being the one who'd brought Starr into the band, was the instigator of this member-shuffling hotel arrangement. 'I thought that rather than me hang out with Ringo,' he reasoned, 'it would be best if he shared with one of them because that would integrate him better.'

By this time, their second single, 'Please Please Me', was out and making its leisurely way up the charts. Ringo had played on a rehearsal version at his first session with the band at EMI Studios the previous September. Terrified of the recording environment, he'd manically overplayed: a maraca in one hand and a tambourine in the other, smashing the cymbals with them, while madly pedalling the hi-hat and kick drum. The week after, he turned up at the next session, for the A-side recording of 'Love Me Do', and found that George Martin had installed session drummer Andy White in his place.

'That's the end,' he thought. 'They're doing a Pete Best on me.'

But while the other Beatles had zero influence on the producer's decision, their loyalty to their new drummer was strong. Ringo's subsequent performance on the definitive 'Please Please Me', recorded in November '62, was undeniably powerful, fluid and inventive. Martin had confidently predicted to the group on the night, 'Chaps, you've got your first number one. I'm sure of it.' Still, Starr secretly harboured a grudge against the producer for years.

On 11 February, the Beatles hammered out the other songs for their debut long-player in an intensive shift just shy of ten hours, brilliantly capturing on tape the sound of their nervous energy and nascent expertise. Ringo got a turn at the microphone, his first lead vocal in a studio, reprising his 'Starr Time' turn on 'Boys', practised nightly at Butlin's and in Hamburg, and nailed in one take. 'We just had to run, run them down,' he noted. George said the Beatles 'were permanently on the edge' during the session.

Eleven days later, 'Please Please Me' hit number one on the *New Musical Express* and *Melody Maker* charts (although only number two on the *Record Retailer* trade mag chart). The following night, backstage at the Granada cinema in Mansfield, the band gathered around the TV set in Helen Shapiro's dressing room and watched themselves performing the song, for an audience of around six million, on ITV pop show *Thank Your Lucky Stars*.

Going to number one had a pronounced effect on the Beatles' heads. 'Swelled them a bit, y'know,' McCartney admitted. 'It was really great, man. You've got [the charting of "Love Me Do"] originally, which is good enough, and then "Please Please Me" is number one, y'know. That's like, "Hey baby".

It's what you've been aiming for and it's what you've been dreaming about. You've watched everyone else get there, but when you get there yourself … I don't think there's many feelings quite like it.'

Almost overnight on the Helen Shapiro tour, the Beatles became the main attraction. 'It was embarrassing because she was a very nice person,' George sympathetically noted.

Even amid this excitement, it was still all about the graft. The theatre tour ended and, five days later, another began, the Beatles billed below US rockers Tommy Roe and Chris Montez. Both were quickly overshadowed.

But ten weeks of trudging around the frozen UK had taken its toll on the band. As the snows finally began to melt in the first weeks of March, Lennon was left with a stinker of a head cold that killed his voice and forced him to miss three shows: Bedford on the 12th, York on the 13th, Wolverhampton on the 14th. One man down, the other three were forced to divvy up his vocal parts and play harder.

~

From here, the Beatles went everywhere, zipping around the country, fulfilling engagements that Brian Epstein had made for them prior to their new-found number-one status. Often, these were fifty-quid bookings when they could have been making five grand. The Riverside Dancing Club at the Bridge Hotel in Tenbury Wells. The Floral Hall in Southport. The Music Hall in Shrewsbury.

'We played every gig,' Ringo stated with some pride. 'We'd play some daft club in Birmingham because we'd been booked. I'm glad we did that and not drop the little clubs for the Palladium and say, "Fuck you".' Neil Aspinall was amazed to see how their 'popularity was escalating madly, day by day'.

When they played a handful of 'Mersey Beat Showcase' nights along with Gerry and the Pacemakers, the Big Three and Billy J Kramer, the Beatles had something *other* and easily upstaged the lot of them. At the Fairfield Halls in Croydon on 25 April, promoter John Smith hedged his bets, booking a 'guest star' headliner, 'Johnny Remember Me' singer John Leyton. Leyton fell ill on the day and news of his non-appearance was announced to the queuing crowd. They cheered. Everyone was there to see the Beatles. It was a changing of the guard.

At the same time, they now had competition. Eleven days earlier on 14 April – after taping their third appearance on *Thank Your Lucky Stars* at Teddington Studios, lip-syncing their way through their cutesy third single, 'From Me to You' – they drove to Richmond to watch a new band they'd heard about, who were playing at the Crawdaddy Club in the back room of the Station Hotel. The Beatles were all about re-energising rock 'n' roll and American R&B pop. The Rolling Stones peddled thrilling, dirty blues.

Ringo vividly remembered his first experience of seeing the band who would become his group's greatest rivals in 'some sweaty room. Keith and Brian – wow. I knew then that the Stones were great. They just had *presence*.'

Halfway through May, the Beatles embarked upon their third package tour, co-headlining with one of their heroes (and one of John's, in particular): the king of the heartbreak crescendo, Roy Orbison. The first few dates saw 'The Big O' close the show, until public demand made it obvious that the Beatles had to perform last. In three months, they'd gone from the bottom of the bill to the top. Unaccustomed to being theatrical headliners, in the wings before they went on, they'd nervously whisper a much-repeated catchphrase amongst themselves: 'Guess who's next, folks. It's your favourite rave!'

Being the headliners on the tour wasn't as easy as it looked, though. Ringo said 'it was terrible' following Orbison, because he'd 'slay them and they'd scream for more'. 'They ended up at the top of the bill,' noted Danny Thompson, bassist with Orbison's backing band for the tour, the Sons of the Piltdown Men. 'But they used to go on stage, and you couldn't hear 'em. They could've been singing the national anthem.'

But, the same month – and emblematic of the Beatles' fast-growing celebrity – they were given their own BBC radio series, *Pop Go the Beatles*. The first episode was recorded at the grand Aeolian Hall on New Bond Street on 24 May. On air, they sounded just as sharp as they did on their debut album, which had been out for two months but was only now beginning a thirty-week run at the top of the chart. In the songs recorded specifically for the wireless, Ringo drove the band hard, kicking into the fills of 'You Really Got a Hold on Me' and hammering away at 'The Hippy Hippy Shake'.

Then, on 1 July, at EMI Studios on Abbey Road, the Beatles bottled lightning. 'She Loves You' had been written by Lennon and McCartney on

Wednesday 26 June, facing one another, 'eyeball to eyeball', on twin beds in a room at Newcastle's Royal Turk's Head Hotel after a show at the city's Majestic Ballroom. Five days later in the studio, it exploded into life with a super-charged Starr performance replete with a wristy opening tom roll, fizzing hi-hats, gun-crack snares and syncopated rolls that were to become almost as famous as John, Paul and George's 'Yeah, yeah, yeah's. It was the beat that helped to sell a million singles.

In the last week of July, seventeen-year-old Mark Tilley was down at the beach at Brean Sands in Somerset, when he spotted four lads clowning around for the benefit of a photographer. He wandered over and was immediately pulled into the action when they nicked his straw sombrero from him and carried on gooning.

'I got it back,' Tilley said. 'They weren't rotten. They didn't take it away from me.'

In the summer of 1963, the Beatles were playing a six-night residency at the Odeon up the coast at Weston-super-Mare. Czech-born, London-based photographer Dezo Hoffmann, a bespectacled fatherly figure already in his fifties, visited them there and snapped pictures of them playing leapfrog on the beach wearing Victorian-styled stripy bathing suits. Hoffman also took colour Super 8 film footage that caught them doing daft music-hall dances, mock-fighting and pulling strongman poses. They were already showy naturals on screen.

Girl fans in their summer dresses milled around outside the venue, peering over a wall to see the Beatles sunbathing – with their tops off, but trousers on, and Ringo smoking fags while displaying his pasty, whippet-thin torso. Not that he would remain so waif-like for long.

Everything they now did was being scrutinised, even what they ate. Ringo's diet richly expanded that year and there were reported sightings of him tucking into, among other things, smoked salmon, rainbow trout, fillet steak, banana fritters, crème caramel, pints and pints of milk and generous dollops of ice cream. 'Our weight went right up,' he said, 'because we were eating all this food.' (But never, for him, Chinese food. He'd told teen magazine *Romeo* back in April that it was one of his major dislikes, along with Donald Duck.)

In another seaside town, Bournemouth, they posed for a different photographer, the artful Robert Freeman, who shot them – just as their friend Astrid Kirchherr had in Hamburg – in black and white with their faces half-lit and moody. For the hour-long shoot in a low-lit corridor at the Palace Court Hotel, Ringo was positioned in front of the other three, mainly to fit the square framing, but also, as Freeman noted, 'since he was the last to join the group'.

If the drummer was sometimes an afterthought, it was underlined by the fact that John and Paul were happy to give away to the Rolling Stones the track he was set to sing on their second album, *With the Beatles*. It came about after the pair bumped into Mick Jagger and Keith Richards on West End music row Denmark Street in early September and cadged a lift in their cab.

Keen to hawk tunes to other acts as a sideline, Paul told Mick, 'Ringo's got this track on our album, but it won't be a single and it might suit you guys.' Lennon and McCartney later taught the Stones the basic structure of 'I Wanna Be Your Man' in the studio, before the duo went off into a corner to finish it, astonishing the still non-songwriting Jagger and Richards with their skill and spontaneity.

The very next day, the Beatles recorded their version for Ringo. 'It was a throwaway,' Lennon later remarked, before adding, a touch cruelly but revealingly, 'the only two versions of the song were Ringo and the Rolling Stones. That shows how much importance we put on it. We weren't going to give them anything great, right?'

At the same time, inviting the rival band to have a go at the track was almost a throwdown: the Beatles versus the Stones in a race to see who could cut the definitive version. In end, it was probably a draw: Ringo's version was punchier and pacier, and he delivered the lyric as if he fancied an innocent cuddle on the dancefloor. The Stones' interpretation was messier, and filthier, like a whispered proposition from a dark alley. It may have been a 'throwaway' number, but it set the stylistic dividing line.

∼

In the hairdressing department of the Horne Brothers clothing store on Lord Street in Liverpool, Ringo walked past a line of girls, sat with their heads stuck under domed blow-dryers, as a film cameraman tracked his movement.

'I've always fancied having a ladies hairdressing salon,' he deadpanned in the interview preceding the scene in BBC documentary *The Mersey Sound*. 'Y'know,' he added, grinning, 'a string of them in fact.' Someone, presumably another Beatle, cackled offscreen. 'Trot round in me stripes and me tails,' Ringo envisaged. '"Like a cup of tea, madam?"'

He was only half-serious, but it was an option. The Beatles surely couldn't last, so he was 'saving like mad' to start a business. Possibly the idea had come to him after he'd started seeing a new girl the previous year, Maureen 'Mo' Cox, an assistant hairdresser at the Ashley Du Pre Continental Hair and Beauty Salon.

To Starr, fame felt bizarre and was bound to be fleeting. Elsewhere in the BBC documentary, he was filmed leaving 10 Admiral Grove, pushing through a crowd of shrieking kids and making his escape by zooming off with George in the guitarist's open-topped sports car.

In this first flush of celebrity, and even after their eye-popping education in Hamburg, the Beatles remained decidedly unworldly. It was easy to forget that, even as the eldest band member, Ringo was still only twenty-three – and George the youngest at a mere twenty. Out at night in '63 in the Soho clubs, the drummer was 'mortified' to discover that Ad Lib owner Brian Morris would greet him by kissing him on the check. Eventually he accepted that 'that was just the London way'.

Sometimes, he was screamingly naïve. On an overbooked flight from London to Glasgow in October, Ringo offered to stand for the duration, only to be gently informed, 'I'm afraid you can't do that, Mr Starr.'

Becoming local heroes back in Liverpool 'made us nervous', said Lennon. The Beatles believed that their fellow Scousers would reckon they'd sold out ('Which we had in a way,' he confessed). Conversely, as far as Middle England was concerned, they were still rough-arsed lads from the north. 'But we didn't try and change our accents, which in England were looked down upon,' Lennon stressed. As Paul was to later observe, the Beatles 'became part of the working-class explosion, making it OK to be common'.

Yet they still encountered snobbery. Even the lord privy seal (and future prime minister), Edward Heath, made a sniffy comment about how the Beatles didn't speak the 'Queen's English'.

'We're going, "Yeah, alright, fuck off",' said McCartney. 'The ideology then was anybody who spoke with anything other than a plummy BBC accent was stupid. Not just common, but probably very stupid. We got a lot of that.

'In the end, you got a hard shell,' he added. 'And the great thing about the Beatles, remember, is it was the unity of the four … the gang. We could always just say, "Aw, *fuck off*."'

If they were still made to feel like outsiders, month by month, they were drawn further into the establishment. In Ringo's mind, the big moment when he 'made it' came when the Beatles were invited to perform on ITV variety show *Sunday Night at the London Palladium* on 13 October.

Back in Liverpool when he was playing with the Eddie Clayton Skiffle Group, his mum Elsie's friend Annie Maguire would often jokily say to him, 'See you on the Palladium, son.' Now it was actually happening. 'I always wanted to play there, to get on that roundabout stage,' he said. 'There was nothing bigger in the world than making it to the Palladium. It was *dynamite*. Before the show, I was so nervous with craziness and tension [that] I spewed into a bucket.'

The show was watched by an estimated 15 million viewers and the next morning saw the term 'Beatlemania' being minted by the *Daily Mirror*, following the apparently deranged fan scenes outside the venue. There were, however, conflicting reports about what exactly happened that night: some people said there were actually only around nine girls in attendance; others claimed the band's car was parked 50 yards away from the stage door and the Beatles had to make a dash through a frenzied crowd.

'I can't actually remember what the fan situation was,' McCartney hazily reflected, decades later. 'But I'm gonna say there was millions of them…'

While there had been incidences of fan madness earlier in the year – not least on 19 May when three girls were taken into police custody after scaling 100 feet up a ladder in an attempt to gain access to the band's dressing room at the Gaumont in Hanley – in the wake of the Palladium performance, there were uproarious scenes up and down the country.

Rather than being thrown by the chaos, the group seemed to thrive on it and, with their fame skyrocketing, they began revealing more and more of their true characters, becoming a playfully cheeky and gently subversive anti-establishment force.

Playing for the Queen Mother and Princess Margaret at the Royal Variety performance at the Prince of Wales Theatre on 4 November, Lennon introduced a raucous 'Twist and Shout' with his soon-to-be legendary quip, 'For our last number, I'd like to ask your help. Will the people in the cheaper seats clap your hands? And the rest of you… if you just rattle your jewellery…'

'Driving there, we're thinking, *OK, what are we gonna say?*' McCartney recalled. 'And it was like, "OK, well, you say the first thing there and you do that, and you do that." We assigned each other a couple of jokes. And John came up with the "rattle your jewellery" thing, so it was like, "Oh yeah … that's the one." We just figured it out in the car on the way there.'

Ringo's face during the filmed performance remained fixed with his show-biz grin, with his sideways head wobbles animating his fringe, as was fast becoming his visual trademark. With just a sole microphone positioned above his drums, he threw himself at 'From Me to You', 'She Loves You' and 'Twist and Shout', ensuring the Beatles were *loud* in comparison to any act the royals had experienced before.

Still, these four rock 'n' roll rebels obediently fell into line when they returned to the stage for the showbizzy curtain call at the end of the show, where all of the performers were reintroduced to the audience, act by act. Compere Dickie Henderson yelled 'the Beatles!' and they trooped on. Ringo gave another groovy head shake, before Henderson announced, 'Hattie Jacques and Eric Sykes!', 'Harry H. Corbett and Wilfrid Brambell!'.

For years, the main memory of the event that stuck in Starr's mind was seeing a certain fellow performer up close: the sixty-two-year-old Marlene Dietrich, an international and iconic star of stage and screen back when he was a kid. He couldn't help himself 'staring at her legs as she slouched against a chair. I'm a leg man: "Look at those pins!"'

Five days later, on 9 November, the Beatles were backstage at the Granada Cinema in East Ham when Brian Epstein came to the dressing room to give them the jaw-dropping news that it looked as if their fifth single, 'I Want to Hold Your Hand', was going to shift more than a million copies on pre-sales alone. When it did, it was kept off the number one slot for a fortnight because 'She Loves You' was still firmly lodged there.

Atop a rickety circular podium that looked like some kind of huge industrial spindle, his drums shaking, Ringo pounded through 'I Want to Hold Your Hand', ending with a double cymbal smash and bowing his head in unison with the others before Ernie Wise walked onto the set clapping his hands in appreciation.

Lennon, McCartney and Harrison stepped forward to the front of the stage to greet the comedy straight man, as his wisecracking, faux-gauche partner Eric Morecambe appeared, exclaiming, 'Eyyyah, it's the Kaye Sisters'.

'The Kaye Sisters?' Wise corrected him. 'This is the Beatles.'

'Hello, Beatles,' Morecambe said in a daft singsong voice akin to *The Goon Show*'s Bluebottle, before walking towards the back of the stage. 'Where is he? There is... 'allo, Bongo.'

'That's Ringo,' said Wise.

'Oh, is he there as well?' said Morecambe.

The occasion was the taping of *The Morecambe and Wise Show* for ITV at Elstree Studios on 2 December, a TV appearance that wouldn't be aired for another four months, but that seemed to fully cement the Beatles into the world of light entertainment. Amid the semi-improvised banter that followed, Morecambe broke off to shout at the drummer once again.

'Alright, Bonzo?'

'That's Ringo,' Wise mock-persisted.

'Yeah, him as well.'

Much later, Starr pointed out that the Beatles' route to the top had been via the sometimes cheesy world of variety: 'We had to go through the Shirley Bassey school, that was our battle.'

But at the same time as the Beatles' world appeared to become safe and cosy, it also grew increasingly hazardous and terrifying. At the Wimbledon Palais on 14 December, at a convention held by the southern branch of their swiftly established official fan club, the four stood behind the venue's bar and shook hands with around 3,000 of their starry-eyed devotees (many of whom doubled back to the end of the queue and waited to meet them again).

At 4 p.m., the group jumped onstage for a short set, at which point utter chaos ensued. Firstly, they were pelted with jelly babies (John had said in an interview that he had a taste for the colourful gelatine sweets, but that George usually nicked his). More distressingly, girls horrifically crushed themselves up against wire mesh barriers that the organisers had placed in front of the stage, causing Lennon to carp: 'If they press any harder, they'll come through as chips.'

Up on the drum riser, Starr felt trapped. 'It was like being in a zoo,' he said. 'It felt dangerous. The kids were out of hand. It was the first time I felt that if they got near us, we would be ripped apart.'

Ten days later, on Christmas Eve, their fans mobbed the streets of north London, outside the Astoria Theatre in Finsbury Park, for the opening night of *The Beatles' Christmas Show*, an Epstein-devised festive revue that was set to run for sixteen nights, into the new year. The plan was for the four to perform comedy routines in between the sets by the various support acts on the bill, including the Barron Knights, Billy J Kramer and the Dakotas, Cilla Black and the later-disgraced wobble board-playing singer/artist Rolf Harris.

At the start of the show, the acts arrived on the stage by pretending to climb out of a pantomime-styled cardboard helicopter, before the Beatles appeared to screams that didn't stop for the entire evening. In one sketch, John played a top hat-wearing, wax-moustached villain, who tied George – in dress and headscarf, as the hapless Ermyntrude – to invisible rail tracks, only to be saved by the fearless, handsome signalman Paul. Ringo was relegated to throwing fake snow around from a sack with the word 'Snow' on it.

It was a mess, and they hadn't really bothered rehearsing. They were performing a daft sketch they hadn't properly learned and that no one could hear anyway. In a year, they'd gone from playing to gangsters and off-duty strippers on the Reeperbahn to performing for legions of worryingly demented teenagers.

Befitting of their elevated position, after the show, the Beatles boarded a Vickers VC.1 Viking aeroplane, charted by Epstein, for a private flight home to Liverpool. Ahead of take-off, Ringo was photographed mock-fainting as a foxy air stewardess helpfully fastened his seatbelt. It had been less than twelve months since he and the others had been nervously sliding around on remote Scottish roads in their Bedford van.

9

HOLIDAY(S) '63

Spain and Greece, 1963

In the midst of all the madness, Ringo enjoyed two Beatle-shaped holidays in 1963.

On Sunday 28 April, the day after the group played the Memorial Hall in Northwich, a fortnight's break stretched out ahead of them. Being a self-confessed 'bastard' and leaving wife Cynthia and their three-week-old son Julian behind, Lennon flew to Barcelona with Brian Epstein for a trip that would prompt much sexuality-speculating tittle-tattle back in Liverpool. Meanwhile, McCartney, Harrison and Starr jetted off to Tenerife for a lads' holiday.

It was the most exotic experience of Ringo's life so far. He'd never seen black volcanic sand before. He bought himself a wide-brimmed black bolero hat and had his photograph taken posing in it, 'hanging out ... looking dramatic'. Other pictures showed Paul, George and Ringo in swimming trunks, shades and sandals, but still wearing nice shirts.

Out there, they met up with their Hamburg pals, Astrid Kirchherr and Klaus Voormann, and together they all stayed in Voormann's parents' villa. The house had no electricity, which strangely added to the appeal. 'We really felt like bohemians,' said Ringo. Voormann gave Harrison the keys to his open-topped Austin-Healey Sprite sports car and George and Paul drove it up the Mount Teide volcano where the pair marvelled at the astronomical observatory and cruised through the barren landscape feeling as if they'd landed on the moon.

But, like typical first-time British holidaymakers, Paul ended up with acute sunburn and Ringo and George both suffered sunstroke, which kept them up all night with shivery flu symptoms. More worryingly, one day an overly confident McCartney swam too far out into the sea and found himself in trouble.

'I got caught in a riptide,' he said. 'I thought, *Now I'll swim back in*, but I realised I wasn't getting anywhere. In fact, I was getting further away...' It might have been the end of the Beatles there and then, but Paul somehow managed to anxiously scramble his way back to the shore.

Naturally, while in Spain, the three wondered if their Beatles fame had travelled too. It hadn't. 'We were a bit put off,' McCartney said. '"You know us? The Beatles?" And they were saying, "No, no..."'

~

Later that year, in the middle of September, the Beatles squeezed in another break. Becoming the first band member to set foot in the US, George and his elder brother Peter visited their sister Louise, who'd moved to Benton, Illinois nine years earlier. The trip also worked in detours to New York and St Louis. John, taking Cynthia along with him this time, went to Paris, where they met up with Epstein.

Meanwhile, Ringo and Maureen went to Greece with Paul and his new girlfriend Jane Asher, a sharp and already seasoned seventeen-year-old film and TV actress who'd met McCartney back in April at the Royal Albert Hall during the 'Swinging Sound of '63' concert, where the Beatles made an appearance. On the day, she was photographed for the *Radio Times*, mock-screaming at the group.

The four spent the first week of the holiday on Corfu. They stayed in chalets, rising around ten and heading out to sunbathe, before retreating back indoors an hour later due to the intense, intolerable heat. Here, Ringo, due to his delicate constitution, spent his mealtimes wearily picking bits of garlic out of his meals and longing 'for a good old steak and chips, or a few cheese slices'.

Next, the party ventured south-west to Rhodes for a few days. Starkey was keen to see the Colossus, only to be informed by a British lady in their hotel bar, 'It's gone now, son.' (The towering 108-foot statue of the Greek sun god Helios had in fact been destroyed back in 653 BC.) Wandering down to the harbour, Starr and the others were disappointed to be met by the sight of 'two little plinths with two deers on, supposedly where the Colossus was'. The two-week trip ended at the Acropole Palace Hotel in Athens, where, on the last night, Ringo and Paul, likely sloshed on the local ouzo, joined in with the house band, Trio Athenia.

For Ringo, this second jaunt was ultimately a far less satisfying experience than Tenerife. He remembered 'going around the Parthenon three times – I think to keep Jane happy – and it was really tiring.'

10

WEIRDLAND

Fame, 1963 on

In a split second, Ringo realised he'd slipped into some kind of parallel universe. He was at a family gathering back in Liverpool, sometime early in the days of his bright white fame as a Beatle, when someone accidentally nudged the coffee table and the tea in his cup slopped into the saucer.

'Everyone's reaction was, "He can't have that. We have to tidy up",' he disbelievingly recalled. 'That would never have happened before. I thought then, *Things are changing*. It was an absolute arrow in the brain.

'In 1963, the attitude of my whole family changed. They treated me like a different person. Suddenly I was "one of those" … and it was very difficult to get used to. I'd grown up and lived with these people and now I found myself in weirdland.'

In direct contrast to the cartoony version of the fan scenes around Admiral Grove depicted by the BBC in *The Mersey Sound* documentary – excited kids in the street goofing around and going daft – the reality quickly turned darker, particularly for Elsie and Harry Graves who found it hard to cope with the sheer intensity and strangeness of Richy's sudden fame.

At first, it was novel – and funny. Ringo would have to sneak out the back door to avoid the twenty or thirty fans waiting outside. Then they started repeatedly knocking on the front door and wouldn't believe Elsie when she said her son wasn't around. She tried to placate them with peace offerings – handing over his old socks, shirts and shoes until they were all gone – but it only made things worse. Before long, there might be a couple of hundred kids hanging around, taking turns peeking through the window and rattling the knocker.

When Ringo was back at Admiral Grove, he'd have to slope in and out of the rear entrance under the cover of darkness and even crouch down as he walked around indoors. The two aspects of his life that he feared being altered – his home, his family – were slowly being bent out of shape by his celebrity. Fans began gouging souvenir wooden chips out of his front door; one made off with the letterbox. The family returned home one night to find 'We Love You, Ringo' scrawled in paint across the front of the house.

Elsie began to buckle under the constant pressure and attention; after two years of this, she became, as her son put it, 'ill ... terrified out of her life'.

It was all too much, so, in 1965, Richy bought his parents a bungalow for £8,000 (roughly £200,000 in 2025) in the leafy calm of the suburb of Gateacre, five miles further inland from Admiral Grove. Official Beatles biographer Hunter Davies travelled there two years later to interview Elsie and Harry, and found them to be nervy and 'completely isolated, knowing nobody, not knowing what to do with themselves all day'.

The bungalow was situated away from the road, amid lawns and rose bushes, and away from prying eyes. Gold and silver Beatles discs hung on the wall, the house smelled of fresh paint and the modernist furniture was all new and bought by Richy. But, still, the couple seemed lonely out there all on their own and a general air of oddness lingered.

'I always said I'd never ever move,' Elsie offered. 'I liked my neighbours so much down the Dingle.

'It's still very difficult for the boys, though,' she added. 'I've seen Richy sit in here 'til it's dark because he's scared to go out in the light. Isn't it terrible? But you can't have everything, can you?'

11

RINGO FOR PRESIDENT

On the Campaign Trail in the US, 1964

Flying into New York on a Pan Am Boeing 707, Ringo could almost feel the magnetic pull of the city below. In his mind, it was as if there was an enormous octopus on the ground 'wrapping its tentacles around the plane and bringing us down'. If it was a characteristically surreal thought, it was a vivid metaphor for what awaited him and the others in the US.

The Beatles had thought they'd no hope of cracking the States. That was until the month before, when Brian Epstein had broken some stunning news to them at the Hotel George V in Paris, where the group were staying during an eighteen-night run at the Olympia Theatre, hacking it out on a nine-act bill with Sylvie Vartan and Trini Lopez. Epstein had just received a telegram from Capitol Records. In the US *Cashbox* chart, 'I Want to Hold Your Hand' had leapt from number forty-three straight to number one. The single had been selling 10,000 copies an hour in New York alone. The four instantly exploded with laddish joy, screaming 'Way-hay!' and all taking turns riding on the back of 'Big Mal' Evans for victory parades around the room.

The prospect of actually going to the US, though, was another matter. They fretted about the reception they might meet. 'Cliff went to America and died,' Lennon darkly observed.

But now there was *this*: Friday 7 February 1964, 1.20 p.m., touching down at John F Kennedy International, renamed in honour of the assassinated president, murdered only eleven weeks before. Some 4,000 fans were there to meet them, hanging over the railings of the outdoor arrivals balcony, screeching like disturbed birds and waving homemade placards: 'We Loves You Yeh

Beatles', 'PS I Need You', and even, weirdly and brilliantly, 'Beatles Unfair To Bald Men'.

Shortly after, a police motorcade safely ferried the band from Queens to Manhattan, and the Plaza Hotel, as if they were visiting royalty rather than the 'shaggy minstrels' of one reporter's estimation. 'We got to the hotel and it was madness,' Ringo incredulously related. 'There's barriers and horses and cops all over the place ... with the four of us in the car, giggling.' Fans lined Central Park South, wielding other scribbled signs: 'Elvis Is Dead, Long Live the Beatles', 'We Love You, Never Leave Us'.

Before they'd even left the airport, Ringo had made his star-making performance at the Beatles' press conference for a rabble of print, TV and cine news journalists. When asked by one what they made of the comment that they were 'nothing but a bunch of British Elvis Presleys', the drummer led the dancing, curling his lip and convulsing and shouting 'It's not true! It's not true!', as John leapt into his own jittery routine.

'How many of you are bald, that you have to wear those wigs?' asked another.

'All of us,' Ringo shot back.

'Aren't you afraid of what the American Barbers Association is going to think of you?'

'Well, we've run quicker than the English ones,' he quickly retorted. 'We'll have a go here, y'know.'

'What do you think of Beethoven?'

'Great. Especially his poems.'

Although flanked by Lennon and McCartney, Harrison and particularly Starr dominated the exchanges. Instantly, the States fell in love with Ringo. He was short, cuddly looking, had a runtish charm and an unusual name for a drummer (if not for a character in a Western). His wisecracking personality, along with his prominent schnozzle, even attracted comparisons to Groucho Marx.

Developing his easy-going and cheeky way of dealing with reporters was to serve him very well in the months to come. Someone would enquire as to his exact height and he'd instantly and precisely respond, 'Two feet, nine inches'.

'Ringo, why do you get the most fan mail?'

'I don't know. Perhaps 'cos more people write to me.'

~

This playful relationship between the press and the Beatles was firmly established two days after an estimated 73 million people, the biggest American TV audience recorded, watched Ringo grin and bashfully shake his fringe while perched atop another worryingly tiny circular drum riser on *The Ed Sullivan Show*.

On Tuesday 11 February, they jumped on a train from New York to Washington, DC, sharing their carriage with a pack of journalists. Wholly impressing the hacks, the Beatles swore, drank, smoked and, in terms of banter, gave at least as good as they got.

'The guys from the press had come to bury us,' Ringo reckoned. 'These reporters, being New Yorkers, would yell at us, but we just yelled back. Up until then, pop groups had been milk and honey with the press: "No, I don't smoke", that kind of thing. And here *we* were, smoking and drinking and shouting at *them*. That's what endeared us to them.'

The band's first-ever live US show, that night, was a strange one. They arrived to play in the round at the Washington Coliseum amid a gale of screaming, only to find a shonky stage set-up. Facing in the opposite direction from the amps, Ringo's drums were positioned on a small revolving platform that visibly wobbled as soon as he stepped on it. The cameras from CBS, filming the event for a special closed-circuit broadcast in US cinemas the following month, caught him fiddling with his kit on this rickety sub-stage, as he and the others were pelted with the US equivalent of jelly babies – jelly beans, much harder – forcing Starr and Lennon to bow their heads to protect themselves from the hail.

Ringo alone struggled to try to spin his kit around to face the audience, as the MC singled him out for introduction – 'In case you don't know who this is ... that's Ringo Starr' – and the girls howled in response. Looking nervous and disgruntled, the drummer stood up to appeal for the assistance of Mal Evans to help whirl the precarious contraption around to meet the crowd.

When their set kicked off with 'Roll Over Beethoven', sung by George, he found his microphone wasn't working, forcing him to quickly move over to use

John's. Three songs in, ahead of 'This Boy', Mal Evans arrived onstage to gyrate the drums as the band turned to face the section of the audience 180 degrees behind them. Then, again, before 'Please Please Me', they turned back around. For 'I Want to Hold Your Hand', they even rotated 45 degrees for the benefit of the fans watching on from the side. Starr smashed through the song, even though his kit was shaking violently, up and down, side to side on the flimsy stage, as if he was piloting a small boat through a storm, or as if the Beatles had caused an actual earthquake.

It was poor organisation colliding with pandemonium, and a taste of what was to follow post-show at the British Embassy, where the group were invited as special guests at a charity ball hosted by the UK ambassador David Ormsby-Gore. Arriving just before 1 a.m. – and after handing out raffle-won autographed Beatles records (Ringo: 'If you don't like it, we can exchange it for a Frank Sinatra') – the band milled around amid the upper-crust participants, many of whom were roaring drunk.

In what was to become a notorious incident, the truth of which was increasingly blurred in the aftermath, one of the partygoers walked up behind Ringo and cut off a lock of his hair. 'One guy ... he was such a pig ... I had my back to him and suddenly, I just felt *snip*,' he recalled. 'I just started screaming at him and we didn't stay there that long.'

'Some bloody animal cut Ringo's hair,' Lennon fumed, six years later, in 1970. 'I walked out of that, swearing at all of them, I just left in the middle of it.'

But while Starr's account had the culprit as being a man, American news journo Michael Braun, shadowing the Beatles for what would become the first book written about them (*Love Me Do! The Beatles' Progress*), reported 'a British debutante walks up to Ringo, removes a pair of nail scissors from her purse, and snips off a lock of his hair'.

Meanwhile, eighteen-year-old Beverly Markovitz, there at the Embassy bash with her date, a local disc jockey, later claimed that she'd been the one to lop off the back of Ringo's mop, using her nail scissors. She was subsequently interviewed in a Beatles fan mag and photographed with a lock of hair ceremoniously mounted on a white index card the drummer had signed for her earlier that evening.

'I pulled out little scissors from my purse,' Markowitz claimed. 'I just went clip clip clip clip clip all around the side, and he didn't feel it at first. Then he turned around and grabbed my shoulder.' *Newsweek* further muddied the waters with its reporter's assertion that the assailant was a 'matron [who] whipped out scissors … and disappeared in the crowd'.

If the exact details of the incident were lost forever in the mists of time, what was certainly true was that, as soon as the Beatles hit the States, Ringo was in the thick of the action, and never dismissed as merely the drummer.

'They loved Ringo over there,' he noted, strangely referring to himself in the third person, as if he was an entirely distinct character that Richy Starkey had created (which, in a way, he was). 'It wasn't John, Paul, George and Ringo. Half the time it was Ringo, Paul, George and John, or whatever. Suddenly, it was equal.'

In March '64, the US magazine *Saturday Evening Post* went further, declaring Ringo to be 'the most popular Beatle in America, [who] evokes paroxysms of teenage shrieks everywhere by a mere turn of his head, a motion which sends his brown spaniel hair flying. When he flips his hair, the kids flip theirs.'

~

Five months on from the Beatles' monumental first visit to the US, a group of student protesters stood outside the 1964 Republican National Convention – being held that summer at the Cow Palace in Daly City, south of San Francisco – wielding artfully scribbled banners. 'Ringo for President!!' read one. Another proclaimed, 'We Will Be in Misery Until Ringo Starr Gets Nominated For President!' Yet another insisted, 'The Movie Profits Alone Will Pay the Campaign Costs! Ringo For President!'

Four weeks later, the Beatles landed back in the US for their first full tour, coincidentally also kicking off at the Cow Palace. During a press conference at the San Francisco Hilton on 18 August, Starr was asked how he felt about the Ringo For President campaign.

'It's marvellous!' he stated, clearly bemused but tickled.

Reporter: 'Assuming you were president of the United States, would you make any political promises?'

Ringo: 'I don't know, y'know. I'm not sort of politically minded.'

John: 'Aren't you?'
Ringo: 'No, John. Believe me.'
Paul: 'I think you should be president.'
Reporter: 'Ringo, would you nominate the others as part of your cabinet?'
Ringo: 'Well, I'd have to, wouldn't I?'
George: 'I could be the door.'
John: 'I could be the cupboard.'

~

Still, 'Ringo for President' was a daft idea, phrase and comedy concept that was set to endure for decades. Even today, there are an array of T-shirts available bearing the slogan, including a reprint of the original protest sign declaring, 'We Will Be in Misery Until Ringo Starr Gets Nominated For President!'

A quick online search reveals a variety of designs: a simple stars-and-stripes motif framing the words 'Ringo for President'; another with a crude pencil drawing of the drummer looking glum and not entirely presidential (available in white, pink or blue). One, perhaps more appropriately, features the famous 1967 shot of Starr by Richard Avedon with a white dove of peace perched on his finger. Another is a black-and-white pen-and-ink portrait of his face looking misshapen and slightly troubled, like a bad tattoo, sandwiched by the legend, 'Ringo Starr … for President'. There are many more besides.

'Ringo for President?' McCartney said in 2024 when asked about the ongoing popularity of the notion. 'Yeah, absolutely! He would do a great job. President of *what* is the question.'

12

SOME OTHER GUY

Ringo and Jimmie Nicol,
1964–2011

In the middle of a Beatles photo shoot at Prospect Studios in Barnes, south-west London, on the morning of 3 June 1964, Ringo collapsed. As road manager-cum-PA Neil Aspinall remembered, the drummer suddenly 'sank to his knees'.

Since arriving at the studio, Starr had been battling a sore throat and high temperature, but had told the others that it was just a bad summer cold. Then, as *Saturday Evening Post* photographer John Launois clicked away, Ringo suddenly felt dizzy and his legs gave out.

A doctor was quickly summoned and Ringo was sped to a private room at University College Hospital in Fitzrovia, where his temperature was recorded as a dangerously high 103°F. Following further examination, he was diagnosed as suffering from a viral infection that had caused both tonsillitis and pharyngitis.

Not that there was ever a spare moment in the Beatles' schedule at this point, but the timing couldn't have been worse, since the group were due to set off on their first world tour the following day, heading first to Europe, then Hong Kong and on to Australia.

George Harrison, ever loyal to Ringo, was dead set against replacing him with a stand-in for the trip, but Brian Epstein and George Martin argued that it was too late to cancel the dates. Harrison later disbelievingly recalled 'how we were bullied … into accepting that situation that we had to go. We should have been more forceful and said, "No, we're not doing it."' Nonetheless, the decision was made and the tour was back on.

Next, there was a scramble to find a replacement drummer at impossibly short notice. Raye Du-Val, holder of the Guinness world record for non-stop drumming (100 hours, one minute and fifteen seconds) was at the Top Ten Club on Berwick Street in Soho, getting ready for a show with the Blue Notes, when a Beatles messenger arrived to offer him the gig. Du-Val sent him away, saying, 'It's not for me'. Epstein then called Bobby Graham, drummer for Joe Brown and Marty Wilde. Graham told the manager that his diary was filled with studio session bookings that he couldn't cancel at short notice, but suggested another player, Jimmie Nicol.

Meanwhile, Ringo was stuck in hospital, his health once again having failed him as it had done for the extended stays of his youth. It was a grim reminder of his vulnerability. At the same time, his inability to fulfil his commitments with the band played into his insecurity as the last Beatle to join, less than two years before.

'My illness was a real big event,' he reflected. 'It was miserable. My throat was *so* sore and I was trying to live on jelly and ice cream.' Still 'hooked on the weed', as he put it, he didn't help himself by continuing to puff away on cigarettes.

Inevitably, a photographer was dispatched to UCL and snapped Starr in bed, wearing brown striped pyjamas, lying back with his hands knitted behind his head, and looking morose.

~

Jimmie Nicol was at home in Barnes – by spooky coincidence the same area of London where Ringo had suffered his collapse only a few hours earlier – and waking from a post-lunch nap when his phone rang. It was George Martin, calling to offer him the temporary gig in the Beatles. Nicol, as he vividly noted, 'nearly shit in me pants'.

The drummer was already busy, with a growing reputation. Only the month before, he'd enjoyed his biggest break yet, joining Georgie Fame's Blue Flames, the slick jazz and R&B mainstays of the Flamingo Club in Soho. Epstein remembered Nicol playing on a session for one of his other management charges, Liverpool rock 'n' roll singer Tommy Quickly, at Pye Studios three months before.

What swung it for Nicol, though, was the fact that he'd been the uncredited drummer on a cash-in cover version album, *Beatlemania*, released earlier in '64 on UK budget label Top Six. As a result, he knew most of the material already.

Mid-afternoon, Nicol was brought to EMI Studios on Abbey Road to meet the Beatles. 'My mind was blown,' he said. 'I shook all their hands and blurted out tones of admiration [sic] that I think made them embarrassed.' He then rehearsed with the band, confidently running through six songs, including four – 'Long Tall Sally', 'I Saw Her Standing There', 'This Boy' and 'Can't Buy Me Love' – that he hadn't played on the knock-off Beatles covers LP.

The press descended on the studio and John, Paul, George and Jimmie answered a few questions. 'I wouldn't be human if I didn't admit I was nervous,' Nicol told the assembled journalists. 'But they put me at ease straight away.'

One wag of a reporter asked why the Beatles hadn't called up Pete Best to come to the rescue. 'He's got his own group,' said Lennon, empathically adding, 'and it might have looked as if we were taking him back, which is not good for him.'

Wide-featured and with a toothy grin, Nicol didn't fit the Beatle profile, but had already undergone an emergency comb-forward-and-fringe-trim haircut. He was filmed by ITN bashing away at Ringo's Ludwig kit, framed by acoustic screens, before the other three joined him: Paul helpfully carrying a suitcase, George mock-thumping him. It was clearly an odd situation, but Nicol seemed the ideal substitute, being a solid musician but not a 'star' drummer who could be viewed as a possibly upstaging or permanent replacement for Ringo.

'I would have played for free for as long as they needed me,' Nicol later said. Down the years, there were to be contradictory reports about exactly how much he was paid. In 1965, Nicol would tell the *Daily Mirror* that he'd been given £500 in total (just under £13,000 in 2025) for what turned out to be six dates. Two decades on, he upped the figure, claiming he had been paid '£2,500 per show and a £2,500 signing bonus'.

All the while, in that first week of June 1964, with the temperature in London creeping up towards a stifling 32°C, Starr remained down in the dumps in his hospital bed. A press statement was issued, reassuring fans that the drummer's health was improving: 'His condition is not serious, and he should be discharged in a few days.' But at the same time, he felt unsettled lying there watching TV news footage of the Beatles arriving in Europe with their imposter drummer.

'It was very strange, them going off without me,' he confessed. 'They'd taken Jimmie Nicol and I thought they didn't love me anymore. All that stuff went through my head.'

~

Over in Copenhagen at the K.B. Hallen on 4 June, Jimmie Nicol was struggling to keep his beat steady amid the screaming. Just before a closing 'Twist and Shout', Paul introduced him to the manic crowd – 'We'd like you all to clap and give a big hand for our drummer, Ring... ah ... *Jimmie!*' – prompting an even greater wave of squeals.

If the three remaining Beatles were highly complimentary about Nicol in public, they weren't quite so generous in private. Paul and George later carped that his playing wasn't tight and that he was too busy looking at the girls. Jimmie, for his part, found the reality of being a Beatle wasn't quite as glamorous as he'd anticipated and said that, onstage at that first show in Denmark, Lennon was still suffering a hangover from his previous night's drinking – quite possibly fuelled by the stress of finding a new drummer – and was 'sweating like a pig'.

It soon became apparent that the hastily assembled collective of Lennon, McCartney, Harrison and Nicol was an uneasy arrangement for all involved. Paul sent Ringo a telegram, telling him 'We didn't think we could miss you so much'.

Footage from the second of two Beatles shows at the Veilinghal in the Dutch village of Blokker on 6 June shows Nicol to be a gangly presence behind Starr's kit: hunched over, his shoulders bouncing as he thumps away, gamely giving the odd Ringo head shake. Clearly buzzing with adrenalin, he flails wildly, pushing the tempo and sometimes making the others sound as if they were falling behind.

Back in England, Elsie had spoken to her son and told the press he 'sounded disappointed' that the tour was continuing on to Hong Kong without him. Still, the drummer didn't miss much: the audience responses to the band during their two shows at the Princess Theatre in Kowloon were oddly muted. These were, however, increasingly rare incidences of the Beatles actually being able to hear themselves play onstage.

Three days later, while Ringo was comfortably tucked up in bed, his band-mates were some 10,000 miles away in Sydney, arriving during an almighty storm. But the torrential downpour didn't lead to the cancellation of the Beatles' scheduled parade on a flatbed trunk outside the airport, which ended with them utterly soaked.

The Australian tour quickly became a whirlwind of excitement and chaos and unbelievable scenes. In Adelaide, ahead of the first of four shows at the Centennial Hall, 200,000 fans lined the route from the airport along the Anzac Highway to the Hotel South Australia, where another 30,000 were waiting.

Filmed news reports of the scenes of mass hysteria in Britain and the US had travelled to Australia, where they were now being amplified and relayed back around the world. Leaving Adelaide for Melbourne, McCartney was clearly overwhelmed. 'I nearly cried in the car,' he told a DJ. 'Nothing like this has ever happened to us before.'

~

On Thursday 11 June, Ringo was discharged from hospital. Accompanied by Brian Epstein, he faced a horrendous journey to the other side of the globe, involving multiple stopovers. The trip didn't get off to a great start when he forgot his passport, although his near-diplomatic status as a Beatle meant he was allowed to board the plane for the first leg to the US, with his documentation being sent on after him.

When he landed in San Francisco, he talked to the waiting press, telling them he was 'raring to go'. Flying on to Hawaii, he was greeted by girls in hula costumes and had an hour-and-a-half wait in the airport before jetting off to Sydney. Reporters at the airport there asked him if he was looking forward to reuniting with his bandmates in Melbourne. 'Yeah, can't wait. 'Cos, y'know, we've been together for ninety years. It's a bit funny being on your own.'

Finally, on Sunday the 14th, he arrived in Melbourne and had to push through a crush of 3,000 fans outside the Southern Cross Hotel. A policeman lifted Ringo up on his shoulders, then lurched into a woman who'd tripped over in the melee, sending the drummer flying to the ground and within the reach of the clawing fans. He began to panic, scrambled to his feet, rushed into the hotel and gasped, 'Give's a drink. That was the roughest ride I've had.' The hotel's PR, there to guide him upstairs, saw that the drummer was 'shaking like a leaf'. After being handed a whisky, Ringo noticed that clumps of his hair had been pulled from his scalp.

Slowly, outside the hotel, the mass of fans began to grow and grow until it was estimated there were around a quarter of a million people present, some hanging in the trees, waiting to catch a glimpse of the Beatles.

They got their chance when the reunited Fab Four, plus Jimmie Nicol, stepped out onto the first-floor balcony at the Southern Cross, waving to the colossal crowd. In a wrong-headed parody of Adolf Hitler, Lennon pointed his left hand under his nose and hoisted his right arm into a Sieg Heil salute.

At the inevitable press conference, Ringo was introduced by the host as someone who'd gone through a 'brief, but very grave illness', causing the drummer to slide, slapstick-style, off his chair and under the table, before emerging to stuff multiple fags in his mouth, causing a gale of laughter. He was asked if he thought his 'tonsillitis might change the group's sound'.

'I don't think so, no,' he responded. 'Only for a few days when I don't sing … if you can call it singing.'

Nicol – whom Starr had thanked via the *New Musical Express* before leaving England for being a 'great drummer and a friend' – remained silent during the interrogation, until he was asked what he intended to do back in the UK and if he had any engagements lined up.

'Um, well, I'll just stop in Australia first,' he averred.

But he didn't. The next day, he was driven to the airport, where he was handed his last cheque by Epstein, along with the gift of a gold wristwatch, etched with the bland inscription: 'From the Beatles and Brian Epstein to Jimmie – with appreciation and gratitude'.

A photographer caught one last frame of the drummer waiting for his flight home, sitting solo on an empty row of seats, staring into space and looking lonely and bemused.

⁓

In the months that followed, Nicol tried to use this enormous flash of exposure to light up his own career. Pye Records reissued a single he'd played on with the Shubdubs, prefixing his name on the credits of what was a ropey, quasi-ska novelty single titled 'Humpty Dumpty'. It flopped, as did its rush-released follow-up, a jazz-swinging comedy number called 'Husky', issued solely under his own name.

In April 1965, Nicol was declared bankrupt and the *Daily Mail* ran an interview with him under the headline, 'The Rise and Fall of the Fifth Beatle'. 'Standing in for Ringo was the worst thing that ever happened to me,' he bemoaned. 'After the headlines died, I began dying too. No one wanted to know me anymore.'

'I didn't think he could fail,' Ringo commented in the article. 'No one did.'

McCartney took pity on Nicol and secured him a short-lasting gig playing with pop duo Peter and Gordon. Later, in '65, Nicol accepted a job drumming for Swedish instrumental rockers the Spotnicks and moved to Gothenburg. By '67, he was living in Mexico, playing with local groups. Through the ensuing years, he rarely agreed to be interviewed about his brief time with the Beatles and seemed happy to drift into obscurity.

In 1988, rumours of his death began to circulate, although they were later believed to have been started by Nicol himself, keen to put an end to enquiries about his days as a temporary Beatle. In 1996, he was papped by a newspaper photographer in Kentish Town, north London, looking like the scruffy builder he'd become.

The last-known sighting of Jimmie Nicol was in 2011, in Utrecht, when a Beatles fan who'd just visited a record fair thought he recognised the man emerging from a construction site. He approached him and asked if he was 'Jimmie Nicol, the drummer'. Nicol, clearly rumbled, nodded and grinned, then wordlessly signed a piece of paper for the fan before swiftly disappearing.

The spectre of Jimmie Nicol sometimes returned to haunt the Beatles, too. On 2 January 1969, day one of the cold and fraught making of *Get Back/Let It Be* at Twickenham Studios, McCartney and director Michael Lindsay-Hogg were discussing the possibility of filming an outdoor Beatles show in a Libyan amphitheatre. The only problem, Paul explained, was that Starr didn't want to travel anywhere.

'Ringo ... doesn't want to go abroad, and he put his foot down,' he said, before punctuating his statement with a loaded quip. 'So, us and Jimmie Nicol might go abroad.'

13

AWOL IN INDIANAPOLIS

Pills and Cops and Stormy Weather, 1964

The psychic predicted that the Beatles' chartered Electra plane would crash somewhere between Philadelphia and Indianapolis, killing everyone on board.

The same clairvoyant and astrologer, Jeane Dixon, claimed to have prophesied, in 1956, the killing of John F Kennedy, writing in the US national Sunday magazine *Parade* that the next American president, elected in 1960, would be a Democrat who would go on to 'be assassinated or die in office though not necessarily in his first term'. (The fact that she later changed her mind and predicted Richard Nixon as the winner appeared to be neither here nor there.)

In the band's dressing room at the Convention Hall in Philadelphia on 2 September 1964, only hours before the night flight was due to take off, George Harrison joked to Beatle-trusted journalist and broadcaster Larry Kane that he was 'going to ride a bicycle' rather than get on the aircraft. In the end, of course, the plane landed safely in Indiana, although Kane reported that it was a white-knuckled experience for all and that Harrison, the nerviest flier, led the 'loud applause' for the pilots.

But, much like her hazy Kennedy prediction, Dixon was halfway proven right in the end. The Lockheed L-188 Electra four-engine turboprop that flew the Beatles around the States during their August/September tour was indeed doomed, skidding off the end of the runway less than two years later at Ardmore Municipal Airport in Oklahoma, before smashing into a hill and exploding, killing 83 military personnel on board.

The Beatles' flight to Indianapolis in the Electra saw them downing whisky and Coca-Cola to take the edge off the amphetamines they were regularly popping to help them keep pace with their demented schedule. Back in April, when without Ringo they'd been heading from Holland to Hong Kong, the punishing long-haul flight had zipped by due to the remaining Beatles' collective imbibing.

'We'd been sitting on the floor drinking and taking Preludins for about thirty hours and it seemed like a ten-minute flight,' Harrison said. 'On all those flights, we were still on uppers.'

Preludin, the go-go-go diet pill that the Beatles had first been introduced to back in Hamburg, had since been joined by various other items on the mood-altering menu: Dexedrine (or dexies), Duraphet (black bombers) and Drinamyl (purple hearts). It was the latter variety of speedy pick-me-up that the group were taking when, in the middle of this thrilling, claustrophobic, weird and jumpy tour, Ringo disappeared.

⁓

In the early hours of 3 September, sometime around 4 a.m., the drummer was sitting at the pool at the Speedway Motel in Indianapolis, alone and totally wired, when he was spotted by two local cops, Jack Marks and Jack MacDonald.

'Let's throw him in,' one joked to the other, before approaching Starr and asking him if he'd like a tour of the city.

'Well, I can't sleep,' Ringo said. 'I might as well.'

The three jumped into the police cruiser and set off, first for a spin around Monument Circle and the Indiana governor's residence, before heading back in the direction of the Indianapolis Motor Speedway, scene of the world-famous Indy 500 car race. The two policemen sweet-talked a night watchman into opening up the gates to the track and then let the Beatle take the wheel of the cruiser, allowing him to zip around the course with the siren blaring and lights flashing.

Now confident that Ringo was a reasonable driver, and clearly feeling mischievous and thrilled at having a celebrity in their company, the cops then permitted him to take the police car out into streets where, as he remembered, he proceeded to go 'screaming all over the city'. At one point, they were pursued by two officers in another cruiser, who presumably believed the vehicle had been stolen. Ringo was quickly instructed by his new pals to pull up into a dark alley and kill the lights, while the three of them hid.

'This other cop car goes past us,' he remembered, 'and then the guys said, "Well, we got out of that one, so what else are we gonna do?"'

Instead of landing themselves in further potential trouble, the trio drove to a diner on the edge of town, where one male customer, having spotted Ringo but not identified him, was overheard saying to his wife, 'Did you see that jerk with the Beatle wig on?'

Marks then invited Starr out to his ranch twenty-five miles north of the city. Upon their arrival, his eleven-year-old daughter Karen looked out of the window and, stunned, turned to her brothers and said, 'I think Dad brought home a Beatle.' The policeman's wife was in the barn getting some of her horses ready for display at the state fair that day. When Ringo wandered over, having been egged on by Marks to cheekily enquire whether she'd rustle them up some breakfast, she was unfazed, telling him, 'You'll just have to hold your horses until I finish with mine.'

As a side order to their breakfast, Ringo and the cop drank cognac and Coke, before the drummer had a ride around on a dirt bike and indulged his old cowboy fantasies by firing off a few target rounds. Before leaving, he signed an autograph for Karen and gave her a peck on the cheek. Later, her mother swore her daughter to secrecy about the incident, fearing that rabid fans would swarm the family's home looking for souvenirs.

Meanwhile, back at the Beatles' camp, with the group due to play two shows at the Indiana State Fairgrounds, and Starr still missing, the mood was growing increasingly frantic. Ringo turned up just before stage-time, slightly dishevelled and still speedily buzzing to the extent that, when he started playing, he realised that he couldn't control his right leg to pedal kick the bass drum.

'I was up three days and nights, and I was with the cops, and then I got onstage and lost the use of my legs. This leg started hopping ... I couldn't control it. It frightened me.'

~

Another shock was to face him six days later when he stepped off the Electra in Montreal and was immediately approached by Canadian police. The Beatles had attracted frequent death threats on the tour, largely taking them in their stride, but there had been a serious one made against Ringo specifically.

'Some people decided to make an example of me, as an "English Jew",' he wryly noted. 'This was one of the few times I was really worried.'

Onstage at the city's Forum that night, feeling exposed on his riser, Starr tilted his cymbals higher to use as potentially bullet-stopping shields. During both of the evening's performances, a plain-clothes cop was stationed by his side. In his anxious state, Ringo found this puny security presence increasingly hilarious.

'I started to get hysterical because I thought, *If someone in the audience has a pop at me, what is the guy going to do? Is he going to catch the bullet?* This was getting funnier and funnier all the time and the guy just sat there.'

The Beatles had planned to stay in Montreal that night, but as McCartney vividly explained, 'We'd thought Ringo was going to get shot. We thought, "Fuck this, let's get out of town" and we flew a day early.'

When the Electra took off that night, it was initially headed for Jacksonville, Florida, before it was suddenly diverted more than 500 miles further south to the island of Key West to avoid the path of Hurricane Dora. On approach to the airport's worryingly short runway, the captain warned the Beatles to fasten their seatbelts, as he was going to be forced to employ full reverse thrust to land safely.

Marooned for a couple of days at the Key Wester motel, the Beatles blew off steam, going on a drinking bender. Paul, who so over-indulged that he ended up puking into a toilet bowl, remembered the overwhelmed band members growing uncharacteristically emotional, temporarily relieved from the constant stress and attention: 'We ended up crying about, y'know … how much we loved each other.'

The worst of the storm had passed by the time they flew into Jacksonville on Friday 11 September, although Dora had wreaked enormous visible damage on the city. Harrison said it remained 'as windy as hell … dark with heavy black clouds all over … palm trees fallen over and mess laying everywhere'.

Ahead of the show at the outdoor Gator Bowl, the Beatles at first refused to play, having learned that the audience was to be racially segregated. Only after being assured by officials that the crowd would be integrated did they take to the stage. Conditions within the decrepit, near-forty-year-old football stadium were less than ideal, however, and the weather remained bad. Mal Evans was forced to nail Ringo's kit to the high, precarious stage, and the drummer hammered through the Beatles' set, in the face of howling 45 mph winds, in a fitting end to a stormy fortnight.

14

'RINGO, I LOVE YOU'

Tribute Records, 1964–1965

Still in her late teens, California-born Cheryl Sarkisian was already making a name for herself as a backing singer, performing on Phil Spector-produced hits such as the Ronettes' monumental 'Be My Baby' and Darlene Love's later perennial 'Christmas (Baby Please Come Home)'. Her boyfriend and soon-to-be-husband Salvatore Bono felt she had the talent to step into the solo spotlight and kept pushing the producer to give her a shot at a lead vocal.

Spector was in cahoots with three songwriters – Vini Poncia, Peter Andreoli and Paul Case – and together they'd written a Beatlemania cash-in record focusing on the Cuddly One, titled 'Ringo, I Love You'. Opportunistically capitalising on the Fabs phenomenon before it inevitably died, the track featured a rattling Starr-like beat and audaciously stitched together melodic elements of 'She Loves You' and 'I Want to Hold Your Hand'.

At eighteen, Sarkisian was just at the upper limit of the right age to be a convincing Beatles fan and so was given the gig to sing 'Ringo, I Love You', in which she pledged her devotion to the drummer in a confident but unusual contralto voice (typically the lowest in the female range). Spector thought that the singer's name should sound more American to appeal directly to the nation's teen screamers and insisted the single was released under the pseudonym Bonnie Jo Mason.

When it was issued to radio stations in the spring of 1964, however, there was immediately a problem. Many programmers believed that the low tones of 'Bonnie Jo Mason' actually belonged to a man.

'The single just died,' Cher later remembered of her first-ever solo release.

81

'My voice was so deep that a lot of people thought I was a gay guy singing a love song to Ringo, and the DJs weren't about to play a homosexual love song.'

~

Confirming his status as the most popular Beatle to American eyes, Ringo was the subject of a flood of novelty songs written in his honour and rush-released between 1964 and 1965 in the hope that they would get the cash registers ringing. Most adhered to a similar formula as the one used on 'Ringo, I Love You': a clattering beat and a girl singling out the drummer for her absolute adoration.

On 'Ringo Did It', Veronica Lee, backed by the Moniques, sounded suitably pining, but ultimately a touch creepy and stalkerish as she insisted that if she had her way, she'd never let Ringo 'go'. On the festive 'Santa, Bring Me Ringo' – co-written, arranged and orchestrated by future David Lynch-affiliated screen composer Angelo Badalamenti – Christine Hunter came over as a spoiled and demanding brat in the throes of a tantrum. The similarly seasonal 'Ringo Bells' by Three Blonde Mice (written as a side hustle by esteemed jazz journalist George T. Simon) was entirely dopey, being a beat group rendition of 'Jingle Bells' rendered in Chipmunk-styled voices with dodgy British accents.

The Starlettes' 'Ringo' was a rocker with a more mellifluous girl-group approach, replete with Fabs-fashioned 'woos', a collective admission that the drummer made the strings of their hearts go 'zingo' and a shared observation that the drummer's hair was longer than theirs. 'My Ringo' by the Rainbows – a fake group name for the overdubbed lead and backing vocals of session singer Jackie Ward – was a haunting doo-wop tune that found the singer taking a sharp interest in the fact that the object of her affections didn't (yet) wear a wedding ring.

More atrocious accents, and tune-free whistling, were the central features of the Whippets' 'Go Go Go with Ringo', a clip-clopping ballad in thrall to the band who hailed from 'Merrie England', but clearly their Teddy Bear drummer most of all. At least the Whippets weren't a manufactured group like most of the others, comprising three twelve-year-old New York 'street kid' delinquents: Jan Kerouac (daughter and only child of *On the Road* author and beatnik icon Jack), Bibbe Hansen (future Warhol film 'superstar' and mother of Beck) and their friend Charlotte Rosenthal.

One day in 1964, the trio were begging for change in downtown Manhattan when they managed to hustle bus money from songwriter Neil Levenson, who immediately spotted the girl-group potential in these cocky pre-teens. He told them he'd written a response song to 'I Want to Hold Your Hand', a snappy little number he'd titled 'I Want to Talk with You'. 'It was a classic girl-group riff,' Hansen said, 'and we dug it.' 'Go Go Go with Ringo' was set to be the disc's woeful B-side. 'We loved the A-side, but weren't too wild about the Ringo song,' Hansen confessed.

Pat Wynter's 'Ringo, I Want to Know Your Secret' took the Lennon/McCartney-written, Harrison-sung 'Do You Want to Know a Secret' and stretched the point by dedicating it to Starr and amplifying its lounge-y aspects. Rex Miller meanwhile stuck to the 'comedy' on 'Ringo's Doctor', playing the role of the titular mock physician relating the details of his appointment with the drummer, his monologue interspersed with snippets of Beatles songs played by a soundalike group. It was altogether non-hilarious: 'We could give you some medicine, what would you like?', followed by a snippet of 'A Taste of Honey' etc.

More knowingly tongue-in-cheek was the Spector-esque stomper 'I Want to Kiss Ringo Goodbye' by one Penny Valentine, the London-based *Disc* music journalist. The Beatles had peddled their first records directly to Valentine, who they reportedly used to 'ogle and fawn over', making the premise of the song – the singer lamenting the fact that in February 1965 Starr married Maureen Cox – something of an in-joke. Still, it was a hopelessly weak record and duly stiffed.

~

Released to coincide with the 1964 US election contest between Lyndon B Johnson and Barry Goldwater, the Young World Singers attempted to exploit the summer's Californian student mini fad with their 'Ringo for President'. Overly perky, with a cheerleader chant, it nonetheless presented Starr as being anti-war, presciently anticipating his promotion of peace and love. The song was swiftly covered and released in the UK by the Beatles' mucker, the later disgraced Rolf Harris, thickening his antipodean accent to rally a troupe of youthful backing singers in a manner that was only to seem all the more unsettling in retrospect.

83

The Ringo novelty single gold rush did, however, yield one US hit, albeit inadvertently. In December '64, Lorne Greene, the forty-nine-year-old star of Western TV series *Bonanza*, scored a *Billboard* number one with 'Ringo', a spoken-word cowboy tale detailing the dangerous bromance between a lawman and the outlaw of the title. It was an unlikely chart-topper, doubtless pushed up the charts by gullible Beatles fans. Greene later accepted the fact, but hoped that some of them had enjoyed the record, nonetheless.

More recently, in 2021, the flame of the Ringo tribute single briefly flickered back to life, rekindled by Danish/Brazilian '60s-phile garage-rock duo the Courettes. 'R.I.N.G.O.' was a rollicking tub-thumper that wore its kitsch proudly, yet was clearly sincere in its love for 'Richard Starkey'. If a time machine could somehow have been built to transport the pair back to 1964, it might have been the most successful record of the lot.

15

SUNNY HEIGHTS

...And the Flying Cow Pub, 1965

Throughout 1963 and '64, when he wasn't on tour or in the studio, Ringo was being a gadabout around London.

Since autumn '63, the Beatles had all been resident in the capital, initially sharing Flat L on the top floor of 57 Green Street in upmarket Mayfair, a far cry from any of their living circumstances growing up back home in the northwest. 'It was such a buzz,' said Harrison, 'because we'd been brought up in little two-up, two-down houses in Liverpool.' John, with wife Cynthia and infant son Julian, then moved to a rented flat at 13 Emperor's Gate in Kensington that November, while the following month Paul – who hated Mayfair, saying 'the place had no soul' – became an attic bedroom lodger of the Asher family at 57 Wimpole Street in Marylebone.

Ringo and George stayed on Green Street for a few months longer, moving into Flat I on the third floor, before relocating to the posh Whaddon House block in Knightsbridge where Brian Epstein kept his tidy fifth-floor bachelor pad.

Starr was still in a relationship with Maureen Cox. If he was free on Mondays – Cox's day off – his girlfriend would travel south from Liverpool to see him. At the same time, claimed Cynthia Lennon, Ringo was also having a semi-secret fling with model Vicki Hodge. 'She was the girl,' said Cynthia, 'that he had to dispose of when Maureen came down to visit.'

Cox remained blissfully unaware of any sexual shenanigans that Ringo might have been involved in amid the dizzying whirl of his new social circle in London. 'I didn't feel threatened ... because I had no knowledge of that kind

85

of life,' she later said, reflecting back to a time when she was clearly naïve or in denial. 'It just didn't occur to me.'

In January '64, Ringo temporarily broke up with Maureen, for a period of four days in which the latter said she 'went apeshit. All I did was sit on the end of my bed and rock.' Worse, she heard that the Beatles – or at least three of them – had been partying with the visiting Ronettes at Decca Records plugger Tony Hall's flat in Mayfair. But while Veronica Bennett (the future Ronnie Spector) later admitted that she'd had a minor smooch with Lennon, and Harrison had a brief relationship with her sister Estelle, there clearly wasn't a spark between Starr and the Ronettes' third member, Nedra Talley.

Starr made up with Cox, who said he told her: 'I had to test our relationship, Maureen, [to see] whether I needed you or whether I didn't.'

'It's not a bad line to use, actually,' Cox reasoned. 'And I fell for it hook, line and sinker.'

However, Cynthia Lennon credited 'tough cookie' Maureen with more tenacity when it came to holding on to her relationship with Ringo. 'She was very possessive about him. She wouldn't let go. She turned up in London and she got pregnant.'

On the night of 20 January 1965, at the Ad Lib club in Soho, Ringo proposed to Maureen. (Their first-born, Zak Richard Starkey, arrived a week short of eight months later on 13 September.) On 11 February, bright and early at 8.10 a.m. at the register office at Caxton Hall in Westminster – the early timing chosen in an attempt to elude both fans and the press – the pair were married. Elsie and Harry, of course, travelled down for the big occasion, along with Cox's parents. The best man was the authoritative figure of Brian Epstein; John was there with Cynthia, and George with his new girlfriend of nine months, Pattie Boyd. Only Paul was absent, on holiday in Portugal at the time.

Maureen – 'Mo' to those close to her – was to be a grounding presence in Ringo's life. Not that she believed he needed bringing back down to earth. To her mind, fame and fortune hadn't changed him at all.

'No, barely,' she attested. 'Everybody changes, I think, but no, he was always the same.'

That summer, Starr paid £37,000 (close to £900,000 today) for his first house. Sunny Heights was a six-bedroomed mock-Tudor mansion on South Road in a private, gated community called St George's Hill, situated in Weybridge, twenty miles south-west of London. Ringo was the last of three Beatles to follow their accountants' advice to invest in property in the commuter belt, John and George both having done so in summer '64. The Lennons lived at Kenwood, a similarly proportioned abode fifteen minutes' walk away on the same estate, while Harrison's large bungalow Kinfauns was only a twenty-minute drive from Starr's home. McCartney had elected to stay on in London, increasingly going his own way.

Like John, Ringo was now a family man, so he felt the relocation out of the heart of the capital was a necessity. Spending like an over-excited pools winner, he was to eventually sink more than £50,000 in renovating and redesigning the house's interior, landscaping the vast, terraced gardens and having an enormous extension built adding various other rooms, including a billiards-cum-cinema space and a couple of man caves in which he could store his growing collection of cine cameras and film-editing gear. His ever-expanding home was clearly a money pit.

'Buying the house and doing it up was probably the daftest thing I ever did,' he lamented.

Ringo had come up with what seemed to be an ingenious plan when negotiating the remodelling of Sunny Heights: he went into partnership with builder Barry Patience, forming the Brickey Building Company. But, if anything, it only served to heighten his ambitions for the redevelopment and sent the costs skyrocketing. 'It had cost me £90,000 by the time we'd finished it,' he grumbled.

By the end, Sunny Heights boasted various pop-star home features, such as a go-kart track, a koi carp pond, a hedgerow maze and, best of all, a pub above the garage, which Ringo surreally christened the Flying Cow. He couldn't go to normal boozers anymore, so he simply had one built, with his own pool table, jukebox, mirrored bar, branded ashtrays and even a working till. There was usually a television set playing in every room of the house.

'When I walk around,' Ringo told Beatles biographer Hunter Davies when the writer visited Sunny Heights, 'I often think, *What's a scruff like me doing with this lot?*

'But it soon passes,' he added. 'You get used to it.'

16

'CALM DOWN, RINGO'

The View from Behind the Kit, 1966

U p on the silver screen flickered the Beatles, five months earlier, performing into a hurricane of hysteria at Shea Stadium. Now, here they were, in the flesh, in the calm of Cine-Tele Sound studios in Bayswater, London W2, on Wednesday 5 January, their first workday of 1966, watching the footage of themselves and attempting to mimic – note by note, syllable by syllable – exactly what they'd sung and played the previous August on that head-spinning night.

CTS was the premier facility in Britain for film dubbing and scoring. Four years before, the studio had reverberated with the sound of Monty Norman's twanging theme for James Bond's *Dr No*. Since then, the facility had been the setting for landmark soundtrack recordings composed and conducted by John Barry (the jazzy, haunting *The Ipcress File*, the sweeping orchestrations of *Goldfinger*). Now it was the Beatles' turn to play live-to-picture.

When it came to the post-production for the Brian Epstein/Ed Sullivan-produced concert documentary film *The Beatles at Shea Stadium*, the tapes recorded on that monumental night in New York had proved sorely lacking in sonic clarity. Today, watching his fingers moving on the screen, McCartney added fresh basslines to four songs, including 'Can't Buy Me Love' and 'I'm Down'. Then the four collectively aped their performances on 'I Feel Fine' and 'Help!', re-recording the songs entirely and effectively taping over poorly recorded history.

However, the live tape of Ringo's sole contribution to the set, his bluff reading of Buck Owens' '63 US country chart-topper 'Act Naturally', was unsalvageable. On the night, as his voice ricocheted around the bleachers from the stadium's inadequate PA system, he'd struggled to hear himself and stay in tune, the result being an unfortunate honker of a performance, particularly in his pancake-flat opening lines.

In the end, the engineers at CTS performed a botched job on the song for the documentary, taking the studio version of 'Act Naturally' that he'd recorded the previous summer, speeding it up and then butchering the onscreen footage with crude edits to try to make it fit. At one point in the completed film, as if in a strange dream, Starr's voice could be heard singing, even if his mouth wasn't moving.

~

Having had to recreate themselves in the recent past, in April the Beatles took a quantum leap into the future, their minds forever altered by LSD.

Ringo's first acid trip had been in Los Angeles the previous year, nine days after Shea Stadium, in a house at 2850 Benedict Canyon Drive, rented from its owner, the Hungarian film star Zsa Zsa Gabor. George and John first experienced the consciousness-warping effects of lysergic acid diethylamide in London in the spring of '65 and were zealous in their desire to take the drug with their other bandmates. The pair had scored LSD, absorbed in sugar cubes, in New York, and held onto them, wrapped in tin foil, planning an intra-Beatles trip for a day off in Hollywood.

McCartney was wary and demurred (at least until later that year, back in England). Starr, however, was very much up for it. 'I'd take anything,' he said, while pointing out that in his recollection it wasn't Harrison and Lennon's acid that he'd swallowed; instead he'd been given it by 'a couple of guys [who] came to visit us' who'd insisted 'Man, you've got to try this.'

After coming up on his trip, Ringo found himself 'swimming in jelly' in the mansion's pool and discovering a newfound appreciation for 'the force of nature and its beauty. You realise it's not just a tree … it's a living thing.' The effects of the drug were surprisingly long-lasting, though. Exhaustingly so. 'It felt like it was never going to wear off,' he said. 'Twelve hours later and it was, "Give's a break now, Lord."'

At EMI Studios, on 6 April 1966, the Beatles channelled their collective experiences into Lennon's newest song, a one-chord mantra for inner voyaging inspired by his reading of Timothy Leary, Ralph Metzner and Richard Alpert's 1964 book, *The Psychedelic Experience*, with its post-lysergic reimagining of the 1927 spiritual text, *The Tibetan Book of the Dead*, particularly its introductory instruction: 'whenever in doubt, turn off your mind, relax, float downstream'.

As revelatory as the song would prove to be, both narratively and sonically, Lennon admitted he felt 'a bit self-conscious about the lyrics'. In the same way as he had done with 'A Hard Day's Night', using one of Starr's character-istic malapropisms – or what John called a 'Ringoism' – he found the track's 'throwaway' title in a nonsensical phrase Starr had used in a 1964 interview with the BBC. Reporter David Coleman was enquiring about their first trip to the US, specifically the controversial hair-cutting incident at the embassy in Washington.

'Now, Ringo, I hear you were manhandled at the embassy ball,' said Coleman. 'Is this right?'

Starr: 'Not really. Someone just cut a bit of my hair. I was talking away, and I looked 'round and there was about 400 people just smiling. So... what can you say?'

Lennon: 'What can you say?'

Starr: 'Tomorrow never knows.'

At this, Lennon wheezed with laughter.

In the studio two years on, the session started with the making of a woozy tape loop: John playing a hypnotic lead guitar riff and Ringo playing a straight 4/4 beat, his drums fed through an echo chamber. The tape machine was then slowed down, making the two parts together sound as if they were moving through murky water. Over this unsettling sonic bed, Lennon sang his first take of the vocal through the spinning Leslie speaker of a Hammond organ, while Starr laid down a thick *boom, bap, boom-boom, bap* beat, not dissimilar to the loping rhythm he'd played on 'Ticket to Ride'. Listening to Ringo's beat, Paul suggested he change the second snare *bap* to a stuttering double hit on his high tom, enhancing the disorientating effect.

Three takes later, the backing track for the appropriately perception-distorting 'Tomorrow Never Knows' was in the bag, replete with a punchy drum sound the like of which had never been heard before. This was due to the presence of twenty-year-old Geoff Emerick, who already had four years of experience as an assistant engineer at Abbey Road under his belt (on his second day, aged sixteen, he'd been a lackey on the session when the Beatles had recorded their version of 'Love Me Do' with Ringo behind the kit). Ahead of this key session, he'd been promoted by George Martin to the enviable position of the band's main recording engineer.

Emerick was inventive, a mischievous rule breaker amid the buttoned-up EMI studio personnel. Having been warned by his bosses that no microphones should be positioned within two feet of drums for fear of damage to their sensitive diaphragms, he nonetheless moved the mics mere inches away from Starr's kit and removed the front head of his bass drum, dampening its sound by stuffing it with a huge woollen jumper (with four neck holes) he found lying around that had been knitted for the Beatles by a trio of Swedish fans. Then, back in the control room, he squashed the drum sounds – by rebelliously overloading the circuitry of a Fairchild 660 compressor/limiter – until they pumped hard out of the speakers.

'What on earth did you do to my drums?' a thrilled Ringo asked him. 'They sound fantastic.'

As the sessions progressed, Emerick pushed Starr to play more and more forcefully. 'If I hit them any harder, I'm going to break the skins,' Ringo warned him, before virtually pulverising the kit, to the point that the floor surrounding it was soon covered in wooden splinters from his destroyed sticks.

Eight days later, clearly enlivened, Ringo performed what he would later consider to be his best-ever drum track, on 'Rain' (set to be the flipside of 'Paperback Writer'). Dabbling further with tape experiments, the group decided to record the song at a much faster clip, before slowing the track down considerably, by around 30 beats per minute, until the sonics were thick and fat.

Throughout, Starr infused the rhythm with ever-changing rolls that almost amounted to a drum solo and were all the more impressive considering the original tempo they were recorded at. 'I feel as though that was someone else playing,' he reflected. 'I was possessed.'

But the most enduring Ringo moment – at least in popular memory – on the album that was to be *Revolver* involved the one track featuring his lead vocal. Sketched by Lennon in a home-recorded demo, it began life as a

91

mournfully confessional acoustic song, lamenting his troubled early life back in Liverpool. By the time it had been worked up with McCartney and was ready to record, 'Yellow Submarine' had morphed into a singalong oom-pah lark, set to appeal to both kids and 'heads' (who believed its title was a reference to the yellow-encased barbiturate pill Nembutal).

Recorded amid fits of laughter by the Beatles on 26 May, the track was originally designed to feature a half-minute-long spoken-word introduction, written by John and narrated by Ringo, involving a walk from Land's End to John O'Groats, the furthermost tips of mainland Britain (twisted in Lennon's words into Land O'Groats and John O'Green), all to the accompaniment of crunching sound-effect footsteps. In spite of the fact that the Beatles worked on the intro for hours, it ended up on the cutting-room floor.

But, as a surreal sea shanty, 'Yellow Submarine' was perfect for Ringo. As he slipped into his spirited first verse, he might have been taking a singing turn once again at one of the old boozy Starkey parties back in the Dingle. In the studio, his and the other Beatles' voices were recorded slightly slower, then sped up, to make them sound a tad more youthful yet bizarre.

On Wednesday 1 June, EMI's Studio Two became the setting for a stoned party involving the Beatles, George's now-wife (as of 21 January) Pattie, elegant boho singer Marianne Faithfull and the Stones' druggiest member, Brian Jones. Together they delved into the studio's percussion and sound oddities cupboard for a Goons-like FX overdub session that variously involved swirling water around in an old tin bath, chinking glasses (Jones) and blowing water bubbles in a bucket using a straw (Lennon), all while shouting ocean-voyaging orders and singing along to the choruses, each growing rowdier in tone.

But, ever the professionals, order remained within the disorder. 'The drugs were kicking in a little more heavily,' Ringo said. 'The grass and the acid. Though we did take certain substances, we never did it to a great extent at the session. We were really hard workers. We worked like dogs to get it right.'

For the first time breaking with their self-imposed, value-for-money protocol of never releasing a single that also featured on a long-player, the Beatles issued 'Yellow Submarine'/'Eleanor Rigby' as a double A-side on 5 August 1966, the same day as *Revolver* arrived in the shops. A week later, the single made the top of the charts in Britain, Ireland, Belgium, the Netherlands,

Norway, Sweden, West Germany, New Zealand, Australia, Canada and on the American *Cash Box* listing.

Ringo had his first number one.

~

It was a time of new beginnings and, also, endings.

On 1 May 1966, the Beatles, all dressed in funereal black suits and turtle-neck sweaters, knocked out a fifteen-minute set – powering through five songs: 'I Feel Fine', 'Nowhere Man', 'Day Tripper', 'If I Needed Someone' and 'I'm Down' – on a bill alongside the Who, the Yardbirds and the Rolling Stones at the Wembley Empire Pool for the *New Musical Express*'s Annual Poll Winners All-Star concert. When the inevitable screams died down, no one was to know that they'd just witnessed the band's last-ever (at least last-ever pre-announced) live concert performance in the UK.

The following month, on 26 June, they returned to Hamburg for the first time since leaving three-and-a-half years earlier, on New Year's Day 1963, as a bunch of scruffy rock 'n' roll reprobates. This time, after shows in Munich and Essen, they arrived in Hamburg in regal fashion, overnight in a luxury train – boasting a marble bathtub for each Beatle – that had been used by Queen Elizabeth II only the previous year. Shortly after 6 a.m., the band and entourage were police-escorted twenty-five miles north of the city to the grand Hotel Schloss in Tremsbüttel Castle.

A host of familiar faces attended the two shows that night at the 5,600-capacity Ernst-Merck-Halle, including Astrid Kirchherr and writer/ producer Bert Kaempfert. (Kaempfert had, two months before, scored a hit with Frank Sinatra's reading of his 'Strangers in the Night', which – if only for one week – held 'Paperback Writer' off the UK number one spot on the *Record Retailer* chart.) Even Bettina Derlien, the garrulous barmaid at the Star-Club, was there to greet them.

George harboured mixed feelings about the group's return to Hamburg as big international stars, saying that while it was gratifying, it also involved encoun-ters with 'people you didn't necessarily want to see again, who had been your best friend one drunken Preludin night back in 1960. It's 1966, you've been through a million changes, and suddenly one of those ghosts jumps out on you.'

The madness that followed the four everywhere now had inevitably reached Germany. In Hamburg, more than forty youths were arrested for rioting inside and outside the venue. At a press conference in Essen, the group were asked about Japanese nationalist students who were protesting their upcoming series of shows at the Nippon Budokan in Tokyo (which, they claimed, would desecrate the purpose-built traditional martial arts venue). They'd even threatened to cut off the Beatles' hair when the band visited Japan. 'No, they won't,' Paul defiantly insisted.

Security around the Beatles was, however, oppressively tight from the second they landed at Haneda Airport on 29 June. During their five-day Japanese stay, they were protected by a 35,000-strong army of guards, virtually imprisoned at the Tokyo Hilton and even subjected to a minutely timed, military-styled schedule (which they almost instantly messed up, being inherently laid-back). Ringo was asked how he felt about being surrounded by so much official fuss. 'Very safe,' he quipped.

From the stage at the Budokan, the drummer viewed a bizarre spectacle: 3,000 police personnel stood in the aisles – 'a cop on every row', as he put it – keeping a close eye on the 10,000 fans. It was a wildly overprotective, almost one-to-three ratio. As a result, the atmosphere during the shows was unusually subdued and, for once, the Beatles could hear themselves with absolute clarity, which, during the first performance, only revealed the flaws in their live playing. 'The band suddenly realised they were out of tune,' Neil Aspinall remembered. 'They had to get their act together.'

Even greater scenes of strangeness, turning to horror, awaited them on the next leg of the tour, which took them to the Philippines. As soon as the Beatles' plane touched the tarmac in Manila, they were surrounded by rifle-toting soldiers from the Philippine Army, instructed to leave their bags on the ground and get into a car, separating the four from Brian Epstein and the rest of their small entourage. Ringo felt that something was off from the beginning: 'It was a little dodgy … everyone had guns.'

The band were sped off to Manila Bay and marched onto a waiting boat, the *Marima*, owned by Filipino businessman Manolo Elizalde, the co-founder of the Manila Broadcasting Company, for an unscheduled and enforced meet-and-greet with the mogul's son, Frederick, and a host of his friends, gathered together for a party to celebrate the twenty-four-year-old's birthday. Epstein was incensed by this effective abduction of his charges and insisted on being oared out to the *Marima* on a skiff to retrieve the band.

The Philippines, where the previous year President Ferdinand Marcos of the increasingly populist Nacionalista Party had been elected for his first term, was not yet a dictatorship, but certainly felt like one. (Marcos would seize absolute control by declaring martial law at the end of his second term in 1972.)

In the itinerary for the following day, 4 July, prepared by local promoter Ramon Ramos ahead of the Beatles' two performances for 80,000 fans at the Rizal Memorial Football Stadium, there was an entry for a 3 p.m. visit to the Marcos family's Malacañang Palace. Epstein, likely still miffed by the previous day's quasi-kidnapping, told the angry officials who knocked on his hotel room door that morning that there was no way the group was going to make the reception, since their first show was due to begin only an hour later at 4 p.m. After the gigs, which were crazed and dangerously oversubscribed – Harrison reckoned there to be 'about 200,000 people on the site' – the band returned to their hotel, jet-lagged and dejected.

The next morning, Starr and Lennon, who were sharing a room, were lying around in their beds chatting, before they called room service to order breakfast. 'Time went by, so we called down again,' Ringo remembered. '"Excuse me, can we have the breakfast?" Still nothing happened, so we put the TV on.' The televised scenes the pair witnessed threw them into shock – footage of the Marcos family's children crying over empty plates at the palace. The Beatles' no-show had been taken as a horrible snub and caused an almighty furore.

Before long, death threats and bomb warning calls were being made to both the hotel and the British Embassy by incensed Filipinos. The Beatles party immediately scrambled their belongings together and made for the hotel exit. 'We really had no help,' said Ringo. 'There was only one motorbike, compared to the huge motorcade that brought us in.'

At the airport, things turned ugly, with the Beatles and their team being pushed and shoved and even spat on by angry members of the public from a balcony above them. A subsequent report in the *Manila Sunday Times* amped up the drama, falsely claiming that 'drummer Ringo Starr was floored by an uppercut. As he crawled away, the mob kicked him.'

Nonetheless, Ringo and John were comically forced to hide behind a group of nuns, with Starr figuring that 'it's a Catholic country ... they won't beat them up'. By the time the band and entourage had all safely made it onto their plane, other, more serious problems presented themselves. The authorities were refusing to let the flight take off until tax was paid on the Beatles' share of the concert fees (which Ramos was now withholding). Worse, customs officials were claiming that there was no paperwork record of the British cohort having ever arrived in the country and so they were to be treated as illegal immigrants. Epstein, Mal Evans and publicist Tony Barrow were then trooped back into the airport as the Beatles sat nervously on the aircraft, for close to an hour, awaiting their fate.

'We had fantasies that we were going to be put in jail,' Ringo said. 'So we weren't going to get off the plane.'

Finally, President Marcos intervened, issuing a press statement claiming the whole thing had been a 'misunderstanding' and insisting that the ructions at the airport 'shouldn't have happened since they were a breach of Filipino hospitality and totally disproportionate to the triviality of the whole matter'. Epstein, Evans and Barrow got back on board and the flight was permitted to leave.

As the plane began to move down the runway, a rattled Epstein turned to his and the band's personal assistant Peter Brown and said, 'I'll never forgive myself. I put the boys in danger.'

'It was the most frightening thing that's happened to me,' Ringo admitted.

More than anything, this hairy incident was proof that it was becoming almost impossible to protect the Beatles; the cultural tsunami they'd created was by now also washing up all the bad stuff, too. Unofficially anointed as international sociocultural commentators, the four were now canvassed for their opinions on *everything*. This was particularly dangerous when it came to the mouthy, impulsive and increasingly iconoclastic Lennon.

Back in March, Maureen Cleave, a band-trusted reporter for London's *Evening Standard*, had spoken to all four Beatles for a series of individual profiles in the paper. In the eighth paragraph of the article focused on Lennon, he mused, 'Christianity will go. It will vanish and shrink. We're more popular than Jesus now.'

When the story ran in the UK, it caused no greater ripples of dissent than a handful of letters written to the paper. In the US, teen mag *Datebook* republished Lennon's words, quoting them out of context in a cover strapline that blared another of his off-hand comments: 'I don't know which will go first – rock 'n' roll or Christianity!' Uproar followed, led by a radio station in the Bible Belt city of Birmingham, Alabama, immediately banning all Beatles music, followed by close to two dozen others, particularly in the Deep South.

Heavy scenes met the group when they arrived in Chicago on 11 August for the beginning of their third US tour: record burnings, Ku Klux Klan protests, more death threats. At the obligatory press conference, held on the twenty-seventh floor of the Astor Tower Hotel, John tried to pour water over the controversy, insisting, 'I'm not saying that we're better, or greater, or comparing us with Jesus Christ as a person or God as a thing or whatever it is. I just said what I said, and it was wrong, or was taken wrong. And now it's all this.'

One reporter pointed out, 'Mr Starr, you haven't said a thing.'

'Well, I just hope it's all over now,' the drummer offered, clearly keen, like the others, for the fuss to die away. 'I hope everyone's straightened out and it's finished.'

But it was far from over. The tour progressed in an atmosphere of further threats to their lives, general mania and dwindling audiences, the hullabaloo visibly denting the Beatles' popularity, particularly since this time around they were booked into arena- and stadium-sized venues.

In Memphis on 19 August, outside the Mid-South Coliseum, the KKK encouraged crew-cut-wearing all-American kids to torch piles of records. Inside, three songs in, during 'If I Needed Someone', one individual in the audience threw a cherry bomb firework onto the stage, creating a *bang* as loud as a gunshot, causing instant panic among the band members and screams of fear from the crowd, including a cry of 'No, no!' from one girl fan.

Commenting later on this terrifying moment, in a quote that was all the more chilling in retrospect, John said that all of the Beatles instantly scanned the stage 'because each thought it was the other that had been shot'.

Four days later, back at Shea Stadium in New York on 23 August, 11,000 of the 55,000 tickets remained unsold: a statistic that would have been unthinkable at their record-breaking show there only a year and a week earlier.

Five days on, at Dodger Stadium in LA, just as the band launched into their closing song 'Long Tall Sally', around 7,000 of the 45,000 fans broke through security barriers, overwhelming the mere 100 security staff, rushed towards the stage and surrounded the armoured van that the Beatles had arrived in. The band struggled back into the vehicle, which then took off at high-speed, in reverse, forcing fans to leap out of its path, before it accelerated forwards towards a dugout, where the group jumped out and raced underground through a tunnel. They were then locked in their dressing room for two hours before it was declared safe for them to leave. Tony Barrow remembered a despairing Ringo lifting the tension by adopting a baby-ish voice and mock-pleading, 'Can I please go home to my mummy now?'

In Candlestick Park in San Francisco, on the fateful date of 29 August, the Beatles acknowledged that the game was up. Playing live, for them, had become an impossible situation, both musically and logistically. 'There was a big talk at Candlestick Park that this had got to end,' said Starr.

On that unseasonably cold, windy and foggy night, Lennon and McCartney stopped in between songs to snap self-portraits of themselves and their band-mates. The final photograph involved John positioning his camera on an amp, Ringo stepping down from his riser and the quartet lining up with their backs to the almost half-capacity crowd of 25,000.

'It seemed that this could possibly be the last time,' the drummer recalled. 'But I never felt 100 per cent certain 'til we got back to London.'

~

On their return to Britain, they effectively disappeared and, with the news-papers reporting that the Beatles had quit touring, rumours began to swirl that they'd in fact broken up. In October, Ringo and Maureen travelled to Spain to visit John, there filming his starring role as Private Gripweed in Richard Lester's military satire, *How I Won the War*. In his downtime, Lennon was developing a whimsical, haunting song that would take its name from Strawberry Fields, a Salvation Army children's home back in Liverpool.

It wasn't until the end of November that Ringo was back behind the drum kit in the EMI Studios. On the evening of Thursday the 24th, he played a muted tom-tom beat, with cocktail lounge-styled syncopated fills, along to

John's new song, 'Strawberry Fields Forever'. Four nights later, they reworked the arrangement, Ringo contributing a tougher beat and fluid rolls, in a take nailed the next day. More than a week on, they tried a different, faster approach and an end piece that featured heavy, polyrhythmic drum overdubs and Lennon exclaiming, 'Alright, calm down, Ringo.'

After all that they'd been through in 1966, Studio Two on Abbey Road did indeed feel to them like an oasis of calm. On 20 December, the four arrived there one by one and were interviewed in the car park by John Edwards, a reporter with ITN, for a TV news special originally set to be titled 'Beatles Breaking Up', but which ended up being more fittingly named, 'End of Beatlemania'.

Starr, similar to the others in now sporting a moustache (George had a full beard), grinned and yelled 'Merry Christmas' to waiting fans.

'You're looking very smart,' Edwards offered.

'Yes, I am,' the drummer agreed. 'Well, I had a bath.'

'Have you got anything lined up on your own?' prodded the journo.

'I've just been sitting around,' Ringo fibbed.

'Getting bored?' Edwards wondered.

'Getting fat,' Starr laughed.

The truth was far more tantalising but, for now, no one was revealing it. As Ringo later vividly described it, the plan was for the Beatles to remain in the studio, where they 'could hear each other and create any fantasy that came out of anyone's brain'.

17

BILLY SHEARS

A Singular Voice, 1963–1969

'**M**an, the Beatles were so high, they let Ringo sing a couple of tunes.'
So wisecracked American comedian Bill Hicks in one of his early
'90s stand-up routines, as he instructed anyone who was anti-drugs
to go home and burn their entire music collection. He then launched into a
saucer-eyed rendition of 'Yellow Submarine' in a cod English accent.

'D'you know how fucking high they were when they wrote that? They had
to pull Ringo off the ceiling with a rake to sing that fucking song.'

But even after their embracing of marijuana, which enhanced the musical
shapes of *Rubber Soul*, the Ringo Track was typically an afterthought for the
Beatles. In their early days, they simply followed the 'Starr Time' blueprint:
Lennon and McCartney's 'I Wanna Be Your Man' was a souped-up rocker in
the vein of the Shirelles' 'Boys'; Ringo's rendition of Carl Perkins' 'Matchbox'
(fourth track on the *Long Tall Sally* EP) was a rockabilly swinger sung gruffly in
the studio in June '64, two days before he was felled by tonsillitis and pharyngitis. Repeating the simple formula, another Perkins tune, the skiffle-y 'Honey
Don't', was chosen to be Starr's feature track on *Beatles for Sale*.

Then, things took a turn towards country and western: firstly via 'Act
Naturally', and then with 'What Goes On' on *Rubber Soul*, the latter credited
to Lennon/McCartney/Starkey, with Ringo shruggingly explaining that he'd
written 'about five words' to earn his co-credit on the song.

If there was a sense that everyone involved in the making of the Beatles'
records felt an obligation to give Starr a number to sing on (most of) their
LPs, it was one later underlined by Geoff Emerick. 'Almost every Beatles album

had one song with a lead vocal by Ringo, despite the fact that he could barely sing,' he loftily opined in his 2006 memoir, *Here, There and Everywhere*. 'But the fans ate it up and I have to admit there was something endearing about his voice – even if it was just the fact that you could hear him constantly straining to stay on pitch. Aware of those limitations, John or Paul would try to write him a song that had only a few notes in the melody line.'

During the making of the *Help!* album, this approach resulted in what is widely considered to be the weakest of all of Lennon and McCartney's compositions. 'If You've Got Trouble' was knocked off in the studio in February '65 – on the same day as 'Tell Me What You See' and 'You've Got to Hide Your Love Away' were more carefully recorded – and was a propulsive rocker featuring a back-breaking beat from Ringo, who also gamely tackled its ho-hum melody and unsympathetic, arms-race-of-moaning lyric. It was formulaic Merseybeat at best, duly dumped in favour of 'Act Naturally' (and left in the vaults until it was dusted off for the *Anthology 2* out-takes compilation released in 1996).

As his contributions to the Beatles' records progressed, Ringo's voice didn't develop as much as increasingly underline his character and his distinctive role within the band set-up. Arguably none of the others could have sung 'With a Little Help from My Friends' – or inhabited the persona of 'Billy Shears' – with quite the same jocular charm. Or, indeed, gone for his big two-bars-long note at the end of the song with the everyman gusto of a last-orders pub singer.

From *Sgt. Pepper* on, Starr was always brought in whenever a rousing chorus was required, starting with the Side Two reprise of the title track, where all four were pressed into vocal action. From there, a pattern developed, involving the quartet on the microphone for the kiddie sugar-rush singalong of 'All Together Now', the amateur dramatic society 'la la's' of 'Flying', the demented tiger hunter-interrogating chant of 'The Continuing Story of Bungalow Bill' (where they were joined by Maureen Starkey and Lennon's new girlfriend, of five months, Yoko Ono). Naturally, when it came to adding the 'chikka-cha' vocal percussion to 'Ob-La-Di, Ob-La-Da', Ringo was roped in to help overdub the proto human beatbox performances.

Elsewhere on *The White Album*, like the discarded spoken-word introduction for 'Yellow Submarine', in rehearsal Ringo improvised a never-used preamble for Lennon's lullaby 'Good Night', gently telling a child to pack away their toys and climb into bed. In the final recording, amid an elaborate and twinkling vintage Hollywood score (Lennon directing George Martin to make it 'corny'), Starr performed without the other Beatles, but with the support of a full orchestra and easy-listening stalwarts the Mike Sammes Singers.

When Ringo began writing his own material for the band, he cast himself in familiar roles as snug-bar performer ('Don't Pass Me By') or weird children's entertainer ('Octopus's Garden'). However, the notion of the Ringo Track hadn't yet entirely died in the writing minds of his bandmates, with Paul imagining 'Carry That Weight' might be one for the drummer to sing, his original verses narrating a series of 'trivial' problems in the resigned-but-cheery country style of 'Act Naturally'. Even when it was cut-and-shut with 'Golden Slumbers' and recorded as a mass-voiced group version for *Abbey Road*, it was Starr's unmistakable tones that cut through most prominently.

Of course, Ringo's singing was easily parodied, best of all by English session drummer John Halsey, in his role as Barry Wom in the Rutles, particularly with the affectionate, if sometimes cruelly accurate 1978 Beatles send-up mockumentary *All You Need is Cash* and accompanying soundtrack LP. In 'Living in Hope', a loping 'Don't Pass Me By' soundalike, the lyric of the song nailed Starr's pragmatic optimism, as Halsey/Wom sang in a loud, flat, yet blithely confident bellow.

But it was satire as skewed flattery. Ultimately, it's now impossible to imagine the Beatles without the sound of Ringo's voice.

18

RICHY AND PRISCILLA

Ringo and Cilla, 1961–1973

Tuesday 6 February 1968, and in Studio One at EMI on Abbey Road, the Beatles were hard at it, putting in a ten-and-a-half hour shift that involved George dubbing his vocals onto 'The Inner Light' – his third and deepest journey into eastern sounds, recorded with a group of Indian musicians in Bombay the previous month – and Paul double-tracking his voice on the playful, vamping 'Lady Madonna'.

Ringo wasn't there. The studio diary recorded that the others took a break between 8 p.m. and 9 p.m., presumably to watch their drummer's live appearance on the second episode of BBC1's new primetime show, *Cilla*, for a TV audience of around 13 million viewers.

He popped up at first in the opening credits, flashed as one of that week's guest stars, alongside mischievous, surrealist comedian Spike Milligan and ventriloquist Peter Brough, who featured in a subsequent sketch involving Starr. Brough propped his doll – smart-arse schoolboy Archie Andrews – on his knee, while Ringo had his own 'dummy' named Ariadne (Cilla Black as a gymslip-wearing, pigtailed schoolgirl) perched on his lap. Together, the latter pair sang the hoary old pub standard 'Nellie Dean', as Ringo glugged down a gottle o' geer. Cue canned laughter.

Later, dressed like a wartime spiv in homburg, black suit, white tie and snazzy two-tone black-and-white shoes, Ringo joined Cilla for a tap-dancing routine as they cooed their way through 'Do You Like Me?', an old-timey music-hall duet written by comedian Herbert Darnley back in 1917. The song was in fact suggested to Starr and Black by none other than Paul's dad, Jim, who used to perform it in his jazz band in the '40s. Emphasising the McCartney influence, Paul had written the theme tune for the *Cilla* show, the dreamy-to-brassy bossa nova of 'Step Inside Love'.

In some ways, the events of this day illuminated the growing schism between John and George, Paul and Ringo: torn between the inner light and light entertainment.

～

Back in Liverpool, at the start of the decade, Priscilla White had been close to the Starkey family. She and her friend Pat Davies (Richy's sometime girl-friend) were aspiring hairdressers and would arrive at 10 Admiral Grove every Wednesday to shampoo and set Elsie's hair, in return for a free tea of fried Spam, chips and beans. 'We didn't say anything at the time,' Harry let slip to Cilla many years later, 'but you used to make a right bloody mess of poor Elsie's hair.'

Known to her pals as Swinging Cilla, White was also a powerful, gutsy singer who, at the age of seventeen in the spring of 1961, was pushed by a friend up onto the stage at the Liverpool Jazz Society club on Temple Street for a guest spot with the Beatles. She turned in a fine performance of Sam Cooke's R&B take on Gershwin's 'Summertime', before Lennon told her, 'OK, Cyril, you've had your turn, now gerroff...'

Richy and Cilla became pals during her visits to Admiral Grove and she'd sometimes be invited onstage at Rory Storm and the Hurricanes gigs to belt through 'Boys' with their drummer, singing alongside him behind his kit. In the summer of '61, she was part of the horde that descended on the Starkeys' two-up, two-down on the occasion of Richy's twenty-first. Somewhere between sixty and seventy of his pals, mostly from the Liverpool music scene, crammed into the small terraced house, including members of the Hurricanes, the Dominoes and the Pacemakers. Richy and Cilla reprised their version of 'Boys' for the assembled and at one point everyone piled out onto the waste ground opposite the house for a group photo capturing them looking young and groovy and daft and drunk, with the middle-aged figures of Elsie and her friend Annie Maguire grinning out from the centre of them.

Though never officially an item, Cilla later hinted that there was more to her and Ringo's relationship in the early days of the Beatles. 'He was like a best friend,' she said. 'Even though he did ask me to marry him, but just for a giggle.

'Well, he was desperate actually ... 'cos all the other Beatles had girlfriends,' she added, seemingly having no knowledge of Maureen Cox at the time. 'I guess he was the odd one out. And I called his bluff. I said, "Well, call the banns in forty-eight hours, and I'll do it."'

White had increasingly impressed the crowds on the pub and club circuit, before a happy accident inspired her stage name when a *Mersey Beat* article mistakenly referred to her as 'Cilla Black'. In the summer of 1962, at Lennon's urging, she auditioned for Brian Epstein, backed by the Beatles once again, at the Majestic Ballroom in Birkenhead. Attempting to showcase her rendition of 'Summertime', she blew it through a combination of nerves and the band playing the song in too low of a key. Epstein, unconvinced, passed, for now.

A year later, the manager caught her act at the Blue Angel, updated his assessment and, in the autumn of '63, signed Cilla to his NEMS Enterprises as his sole female singer. Black was then pulled along fast in the Beatles' slipstream: an introduction to George Martin; a deal with Parlophone; her first hit with the Lennon/McCartney-written 'Love of the Loved'; and her first number one, with Bacharach/David's haunting showstopper 'Anyone Who Had a Heart', in which she moved between achingly tender verses and super-lunged chorus crescendos.

Fame brought with it a certain self-assurance for Black and she initially turned down the opportunity to sing Bacharach and David's 'Alfie' – written for the 1966 film of the same name starring Michael Caine as a Cockney lothario – unless the former flew to Abbey Road to conduct the orchestra for the session. Bacharach complied but pushed the singer hard on the day (she remembered eighteen takes; he said it was closer to thirty) until she'd nailed the emotional dynamic of the song to his satisfaction, her voice growing from a whisper to one that could strip paint when she went for the big notes. In the May of '66, it entered the top ten, becoming her eighth big hit, only weeks before the Beatles put out 'Paperback Writer'.

For Ringo, still acclimatising after the Beatles' rapid ascent, it was good to have a familiar face on the scene in London. One night at the Ad Lib club in Soho, he broke the mind-blowing news to Cilla that when the Beatles had met Elvis Presley in Los Angeles during the acid summer of '65, he'd spotted her sweeping power ballad 'You're My World' listed on the king of rock 'n' roll's jukebox. At that uneasy summit, where Elvis, idly plucking away at a bass guitar, had seemed drugged and aloof, the ice had been broken when the others picked up guitars and proceeded to jam together, with Ringo tapping along, to songs on the jukebox, including Cilla's Presley-loved hit.

⁓

May 1971. Almost ten summers after Richy's mad, mobbed twenty-first party in Liverpool, some 800 miles away in the south of France, Ringo was acting the millionaire playboy, renting a luxury yacht, the SS *Marala*, for the two-week duration of the Cannes Film Festival. Staying on in the country after attending Mick Jagger's high-society wedding to Bianca in Saint-Tropez, he'd set aside the fortnight for the purposes of general lazing and hobnobbing, with one eye on his burgeoning movie career.

Aboard the super-classy, '30s-built yacht, used by international royalty and also hired at different times by Salvador Dalí and Frank Sinatra, Ringo and Maureen were joined by Pattie and George, plus Cilla and her husband/manager Bobby Willis. One evening in this idyllic and laid-back setting, Starr and Harrison began casually developing a song, set to be the catchy and sentimental 'Photograph'. Black later claimed to have pitched in lines amid the boozy sing-along atmosphere (although she'd receive no writing credit when Ringo released the song and took it to the top of the US charts two years later). On the night, Cilla told Ringo she wanted to record 'Photograph' herself and release it as a single later in the year. 'No, it's too bloody good for you,' he said. 'I'm having it myself.'

Another scheme was hatched during the leisurely cocktail hours on board the *Marala*. The following month of June, Black was due to film a BBC TV special, *Cilla in Scandinavia*, and she asked Starr to join her there for a guest spot. Kicking off his subsequent seven minutes of screen time in the show, filmed in the snowy Hallingdal valley in the Norwegian winter resort town of Geilo, Ringo, in woolly hat and on skis, skidded to a respectable stop beside Cilla, before the two launched into some scripted dialogue that was as wooden as the trees seen in the distance.

'So you don't think I'm ready for the Olympic Games, then?' he asked her, before she turned to the camera and grinned, 'Ladies and gentlemen, Ringo

Starr', to a soundtrack fanfare of showbiz brass and canned applause. There followed some brief, mirth-free repartee about Ringo's skiing skills before Cilla said, 'Hey Ringo, did you know there was an echo in this valley?'

'So that's what it is?' he flatly responded. 'I thought it was me answering meself back.'

Cupping his hand to his mouth, he yodelled, 'Hello-eee-oh-eee-oh-eee-oh-eee'.

A second later, a cry of 'Hello-eee-oh-eee-oh-eee-oh-eee' could be heard resounding around the mountains. Then Cilla had a go. The same boom-booming, reverberating result. The action cut to reveal the echoing voice belonged to none other than Basil Brush, the Beeb's cravat-wearing puppet fox with his posh, know-all ways, sat on a waist-high mound of snow.

'Well, if it isn't my furry friend, Basil Brush,' Ringo exclaimed, before the three showbiz pals got together for some more toe-curling, jokes-deficient banter. A polystyrene snowman was crudely shoved into the frame and the trio then launched into 'Snowman Song', a perky World War II-styled marching song concerning the frustrating impossibilities of melting the cold, hard heart of a creature made of ice.

With his own credibility puddling around his feet, Starr's cool was imme-diately restored in the next segment. Sat at an upright piano positioned in the snow, he cut a hip figure in his mirrored ski shades, with his long hair flying in the breeze and his gloved hands prodding the keys as he sang 'It Don't Come Easy', his US and UK top-five solo hit of earlier in '71 that had been produced (and, some suspected despite the sole 'Starkey' credit, written) by Harrison. In intercut shots, Ringo zoomed around the slopes on a yellow snowmobile.

Earlier, underlining the vaguely Beatle-y theme to the show, in a TV studio-shot clip Cilla performed a hippie folk 'Norwegian Wood' with post-Shadows troupe Marvin, Welch & Farrar, accompanied by the wonky strains of Ronnie Hazlehurst and his orchestra. Elsewhere, Black risked her neck while being hurtled along Finnish dirt tracks in a white Ford Escort driven by rally cham-pion Hannu Mikkola to the lite R&B sound of her version of 'Drive My Car'.

It was, for the most part, thoroughly cheesy stuff. But when the show was broadcast later that year on 27 November, once again millions upon millions tuned in to watch these two rich Scouse celebrities take over BBC1. It was a long, long way from Spam and chips and Admiral Grove.

19

BUTLIN'S RISHIKESH

An Indian Holiday Camp, 1968

It's widely believed that Ringo hated the Beatles' sojourn to India in the February of 1968 that, for him, lasted less than a fortnight. But that's not entirely so.

After arriving in Delhi on Tuesday 20 February, with Maureen, Paul and Jane, he and the others embarked upon the near-six-hour taxi ride to Rishikesh and the Transcendental Meditation retreat of the Maharishi Mahesh Yogi. Rattling along for some 160 miles northeast in a boxy '50s-era Morris car, they arrived at the Ganges, crossing on foot via the Lakshman Jhula suspension bridge before ascending the steep hillside to the Maharishi's ashram, a fourteen-acre compound surrounded by thick jungle. There they joined John and Cynthia, and George and Pattie, who'd arrived four days earlier.

'We'd been sent lists of what to take with us, like blankets and camping things,' Ringo remembered. 'But we didn't need any of them. It was all very luxurious.'

Starr's main worry was his aversion to spicy food. A health hangover from his childhood peritonitis meant that his insides remained delicate: onions, garlic and definitely curries were off the menu for him. 'I always took a suitcase full of clothes,' he said, 'and a suitcase full of beans.'

~

Ringo was the last of the four Beatles to fall under the influence of the Maharishi. In the summer of 1967, Pattie Harrison had spotted an advert in *The Times* for the Indian guru's Spiritual Regeneration Movement Foundation, attending a subsequent introductory TM lecture at Caxton Hall (where, coincidentally, the Starkeys had married two years earlier).

George, John and Paul followed her lead, meeting the Maharishi at the Hilton Hotel on Park Lane on 24 August, and leaving, according to Pattie, 'spellbound'. Post-acid, the Beatles felt that they'd been given a glimpse of the bigger picture, but now sought to connect to a form of spirituality that was both drug-free and beyond the scope of their Christian upbringings. And so, they looked east. But, first, north-west to Wales, where the Maharishi was holding a ten-day conference in Bangor.

One day in the third week of August '67, Ringo returned home from Queen Charlotte's Hospital in Hammersmith, where Maureen had given birth to their second son, Jason, on the 19th. At Sunny Heights, he played back messages from John and George on his new-fangled answering machine, urging him to come to Bangor. Where one Beatle went, the others inevitably followed and so, the next day, the drummer and his bandmates, trailed by reporters and photographers through Euston station, boarded the train to north Wales that the press later dubbed 'the Mystical Special'.

The Maharishi caught the Beatles at a transformative but also vulnerable time, not least because of the devastating news that arrived two days into the trip that Brian Epstein had died in his sleep at his home in London.

Epstein had been increasingly troubled and aimless, particularly after the Beatles quit touring in 1966. Suffering from profound insomnia, worsened by his addiction to amphetamines, he had in the days before checked out of the Priory clinic, where he'd attempted to rest and rid himself of his dependencies. The last time he saw the Beatles was on 23 August at Chappell Recording Studios on New Bond Street, where they were working on 'Your Mother Should Know'. The manager had seemed low and distant, listening to the playbacks of the track from the back of the control room and saying little.

On 27 August, Epstein's butler knocked on the manager's locked bedroom door, receiving no response. After summoning a doctor, the two together barged the door open and found Epstein dead. A pathologist's report later recorded that the thirty-two-year-old had succumbed to a 'low fatal dose' of the tranquilliser Carbrital, which Epstein had been using as a sleeping aid.

His body's tolerance to the drug had been lethally diminished by combining it with alcohol.

A camera crew in north Wales filmed Lennon and Harrison's reactions to the horrific news. Both, but particularly John, appeared vacant and haunted by grief. Ringo later said the Maharishi had advised them 'not to hold onto Brian ... to love him and let him go, because we are all powerful forces, and we could stop him going on in the natural progression up to heaven. He said, "You know you have to grieve for him and love him, and now you send him on his way." And it really helped.'

In the face of much conjecture that Epstein had committed suicide, Starr believed the manager's death to be an accidental overdose of 'downers', reckoning that the manager had probably taken the pills, fallen asleep, 'then woke up and took some more'.

~

Six months on at the ashram in India, for this and various other reasons the Beatles remained hollow. 'We were all a bit exhausted, spiritually,' McCartney reflected. 'I think generally there was this feeling of, "Yeah it's great to be famous, it's great to be rich ... but what's it all for?"' For Starr, this brief period of isolation was to temporarily relieve 'all that pressure of being the Beatles'.

Far away from the outside world, they settled into a daily routine. A vegetarian breakfast was taken at an outdoors communal dining area where the main challenge was to avoid the marauding grey langur monkeys who'd arrive to steal their food. Group meditation exercises were then conducted on the rooftops, with Ringo entirely dedicated but lacking the marathon mental stamina of the others, being able to internally focus 'for an hour at the most'.

There were other, more ordinary distractions, mainly involving shopping trips into Rishikesh where Ringo (ever style-minded) had clothes tailor-made for him: Nehru-collared shirts and what he described as 'huge silly pants with very tight legs and a big body that you'd tie up tight'.

Back up the hill, bathing became a problem and involved having to shout and stamp to frighten away 'the scorpions and tarantulas'. This terrified Maureen, who suffered from a general phobia of insects. Paul comically remembered her at one point being 'trapped in her room because there was a fly over the door'.

Ringo moaned to the Maharishi about the living conditions and was told that 'for people travelling in the realm of pure consciousness, flies no longer matter very much.'

Starr shot back, 'Yes, but that doesn't zap the flies, does it?'

What with the exotic creepy crawlies and limited food options, life at the ashram quickly began to pall for the Starkeys. Ringo had requested eggs for breakfast – which are seen as a violation of the ahimsa (or non-violent) principle adhered to by many Hindus – and was surprised to see the cook burying their shells. He thought to himself, *Can't God see that too?* and began to suspect that all was not as rigorously religious as it seemed.

After ten days, on 1 March he and Maureen, homesick and missing their kids (who'd been looked after by both a nanny and the latter's mother while they were away), packed up and flew home to England. 'I wouldn't want anyone to think we didn't like it there,' he stressed to a reporter on his return, before knowingly adding, as someone who had experienced summer seasons bashing the drums onstage at the resorts of Pwllheli and Skegness, 'it was like a Butlin's holiday camp'.

Starr nonetheless had left India with one important tool that would prove invaluable in his future life. 'I feel so blessed I met the Maharishi,' he commented, thirty-six years on, in 2004. 'He gave me a mantra that no one can take away and I still use it.'

20

34 MONTAGU SQUARE

The Curious Tale of a
Marylebone Flat, 1965–2010

Just before his wedding to Maureen in the February of 1965, Ringo took out the lease on a split-level terraced flat in the north-western corner of a quiet square in the affluent area of Marylebone in London's West End. Flat 1, 34 Montagu Square was accessed either via its imposing ground-floor Regency front door or, more often, through a railing gate and down a narrow set of steps to its basement.

It was a swish pad, with a living room (featuring an original nineteenth-century fireplace), bedroom and en-suite bathroom (boasting a sunken pink tub) on the top level, and a kitchen and sitting room-cum-second bedroom on its lower level. Perfect, then, for a Beatle and his new bride.

As a measure of how far they were going up in the world, even hereditary Tory peer Lord Mancroft, a resident of Montagu Square who had served under both Winston Churchill and Harold Macmillan, welcomed the Starkeys to the area. In a signifier of how the Beatles were now warmly accepted by the establishment, he told a journalist: 'We're a very distinguished square and I'm sure we'll welcome such a distinguished gentleman and his lady.'

Maureen, however, hated living there, particularly when she was alone and left entirely undefended against the feral girl fans who lingered outside on the pavement, staring into her front window or taking turns to buzz the intercom. 'Some of them were basically little cows,' she later fumed. 'They used to do it on purpose to terrorise me when he wasn't there. It used to frighten me sometimes.'

The Starkeys didn't last long at Montagu Square, before they moved out to Sunny Heights. Ringo clearly loved the place, though, and cannily decided to keep the lease on and sub-let the property. Further proof of how 34 Montagu Square was an upmarket address befitting of his fast-rising status came on 26 October that same year. He and Paul were photographed standing on its front steps, grinning and smoking fags, as they waited for John to pick them up in his Rolls-Royce, en route to Buckingham Palace to be given their MBEs by the Queen.

~

The next, short-lived tenants of Montagu Square were the Fool, the Dutch design collective who would later psychedelically daub the exterior of the Apple boutique on Baker Street. As '65 turned to '66, Paul took over the flat and installed a studio in the basement, with the notion of recording avant-garde performers and poets there. McCartney was advised by his friend Barry Miles, co-owner of the Indica Gallery, that Ian Sommerville, sometime boyfriend of wildcard heroin addict poet, author and visual artist William S Burroughs, would be a good person to employ as a studio manager and engineer. Sommerville was duly sent to the Teletape hi-fi shop in Piccadilly Circus where he bought two Revox reel-to-reel tape machines, a small mixing desk, enormous, neighbour-bothering speakers and, crucially, a tape-editing block which they would use to conduct their sound-snipping experiments.

In reality, and likely due to the fog of dope smoke that typically clouded the basement, nothing much got done there. Sommerville moved into the flat, insisting that he was happy to be on call at all times. Miles later noted that 'Ian was in the strange position of playing host in Ringo's expensive apartment, fixing everyone drinks, fussing about, cautioning everyone not to lean against the green watermarked silk wallpaper in the sitting room'.

The only recording to be released from Montagu Square was the voice of Burroughs, drearily intoning 'yes … hello … yes … hello' for nigh on twenty minutes for the soundtrack of his 1966 experimental film, *The Cut Ups*. Down in the basement, McCartney always struggled to connect with Burroughs. 'He was very interesting, but we never really struck up a huge conversation,' Paul said. 'I actually felt you had to be a bit of a junkie, which was probably not true.'

Characteristically, McCartney soon found a more practical use for the studio, taping an acoustic guitar version of the just-written 'Eleanor Rigby', which featured his double-tracked voice. 'I went down there in the basement on my days off on my own. Just took a guitar down and used it as a demo studio.' When Burroughs heard the full-realised version of the song on *Revolver*, he complimented McCartney on how he had managed to compress its narrative into a mere three verses.

But ultimately, the basement studio experiment was a failed one. McCartney gave up his tenancy and, for a few months, Flat 1 lay empty.

Then, in December, Jimi Hendrix moved in. Starr had bumped into the guitarist's girlfriend, Kathy Etchingham, in a club one night, listened to her complaints about the couple's current living situation in a cramped hotel room and offered to let them Montagu Square for £30 a month (the equivalent of less than £700 today and clearly an absolute bargain in terms of modern London pricing). The pair took up residence on the lower level, while the first floor was occupied by Hendrix's manager Chas Chandler and his girlfriend Lotta Null.

That same month, Hendrix released his debut single, 'Hey Joe', and his dazzling reputation in the capital lit up the rest of the UK when the record peaked at number six. One night at Montagu Square, following a domestic row with Etchingham that resulted in her storming out, down in the basement he wrote for her the soulful conciliatory ballad 'The Wind Cries Mary', destined to be his third top-ten hit.

But after only three months, the guitarist fell foul of his Beatles landlord. Another night, while tripping on acid, Hendrix had thrown whitewash over the walls. Ringo, furious, evicted him, and solved the decorative problem by having the rest of the walls painted white. This was to suit the fashionably minimalist tastes of 34 Montagu Square's future, and most notorious, tenants.

John and Yoko had been a conjoined couple since the former's return from Rishikesh, resulting in Cynthia and five-year-old Julian being unceremoniously turfed out of Kenwood, the family's Surrey home. Mother and son moved into the vacant Montagu Square flat, but only for three months, after it became clear that Ono and Lennon were struggling with the isolating effects of life out into the sticks. A house-swap was agreed, and John and Yoko moved into the square in the autumn of '68.

The apartment soon became, by all reports, an utter tip, with records and ashtrays and dirty clothes littering the floors, as the pair blocked out the world and indulged in snorting heroin, in what Lennon vividly described as 'a strange cocktail of love, sex and forgetfulness'. In October, using a camera fitted with a self-timer, the couple photographed themselves in the back bedroom on the ground floor, in stark black and white, fully naked. The shots were to be used as the infamous artwork for their November 1968 experimental album, *Unfinished Music No. 1: Two Virgins.*

'I come from the art world,' Ono later stressed. 'You get a naked model and you do a drawing or whatever. So the idea of physical nakedness is not that controversial in the art world. The cover was something that we thought was a statement in itself, but also it would just carry our music. I mean, usually the cover has to be good so that people buy it.

'But in this case, they bought it, but for what reason?' she laughed. 'You know what I mean? I don't think they listened to any of it.'

Ringo remembered his reaction when John first showed him the photographs. Embarrassed, he pointed to a minor detail: the fact that a copy of *The Times*' business section was in the frame: '"Oh, you've even got *The Times* in it...", as if he didn't have his dick hanging out.' Starr pointed out to his bandmate that, as Beatles, they would all have to answer for this controversial move. Lennon told him, 'Oh, Ringo, you only have to answer the phone' when reporters called.

'Two or three people phoned,' Ringo remembered. 'I said, "See, he's got *The Times* on the cover?"' as if to try to distract them, as he had himself, from his pal's pecker.

The drummer did indeed defend Lennon, telling David Wigg on Radio 1's *Scene and Heard* show, 'It's alright. It's a very nice photo. It's very clean. It's alright being naked ... if you want to be naked. And all those people who don't want to be shouldn't just shout, "Kill, kill". They should just let it go and say, "Alright, he wants to be naked ... I'll keep me trousers on."'

In the wake of the outrage, *Two Virgins* had to be issued by Apple Records in a brown paper bag, like a dirty book.

'I didn't mind that,' Ono said, 'because by then I realised what we did was so controversial that it was getting a bit dangerous for us. "OK, put it in a brown paper bag, it's fine."'

—

At around 11.30 a.m. on Friday 18 October 1968, the police raided Flat 1. Rumours had been circulating that the Beatles were to be the targets of drug busts, with Lennon's journalist pal Don Short, of the *Daily Mirror*, telling him three weeks before that he'd overheard an officer in a pub boasting that he was going to 'get' the band members.

'We got a notice from Apple,' Ono remembered, 'that this irritating sergeant was going around arresting famous people, so just be careful, make sure that you have *nothing*. And so John was going around washing everything…'

Lennon's old Liverpool pal Pete Shotton dropped round Montagu Square that morning and was met by the unusual sight of the Beatle with a vacuum cleaner. He offered to lend a hand to give the place a deep clean. 'Fucking Jimi Hendrix used to live here,' a rattled Lennon told him. 'Christ knows what the fuck is in these carpets.'

Satisfied that the flat was drug-free, Lennon and Ono went back to bed. Then, they were awoken by a sudden commotion.

'There was such a noise,' Ono said, 'and we looked out the window and somebody was climbing down the wall to come in. And we were sort of naked, so we just gathered our sheets around us and immediately went into the bathroom and just peeked. There was a bell ringing at the door and I, like a fool, opened the door. There was a policewoman and I immediately tried to shut the door, but one foot was in there.'

Officers from the drug squad, led by the notorious figure of Detective Sergeant Norman Pilcher, entered the apartment and, with the aid of two Labrador sniffer dogs, Yogi and Boo-Boo, quickly discovered cannabis in two places: a tiny 0.06 of an ounce in an envelope in a trunk in the bedroom, and close to half an ounce in a binoculars case in the living room.

'They discovered this big, big piece of hash in the other room,' Ono said of the latter find, which she insisted was planted. 'We knew that we didn't have that.'

After the pair were led outside through a pack of tipped-off photographers and taken to the nearby Paddington Green police station, Lennon copped to owning the drugs. Later, he insisted that he only did so to protect Ono. 'I thought they'd send Yoko away because we weren't married,' he said, '[that] they'd throw her out of the country.' In the event, at Marylebone Magistrates' Court on 28 November, Lennon pleaded guilty to cannabis possession and was fined £150. 'It's not too bad,' he reasoned, as yet unaware that the stain of his criminal record would prove impossible to remove and would later be cited by the Nixon administration in its attempt to have him deported from the US in 1973.

Things could have been equally hairy for Starr, being Lennon's landlord and arguably guilty by association. On 19 February 1969, the building's owners, Brymon Estates, served him with a writ, forcing him to agree to never allow Lennon and Ono to live on the premises – they'd cleared out by the previous November anyway – and insisting that only the drummer and his family were allowed to occupy the residence. What's more, the making of music was to be banned entirely in the apartment.

Nine days later at the High Court, the hearing was brief. Ringo gave up the lease on Montagu Square and no more remained to be said.

⌒

Four decades later, in August 2010, the seventy-seven-year-old Yoko Ono sat across a table from the author in the kitchen of apartment 72 in the Dakota building in New York. She told me she'd been reflecting on the Montagu Square bust again only recently and had come to a realisation about why the dope had been planted by the police.

'Think about it,' she said. 'If they came in and couldn't find anything, we could sue them. So they had to be prepared with something. It didn't dawn on me until about a week ago.'

However, that didn't stop Ono from returning to Montagu Square two months later. English Heritage had agreed to have a blue plaque denoting a 'building of historical interest' installed on the wall of number 34. She was there to perform the unveiling of the memorial sign, which read: 'John Lennon 1940–1980 Musician and Songwriter lived here in 1968'.

Ono thanked all involved and then offered an 'affirmation' she'd written for the occasion. 'We're now bathing in the light of dawn,' she began, 'standing in the heaven we have created together on this planet. We wish to share this age of joy with all lives on Earth, as we are one united with infinite and eternal love in the name of truth, for the highest good of all concerned. So be it. Thank you.'

No mention of hokey drug busts or full-frontal nudity was necessary. Or, for that matter, the name of their absent landlord.

21

BLISTERS

The White Album and
a Crisis of Confidence, 1968

While Ringo had been somewhat enlightened by his time in Rishikesh, as soon as he got back to England at the start of March '68, he descended into gloom. Speaking on the phone to the *Evening Standard*'s Ray Connolly, for the first time in his near-six years of fame, Starr seemed unsure of himself: where he was at and where he was going.

'Sometimes I feel I'd like to stop being famous and get back to where I was in Liverpool,' he confessed. 'There don't seem to be so many worries in that sort of life, although I thought there were at the time. But ... they counted for very little.'

Now he had everything; more than he needed. The drummer had kept in touch with his old pal Roy Trafford back in Liverpool, who was still working as a joiner. Ringo seemed to somehow envy his friend's simpler life, one that Richy had left behind to become a Fab Beatle.

'He's only got about thirty records,' he said of Trafford, 'but he gets so much pleasure from them. Yet, I've got a cupboard here with about 500 LPs and when I want to play one, I have to close the cupboard again, because I don't know which one to put on anymore.'

Revealing a previously hidden psychological bruise, he admitted that he'd even considered having plastic surgery to fix his nose since, in his mind, it 'was all the papers seemed to write about.

'It didn't hurt me,' he stressed, unconvincingly. 'But I got fed up with reading about it.'

Elsewhere, he spoke of what he viewed as the precarious nature of life as a Beatle. He clearly didn't see it as a long-term prospect.

'I could now afford never to work again, I suppose,' he reckoned. 'But I'd have to be careful and probably have to sell this house in about ten years. I'm rich by working-class standards, but not immensely rich, and not by the standards of those who really do have money. I spend money like water, you see.'

Then, when it came to assessing his own skills as a musician, he offered a quote that was to seem all the more significant given the subsequent events of 1968.

'As a drummer, I'm fair, that's all,' he stated, before ominously adding, 'and I don't care about being good anymore.'

Twelve weeks later, Starr sat at a mixing console at EMI Studios and attempted to explain the record-making process to a camera crew filming him for *All My Loving*, a BBC documentary by director Tony Palmer focusing on the rock scene of '68 and featuring the Beatles alongside the Who, Jimi Hendrix and Pink Floyd.

Looking neat and tidy in a dark suit, smoking a fag, he explained that 'there's more fun in the record if there's a few sounds that you don't really know what they are. And really, they're just instruments, only something happens on here, y'know.' He swept his hands, with a showman's flourish, over the mixing desk. 'I couldn't tell you what because we've got a special man who sits here and does this [mock-twiddles knobs] and the guitar turns into a piano or something, y'know.'

He looked directly into the camera's lens, addressing the future viewers. 'And then you may say, "Why don't you use a piano?" Because the piano sounds like a guitar.'

In reality, Ringo was obscurely describing recording techniques that were by this point becoming increasingly redundant for the Beatles. A week later, they began work on what was to become their self-titled double album, forever known as *The White Album*, in often fraught sessions that typically adopted a live-to-tape approach to production.

On 30 May, in Studio Two, they did eighteen takes of John's 'Revolution', the final one comprising more than ten minutes of loose, bluesy loping, Ringo mutedly beating the kit before growing thumpingly loud as the minutes ticked by, to be matched by John's vocal overdubs, which moved from lullaby tones to throat-shredding screams. Geoff Emerick described the scene in the studio as 'uncontrolled chaos, pure and simple', noting that George Martin appeared 'puzzled and concerned', while Ringo 'looked like he was about to keel over'.

In the background of the track, the sound of someone fiddling with a tape machine could be heard, playing a disembodied voice intoning phrases such as 'Maybe if you become naked…'. This was the first recorded presence of Yoko Ono on a Beatles session, marking the first time John had ever brought her along to one.

None of the other members, for fear of upsetting the delicate balance of the band, faced up to Lennon about Ono's soon-to-be constant attendance at the studio. 'We were all trying to be cool and not mention it,' Ringo admitted. 'But inside we were all feeling it and talking in corners.'

'Let's put it this way,' Ono said of the quietly strained atmosphere, 'they had so much respect for John, they were not outwardly nasty to me. Actually… very delicate. A little jab here and there.'

But it was Starr who first stepped forward to confront Lennon when he managed to get his bandmate alone, telling him, 'John, it bothers me. OK? I don't understand …Yoko is here all the time.'

Lennon argued back, 'Well, when you go home to Maureen and tell her how your day was, it takes you two lines: "Oh, we had a good day in the studio…" Well, *we* know exactly what's going on.'

Starr absorbed Lennon's explanation and immediately 'relaxed a lot around Yoko'. The drummer's acceptance of Ono was ongoing from this point and was quietly appreciated by the couple, not least because, as John said later, Paul and George 'really gave it to us'. Ono in turn clearly liked Starr, the only Beatle that she had been aware of back in the early '60s, mainly because of his quirky name.

'When I was [living] in New York,' she remembered, 'I heard Ringo's name. It was easy for me to catch because "Ringo" in Japanese is "apple".'

Moving into June, the sessions for the album became fractured and were increasingly characterised by members splintering off into different studios at Abbey Road, whether solo or in pairs. There was, however, still group fun to be had, such as Ringo pelting the kit on 'Everybody's Got Something to Hide Except Me and My Monkey' as Paul stood beside him clattering out a metallic rhythm on a fireman's bell and interjecting mad screams.

However, George Martin and Geoff Emerick were surprised when the group decided to focus their energies so early in the sessions on Ringo's first self-penned contribution to a Beatles record, the jaunty, if gently weird, 'Don't Pass Me By'. 'The only [reason] we could come up with,' Emerick reflected, 'was that, behind the scenes, the others must have known that Ringo was getting fed up and they were trying to keep him happy.'

If so, the gesture didn't work and Starr fell into a state of silent disgruntlement, which came with a paranoia that he – the last man into the Beatles – was once again becoming the outsider. Still, through July and into the beginning of August, there remained some real highpoints for him during the recordings: the moment when 'Hey Jude' 'just clicked' after the Beatles had decamped to Trident Studios in Soho, lured there by the facility's fancy eight-track machine; recording the blistering 'Yer Blues' while the four were crushed together with their gear in a fifteen-by-eight-foot storage cupboard adjacent to Studio Two in Abbey Road. 'You can't top it,' he enthused of the latter experience, which effectively recreated the small club stage conditions that for the Beatles were now a distant memory.

But, increasingly, there were drearier days. Monotonously pounding out a troglodyte rhythm on the four beats of the bar for an early version of 'Helter Skelter'. Tackling the slippery time signatures of George's 'Not Guilty', which ran to more than 100 energy-depleting takes – the most of any Beatles recording – but was still left on the cutting room floor.

Further denting his confidence, McCartney was increasingly encroaching on Starr's territory in trying to shape or dictate his drum parts. 'Every time I went for a cup of tea,' Ringo later moaned, 'he was on the drums!'

Things came to a head on 22 August when they were running through Paul's Chuck Berry-via-the Beach Boys homage, 'Back in the USSR'. McCartney kept pushing and pushing the drummer to achieve a certain feel. Suddenly feeling he was 'playing pretty shitty', Ringo walked out.

Maureen Starkey later said that her husband had already been thinking of quitting the Beatles. In one moment when they were together at home in Sunny Heights, he'd confided to her, 'I can't do this anymore.'

'That's OK,' she remembered reassuring him. 'If that's the way you feel, you have to go … Carry on and do whatever you want.'

'I know,' he said, 'but the money will be different.'

The day after he stormed out, Ringo went to visit John at Montagu Square and told him he was leaving the group because he felt 'unloved and out of it'. Lennon shocked him by saying that *he* believed he was the one who'd been excommunicated and told the drummer, 'If you go, I go.' Starr then went to see McCartney, who expressed a similar sense of remoteness from the others. In the end, it was suggested that the drummer take a break somewhere to think it over. Harrison was simply told, 'Oh, Ringo's gone on holiday.' The guitarist, too, subsequently admitted he'd been thinking, 'What's the point in me being round here? They all seem so cool and groovy, and I just don't fit.'

Ringo, Maureen and the kids flew to Sardinia, staying on a yacht borrowed from Peter Sellers. In the drummer's absence, the other three Beatles soldiered on, all contributing to the composite beat on 'Back in the USSR', while Paul provided the simple, circular rhythm, replete with some flabby impersonations of Ringo's trademark fills, on 'Dear Prudence'. Meanwhile, any talk of Starr's departure, outside of the inner circle, was strictly verboten.

Lennon meanwhile came up with a weird idea for a belated birthday present for Ringo, commissioning a bespoke artwork from celebrated Spanish surrealist Salvador Dalí. The artist asked for $5,000 in cash and, in return, handed over a strange *objet d'art* that looked like a coconut sawn in half, lined with sponge implanted with what he claimed was a coiled black hair he'd plucked from his iconic upturned waxed moustache. If the sponge was wetted with a drop or two of water, the hair slowly uncurled. John, of course, loved it and never did give it to Ringo.

The Beatles sweetened Starr up by sending him a telegram in Sardinia, which, in his recollection, stated: 'You're the best rock and roll drummer in the world. Come on home, we love you.' On his return to Abbey Road on

Tuesday 3 September, he found his drums covered in flowers, as arranged by Harrison. A banner above them read: 'Welcome Back'.

Still, there was no actual playing required of him until the following day, when the quartet reassembled, at Twickenham Film Studios, to videotape performances of their just-released single 'Hey Jude' – the band engulfed by an all-singing audience surrounding them on all sides during its crescendo – and the thrillingly distorted remake of 'Revolution' that featured on its B-side.

Even if he was only miming, during both performances Starr was visibly in his element, clearly happy to be back in the Beatles-shaped frame.

In the days and weeks that followed, the four threw themselves back into band-based recordings, starting with George's 'While My Guitar Gently Weeps' and, four days later, twenty-one takes of the newly turbo-charged 'Helter Skelter', the final one ending with the drummer screaming 'I've got blisters on my fingers!'. On Wednesday 18 September, they jammed and taped a pacey and intense twelve-bar blues together, then took a break to nip round to Paul's house on Cavendish Avenue to catch a 9.05 p.m. BBC2 screening of the 1956 rock 'n' roll film *The Girl Can't Help It*, featuring Little Richard, Eddie Cochran and Gene Vincent. Having tapped back into the source, they returned reinvigorated to Abbey Road where McCartney and Lennon quickly wrote and then sang the uproarious 'Birthday' over the recording of the earlier blues jam.

Next, five days on, and over three nights, they nailed the concentrated, multi-movement 'Happiness Is a Warm Gun' – after seventy takes. 'Now *I'm* playing on a blister,' Lennon noted after take sixty-five, echoing the drummer's painful 'Helter Skelter' complaint.

~

Close proximity to an audience during the 'Hey Jude' Twickenham filming had whetted Paul's appetite for live performance, although the others remained unconvinced. Nonetheless, reports appeared in the press that the Beatles were set to return to the stage for the first time in two years, for three charity shows on consecutive nights, starting on either 15 or 16 December. The chosen venue was the Roundhouse in Chalk Farm, the former railway shed and gin warehouse that had become the happening hard-rock venue in London by 1968.

The plan was for the band to play for an invite-only audience of 1,500 for each of the three performances: the first a run-through, the second a dress rehearsal and the third the final, polished presentation. The *NME* teased that a 'one-hour TV spectacular may be built around the shows'.

'These concerts will be a mind-bender!' promised Apple exec Jeremy Banks, revealing that the setlist would centre on the group's new, thirty-track album. 'Negotiations for the Roundhouse are at an early stage,' he added, 'but will be completed this week.' Beatles publicist Derek Taylor was meanwhile quoted in *Melody Maker* saying, 'The group will be playing tracks from their album, old rock and roll tunes, anything they feel like or can play. It'll be informal and flexible.'

'We ended up being a band again,' Ringo subsequently said of the latter half of '68, 'and that's what I love. I love being in a band.'

These Roundhouse gigs, never to be realised (but morphing into the vague concept for the *Get Back* project), might have charted a different future for the Beatles. But, in the end, all of this band-based activity proved that, despite its later reputation as the album where the Beatles began to fall apart, *The White Album* was also where, for a time, they pulled back together. Once again, they became far more than the sum of their four parts, the rituals of their mysterious musical brotherhood conjuring what McCartney enigmatically described as 'the magic circle within the square'.

22

PUT ME IN THE MOVIES, PART ONE

The Route to *Candy*, 1964–1968

Mopey and unshaven, his hangover beginning to kick in, Ringo wandered moodily down the river towpath. It was Thursday 9 April 1964 and he'd been up all night, staying out in a London club until dawn, before arriving on location for another day's filming on the first Beatles feature film, *A Hard Day's Night*. In truth, he was still a bit pissed.

'I had no brain,' he later confessed. 'I'd gone.'

Director Dick Lester and his crew were waiting for Starr beside the stretch of the Thames that runs past Kew. At first, they attempted to shoot a scene wherein the drummer bantered with a truanting boy, played by David Janson, but it soon became apparent that the drummer didn't know his lines and was in no fit state to act anyway.

Lester, frustrated, said, 'Let's do *anything*.'

Starr suggested, 'Let me just walk around and you film me.'

In the movie, this solo spot for Ringo was to be preceded by a scene in a TV theatre where he is forced by the Beatles' manager (played by Norman Rossington) to look after Paul's gurning, perma-complaining grandfather (Wilfrid Brambell). The drummer takes him to the café where the grandad has a go at him for having his 'hooter' stuck in a paperback of Robert Traver's *Anatomy of a Murder* and urges him to stop filling his head with books and to go outside to experience real life.

Thus inspired, Ringo heads off into the street with his Pentax camera, snapping pictures, before he's chased by two girls. Ducking into a second-hand shop, he emerges in a disguise comprising a trendy peaked cap and long mac. Trudging along by the river, he throws a brick into the water and is told off by a policeman and is then hit by a tyre rolled by Janson. The two engage in some chitchat about them both being 'deserters'. Then, like two kids, they skim stones across the Thames.

As unlikely as it seemed, it was set to be a standout moment in *A Hard Day's Night*, making the hearts of Ringo fans flutter to see their pin-up looking so lonely and sad. Even its soundtrack, a syrupy instrumental of 'This Boy' led by the twanging guitar of Vic Flick (best known for the 'James Bond Theme') and orchestrated by George Martin, managed to make number fifty-three in the American chart when it was released as a single titled 'Ringo's Theme'.

It may have appeared to be an inauspicious beginning to a life in film, but because Ringo did indeed act naturally – fed-up, intoxicated – in the process he unwittingly opened up a whole new career path for himself.

Of all the Beatles, Ringo was the one whose mind was blown by the fact that they were making an actual movie. It zapped him back to his childhood memories of going to the Gaumont and Beresford cinemas in Liverpool and emerging with his head full of fantasies of being a cowboy or a pirate or one of the Three Musketeers.

Reviews for *A Hard Day's Night* singled Starr out for praise. 'Ringo emerges as a born actor,' reckoned Penelope Gilliatt in the *Observer*. 'He is like a silent comedian, speechless and chronically underprivileged, a boy who is already age-less, with a mournful, loose mouth, like a Labrador's carrying a bird.' Leonard Mosley in the *Daily Express* described the drummer as 'a natural clown in the Chaplin-Harpo Marx class', before blowing the compliment by focusing upon his 'sad face crowned by the most elegant nasal organ since Schnozzle Durante and Cyrano de Bergerac'.

'I know people said I was OK in *A Hard Day's Night*,' Ringo modestly reflected, 'but I had no idea what was going on. That little scene with the little boy on the canal that they said was good … I was stoned out of my mind when I did that. I had a real thick head. I was still in a haze.'

But such was Starr's significant contribution to the production that even the name of the movie was inspired by a 'Ringoism'. After a long day of working indoors, the drummer walked outside to discover to his surprise that it was already dark. 'We've had a hard day's... *night*,' he said, in a characteristic jumbling of words. Lennon nicked the phrase, using it in a story, 'Sad Michael', in his 1964 book of prose and poetry, *In His Own Write*.

During filming, Lester heard Lennon use the term and told the Beatle, 'We are going to use that [as the] title.' 'The next morning,' John casually noted, 'I brought in the song.'

~

The entire plot of the Beatles' next film revolved around Ringo, although, initially, Dick Lester had conceived an entirely different Starr-centred story than the one that featured in *Help!*. The original concept had the drummer, already typecast as downbeat, deciding that he can no longer go on. He reveals his desperation to man in a bar who, as it neatly transpires, is a professional assassin. He offers to put Ringo out of his misery if the drummer takes out a contract on himself.

'So Ringo agrees,' Lester recalled, 'and gives him a cheque, only to wake up the following morning to realise what a dreadful mistake he's made. The rest of the plot is obvious.'

Too obvious, perhaps. Lester had in fact dreamed up a plotline that, unbeknownst to him, was similar to French director Philippe de Broca's in-production 1965 film *Les Tribulations d'un Chinois en Chine*. Back at the drawing board, Lester came up with a different story. Starr is sent a gift by a girl fan: a sacrificial ring belonging to an Indian cult, which she is due to wear in a horrific ceremony. Ringo ends up with it stuck on his finger and madcap adventures ensue when he is pursued by members of the sect, intent on killing him, as his bandmates come up with daft schemes to have the ring prised from their drummer's digit.

In reality, the Beatles already had a half-arsed approach to movie making. As Lennon pointed out, they were by this point 'smoking marijuana for breakfast' and were typically trying to learn their lines while stoned in the car en route to the set or location.

'A hell of a lot of pot was being smoked while we were making the film,' Starr confessed. 'It was great. That helped make it a lot of fun. I had the central part. I think it helped that I'd been enthusiastic about the first film.'

Even if *Help!* was a bit ropey, Ringo nonetheless threw himself into the making of it and, for the first time, began to ponder an alternative career on the screen. He'd already had one film offer, in the wake of *A Hard Day's Night* – from none other than seasoned Hollywood director Billy Wilder – to play Dr Watson in his long-gestated *The Private Life of Sherlock Holmes* (which finally appeared in 1970).

For Starr, it felt like too much pressure. 'I thought it was too big,' he said. 'I don't want to try and carry anything yet. It would be awful if it was a flop. But a minor part would be OK, then I wouldn't have the responsibility. If that was OK, I could try bigger stuff.'

As such, his and Maureen's trip to Almeria in southern Spain in autumn '66 to observe John filming his scenes as Private Gripweed in Lester's *How I Won the War* was partly a reconnaissance mission. 'Ringo is spending a week or so in Spain to watch me act,' Lennon told a journalist on set. 'Each one of us has more or less the same dilemma … what to do in the future.'

A year on, Starr was further encouraged by his key role in the Beatles' acidic knockabout TV movie *Magical Mystery Tour*. Appearing as 'Richard B Starkey', his argumentative improvisations with his matronly Aunt Jessie (Jessie Robbins) were a stabilising comedy element in the wacky compound. There was little concern that he was morphing into a cartoon representation of himself, since that had already been done.

Running over thirty-nine episodes screened by ABC TV in the US between 1965 and 1967, *The Beatles* was an animated series that entirely transformed the group into two-dimensional goofballs. Ringo was generally depicted as lovable and dopey, the latter perhaps as a result of the fact that as a baby – as he revealed in a season-one episode entitled 'Money' – 'me mother dropped me once'.

The team working on the series were given bullet point guides to help them to draw and animate these exaggerated Beatles. One advised that 'Ringo always looks a bit disjointed whether walking or standing'; another that 'Ringo walks in a Grouch Marx pose'. Most telling of all in terms of the perceived character of the drummer was the directive at the top of the list: 'Ringo is the nice gentle Beatle, although he always looks rather sad.'

It was Sad Ringo who popped up at first in *Yellow Submarine*, the Beatles' third, contractual-obligation film released in 1968, produced by Al Brodax who'd conceived the ABC series. In the animated film, Starr is depicted gloomily hoofing along a Liverpool street and wondering whether he should throw himself in the Mersey. The titular submarine then magically arrives to whisk him, and the other Beatles, off for adventures and misadventures in Pepperland, a peaceful faraway idyll that has been invaded by the Nazi-like Blue Meanies.

The Beatles were so entirely uninvolved in the process, aside from Lennon tossing in plot suggestions and the group appearing for a skit ahead of the 'All Together Now' finale, that they didn't mind their parts being voiced by actors. Ringo later stated that 'Eddie Yeats from *Coronation Street* [actor Geoffrey Hughes] did the voices for John and me. They sound the same to me. I can't see any difference between them.'

Strange, then, that he wasn't aware that it was in fact actor Paul Angelis who mimicked his voice in the film, and that Hughes was actually McCartney. Still, overegged Scouse accents didn't kill the drummer's love for *Yellow Submarine*, which he deemed to be 'really innovative, with great animation'.

At one point in the action, when the group were travelling through the nightmarish Sea of Monsters, Ringo took the controls of the vessel and, despite a warning from their guide Old Fred, pressed a button that ejected him out of the submarine and onto the back of an ocean-dwelling brontosaurus that tried to eat him.

Starr said that, after the film hit cinemas internationally in '68, 'kids from all over the bloody world kept shouting, "Why did you press the button?" at me as if it was real. They actually thought it was me.'

$\sim$

That same year, Ringo's first extracurricular film role was brought to the screen. *Candy*, based upon Terry Southern and Mason Hoffenberg's hip 1958 novel, was a sex comedy that was very much of its time, its storyline involving the central character, a moon-eyed blonde innocent played by Ewa Aulin, being seduced, or assaulted, by a procession of lecherous men. It starred Charles Aznavour as a 'Hunchback Juggler', Richard Burton as the Devil ('MacPhisto'), Marlon Brando as 'Grindl' (an Indian guru not unlike the Maharishi) and Starr as 'Emmanuel', a Mexican gardener.

'I took Candy because it wasn't too big a part,' he said, 'and there was them other stars – Marlon Brando and Richard Burton. I thought, *They'll be carrying the film, not me, and I'll learn from them.* It was only a ten-day part, as the Spanish [*sic*] gardener, with not much dialogue.'

'Oh no, dis no good,' he remarked in his opening line in the film, as he hid behind a bush watching a drunken and amorous Burton trying it on with Aulin in a car. It was an observation that was more widely suited to the entire film. In his second scene, Emmanuel met Candy in a basement and ended up horizontal with her on a pool table, ripping off her dress in spite of her struggles and protestations, before she inevitably succumbed to his charms. Despite its lumpen comedy overtones, it was an uneasy scene in a wrongheaded film (which, even in the light of its star power, lost money).

But in terms of non-Beatle movie experience, it was at least a start. 'It's just guessing, isn't it?' Ringo said of screen acting. 'Hoping it's going to come off and you've got something good.

'But I'm quite interested in films,' he added. 'I might as well get in there if I can.'

23

'MAUREEN IS A CHAMP'

An Apple Records
Private Pressing, 1968

The needle hit the groove and there followed a jaw-dropping surprise: Frank Sinatra – *the* Frank Sinatra, not some two-bit impersonator – singing a song to Maureen Starkey.

'There's no one like her / But no one at all,' Ol' Blue Eyes crooned. 'She married Ringo / And she could have had Paul...'

The very first single in the Apple Records catalogue – listed as 'Apple 1' – was a one-off pressing of 'Maureen is a Champ', recorded in Sinatra's spiritual recording home of the Capitol Records basement studio in Hollywood and gifted to an astonished Mrs Starkey for her twenty-second birthday on 4 August 1968.

Mo was a huge Sinatra fan and this grand gesture had been secretly organised by Ringo, who asked Apple's chief operating officer Peter Brown to get in touch with the singer's management to ask if he might perhaps send a written birthday message to her. Sinatra went one better, employing lyricist Sammy Cahn (whose most famous songs included 'Three Coins in the Fountain' and 'Ain't That a Kick in the Head?') to redraft the words for Rodgers and Hart's 1937 show tune 'The Lady Is a Tramp' – sung by him to Rita Hayworth in the 1957 musical comedy *Pal Joey* – with a Beatle wife slant. Cahn played piano on the master tape of the song, which was subsequently destroyed after the bespoke disc had been pressed.

'It was early in the morning and Sinatra was a little tired,' Cahn recalled of the recording, explaining Frank's audible croakiness. 'No matter ... it's great.'

It was also acutely cheeky, which only added to the appeal, not least with the lines, 'I've lots of fans / Well, at least one or two / But Peter Brown called me to tell me it's true / "She sleeps with Ringo, but she thinks of you..."'

While the exact whereabouts of the original record is unknown, a hissy tape copy of the track (believed to have been made by Cahn) mysteriously appeared online in 2010, ensuring that proof of Maureen's champion qualities, as expressed by a singing legend, was preserved for posterity.

24

ROR

Adventures in Design,
1969–1986

It began with a set of small, clear-plastic, mercury-filled discs that could be used as executive stress toys or as the pieces of a simple board game. Memories were blurry, but either Ringo gave them to Maureen, or Maureen gave them to Ringo, for Christmas in 1970.

Devised by Robin Cruikshank, they were an arty complement to the interior design work that the former student of London's Central School of Art and Design was doing for the Starkeys. The family had moved from Sunny Heights in November '68, buying Peter Sellers' house, Brookfield, twenty miles southwest in Elstead, Surrey. At £70,000 (£1.5 million today), it was something of a steal, being a fifteenth-century – actual as opposed to mock Tudor – redbrick mansion, replete with original stone flooring, sturdy beams and windows latticed with lead. Out in the vast twenty-three-acre grounds sat a lake and a walled garden, while Sellers had kitted out one barn as a private cinema. It was a house entirely fit for a bona fide rock star.

The problem with Brookfield was that it was forty miles outside London, meaning Ringo soon realised that it was a 'drag coming to town every day in the car' when he had to go to work, while Maureen was left at home 'getting a bit fed up with being stuck out in the country'. Their solution involved buying Round Hill, an enormous three-storey, mid-century property in a private cul-de-sac on Compton Avenue in Highgate in north London (and only a few minutes' walk from Hampstead Heath) where they relocated in the December of 1969.

Starr first met Robin Cruikshank at the Apple offices on Savile Row the year before. In a stroke of serendipity, the young designer had been working for the Conservative Party leader (and future prime minister) Edward Heath, whose apartment overlooked the Beatles' new headquarters. Before long, partly due to his proximity, Cruikshank was commissioned by Apple, initially redesigning the office of the company's president, Ron Kass. Ringo then asked for his help to realise some of his own interior designs he'd been idly sketching, including a super-modernist, stainless-steel fireplace that became a centrepiece of the Highgate house.

'I wasn't making a huge amount of money,' Cruikshank admitted. 'But it was fun.'

When it came to the plastic space-age discs Cruikshank had made, Starr didn't really know what to do with them and, inspired, imagined them as a working part of a futuristic artwork that he had the designer build for him. Housed in a Perspex frame was a sloping zigzag runway, down which the discs rolled, before being hoisted back to the top via a side shaft powered by a motor, creating an endless looping movement. It was an *objet d'art* that offered the same reverie-inducing qualities as the swinging metallic pendulum balls of the then-chic Newton's Cradle.

Both were thrilled by their creation and decided to start a business together, ROR, an initialism that stood for 'Ringo Or Robin'. Starr owned a 51 per cent share, Cruikshank 49 per cent, and it was agreed by both that any differences between them would be settled by the toss of a coin.

'I had the conventional art school training,' Cruikshank said at the time. 'But he comes up with some very unusual ideas.'

Starr named the disc-rolling contraption 'Another One', impishly imagining prospective buyers approaching storekeepers. 'I want to cause confusion when people go in and say, "Could I have Another One?"' he told a reporter from *Reuters*. 'And the woman will say, "Have you had one already?"'

~

Given the partnership's combined world-famous rock star/trendy interior designer appeal, it wasn't long before ROR attracted its first commission. The chairman of British shipping operation Cunard approached the pair with a view to their designing a nightclub for a London hotel owned by the company.

Ringo remembered Robin asking, '"Got any ideas for a discothèque?" And seeing how I've lived half my life in them … I gave him a few ideas which lost him the job.'

But if it was a project later scrapped, it strengthened the creative bond between Cruikshank and Starr. ROR moved into offices on the top floor of Apple in Savile Row, putting an architect and secretary on the payroll. The company's first standout creation arrived with a lightbulb moment when Starr and Cruikshank were one day returning from a lunch meeting and passed an upmarket car accessory shop near the Roundhouse in Chalk Farm. There, in the middle of its window, sat a gleaming silver Rolls-Royce radiator grille.

Cruikshank remembered Starr turning to him and saying, 'What if we were to put one each end of a stainless-steel panel? We would have a really great coffee table.'

The trouble was, you had to own a Rolls-Royce to buy its parts, as Ringo and Robin discovered when someone called the luxury car company and were asked for their vehicle's chassis number. Instead, according to Starr, they turned to more furtive methods. 'We found this man who got them,' he said. 'I don't know how he got them. But he sold them to us. He ran in with them in a little bag and said "Give us me money" and off he went.'

The finished product was a five-and-a-half-foot-long, rectangular, twin-level table topped with polished amboyna wood and bookended by the Rolls-Royce grilles, both crowned with their iconic 'Spirit of Ecstasy' winged figure statuettes. From here, ROR's design vision began to pull into focus and become clearer: modern, artful, flashy furniture for the wealthy hipster. Both Starr and Cruikshank were also interested in high-end hi-fi and together designed a tall, steel tube column that could incorporate the parts of a state-of-the-art sound system (with a handy drinks cabinet sitting on top).

Ringo was more than happy to use his celebrity to sell these products. When another modern design company, Zarach, opened a new shop on Sloane Street in May 1971, he made a personal appearance there to tout 'Another One', which was described in its blurb as a 'rich man's plaything'. Two months later, ROR was given its own black-walled, third-floor exhibition/sales space in the Liberty's luxury department store on Great Marlborough Street near Oxford Circus. Here, Starr was particularly hands-on, helping to put the finishing touches to the displays right up until a few minutes before the opening of the official launch.

Starr and Cruikshank were filmed at Liberty's by a crew from German public service broadcaster ZDF. The two were seen sitting on the pavement-level ledge outside their ground-floor window display, which featured almost *Pepper*-esque black-and-white photographic cut-outs of the pair, showing Cruikshank conspicuously pointing a finger at Ringo, as if to reveal the duo's power dynamic or simply highlight the drummer's involvement to passers-by. Inside, Ringo, in denim jacket, mauve shirt and matching scarf, gave a demonstration of their trademark kinetic sculpture, now being sold with a price tag of £60 (just over £1,000 in 2025).

Then, on 16 September 1971, he made an appearance on *Blue Peter*, the BBC's flagship teatime children's magazine show. Introduced by presenter John Noakes as 'a very famous gentleman' responsible for 'the latest thing in furniture', Starr walked onto set in a psychedelic patchwork dream coat and explained that at the Liberty's exhibition there were 'about forty things ... 60 per cent tables, all different types of tables, storage columns. We've done a big hi-fi column. Lots of small things. You can all walk in and have a look around.'

Plans for ROR were becoming more ambitious, with Starr stating that the company were 'negotiating to get a shop. And then in February we go to France with it. And then we go to America with it.'

~

From 1972 onwards, ROR won several big-name pop star customers, including Marc Bolan, David Bowie, Rod Stewart and Elton John, alongside screen stars Christopher Plummer and Anouska Hempel. That summer, Ringo's buddy Harry Nilsson was relocating from Los Angeles to London and, having bought a two-bedroom, top-floor flat in a black-brick Georgian townhouse at 9 Curzon Place in Mayfair, suggested to the drummer, 'Why don't we let you and Robin run wild?'

While Nilsson was in the US, ROR gutted the apartment and refashioned it with an interior that was a symphony in glass and chrome, felt and velvet.

The final cost was almost double the company's estimate, although Starr footed the bill for (most of) the difference. Nilsson was initially shocked when he saw the results.

'I didn't know what to think,' he recalled. 'And then I thought for a second … and I loved it.' Not all of it, however. Above the twin sinks in the bathroom were two mirrors: one etched with the image of an oak tree; the other a hangman's noose.

The latter, said Nilsson, 'bothered me … Each time you woke up and brushed your teeth, you would look in the mirror and be hanged, and I didn't like it. So I called Ringo and told him, and he didn't like it either. The next day, it was replaced by an apple tree.'

But this morbid insignia was set to become part of the dark myth that was to grow around 9 Curzon Place. In the summer of 1974, having accepted Nilsson's offer to borrow the flat during her run of shows at the Palladium, Cass Elliot, formerly of the Mamas & the Papas, died of a heart attack in bed there, aged thirty-two. Harry subsequently believed the place to be cursed and was reluctant four years later, in mid-1978, to rent it to the unhinged dervish that was the Who's drummer, Keith Moon. The band's guitarist Pete Townshend convinced Nilsson, arguing that 'lightning wouldn't strike the same place twice'. On 7 September, Moon died in the same bedroom, from an overdose of sedatives prescribed to alleviate his withdrawal from alcohol. He was also thirty-two.

Nilsson was with Starr at the Beverly Wilshire hotel in LA when he received the call from Ringo's business manager, Hilary Gerrard, telling him, 'Harry, Keith Moon is dead. He died in your bed and the police are there looking for drugs.' Nilsson couldn't wait to get rid of the apartment, which was bought by Townshend, who absolutely insisted on taking the place, with its heavy vibes, off the American singer's hands. 'The flat at number nine had been the scene of outrageous laughter and fun, and sorrow,' Harry reflected. 'It was no longer a place for joy.'

Bad voodoo aside, ROR's reputation for luxury interior design had continued to grow. Another key client was Paul Raymond, the porn-peddling, nudie club owner of the Raymond Revuebar where the Beatles had filmed the stripper scene in *Magical Mystery Tour*. The self-styled 'King of Soho' lived in a huge seventh-floor apartment in the modern block Fitzhardinge House in Portman Square in Marylebone, which was often likened to the super-stylish lair of a Bond villain.

Raymond asked ROR to come up with a design for his roof terrace, the central feature of which became a steel and glass dome, under which sat a fountain with submerged lights that flashed in disco-style synchronisation whenever music was played. Impressed, Raymond retained ROR to refurbish a £50,000 boat he'd bought, which, on Starr's suggestion, was laid throughout with a blue-carpeted scheme featuring different coloured stripe motifs for each of its cabins.

Then, in 1981, when Raymond moved to another penthouse in Arlington House, tucked behind the Ritz in Piccadilly, ROR were entrusted to bring it up to super-modern standards, which they did by installing beige marble flooring and covering almost every walled surface in mirrored glass. From humble, semi-fumbling beginnings, Starr and Cruikshank had built a highly successful design business, which also exported its products to Europe, the US, Africa and east Asia.

~

As time passed and Starr's interests were scattered elsewhere, Cruikshank and a growing team of associates took over the day-to-day running of ROR. In 1982, partly thanks to the recommendation of Edward Heath, the company won a $10 million contract to design and furnish a guest palace for the then-ruler of Abu Dhabi, Sheikh Zayed bin Sultan Al Nahyan. This highly ambitious undertaking almost bankrupted the firm, but was eventually successfully completed, leading to another lucrative contract in the city, which ended four years later.

By then, 1986, Starr was out, leaving Cruikshank to rebrand the company as ROR International, after which he embarked upon various successful projects in the Middle East and the Caribbean. The company's current website notes of the amicable split between Ringo and Robin that the pair 'decided to cease activities as both owners wished to go their separate ways and this was considered to be a good time to finish on the best possible high note'.

25

'RICHY! SCAB'EAD! ONE MORE!'

The View from Behind the Kit, 1969 (Part One)

Virtually every day of January 1969 saw the Beatles being filmed by director Michael Lindsay-Hogg for the proposed TV special documenting the making of their back-to-basics, live-recorded eleventh album.

Released in cinemas the following year, *Let It Be* the movie – which premiered in New York, Liverpool and London in May 1970 (with none of the Beatles in attendance) – was a weird epilogue to the band's stellar career and one that they immediately disowned. The gnarly, grainy movie then underwent a strange afterlife: released on video tape and LaserDisc in the early '80s; revisited in 1992 ahead of parts of it being used in the *Anthology* TV series, with a DVD release mooted and then scrapped in the mid-'90s, and again in the late noughties. McCartney and Starr, it seemed, were not keen to remind a global audience of a time when the Beatles were bickering.

All of that changed with the arrival of the *Lord of the Rings/Hobbit* trilogies director Peter Jackson and his extensive upgrading and positive-spin reimagining of the footage for the near-eight-hour-long *Get Back* series, released in 2021. As highlighted by Jackson's cut, Ringo was a slightly elusive, semi-detached, typically unsmiling presence, who often faded into the background while the more dramatic interplay between John, Paul and George unfolded before him.

In some ways, by the end, he was almost forgettable (most seemed to mainly recall the scene in which he admits to having farted). Reviewing the footage and audio tapes day by day as the action moves from Twickenham Film Studios to Apple Studios in Savile Row – and really zoning in on the

140

drummer – proves illuminating when it comes to trying to assess Starr's state of mind at the time, during what Lennon called the 'slow death' of the Beatles.

Thursday 2 January

Ringo, wearing a blue suit with a dark red velvet collar and a black polo neck, arrives onto the sparse set at Twickenham, with John, Yoko, George and a sole Hari Krishna devotee (Shyamsundar Das) who proceeds to rock and pray on the floor. Harrison, Starr and Lennon wish each other 'Happy New Year' (it won't be).

Paul turns up and together the four work through his new song, 'I've Got a Feeling'. Behind the kit, Starr plays a shuffling beat, never taking his eyes off McCartney, as he absorbs the arrangement. Clearly this is a well-practised routine.

In a break, Denis O'Dell of Apple Films talks to Ringo about *The Magic Christian*, which he is also producing and in which Starr is set to act alongside Peter Sellers. Filming is due to begin at Twickenham before the month is out. O'Dell tells him the start date has been pushed back to 24 January.

'Why?' the drummer protests. 'This is only going to take two weeks.'

'Well, we don't know yet, do we?' O'Dell sagely points out.

Friday 3 January

Wearing a different dark suit, but perhaps the same polo neck, Starr plays his work-in-progress song to McCartney and Harrison: 'Taking a Trip to Carolina', a characteristically simple ditty with punning words. There is much mirth from George and Paul.

Harrison has surprising news. He's spent some of the winter hanging out with Bob Dylan and the Band in Woodstock where the latter's singing drummer, Levon Helm, told him that his favourite track on *The White Album* was Starr's 'Don't Pass Me By'.

Paul asks Ringo, 'Are you going to write another?'

Ringo proceeds to sing a snatch of a second song he's developing called 'Picasso', in which he's bought a painting by the legendary Spanish artist but can't make head nor tail of it: he looks at it upside down, but he can't see 'a lady' in it, only a 'wooden chair'.

Enlivened by all this talk of his singing, he croons 'Just Fun', an early Lennon/McCartney composition, before he joins in with Paul and John on old blues number 'Midnight Special'.

John and Paul work on the harmonies for 'Don't Let Me Down' as Ringo watches on impassively. They all start to look smokey-eyed and knackered and finally rattle through some old rock 'n' roll numbers: 'All Shook Up', 'Blue Suede Shoes', 'Lucille'. Time for the weekend.

Monday 6 January

Ringo arrives, sporting a black, stained overcoat over a mustard jumper with a brown, cream and white stripey neck. He looks rough. 'I won't lie. I'm not too good,' he confesses. Everyone laughs.

They improvise a never-to-be-released tune called 'You Wear Your Women Out', before getting back to 'Don't Let Me Down'. Paul instructs Ringo to play a different beat in its middle eight ('Should be ... all onto light things and cymbals'). The drummer stares at him and says nothing and nods. He is clearly hungover to hell. He proceeds not to change his previous beat and plods along looking like he might fall off his stool.

The other three start arguing, particularly Paul and George, and Ringo keeps shtum. He is wearing the face of someone attending a particularly tragic funeral. He has a fag, taps on his snare, then they play 'Two of Us' again. This time there's a bit more spirit to his performance.

Tuesday 7 January

George sits with Ringo (lavender grey jumper under a suit jacket) on the drum riser, looks out into the drafty space and says, 'It reminds me a bit of Lime Street station'.

Lennon is late. 'I'm never late,' says Starr.

'He's never late,' McCartney confirms. 'He's a bloody pro is Ringo.'

Paul strums his bass and plucks 'Get Back' out of thin air. Ringo watches intently and taps his foot along. George yawns. As the fledgling song develops, Ringo claps a double-time rhythm while George joins in more enthusiastically with the guitar chords. The next minute, the drummer is behind the kit knocking out a four-on-the-floor soul beat as John arrives and slips into the groove.

The other three quarrel about their general lack of enthusiasm and whether they even want to do a live performance at the end of the TV special. Ringo fiddles with his drum stool and smokes as they work out the chords to 'Maxwell's Silver Hammer'.

At close of play, they jam through their lively version of Chuck Berry's 'Rock and Roll Music', which they cut on *Beatles for Sale* and last played on their 1966 tour.

Wednesday 8 January

As McCartney hopefully tries to coax news of any impending songs from Lennon, Starr stands at a microphone loudly making noises through an echo machine.

'Hello … [whistles] … Paul, Paul, Paul…'

'Stop that goddam feedback!' McCartney grins.

Michael Lindsay-Hogg tries to talk Ringo into going to Libya to perform the finale of the special at the ancient Roman amphitheatre in Sabratha. 'Think of a helicopter shot over the amphitheatre…' the director evocatively suggests.

'One, two minutes, say, of that shot isn't worth me going over there,' the drummer argues.

'But if it's going to be your last TV show…' the director contends.

'Yeah, but you're only surmising that,' Starr points out. 'Just 'cos we get a bit grumpy. We've been getting a bit grumpy for the last eighteen months.'

In terms of the others and the Sabratha idea, Lennon is in. So is Paul. George isn't. Ringo says nothing.

There is talk of alternatively playing on a P&O ocean liner filled with fans, but George hates even the thought of it. Starr is ambivalent.

Thursday 9 January

'I went off the boat, actually, the idea,' Ringo says. 'We all know what it's like on holiday. Y'know, I go a bit crazy.'

Looking glum, he sits beside Paul who's finishing off the lyric for 'The Long and Winding Road'. A camera close-up reveals Starr has an angry-looking spot on his chin.

Paul has an idea for a song for Ringo, 'a comedy'. He starts singing 'Carry

That Weight'. Starr picks it up and sings along. McCartney improvises a verse lyric about a hungover man with a heavy head being nagged by his wife.

John talks about his interest in buying ex-prime minister David Lloyd George's house, Bron-y-de in the Surrey village of Churt, five miles south-west of Ringo's Brookfield. 'So I'll pop in for a cup of tea if I come 'round, Saturday or Sunday,' he says. 'It was built for him in about forty acres. And about three lakes… all joined together. So, sounds good. £45,000.'

'Sounds amazing,' offers Ringo.

Friday 10 January

Ringo sits with Paul and fusty music publisher Dick James who tells them about Vera Lynn's version of 'Good Night', which she is due to perform on *The Rolf Harris Show* on BBC1 the following night.

'Ringo'd like to hear that,' Paul says, presumably because Starr sang the original.

'Yes, love to,' says Ringo.

Later in the day, Paul attempts to describe a lead guitar line to an increasingly wound-up George, which the latter reckons might be better suited to Eric Clapton. Then, after playing 'Two of Us', George says, 'I think I'll be leaving … the band now.'

Harrison flounces off, apparently quitting the group.

'We have to play harder as a trio,' Ringo points out.

Maureen Starkey watches the remaining three jamming, with Yoko wailing into a mic. They all look as if they're having frustrated fun and letting it all out. Ringo goes demented on the kit.

He picks up a mic and addresses one of the film cameras as the racket continues. 'Yeah, rock it to me, baby. It's the big sound of 1969.'

Lindsay-Hogg asks, 'Has anyone ever left as seriously as George before?'

'Well… Ringo,' Lennon admits.

As they get ready to go, a flirty Paul tells Maureen, 'A7, D7, G7 … Get 'em off over the weekend and you're in.'

Monday 13 January

The day after an emergency Beatles summit was held at Brookfield, Ringo is the first to show up at Twickenham. Mal Evans asks him how the meeting went, and Ringo says, 'Fine … A lot of good things but then they all sort of fell apart in the end.'

Paul and Linda arrive. 'We're just carrying on with the documentary,' Ringo tells them, before pointing out he feels it's good that Paul's had them come to work today, otherwise he'd have been lying in bed or doing the garden.

Lennon doesn't appear and Harrison has gone to Liverpool. Ringo looks sad. Paul says, 'And then there were two…' and his eyes brim with tears.

Tuesday 14 January

Together, Ringo and Paul play a three-handed boogie-woogie tune that ends up being titled 'I Bought a Piano the Other Day' (and credited to Lennon/ McCartney/Starkey).

McCartney, Lennon and Starr sit and jape around, pretending to be on a talk show.

'Now we were going to discuss this afternoon what religion means to a pop star,' says John. 'And the pop star we've chosen is Tumble Starker who's sitting here.'

'I feel ill actually,' says Ringo, genuinely, looking as if he'd heartily partaken of the old rock 'n' roll mouthwash the previous evening.

With George Martin, they discuss the songs they imagine being on the album. 'Ringo could put in a long drum break, couldn't he?' quips the producer. Starr nods off.

Tuesday 21 January

The action moves to the newly built Apple Studio in the basement of 3 Savile Row. Ringo (flower pattern shirt and jeans) says to Hogg, 'It was lovely walking in here yesterday after Twickenham', which he reckons was 'too big, for what we were doing, and this is nicer'.

There's a copy of the 16 January edition of ailing tabloid the *Daily Sketch* lying around, containing a gossipy report about the state of the Beatles by Michael Housego under the headline 'The End of a Beautiful Friendship?'. Paul picks it up and reads it aloud in a posh, luvvy accent, savouring the sentence, 'I will deliberately leave Ringo out of it because he has never developed an inclination towards the bizarre.'

145

A mollified George is back and the four play a great take of 'Dig a Pony'. Ringo limbers up for a second one with star jumps, as a super-Scouse John shouts, 'Richy! Scab'ead! Come in! One more!'

At close of play, Starr is visibly perky, pulling dippy Fab shapes for the camera.

Wednesday 22 January

Starr remains bright in mood, pounding through a blistering 'Dig a Pony' where his drums sound powerful and super-fat. He mock-batters a camera shooting him from below.

Electric piano-player Billy Preston – whom the Beatles have known since he was in Little Richard's band back in Hamburg in '62 – arrives. He says hi to the approachable drummer first.

'How you doing, baby?' Ringo says.

'Good to see you, mate,' says Preston. 'Outtasight.'

They launch into 'I've Got a Feeling' and it immediately has added groove and power. Ringo is grinning. He loves this stuff, being in a band. And what a five-piece band.

Thursday 23 January

Ringo argues that they should 'work ten days straight from now'. Paul suggests, 'Let's work Saturday, but not Sunday.'

Starr, in a simple black T-shirt and jeans combo, as if it's dress-down Thursday, develops the skippy beat for 'Get Back'. During a playback of the track in the control room, he moans, 'I'm feeling really tired today'. Later, he howls with laughter as Paul recounts a tale about Jimmie Nicol, onstage with the Beatles in Sweden, missing the opening of 'She Loves You' because he was eyeing up all the girls.

George suggests 'Get Back' should be issued as a single 'now' and they're all in agreement. There's a palpable sense of excitement among them.

Friday 24 January

Ringo – black shirt and jeans – does a lot of staring blankly into the room, giving the odd smile.

Mal Evans takes their lunch orders: 'sparrow on toast' for Lennon, 'boiled testicle' for Paul, and for George 'whatever the vegetables are ... if they've got any cheese sauce for the cauliflower'. Ringo wants 'just some steak' with 'mashed potato'.

'Don't do it, Richy, don't do it,' Lennon advises him, concerned about his bandmate's unhealthy diet, before adding, 'he used to eat chips'.

Michael Lindsay-Hogg is fretting and says, 'I don't know what story I'm telling anymore.'

Ringo flatly informs him, 'You're telling the autobiography of the Beatles, aren't you?'

Saturday 25 January

Ringo is wearing a paisley shirt and rustic Indian waistcoat.

'Been to India have you?' John affectionately jibes.

Lennon launches into 'Act Naturally' and Starr half-sings along. He looks knackered again.

A notion had been floated to do a show at Primrose Hill in north London to conclude the film, but it wasn't possible logistically. Michael Lindsay-Hogg and engineer Glyn Johns suggest the idea of going onto the roof of Apple for the finale. Starr and McCartney climb up there to check out the possible location.

Back down in the studio, as they play through 'Let It Be', Ringo's trip-let rolling beat begins to fall into place. He has a chocolate digestive biscuit to celebrate.

Sunday 26 January

Ringo appears in the same shirt and waistcoat as the previous day, as if he's stayed out all night. Ironically, he asks Johns, 'Did you get to bed last night, Glyn?'

Harrison asks Starr if he's written any more words to 'that one about Picasso'.

'No,' says Ringo. 'Have you heard the octopus one?' He plays rudimentary piano and sings what he has so far of 'Octopus's Garden'. George picks up an acoustic guitar and helps him to shape the chord sequence. Lennon gets behind the kit and thumps along.

Paul and Linda and six-year-old Heather arrive. She joins Starr behind his sonic screens, loudly hits a drum and he pretends to jump out of his skin.

Monday 27 January

Starr dresses to impress in an electric-blue Edwardian-style jacket and red ruffled shirt replete with white dots. Paul gets behind the drums for 'Old Brown Shoe' as Ringo frugs away with George at the piano.

Later, they reach an impasse while trying to tape 'The Long and Winding Road' because the bass is too loud and the piano can't be heard. Studio rearrangements are made.

'It doesn't matter particularly about Ringo hearing the piano, does it?' asks George Martin.

'No, we don't bother about him,' Lennon says. 'We never take any notice.'

Ringo laughs.

There is talk about the rooftop gig, due to happen on Wednesday.

'What if it rains?' the drummer sensibly wonders.

(A gloomy weather forecast does indeed put the concert back to Thursday 30th.)

Tuesday 28 January

They rattle through 'Love Me Do', the drummer happily boom-bapping away in a harlequin green cord suit matched with a ruffled shirt. John enthuses about his meeting with potential business manager Allen Klein that lasted until the early hours of the morning. Ringo smokes, his face unreadable.

Starr then mucks around with a Stylophone and they attempt to use the fizzing proto synth on George's 'For You Blue'. Together, they absolutely nail the version of 'Don't Let Me Down' that will appear on the B-side of 'Get Back'.

Wednesday 29 January

Lindsay-Hogg wonders how many tunes the Beatles will have ready for tomorrow's performance. 'About six,' says Ringo.

After meeting with Klein the previous day, Ringo judges him to be 'a conman who's on our side for a change. All those other conmen are on the other side.'

Later, as a few of them (Starr, McCartney, George Martin and Michael Lindsay-Hogg) are resting in a corner, Ringo confesses, 'I've farted. I just thought I'd let you know.' Paul immediately walks away. Martin says, 'Thank you.'

'I was gonna sit here silent and look at you,' Ringo adds. 'Then I thought, *No, I'll tell you about it.*'

During discussions about the guerilla gig, Starr mischievously wonders, 'What happens if we go on top of the other roof?'

'If it's somebody else's roof,' the increasingly rattled director points out, there's a good chance they could be arrested 'not only for disturbing the peace … but also for trespassing'.

Thursday 30 January

The big day. Half past noon, they step onto the roof. Ringo wears a shiny, tomato-red mac (borrowed from Maureen), wisely thinking ahead in terms of possibly inclement weather. He also looks warm. Paul is in a suit, the other two in roasty-toasty fur coats.

Ringo moves his kit around, saying to Mal Evans, 'You've nailed me down in the wrong place.'

As soon as they kick into 'Get Back', the transformation is startling, as the Beatles turn it on for a live audience. When they move into 'Don't Let Me Down', Starr's fills are flowing, his performance swinging and powerful. He's in his happy place. For 'One After 909', they shapeshift into the Fabs again, Ringo even doing his old head tosses as the muscle memory returns.

Down in the street, a middle-aged Irish woman in a multi-coloured head-scarf is caught on camera, being asked by an interviewer, 'Have you a favourite amongst the Beatles?'

'Em, I think Ringo,' she smiles.

The coppers arrive on the roof during the band's second go at 'Don't Let Me Down'. Ringo watches Mal trying to placate them. The roadie then steps behind the drummer and halfheartedly waves to get them to stop playing. No one's looking at him. Starr powers on and keeps half an eye on the rozzers.

The group quickly segue into a third, defiant take of 'Get Back'. Under pressure, Mal switches the Fender guitar amps off. George switches his back on. Then John switches his back on. Ringo grins.

When the song finishes, Paul's last words are to Maureen, who has been bopping away throughout: 'Thanks, Mo.'

Back down in the control room, they all listen to a playback of 'Get Back'. Then Mo grooves along to 'One After 909' and grins at George.

Friday 31 January

Back in Apple, for the master take of 'Two of Us', which Ringo notes 'sounded lovely'. In a break, he reads to the others a *Daily Mail* report of the previous day's events. 'Mr Davis, 57, director of a clothes wholesaler, said, "All hell was let loose. We are not amused. Work came to a standstill. Our switchboard operators couldn't hear anyone. We have had the police in ... we have had complaints ... but we are not taking any action." Woah.'

At close of play, fittingly, they nail the definitive take of 'Let It Be', over which Starr fluidly follows the piano's slowdown on his final tom-tom beats, and then it is over.

26

ANOTHER DIMENSION

The View from Behind
the Kit, 1969 (Part Two)

Having triggered umpteen angry phone calls to the police during the Savile Row rooftop gig, three weeks later the Beatles attracted another noise complaint. They were down in the basement at Trident Studios in Soho, blasting through John's 'I Want You' – its title later suffixed with '(She's So Heavy)' – when Glyn Johns informed the band that a neighbour was moaning about their late-night racket.

'It's his own fault for getting a house in such a lousy district,' McCartney mock-huffed.

'Well, we'll try it once more very loud,' announced an untypically capitulating Lennon. 'And then if we don't get it, we'll try it quiet.'

After enjoying their time recording at Apple, and subsequently ordering a refit of their new private studio there, the Beatles weren't in any mood to return to the overly familiar spaces at EMI. Instead, they chose to decamp to Trident, where they'd recorded 'Hey Jude' the year before. The heavy-rock carousel of 'I Want You' cut there that night was spliced together from various intense takes and destined to be used for the end section of the track that would close Side One of their next album, *Abbey Road*.

At this stage, though, it wasn't clear exactly what form the forthcoming Beatles LP would take. By spring, Lennon was talking up 'the next great Beatle event' as an album comprising the best of the Twickenham and Apple songs, along with Starr's 'Octopus's Garden' (in John's opinion, a 'Ringalong singalong') and 'a kind of song montage that we might do as one piece on one side'. He didn't hold out much hope of the Beatles ever returning to the stage, blaming their drummer. 'I quite fancy giving some live shows,' he said, 'but Ringo doesn't because he says, y'know, "It'll just be the same when we get on, nothing different."' Presumably, Starr meant utter chaos in the crowds.

In March, Paul married Linda in London and John married Yoko in Gibraltar. The following month, back at Abbey Road, Lennon and McCartney renewed their own vows, the two of them alone recording 'The Ballad of John and Yoko' (George wasn't in England, Ringo was busy filming *The Magic Christian*) and released in May as the Beatles' next single. Lennon sang and played guitars and percussion. McCartney harmonised and played bass and piano and maracas and – significantly – drums.

Their errant bandmates were never far from their thoughts, however.

'Go a bit faster, Ringo,' John told Paul just ahead of take seven.

'OK, George,' Paul shot back.

But no one was really sure of the best way forward for the Beatles. A pragmatic Harrison suggested, 'Let's make a *good* album.' This prompted a return to Abbey Road where, from mid-April and into May, they laid down various new songs, including Paul's throat-shredding doo-wopper 'Oh! Darling' and George's masterful love song 'Something', replete with Ringo's triplet drum rolls echoing the Band's 'Tears of Rage', released on their *Music from Big Pink* the summer before.

Concurrently, Glyn Johns was at Olympic Studios in Barnes attempting to knock the proposed *Get Back* album into shape. In the first week of May, the Beatles piggybacked on its sessions to record 'You Never Give Me Your Money' there. On Friday 9 May, fittingly, given the sadly desperate tone of McCartney's financially frustrated lyric, it was the scene of a business showdown. Lennon, Harrison and Starr had the previous day inked their names to a contract giving Allen Klein control of the group's business affairs. McCartney refused to sign it.

'They really bullied me and ganged up on me,' he angrily recalled. 'I said, "No, I want a good deal out of this guy. I'll wait until Monday before we ratify anything. My lawyer will be present on Monday." So they said, "Oh, fuck off!". And they stormed off, leaving me with a session at Olympic.'

Paul blew off steam by hooking up with American blues rocker Steve Miller, also recording at Olympic. McCartney proceeded to batter the drums for Miller on a track appropriately named 'My Dark Hour'. 'I thrashed every-thing out,' he remembered. 'There's a surfeit of aggressive drum fills.'

~

Four days later, the schism between them not visible, but the passing of time clearly evident, the Beatles regrouped on the balcony at EMI's Manchester Square HQ where, six years and three months earlier, they'd gazed down at photographer Angus McBean for the cover of *Please Please Me*. On that day in 1963, McBean casually asked Lennon how long he thought the Beatles might last.

'Oh, about six years, I suppose,' John told him. 'Who ever heard of a bald Beatle?'

But the group who turned up for the session with the rehired McBean, for a remake of the shot for the cover of *Get Back*, were entirely the opposite of bald, being a positively hirsute apparition. From left to right, Ringo's '63 quiff had been replaced by shoulder-length locks matched with a bushy moustache, while Paul and George were similarly hippiefied. John was the most changed of all, transfigured from a grinning moptop to a penny rounder-wearing Yeti. Harrison and Lennon however nodded to Beatles Past by wearing their grey, orange-pinstriped stage suits from the '66 tour.

They returned to Abbey Road in July, where, on the 21st in Studio Three, John presented the group with his inspired contortion of Chuck Berry into Cubist shapes on 'Come Together'. Ringo responded with a fractured yet soul-ful modern art beat. His drums sounded great on these new recordings: fitted with new calf-skin heads, recorded to eight-track tape and placed in different stereo positions so that his beats moved between the ears of the listener.

Further experimenting with the Side Two montage concept, the four recorded songs in twinned, conjoined pairs: the hypnotic procession of 'Sun King' into the comic-strip figure of 'Mean Mr Mustard'; the sexually deviant, 'mythical Liverpool scrubber' 'Polythene Pam' into the surreal fan intrusion of 'She Came in Through the Bathroom Window'. Lennon got narked by Starr's heavy playing when they were trying to pin down 'Polythene Pam', laughing and commenting that 'it sounds like Dave Clark' (creator of the relentlessly unsubtle stomping groove of 'Bits and Pieces' et al). A miffed Ringo stayed late to perfect and overdub a fresh drum track over the group take.

Then, for one last time, John, Paul and George reprised their beautiful, brotherly harmonies – last heard on the haunting 'Yes It Is', the B-side of 'Ticket to Ride', back in '65 – for 'Because', as Ringo watched on, softly clapping his hands to keep time. 'Ringo was our drum machine,' George Martin later said, highlighting the now ever-reliable, near-metronomic precision of the drummer he'd once doubted.

Elsewhere, the producer even convinced the reluctant Starr to record a drum solo for the album, in the first section of 'The End'. Not since the show-stopping fills he'd performed at the climax of 'Thank You Girl' back in '63 or his solid 4/4 intro to the reprise of 'Sgt. Pepper's Lonely Hearts Club Band' had his drums had a lone spotlight shone upon them on record.

'I don't want to do no bloody solo,' Starr told Martin (and in truth he'd played far better in many other places in the Beatles' catalogue), turning in a self-conscious-sounding, eight-to-the-floor thump with syncopated, if stiff-armed tom-tom interjections.

'Anyway, I did it, and it's out of the way,' he later reasoned.

All the while, they'd been throwing around suggested titles for this entirely new album that had leapfrogged over the *Get Back* project: *Four in the Bar*, *All Good Children Go to Heaven*, *Inclinations*, *Turn Ups*. The frontrunner was *Everest*, inspired by the brand of Zimbabwean cigarettes smoked by Emerick and expanded into a cover-shot concept in which the Beatles were pictured in the Himalayas (Paul was keen to go, Ringo not so much).

Instead, much like the rooftop show, the Beatles stayed local, after McCartney suggested they call the record *Abbey Road* and scribbled a sketch of the quartet walking in lockstep across the zebra crossing outside. On 8 August, the day of the shoot, Ringo turned up in his dark, Tommy Nutter-designed suit and marched second in line between Lennon and McCartney. Photographer Iain MacMillan snapped only six frames, Paul selected one, and the image was forever frozen in time.

～

Two weeks later, and seven years to the day since the four had first been photographed together on stage at the Cavern on 22 August 1962, the Beatles reconvened for the camera for one final time on 22 August 1969.

Eleven days earlier, John and Yoko had finally moved into their Georgian mansion at Tittenhurst Park, the vast Berkshire estate they'd purchased in May for £145,000 and then extensively renovated at twice the cost, including having a lake dug into the grounds.

There, as photographer Ethan Russell captured an array of pictures, the Beatles – looking like four lost American settlers, their visual styling owing something to Elliott Landy's faux-pioneer shots of the Band – wandered from the house to an overgrown field, then under a cypress tree and a pair of weeping blue atlas cedars.

'It was just a photo session,' Ringo said later. 'I wasn't there thinking, "OK, this is the last photo session."'

A shaky sense of togetherness remained and, on 8 September, when Starr was in hospital being treated for his ongoing intestinal problems, Lennon, McCartney and Harrison got together at Apple and taped the meeting so that the drummer could listen to it later.

'Ringo, you can't be here,' John said at the start of the recording. 'But this is so you can hear what we're discussing.'

The conversation was fairly upbeat: there was talk of a post-*Abbey Road* single to be released in time for Christmas and Lennon came up with a formula to further ease the creative tensions. He imagined a new fourteen-track album to follow in 1970: four songs apiece written by himself, Paul and George, and two by Ringo, 'if he wants them'.

Then a stoned-sounding Paul offered the inflammatory opinion, 'I thought until this album that George's songs weren't that good.'

'That's a matter of taste,' Harrison pushed back. 'All down the line people have liked my songs.'

Lennon was blunt but conciliatory, pointing out to McCartney, 'Wouldn't it be better … because we didn't really dig 'em, y'know … for you to do songs you dug, and for "Ob-La-Di" and "Maxwell" to be given to people who *like* music like that? Like [McCartney's Apple Records' protégé] Mary [Hopkin] or whoever it is that needs a song? Why don't you give them to them?'

'I recorded it,' Paul woozily insisted, 'because I liked it.'

Veering from peacemaker to provocateur, Lennon's mood had turned by 20 September. During another, fateful meeting at Apple where the four

– even a wary McCartney – put their signatures to a new, Klein-negotiated deal with EMI/Capitol that increased their royalty rate from 17.5 per cent to an unprecedented 25 per cent, Lennon kept saying, 'No, no, no' to McCartney's suggestions that the Beatles should fully return to their roots, playing small gigs and getting back in touch with their former selves. If that didn't work, then they could quit.

John told Paul, 'I think you're daft. I wasn't going to tell you until after we'd signed the Capitol deal, but the group's over, I'm leaving.' The others, as McCartney remembered, 'paled visibly and our jaws slackened'.

'We weren't really fighting,' Ringo later stressed. 'If that had happened in 1965, or 1967 even, it would have been a mighty shock. Now it was just, "Let's get the divorce over with", really. And John was always the most forward when it came to nailing anything.'

After the meeting, the drummer returned home and 'sat in the garden for a while wondering what the hell to do with my life. You think, *Oh God, that's it then*. It was quite a dramatic period for me… or *traumatic*, actually.'

Abbey Road was released on 26 September and an interview with Starr speaking to Radio Luxembourg's David 'Kid' Jensen was aired the same day. In spite of the fact that Ringo had played out of his skin on the new record, he was still being forced to defend his skills as a drummer.

'Ringo,' Jensen ventured, 'it's been suggested that the reason for the Beatles' prolonged success is that the Lennon/McCartney compositions have not been allowed to get over-progressive because you're basically a straightforward rock drummer and those songs and productions have been built with this in mind. How do you yourself class yourself as a drummer?'

'Yes, I'm holding those guys back, y'know,' Starr laughed. 'Well, it's because I'm a rock drummer, y'know. Basically, we're all just rockers. We like rock 'n' roll. I don't think I hold them back.'

In December, he was the subject of a far more sympathetic and freewheeling on-location TV interview on BBC2's arts programme, *Late Night Line-Up*.

Gently interrogated by host Tony Bilbow, first in the back of a car and then in a rowboat oared by the drummer down a bucolic stretch of the Thames, he was quizzed on a number of subjects, the most newsworthy being Allen Klein's stewardship of Apple.

'What we're really doing now is paying for when we opened it and played around,' he offered, in explaining the current attempts to clean up the company's financial messes. 'It's not a playground anymore.'

Bilbow then addressed how Starr viewed social changes in this last month of the 1960s, specifically 'the drug scene ... Do you think that is going to change radically?'

'Yes,' Starr emphatically responded. 'Everyone will have a right to take them if they want. I don't mean hard drugs because I'm not for them and they're banned. But I think we should all have the right, in our own homes, to smoke pot if we want to. I don't anymore, personally. But, y'know, I did it and I was annoyed that I had to hide.'

Ringo's wide-brimmed black hat then blew into the water and he and the presenter tried to retrieve it with the paddles. Elsewhere, their talk turned spacey, as they pondered the possibility of parallel universes.

'I mean, we know there's three dimensions, and there's theories about a fourth dimension,' said Ringo. 'But there could be fifty dimensions. And ... we're not bright enough to catch 'em all.'

Starr's belief in alternative realities was particularly apt at this point. Shortly, he was about to slip into a new one entirely: the post-Beatle world.

27

PICTURING THE SONG

The Best Drummer for
the Beatles, 1962–2023

Date-stamped 31 January 1969, the final day of the Beatles' *Get Back* sessions at Apple, the postcard from Paul to Ringo, mailed from St John's Wood and addressed to 'Brookfields', simply read: 'You are the greatest drummer in the world. Really.'

It had been the previous summer of *The White Album* when Starr had suffered his crisis of confidence and had been showered (and flowered) with praise. But it seemed that, five months on, McCartney still felt that the drummer needed some reassurance.

'Paul's just making up for lost time here,' Ringo reckoned many years later, after he published the card – featuring on its front a Coldstream Guardsman pictured at Windsor Castle wearing a bearskin hat and beating a marching tom-tom – in his 2004 book, *Postcards from the Boys*.

'He's a year late though!' he added, his arithmetic failing him.

In truth, the Beatles always rated Starr. McCartney later lauded 'his feel and soul and the way he was rock-solid with his tempo'. Lennon, in a partly backhanded compliment, said: 'Ringo's a damn good drummer. He was always a good drummer. He's not technically good, but I think Ringo's drumming is underrated.' Harrison reckoned that – like himself – Starr would be better if he practised more, but that perhaps the drummer's greatest skill was that 'he listens to the song once and he knows exactly what to play'.

Ringo very rarely stuck to the most obvious beats for Beatles songs. While he was never given credit for being as artfully minded as his bandmates, his style involved lateral thinking and approaching the others' songs from obtuse angles. Never flashy for flash's sake – even those wristy rolls that punctuate 'Day Tripper' are there for thrilling, accelerating effect – drumming was for him always a matter of feel and spontaneity.

'I couldn't do the same drum sequence twice,' he said. 'Whatever beat I would put down, I could never repeat identically because I play with my soul more than my head.'

His playing often mirrored, or emphatically supported, the emotions John, Paul and George were trying to convey. With his tense, pacing-in-circles middle-eight patterns in 'Something', for one, he followed Harrison's sudden shift into agitation. Minimalism was important, too. He later named his favourite drummers as Charlie Watts of the Rolling Stones and American sessioneer Jim Keltner. Neither musician played more than was absolutely necessary. Starr noted Watts, in particular, as being 'the only drummer who leaves out more than I do'.

Most importantly, Ringo listened to the lyrics, pictured the song in his mind's eye and tried to reflect that in his playing. The behind-the-beat swing of 'Ticket to Ride' sounds like a jolting locomotive. The crackling energy of the around-the-kit movements of 'Rain' approximate bursts of rolling thunder. 'I play the mood of the song,' he offered, before citing perhaps his greatest contribution to any Beatles record: the shape-shifting beat of 'A Day in the Life'. '"Four thousand holes in Blackburn, Lancashire" – boom ba bom. I try to *show* that … the disenchanting mood.'

~

Yet, it wasn't really until the making of 2006's *Love* – the part elaborate restoration job, part high-concept mash-up album conceived as the soundtrack to Cirque du Soleil's Beatles-endorsed Las Vegas show – that the spotlight was truly thrown on Ringo Starr as a drummer. The project also marked the first collaboration between George Martin and his son, Giles.

At the time, Martin Sr, then aged eighty-one, stressed to me that Ringo had turned out to be the star of the show. 'Listening to this recording, he drives that band right through [it],' he enthused. 'Fantastic stuff. And it isn't just the technique of playing the drums, but it's also thinking up what he's going to play. If you listen to "Come Together", for example, his work on that is very, very thoughtful and very clever. And the stuff he did on "A Day in the Life" with the toms … magic.'

Giles Martin had his own theories as to why people were only now really sitting up and taking notice of Starr's drumming.

'I guess his drums are slightly bigger than they were,' he said. 'I've had the ability to take Ringo off the Beatles' records and put him back on and he plays stuff that you wouldn't imagine a drummer playing. As a producer or a musician, you can go, "Right, what would I have the drummer doing now?" And it's never what Ringo plays.'

Seventeen years later, in 2023, McCartney asked Giles Martin to co-produce 'Now and Then', the third 'new' Beatles track that had been built up from a 1970s Lennon cassette demo for the 1995 *Anthology* project, yet remained unfinished and unreleased due to the latter's vocal being glued to a piano on the original tape. Now, it was possible to separate the two, using de-mixing software. Paul had already began reworking the track, but Giles felt there was something missing: Ringo's natural rhythmic style, his original take having been effectively looped in the '90s by the song's initial producer, Jeff Lynne.

'I said to Paul I didn't think it sounded like Ringo was drumming on it,' Martin said. 'The style of drums then was very much, "Boom, clap".'

'Jeff is very particular and meticulous," Starr explained in 2023. 'He always wants a click track and I keep telling him *I'm* the click. He likes you just to hit the drums or do a short rhythm pattern and then he uses it. He said, "OK, now do some fills." The fill comes when I'm emotionally involved in the track. I think maybe that's what ended the sessions.'

Starr laid down his new parts for 'Now and Then' – quickly and spontaneously, just like in the old days – at his Roccabella West home studio in Los Angeles. 'The way Ringo does things is amazing,' Martin added, marvelling at what, for Starr, was a well-practised technique. 'He just listens to a song a couple of times, and literally plays drums along with it.'

Jim Keltner, who'd by 2023 been a long-time studio and stage collaborator of Starr's, said he was surprised how Ringo was oddly bashful about his own playing skills. It was almost as if being in the most famous band there ever was, and likely ever would be, had forced him into an awkward position of humility.

'We'd hang out,' Keltner said of the time they became friends, 'and I'd tell him, "Ringo, y'know, you changed everything for a lot of people." Because he seemed too overly humble … almost beyond humble … totally unaware that he'd done anything.

'That's what it must have been like to be the drummer with the Beatles.'

27

'WASN'T EVEN THE BEST DRUMMER IN THE BEATLES...'

Untangling the Myth of a Joke, 1981–2022

Sometime, somewhere, an apparent quote from John Lennon began to circulate, scathingly joking about Ringo's skills as a musician. When asked by an interviewer whether he considered Starr to be the best rock drummer in the world, Lennon had supposedly carped, 'Ringo wasn't even the best drummer in the Beatles.'

It's a memorable line, seemingly referencing the fact that, on top of the Beatles tracks that McCartney drummed on ('Dear Prudence', 'The Ballad of John and Yoko'), all three of the others contributed to the composite beats of 'Back in the USSR'. The trouble is that no proof exists, anywhere, of Lennon actually making the joke.

As time passed, the quip was subsequently attributed to British light entertainment comedian Jasper Carrott, and dated to 1983 and his BBC1 show *Carrott's Lib*.

'I had made this passing remark, "Ringo Starr – not the greatest drummer in the world. He wasn't even the greatest drummer in the Beatles",' Carrott later explained. 'But then it started to be credited to John Lennon. That didn't annoy me, but I think it annoyed a lot of Beatles fans because they knew John would never have said that about Ringo.

'Eventually it was traced back to me and I admitted I'd said it sometime in the mid-'80s. But it's taken on a life of its own. If you Google "Jasper Carrott and Ringo Starr", it comes up. But I didn't mean anything bad. It was just a throwaway line.'

The mystery further deepened when it transpired that the comedian hadn't even made the joke in *Carrott's Lib* in the first place. Fresh evidence of the quote's provenance was revealed on social media in 2018 when writer and broadcaster Tim Worthington cited an earlier BBC Radio 4 sketch show, *Radio Active*, which spoofed the frequently cheesy and amateurish traits of regional broadcasts. In the second episode of its first series, aired in the autumn of 1981, the character of bungling studio staffer Martin Brown (voiced by Mike Fenton Stevens) is heard to say, 'Alright, alright, maybe Ringo Starr wasn't the best drummer in the world. Alright, maybe he wasn't the best drummer in the Beatles…'

This meant that Carrott wasn't the first to crack the joke – although, as it turned out, he did indeed use it. In 2022, dogged Beatles YouTuber Andrew Dixon sat and watched through twenty-four episodes of *Carrott's Lib* and its successor, *Carrott Confidential*, finding no trace of the gag. Then, three minutes into the eighth episode of the latter series, broadcast on BBC1 on 21 February 1987, the comedian segued from a previous joke by saying, 'It was the era of the Beatles, eh? Now that is nostalgia, eh? John, Paul, George and dear old Ringo. He wasn't the greatest drummer in the world, was he? Let's face it… he wasn't the greatest drummer in the Beatles.'

The audience duly tittered.

'No, I've never met Ringo,' Carrott later told a journalist. 'But if he was in the same room as me, I might skirt around it very quickly.'

Anyway, Lennon never said it.

29

PUT ME IN THE MOVIES, PART TWO

The Magic Christian, 1969–1970

'It's your eyes, Ring,' Peter Sellers advised Starr on the art of cinematic acting. 'They'll be 200 feet big up there.'

Having awkwardly dipped a toe into a film career with 1968's best-forgotten *Candy*, the next year Ringo threw himself into his first feature-length starring role outside of the Beatles. Taking Sellers' advice a tad too literally, on screen in *The Magic Christian* his eyelids were dramatically widened at every available opportunity to reveal his voluminous blue peepers.

Starr and Sellers were by this stage friends. The previous year, the drummer had borrowed the actor's yacht in Sardinia during his escape from the Beatles during *The White Album*, and also bought the Brookfield house in Surrey from Sellers. Still, Ringo found it tough to keep up with Peter's ever-changing moods.

During filming, the two often went out to dinner together in the evening, typically enjoying an uproarious time. The next morning, on set, Sellers was often utterly changed, and completely remote, leaving Starr struggling to engage him to even say hello. 'There was no continuation,' said Ringo. 'You had to make the friendship start again from nine o'clock every morning.' He bemusedly likened the experience to having to 'knock the wall down'. On a few occasions, Starr was even asked to leave the set on account of his temperamental co-star. 'Peter Sellers was being Peter Sellers,' he noted.

Starr – perhaps because of his own white-hot fame – wasn't in the least intimidated by Sellers, even if, like millions of others of his generation, he'd listened to the latter on *The Goon Show* throughout the '50s. There was also the connection shared by the two of having been produced by George Martin at EMI Studios in Abbey Road, with Peter predating Ringo's time there having made a series of comedy albums from 1958 to 1960 supervised by the future Beatles producer, including '59's number three-charting *Songs for Swingin' Sellers*.

Further bonding the pair, Sellers had been an accomplished jazz drummer in his late teens, touring with the big bands of Oscar Rabin and Henry Hall. He later said of his conversations with Starr, 'I don't think we spoke about anything else other than drums and drumming.'

Sellers was a big fan of *The Magic Christian*, the 1959 novel by *Candy* author Terry Southern. He regularly gifted copies of the book to his friends, including, in the early '60s, Stanley Kubrick (leading to Southern being asked by the director to help rework the script for *Dr Strangelove*). Starr was also tickled by this tale involving Guy Grand, an eccentric billionaire prankster who performs practical jokes on strangers, pushing them to daft extremes to test their all-too-human desire for easy cash. Sellers harboured a notion for a number of years to turn the book into a film. Starr claimed it was him that actually made it happen.

'We got the film together by my knocking on Peter's door,' Ringo recalled. 'I said to him, "Let's make this movie". So, as he was Peter Sellers, three phone calls later, they put the money in and we were off.'

Brought in to oversee the proceedings was Joseph McGrath, one of the five directors involved in creating the confusing mess that was 1967 James Bond send-up, *Casino Royale*. In the screenplay for *The Magic Christian*, co-scripted by McGrath and Southern (with additional scenes written by Sellers and soon-to-be Pythons John Cleese and Graham Chapman, both of whom had brief roles), the novel's location was shifted from New York to London, and a character was created for Ringo: Youngman Grand, the vagrant-turned-adopted son of the demented big spender.

Shot between February and May 1969 on three stages at Twickenham Film Studios – including the one vacated that January by the disintegrating Beatles – *The Magic Christian* was also filmed at various locations in London, Surrey and Hertfordshire. But, as a movie, it was to suffocate under an avalanche of star-guest cameos and a script that was often rewritten on the day to accommodate their appearances.

Starr remembered Southern typing in a neighbouring dressing room and the writer being told by the producers, 'You'll never guess... We've got Yul Brynner', or 'We've got Raquel Welch'. 'Poor Terry would have to write them in,' he said. 'Terry would post the words under my door and then I'd be called in an hour to go down and do them. It was a very strange movie to make.'

The Magic Christian opened with an image of a £10 note and a ball bouncing over the lyrics of 'Come and Get It', the jaunty McCartney number written and multi-instrumentally demoed by him in the summer of '69 during the making of *Abbey Road* (and then later produced by him with Apple Records signees Badfinger performing).

The first scene in the film saw Sellers as the grey-coiffured Grand waking in his plush bedroom, before showing Ringo sleeping rough outdoors and being poked awake by a parkie, looking less like a homeless man and more a dishevelled Beatle. He proceeded to eat a sandwich on a bench and brush his teeth while perched on the edge of the Victoria Memorial fountain outside Buckingham Palace (where, in real life, he'd collected his MBE four years before).

Starr is standing on a bridge, throwing bread to the ducks, when a passing Sellers notices him and, in unheard dialogue, persuades Ringo to wander off with him. Cut to the office of Guy Grand's lawyers, where he legally adopts the long-haired down-and-out as Youngman Grand. After a spot of light Laurel and Hardy-esque physical comedy – Sellers dusts down Starr's manky overcoat and Starr fussily finishes the job – Ringo pulls off his shades, widens his eyes, exclaims 'Father!' and the two hug.

Then it's immediately into the prank-pulling. A helicopter flies the two to the Theatre Royal in Stratford where from the audience they watch an actor – Laurence Harvey – playing Hamlet, who has been secretly bribed by Grand to strip off during his 'to be or not to be' soliloquy. By the time Harvey reaches the line involving 'a bare bodkin', the thespian is entirely in the raw, provoking an aghast response from the toffs in the auditorium.

And on (and on) it goes. Throughout, Starr is striking on screen, until he opens his mouth to voice his scripted lines and his delivery falls painfully flat, his enunciation stilted and over-careful. Better are the scenes where he's improvising, with his ripe Scouse accent bouncing off Sellers' chewy posh intonation. In one scene in the Grands' lavishly appointed sitting room, Sellers shimmies from side-to-side atop a skateboard and Starr wackily urges him on by saying, 'Groove with your space commander, Dad'. By this point, *The Magic Christian* really couldn't be any more '60s.

Most of the cameos are stuffed into the last fifteen minutes of screen time. Aboard the modernist, Kubrickian ship that gave the film (and book) its title, sailing on a madcap maiden voyage from London to New York, Christopher Lee turns up as a Dracula-like butler and Roman Polanski sits at a bar with a drag queen played by Yul Brynner, who lip syncs to Noël Coward's 'Mad About the Boy' (sung by an uncredited Miriam Karlin), before pulling off his wig to reveal his bald pate. In a gratuitous scene, albeit one of the movie's most memorable, Ringo descends to the bowels of the vessel where scantily clad slave-master Raquel Welch whips topless female captives rowing the boat.

For the film's daft denouement, in London, the Grands have an outdoor tank filled with slaughterhouse blood, animal urine and manure. Ringo spray-paints 'Free Money Here' on a white banner, before father and son, wearing gas masks, watch city types in suits, holding hankies to their noses, suddenly clamber in to collect the cash, their greed having overtaken them.

In the final scene, Sellers and Starr end up in sleeping bags back in the park, resorting to a simpler way of life, after having made some point or other about the corrupting power of money.

Reviews for the film were understandably mixed, ranging from Roger Greenspun in the *New York Times* lauding it as a 'superb realisation of the book' and further stating, 'Ringo is fine, and Sellers is finer', to Dave Kehr in the *Chicago Reader* slamming it as 'a curdled, unfunny satire'. Pauline Kael in the *New Yorker* was fairer, and more accurate in her assessment: 'There are funny moments, but they don't add up to enough.'

Fuelling the general confusion surrounding the movie, one print ad for it featured Starr sitting smiling on Seller's lap alongside the cryptic tagline: 'Presenting the most irreverent, irrelevant father and son team since the Frankensteins.'

At the British charity premiere of *The Magic Christian*, attended by a presumably baffled Princess Margaret and held at the Odeon in Kensington on 11 December 1969 (and followed by similar events in Los Angeles and New York in early 1970), Ringo sat alongside Maureen, and John and Yoko, and watched his performance in widescreen. The experience taught him a valuable lesson about his interplay with a co-star.

'There's a scene in the movie where I have all these lines, but on the other side of the screen, he just picked his nose,' he said. 'If you watch the film in the cinema, you see everybody shift from me right over to him. A thousand people think, "Oh, he's picking his nose." It was much more important than the speech I was saying.

'And so,' he added, revealing the true depths of his acting ambition at the time, 'I never let anybody do that to me again in a movie.'

30

RINGO STARDUST

A *Sentimental Journey*, 1969–1970

Ringo stepped out of the shadows and into the spotlight, besuited and wearing a comically outsized pink dickie bow tie. Behind him on the stage at top London cabaret haunt the Talk of the Town loomed a projected image of the Empress pub back in the Dingle (its front entrance situated only steps around the corner from his childhood home at 10 Admiral Grove), as featured on the cover of his first solo album, *Sentimental Journey*.

In true showbiz style, Starr coolly sauntered to the front of the stage, watched by the supper club audience seated around low-lit tables, as he crooned the opening lines of the LP's title track, the slow jazzy number made famous by Doris Day when she took it to US number one back in 1945. He smiled warmly at the patrons as the club's in-house string ensemble sawed away in the background, before white-clad male and female dancers launched into a twinkle-toed routine on either side of him and he joined in. Finally, a platform descended from the roof to reveal three backing girl singers vocally supporting him for the song's big finish.

Filmed on 15 March 1970 and directed by Neil Aspinall, the three-minute promo clip for 'Sentimental Journey' was set to be aired by David Frost on British television and by Ed Sullivan in the States. As the first Beatle to make a solo record bid for mainstream success (as opposed to arty kudos), it was a slightly bizarre move from the drummer-turned-old timey balladeer, particularly in the era of long-haired, confessional acoustic troubadours and progressive heavy rockers.

Ringo had first expressed a passing fancy to record an album of standards during the *Let It Be/Get Back* sessions. But following Lennon's still-secret September '69 quitting of the Beatles, and after Starr experienced a period of feeling 'lost for a while', he firmly resolved to make the album.

'When it was over,' he reflected, 'it was like I had to sit around the garden and think, *Y'know, I'll just enjoy the sun... or a joint, whatever.* And then I thought, *Nah, come on, you gotta get up.* And I talked to George Martin, and we did all the standard songs. Because where I come from, there was a lot of parties and everybody had to sing a song. And these were all the songs that I'd heard, mainly at the house or anybody's house you went to.'

The other Beatles, and his parents Elsie and Harry, encouraged him in his efforts, and the resulting twelve-track album included idiosyncratic takes on big-band staple 'Night and Day', between-the-wars bopper 'Bye Bye Blackbird', slow dance smoocher 'Whispering Grass' and Hoagy Carmichael's haunting, lovelorn classic 'Stardust'. For a time, the working title for the record was *Ringo Stardust*.

Throughout, there was a hint of humour in his voice. It was clear that Ringo wasn't trying to be a proper crooner but more of an everyman, singing down the boozer, albeit one backed by a full orchestra.

$\sim$

Recorded in fits and starts between October 1969 and March 1970, *Sentimental Journey* was a full-scale George Martin production involving arrangements scored by such diverse figures as London jazzer John Dankworth ('You Always Hurt the One You Love'), Hamburg buddy and *Revolver* cover artist Klaus Voormann ('I'm a Fool to Care'), Bee Gee Maurice Gibb ('Bye Bye Blackbird'), Paul McCartney ('Stardust') and bona fide Sinatra collaborator Quincy Jones ('Love Is a Many Splendored Thing').

'They were my first musical influences,' Starr said of the songs he'd chosen. 'So, for want of a better idea, I thought I'd do that. I still had George Martin, so I didn't feel completely alone.'

In fact, it was an international operation, which saw Jones recording orchestral parts at A&M in Hollywood and Ringo shuttling around various studios in London – from EMI to Wessex to Trident to Olympic to Morgan – to realise his symphonic vision, at eye-watering cost, with the bills footed by Apple Records. For the most part, Martin and Starr kept it strictly trad, although Captain Beefheart/Tiny Tim producer Richard Perry's treatment of the title track incorporated a vocal refrain performed through a futuristic, robotic talk box effect.

The recording process wasn't without its challenges. Quincy Jones, unhappy with Starr's initial performance of 'Love Is a Many Splendored Thing', insisted on flying over to London in February '70 to oversee a re-recording of the song at Studio Two in Abbey Road. Even in the final version, Ringo's voice was virtually buried under an avalanche of backing singers.

For his part, Voormann later rated his own arrangement of 'I'm a Fool to Care' as 'terrible'. 'It was so bad,' he said. 'I'd never done anything like that before. And they said, "Oh yeah, come on Klaus, you can do an arrangement." And I had no idea. I had a guy who helped me, Francis Shaw, a very well-known arranger. But it didn't turn out the way I wanted it to. It was completely off the mark. I wanted to be real clever and have a tuba and the bass play the same lick. But it just didn't work, y'know. I'm so embarrassed about that. It was very dilettante.'

Elsewhere on the record, for those soon to be mourning the death of the Fabs, there was some comfort to be found in Starr's wavering if heartfelt rendition of 'You Always Hurt the One You Love'. Still, taken altogether, it was a deeply weird album to bear the Apple Records imprint, especially one following Harrison's '68 experimental film soundtrack *Wonderwall Music* and Lennon/Ono's far-out avant-garde releases, *Unfinished Music No. 1: Two Virgins* and *Wedding Album*. George was notably gracious when commenting upon *Sentimental Journey*, praising it as 'a great album … really nice'. John, however, didn't pull his punches, saying he felt 'embarrassed' about the record.

Two days after its release, on 29 March 1970, Ringo appeared on London Weekend Television talk show *Frost On Sunday* to plug the album. 'First of all,' the ever-genial host ventured, 'you better tell us what *Sentimental Journey* is.'

'Well,' said Ringo, 'it's a lot of tracks, of a lot of songs that were like my initiation to music. It's all the tracks that when me mother and me dad came home from the pub out their 'eads, they'd sing all these songs.'

There followed absolute silence from the studio audience, presumably shocked by Starr's bluff working-class honesty.

'It went better in the dressing room,' he awkwardly noted of the flopped anecdote, and nervous laughter rose into the air.

'And what do you plan after this?' Frost went on. 'What do you plan for the future?'

'I plan to do a country and western album,' Ringo chuckled.

~

The critics, meanwhile, were generally scathing in their appraisal of *Sentimental Journey*. Greil Marcus in *Rolling Stone* deemed it to be 'horrendous', while Robert Christgau in the *Village Voice* reckoned its appeal would be limited to the 'over-fifties and Ringomaniacs'. The *NME*'s Andy Gray was alone in declaring it 'top class'.

In the end, maybe the most memorable thing about *Sentimental Journey* was its vividly nostalgic cover. Featuring a faded, Richard Polak colour photograph that was to lend the towering Empress pub an iconic status – as enhanced by the cut-out faces of Starkey family members peering from its various windows, with a black-and-white image of Starr throwing jazz hands superimposed in the doorway – it was a striking image for those flipping through the record racks to come across in 1970. Perhaps fuelled more by Beatle power than musical merit, the record reached number seven in Britain and sold more than half a million copies in the States within its first two weeks of release.

Looking back, Starr later viewed the album as an essential endeavour for him, if only in terms of getting him back to the recording studio. 'The great thing was that it got my solo career moving,' he reasoned. 'Not very fast, but just moving.' At the same time, *Sentimental Journey* set a trend; the jazz standards album model was later copied by the likes of Harry Nilsson (1973's *A Little Touch of Schmilsson in the Night*) and Linda Ronstadt (1983's *What's New*).

It also opened up an unexpected career path that Ringo chose not to pursue. In early 1970, he was flown out by a promoter to Las Vegas to watch Elvis Presley perform during his second, fifty-seven-show residency at the International Hotel, with a view to Starr staging a similar production there. But the dickie-bowed song and dance man Ringo Stardust was never to be.

'They thought I would be good for Vegas,' he said. 'But I just knew at the time that was not what I wanted to do. I had a very nice couple of days and then I said, "Goodbye, no".'

31

FROM US TO YOU

Ringo the Diplomat, 1970

The letter – addressed 'From Us to You' – sat in the reception out-tray at Apple in Savile Row, waiting for a courier to pick it up and deliver it to Paul McCartney's house in St John's Wood. Ringo knew the message it contained, although he hadn't signed it.

Lennon, Harrison and Starr, together with Allen Klein, had decided they were facing a sudden logjam with the impending release dates of Beatles and solo Beatles LPs. The newly titled *Let It Be* was finally due to come out on 24 April 1970. McCartney's self-titled (and secretly recorded) debut was scheduled for release a week earlier on 17 April.

Handwritten by Lennon and dated 31 March, the note read: 'Dear Paul, We thought a lot about yours and the Beatles LPs – and decided it's stupid for Apple to put out two big albums within seven days of each other (also there's Ringo's and [US compilation album] *Hey Jude*). So we sent a letter to EMI telling them to hold your release date til June 4th (there's a big Apple-Capitol convention in Hawaii then).

'We thought you'd come round when you realised that the Beatles album was coming out on April 24th.

'We're sorry it turned out like this – it's nothing personal. Love, John and George. Hare Krishna.'

At the bottom, Harrison had scribbled, 'A mantra a day keeps maya away' (maya being the Sanskrit word for 'illusion').

Starr looked at the envelope in the tray and, clearly understanding its heavy significance, decided it wasn't fair 'that some office lad should take something like that round'. Instead, he elected to carry the letter around to 7 Cavendish Avenue and personally hand-deliver it, in the process giving himself something of a thorny diplomatic task.

But nothing could have prepared Starr for McCartney's explosive reaction after he'd turned up on Paul's doorstep and been invited inside. 'He went completely out of control, shouting at me, prodding his fingers towards my face, saying, "I'll finish you now" and "You'll pay",' he later incredulously recalled. 'He told me to put my coat on and get out.'

The drummer, shocked by his bandmate's fury, reported back to Lennon and Harrison, suggesting they rethink their position. The result was that *Let It Be* was pushed back to 8 May. If it was a victory for McCartney, it was also the moment he gave up on the Beatles. As an added consequence, the argument was to damage his and the drummer's friendship, which wasn't to be fully repaired for another three years.

~

Sitting in his office at his MPL headquarters in Soho Square almost four decades on, McCartney recalled to me his sudden flash of anger directed at Starr that day.

'I told him to eff off,' he fumed, the embers of his indignation not having fully died even after all that time. 'Everyone to my mind was completely treating me like dirt.'

McCartney still couldn't quite believe that the others had been hypnotised by Klein's big-talking business spiel. He'd always suspected the New York manager to be a crook.

'They were going with this crazy guy,' he added. 'He had his foot in the door and he was about to just run in with a big sack and put everything in it. They were gonna throw everything away and they were just breezing along merrily. I realised that everyone didn't get it, but they sort of felt secure in the middle of this thunderstorm.

'So Ringo just pops round my house, quite innocently, and sort of says, "Oh, by the way, that record, we've agreed on a release date. We'd like you to move it out the way because we're the big guys, we're the grown-ups, y'know."

And I just said, "Well, no way, man. I don't like what's happening in the Beatles' camp at the moment." I just said, "Get out. You better leave."'

At the same time, in retrospect, he recognised the impossibility of Ringo's peace-making mission.

'It was very painful,' he concluded, revealing just how serious this one-off brawl between himself and Starr had been. 'It was not the kind of thing we'd ever done before or, in fact, would ever do again.'

32

THE LAST BEATLE

Ringo Puts Out the Lights, 1970

There was one final Beatles recording session at Abbey Road in the spring of 1970. Ringo was the only member of the group to attend.

Phil Spector had been invited to London and put in charge of getting the *Let It Be* tapes over the finish line and in a presentable state. It was a task he performed in his typically idiosyncratic style. Beginning work at EMI Studios on 23 March, Spector remixed tracks and snipped up the tape for 'I Me Mine' to elongate the song, before making plans to build his Wall of Sound behind the band on key tracks.

On 1 April, Spector hired a small army of musicians – twenty-six string-players, fourteen backing singers, six brass-players and a harpist – and invited Starr to the session to drum along with them. For the producer's Disney-fied 'Across the Universe', with its wordless vocal cooing, strings and harp, Ringo added shuffling maracas and muted tom-toms. More controversially, on 'The Long and Winding Road' – in a treatment that McCartney would always abhor – the producer pressed the session musicians into realising a sugary ballad arrangement that was more befitting of Elvis in Vegas.

Throughout the session, Spector grew increasingly obnoxious and demanding of the EMI studio personnel. In the main, sonic effects were generally added to a track during the mixing stage; Spector demanded to hear all of the tape echoes and plate reverbs as the recording was being done, which was beyond the spec of the facility. All the while, the paranoid producer, shadowed by a bodyguard, kept popping pills. Abbey Road tech Brian Gibson felt that

176

Spector 'was on the point of throwing a wobbly, saying "I wanna hear this! I wanna hear that! I must have this! I must have that!"'

Starr took Spector aside and calmly told him, 'Look, they can't do that. They're doing the best they can. Just cool it.'

In-studio equilibrium was temporarily restored, until Spector began distributing score sheets for 'I Me Mine' to the members of the orchestra, who had only been booked to play on two songs, not three. There was no mention, either, of overtime pay. The hired musos protested and began to pack up.

By this stage, Spector had managed to upset almost everyone involved. Engineer Peter Bown, who knew most of the players on the session, chose to avoid the ugly confrontation by wedging himself into the control room. Then he went home and took his phone off the hook. When he placed it back in its cradle in the small hours, it immediately rang. It was Spector. The wayward producer apologised and Bown returned to Abbey Road in the middle of the night. Arrangements had hastily been made for the orchestra to be paid for their extra time.

In the end, Ringo's politicking saved the day. The bill for this long, cast-of-dozens session amounted to almost £22,000 in today's money – a grand gesture befitting the Beatles, but a big price to pay for such a tense and odd studio swansong.

33

HOME MOVIE

Capering Around
with Maurice Gibb, 1970

The two of them were such big pals that they used to joke about building a tunnel under the garden fence that separated their properties. That way they could hang out and get drunk together without their wives knowing.

Ringo Starr and Maurice Gibb by chance found themselves neighbours in Highgate as the '60s turned to the '70s. It was a strange time for the latter: the Bee Gees had suffered a rift with the solo career departure of Robin Gibb in the spring of '69, leaving the remaining brothers Maurice and Barry to soldier on with the respectable if terribly titled album *Cucumber Castle*. When it flopped, the band seemed to be over, until commercial embarrassment forced Robin to return to the fold and the group to reunite in August 1970.

During this period, Maurice and Ringo grew tighter and almost brotherly, despite the age difference between them (in the summer of 1970, when Ringo turned thirty, Maurice was still only twenty). They shared various interests: music, of course, being one. Starr's tinkering around with a Moog synthesiser in his shed at Round Hill led to the pair recording an unreleased electronic doodle titled 'Modulating Maurice'.

Then, there was alcohol. The duo swiftly became boozing buddies, indulging in growing addictions that it was to take each of them many years to tackle. Gibb had in fact been given his first whisky and Coke by John Lennon and later commented, 'If he had given me cyanide, I would have drunk the cyanide, I was so in awe of the man.' The young Bee Gee regarded his Beatle neighbour with similar wide-eyed admiration. Much idle rock star imbibing ensued.

Their third passion was for surreal humour, one that was seemingly shared by Maurice's wife, Lulu, a primetime TV star and household name. Starr and Lulu were in fact to appear in a sketch two years later in the third series of *Monty Python's Flying Circus*, in which they appeared as guests in a faux talk show, named 'It's…'. In the minute-long skit, as soon as the host – Michael Palin in his returning role as a shredded-clothed tramp – uttered the show's title, the *Monty Python* theme music kicked in and the credits rolled, resulting in Lulu mock-storming off and Starr pretend-wrestling Palin.

In truth, Ringo and Maurice did this sort of stuff for fun, in private, as evidenced by an elaborate eleven-minute home movie, 'Who Goes There?', that the pair made on 30 August 1970. In the first scene, sat in his garden dressed in fifteenth-century garb (baggy breeches, feathered hat), Starr eyes the lens and introduces a chat show pastiche of his own devising: 'Meet the People'.

'We have a very interesting guest for you,' he announces. 'Prince Valentine from Yorkshire. He's travelled all the way down on the 8:30 horse.'

Gibb camply trots into frame in a skin-tight black outfit from the same era matched with a gold, tasselled cap. 'It was a hell of a journey down here,' he says.

'Mmm, yes. How's the road?' Ringo wonders.

'Oh, still there, y'know,' Gibb responds, not missing a beat. 'Nice and bumpy and lovely and comfortable in the old stagecoach.'

'Well, we've had a few interesting parchments from our watchers,' Starr goes on, 'and they've asked us some very interesting questions. As we all know, the battle between the Roses is still going on, between York and was it Doncaster? In all the local tabloids it seems to be that York is winning. I mean, what is your situation on this?'

Maurice: 'They're still fighting the backsides off each other. It's terrible. But they won the last match, which was rather super, y'know. But we're getting there slowly. I mean, the army isn't as big as the other army.'

Ringo: 'Yes, I've heard they have 14 million people on their side.'

Maurice: 'And twelve catapults.'

Ringo: 'And you only have 127 men and a lame dog.'

Maureen: 'Yes, and he's dying.'

For improvised material coming straight off the top of the heads of a couple of non-comedians, it wasn't at all bad. The pair could have perhaps even sidelined into TV gag-writing. Later in the film, Gibb took a turn at being the host, of an item called 'Invention of the Week'.

'Roaming through the ground here,' he began, 'we find somebody that has come up with the most incredible genius of an invention ever invented in the whole of the great universe. This man has invented water.'

Ringo stands with hose in hand, watering a bush.

'You see, it's a very economical thing to have,' Gibb pointed out. 'And this is the brilliant man behind it. Now, what do you think of your invention? I mean, it must be rather exciting.'

'Really very exciting,' Ringo agrees. 'Yes, it's taken me fourteen years to perfect this formula. And this tube-ful [the shot cuts away to a coiled blue garden hose] is all that I've mixed up to now.'

'Can I touch it?' Gibb asks, before tentatively placing his hand under the spray and instantly recoiling. 'Oh I say,' he splutters, 'it's rather...'

'We call that "wet",' Ringo deadpans, revealing the quick wit that served him so well in Beatles press conferences and in his best off-the-cuff bits up on the silver screen.

'Anyway, another great "Invention of the Week",' Gibb concludes, gesturing towards Starr. 'Herbie Groin. Thank you very much, Herbie.'

34

THE GLUE

John, George and Ringo, 1970–1971

The song was called 'Early 1970' and its first three verses addressed each of Ringo's former bandmates. Recorded at EMI in October of that year, this tongue-in-cheek country toe-tapper was in fact a song hopeful of reconciliation. Like millions the world over, Starr was still mourning the Beatles after, in April 1970, McCartney's self-penned mock questionnaire released to the press to accompany his solo album ('Are you planning a new album or single with the Beatles?' 'No.') hammered the final nail into the band's coffin.

'I keep looking around and thinking, *Where are they?*' Ringo admitted to one interviewer in terms of his acute sense of loss. '*What are they doing? When will they come back and talk to me?*'

In reality, Lennon and Harrison were never far away, and the latter even produced this Starr-drawn sketch of the former Fabs (set to be the B-side of his 1971 single, 'It Don't Come Easy'). The opening verse of the light-hearted, if pointed, tune was directed at McCartney, nursery-rhymed 'farm' with 'charm', and publicly wondered if Paul would ever play with Ringo again. The following two stanzas addressed John and George respectively – the former screaming himself 'free' with his Japanese wife, the latter with his spouse picking daisies 'for his soup' – and were assured in their belief that their long collaboration would continue in some form.

In the final verse, Starr made fun of his own musical limitations, despite the fact that he gamely played drums, acoustic guitar, dobro, upright bass and piano, and sang lead and backing vocals on the track. But it was the message that this conciliatory song contained that was key.

'For the first time,' he reflected, 'it was me commenting on the break-up and Paul's attitude towards us at the time ... when he was suing the three of us. So it was good ... I was getting a lot of stuff out then.'

In many ways – his fractured relationship with Paul notwithstanding – cheerful, dependable Ringo was the social and musical glue that held himself, John and George together in the years immediately after the split.

Virtually lost in the sea of faces packed into Abbey Road's Studio Three five months earlier, Starr had agreed to be one of the drummers contributing to Harrison's triple album outpouring of songs, *All Things Must Pass*, often involving a dozen-plus musicians playing at the same time to live-construct a new Wall of Sound for Phil Spector.

A preliminary recording date on 27 May featured Harrison, Starr and Klaus Voormann on bass running through an early, pacier take on 'My Sweet Lord' and a bare-bones, electric rocking version of the gospelly 'Awaiting On You All'. But the following day was when the fun and games began, as a long procession of musicians arrived at EMI at the invitation of Harrison: Eric Clapton, various members of LA R&B rock troupe Delaney & Bonnie and Friends, Billy Preston, Gary Brooker of Procol Harum, Plastic Ono Band drummer Alan White, and more, and yet more.

'Most of the time we were running around looking for headphones,' remembered John Leckie, the future record producer who was at the time a twenty-year-old tape operator at EMI. 'There were twelve, fifteen musicians all playing at once and there were never enough pairs of headphones working.' At one point, when trumpeter Jim Price and saxophonist Bobby Keys arrived and asked 'Where should we stand? Where can we fit in?', Leckie groaned inwardly. 'It was like, Oh no, *more* people.'

The first track to be laid down that day was a remake of 'My Sweet Lord', joyously transformed from the previous day's scratch version into a heavenly mass-strummed mantra. Still, oddness remained evident at the sessions due to Spector's presence. In terms of studio atmosphere, the producer had certain specific requirements: low lighting everywhere; the speakers in the control room set to maximum volume; the air con blasting out in the live room.

'It was freezing in there,' White said. 'He thought people played better when it was cold.'

'We probably finished "My Sweet Lord" at about two o'clock in the morning,' Leckie recalled, 'and they went straight in and did "Wah-Wah", which is pretty live.'

Having renounced drugs in favour of spirituality, Harrison remained clean during the recording of *All Things Must Pass*. In sharp contrast, most of the other musicians indulged in alcohol and dope (and furtive harder drug-taking). 'Everyone else, of course, was completely out of it,' Leckie laughed. 'At the end of the sessions, we used to go round the ashtrays and nick all the spliffs, because a lot of them weren't smoked. They'd roll a joint, have one puff and put it in the ashtray. So, the ashtrays were full of unsmoked, straight-grass American joints.'

These freewheeling sessions rolled on until October. In the final tally, Starr played on several of the standout songs on Harrison's opus, including the elegiac title track and 'Beware of Darkness', a brooding song warning of malign influences and intrusive, negative thoughts. Ringo also drummed on both versions of 'Isn't It a Pity', a lament for destructive human relationships that dated back to 1966, but which was especially poignant after the dissolution of the Beatles.

Still, given the mass of players, the substances taken and a loose, revolving-door approach as to who might be involved in a particular take, it later became difficult for anyone to accurately remember who'd played what. The credits record that both Starr and Delaney & Bonnie's Jim Gordon played drums on 'My Sweet Lord'. Alan White later swore it was him alone, arguing that his memory remained clear due to the initial embarrassment he suffered in the studio.

'George said to me, "I want you to play the drums",' White recollected. 'I said, "Well, Ringo's here." He said, "No, I want you to play the drums and Ringo can play tambourine." It didn't make me feel comfortable at first.'

Later, Starr's own memory failed him when it came to the details of the recording of *All Things Must Pass*. Ahead of the album's thirtieth anniversary edition released in 2001, engineer Ken Scott was tasked by Harrison with interviewing some of the participants for a disc of extras.

'I was living in Los Angeles at the time,' Scott recalled. '[George] said, "Go over to Ringo's and talk to him about the recording of the album, see what he remembers." I go over to Ringo's, I set up the digital recorder and I say, "OK, Ringo, so what do you remember about recording *All Things Must Pass?*"

'He just sort of looked up in the air and said, "Did I play on that?". That kind of shows you where everyone's head was at that point.'

A very different atmosphere descended on Abbey Road when John Lennon began the recording of his stark, confessional debut solo album of purgative songs, *John Lennon/Plastic Ono Band.* The beginning of the sessions dovetailed with the completion of *All Things Must Pass* and John Leckie simply moved from one project to the other. At first, Yoko produced the tracks (or played the 'wind') before Spector arrived to take over.

The core band was a minimal one: John on piano, Klaus on bass, Ringo on drums. 'It wasn't organising lots of musicians like an orchestra,' Leckie stressed, highlighting one of the key differences between Lennon and Harrison's albums. 'It was about getting good takes really.'

When Voormann first turned up at the studio, John handed him the lyrics, scribbled out in a larger print than his normal, elegantly tangled hand-writing. He said he really wanted the musicians to know what these songs were about, to help them to play with appropriate soulfulness to match his pain. There were to be no unnecessary adornments this time: no colours, just stark black and white.

Sat at the piano or behind his guitar, Lennon nailed all of the songs in no more than one or two takes. On 'Isolation', he sang about his and Yoko's remoteness and paranoia. On 'Mother', he screamed for Julia Lennon, twelve years dead. On 'God', he sang about how he didn't believe in the Beatles, or the myth of them at least.

Starr played empathically and expressively throughout, piloting a steady rhythmic course in spite of Lennon's emotional turbulence. 'Suddenly we'd be in the middle of a track and John would just start crying or screaming … which freaked us out at the beginning,' he said. 'But we were always so open to whatever anyone was going through, so we just got on with it.'

Another factor in the urgency of the recording process was Lennon's low boredom threshold. 'John just wanted to get out of the studio,' Voormann chuckled.

It was a productive period for John and Yoko. Recorded concurrently at the studio was sister album *Yoko Ono/Plastic Ono Band*, on which Starr – underlining his acceptance of, and friendship with, the woman so often accused of splitting the Beatles – drummed on almost every track. On the expansively titled 'Greenfield Morning I Pushed an Empty Baby Carriage All Over the City', introduced by Ono's wordless intoning over a tape of Harrison playing sitar, Ringo's drums faded in, playing a proggy, echoing groove that was very 1970. The track's name referenced a line from Ono's 1964 poetry book *Grapefruit*, but also the fact that she had suffered a miscarriage, almost eight months into her pregnancy, earlier that year.

But it wasn't all about the heavy or arty vibes. On Lennon's thirtieth birthday on 9 October 1970, when he, Starr and Voormann were taping the rattling 'Remember', Harrison arrived at the studio with the gift of a recording he'd made titled 'It's Johnny's Birthday': a wonky, organ-led, forty-nine-second version of Cliff Richard's 1968 hit, 'Congratulations' (that Harrison then chose to include on the third 'Apple Jam' disc of *All Things Must Pass*).

~

In the middle of all of this activity, Starr laid down his vocal for 'It Don't Come Easy', over a Harrison-produced backing track recorded at Trident back in March. Stylistically and melodically, the song betrayed the fact that George had had a hand in its writing, although the publishing credit on the label of the single solely named 'Richard Starkey'. A breezy mid-tempo groover, it was topped by a catchy lyric with a resigned, if empowering theme.

'I thought I was so hip with that line "Got to pay your dues if you want to sing the blues",' Starr later admitted, before explaining more of his writing routine. 'I don't spend weeks and months writing a song. I just try to get whatever is coming out at the moment.'

The single, issued on Apple on 9 April 1971, was to seriously compete with, or even eclipse, the contemporary releases of the other solo Beatles: McCartney's 'Another Day' (UK number two, US number five), Harrison's

'Bangla Desh' (UK ten, US twenty-three), Lennon's 'Power to the People' (UK seven, US eleven).

'It Don't Come Easy' reached number four in both the UK and the US, and even made it to number one in Canada. For the first time, it appeared as if Starr might have some unanticipated commercial clout in the pop charts. Those around Ringo noticed that he had a bit more of a spring in his step after the single's, perhaps surprising, success.

~

Starr didn't play on Lennon's next album, *Imagine*, but he did visit the sessions on the day in the summer of 1971 when its most provocative song was being recorded. 'How Do You Sleep?' was an undisguised tirade of abuse aimed at McCartney: accusing him of living with 'straights' and belittling his contributions to the Beatles' catalogue. A film crew captured its making, including an uneasy Harrison contributing guitar to the track and the moment when John seethed at an imagined Paul, 'How do you sleep, ya cunt?'

Ringo felt it was a step too far. Where previously he might have thought twice about confronting the unpredictable, mood-swinging Lennon, he simply said, 'That's enough, John.'

35

PUT ME IN THE MOVIES, PART THREE

200 Motels and *Blindman*, 1971

Descending on fly wires from the roof of a huge soundstage at Pinewood Studios, Frank Zappa, wearing a purple ribbed polo neck and matching coloured jeans, held an Aladdin-styled magic lamp puffing out dry ice. As he sailed down to the floor, he was met by Austrian actor Theodore Bikel, star of *The African Queen* and *My Fair Lady*, playing an MC named Rance Muhammitz.

'And here he is!' boomed Bikel. 'Larry the Dwarf.'

But it wasn't in fact Zappa, or even Zappa playing Larry the Dwarf, who landed beside the actor. It was Ringo, his face caked in foundation, wearing a cheap-looking, long-haired black wig and fake moustache-and-soul-patch combo in imitation of the American musician's Freak Brothers look. It was a disorientating sight: the face of one very famous musician staring out at the viewer wearing the features of a lesser-known other.

'Hi Larry,' Bikel went on. 'I'm sure the people at home would be interested to know why such a large dwarf as you is all dressed up like Frank Zappa?'

His eyes twinkling with comedy mischief, Ringo looked into the camera. 'He made me do it, Dave,' he offered, inexplicably. 'He's such a creep. He wants me to fuck the girl with the harp…'

The shot then cut to a harp-playing Keith Moon – the famously deranged and explosive drummer with the Who – slyly grinning while dressed as a nun.

'He wants you to fuck the girl… *with the harp*?!' the host parroted, with lewd, pantomime emphasis.

'No, *no*, with the *magic lamp*,' Ringo gurned before going into more explicit detail. 'He wants me to stuff it up her and rub it.'

He began cackling wildly, echoed by the sound of canned laughter, reflecting both the triple X nature of this sleazy conversation and the entirely bizarre scenario. It was the opening scene of *200 Motels*, Frank Zappa's first feature film, and this was clearly far-out shit for a former Beatle to be doing, way beyond even the outer reaches of *Magical Mystery Tour*.

Starr had agreed to play Zappa's onscreen doppelgänger after the latter had made an approach through Apple and turned up at the former's house in Highgate. In place of a script, he was carrying a huge book filled with the film's orchestral notation charts. Ringo was temporarily thrown.

'Why are you showing me the score?' he asked Zappa. 'I can't read music.'

Nonetheless, impressed by this idiosyncratic pitch, Starr said he'd do the movie. 'I'd heard Frank's music,' he pointed out. 'In a very musical way it was pretty wacky. It was a nice premise … Ringo playing Frank.' The real reason Zappa hadn't shown him a script was soon to become apparent: there wasn't going to be much of one. 'There was, like, the outline and some script,' Ringo vaguely offered. 'Sometimes you just made it up.'

The plot, as far as it went, involved Zappa's group the Mothers of Invention slowly going crazy on the road, believing that their bandleader – via his alter-ego Larry the Dwarf – is listening in to their conversations and using it as material for songs that he then forced them to play. The rest of the action was made up of mind-bending symphonic pieces, scenes of hippies and groupies who'd delved into the dress-up box improvising spaced-out am-dram nuttiness, musical interludes from Zappa and the Mothers, and even a daft animation. In effect, it was a wigged-out, grown-up kiddie TV show made for Saturday night not Saturday morning.

Shot over seven days at Pinewood in February '71, *200 Motels* had (incredibly) been funded by United Artists and eventually cost $679,000 – more than $5 million today – to make. Breaking new audio-visual ground, it was the first feature-length movie to be shot on video, before being transferred to 35mm film for cinematic release.

'I liked the fastness of it,' Zappa said of the appeal of video. 'You push the button, you tape it. You push another button, you play it back. You don't go to the lab, you don't do anything, it's just there. That's very modern.'

It was also far cheaper than shooting on film, allowing for easy experimentation in a project that was made and remade on the hoof. When the Mothers' bassist Jeff Simmons quit the group after his girlfriend convinced him that he was a serious musician who shouldn't be messing around with a comedy band, Zappa brought in *Steptoe and Son* and *A Hard Day's Night* actor Wilfrid Brambell to replace him and stuck him in a hippie hairpiece, with a view to overdubbing his mimed musical parts later. But Brambell was so horrified on set by the offensive lines he was given to say, and perturbed by the general chaos surrounding him, that he soon flounced off. As Zappa recalled, the actor 'completely freaked out and said that he couldn't handle it anymore'.

In the aftermath, sat in a dressing room with Starr and various cast members, Zappa decided that the next person to walk through the door would be Brambell's replacement. By chance, in wandered Ringo's driver, Martin Lickert, returning from the shop with a packet of cigarettes for his boss. 'Everybody just turned and looked at him and went, "*You*",' Zappa recalled.

As luck would have it, Lickert, who'd previously worked as a gofer at Apple, was in his own words 'a bit of a frustrated pop star' who played a bit of bass. 'He's not astonishing, but he can make the parts' was Zappa's assessment. Acting-wise, Lickert was no worse than the others and respectably handled a climactic scene in which he freaked out after smoking a doctored joint.

Co-directing with Zappa was Tony Palmer, who'd interviewed Ringo back in '68 for his celebrated rock doc, *All My Loving*. Before long, and perhaps inevitably, Palmer and the controlling Zappa were at loggerheads, with the former threatening to take his name off the credits. In the end, their dispute was resolved by Palmer directing the cameras and Zappa the action.

Interviewed on set, Palmer gamely attempted to explain the film. 'Well, I think Frank has had this dream for so long now that I think even he has become unsure as to what exactly the dream constitutes. It's a kind of mixture of childhood fantasies, adolescent fantasies and now grown-up fantasies all somehow strung together to make some kind of enormous nightmare that he may or may not have had at some point in his life.

'One's problem as a director,' he added, knowingly, 'is trying to make some coherent sense of it.'

It was an impossible task. But, in the final cut, some of Ringo's bits were the most memorable, even if simply due to the strange fascination of watching a Beatle amid such a weird set-up. One of his to-camera monologues ended with him standing in front of the massed members of the Royal Philharmonic Orchestra, delivering Zappa's piss-taking observation that 'a pop group can earn a vast amount of money compared to these other kinds of musicians'. Later, he chased Keith Moon the nun through the ranks of the orchestra.

Zappa had been surprised that the RPO could be hired for a mere £1,000 a day (cheap compared to American musicians' rates) and put them to work performing his elaborate, if demented, compositions. In one piece, entitled 'The Girl Wants to Fix Him Some Broth', he forced the female chorus to sing 'tinsel cock!'. Some of the male members of the ensemble, in an act of actual rebellion, ripped their tuxedos in protest.

The phallus fixation continued elsewhere in the operatic cacophony of 'Penis Dimension', a hymn to male inadequacy. At its conclusion, Ringo popped up to confess that he'd 'stuffed three socks and a bar of beauty soap down my pants'. This exhausting circus culminated in the musicians and actors cavorting around to the big ending number, 'Strictly Genteel'. Still holding his magic lamp, Starr frugged away – as the band ground though bluesy rock and sang about how they planned to get 'wasted' – clearly happy in this hippie mad world.

Puerile and plot-free *200 Motels* may have been, but it held a stoned appeal for those 'heads' who frequented its late-night cinema showings (or later bought it on VHS tape). Asked his opinion of the film on its fiftieth anniversary reissue in 2021, Ringo argued, 'it wasn't pretentious ... like some rock 'n' roll movies started to get in the end.'

During a question-and-answer session with an audience some years earlier, Zappa was asked, 'Did Ringo Starr enjoy being in the movie *200 Motels*?'

'Well, it's hard to tell,' he coolly responded. 'Y'know, I never bothered to ask people whether or not they enjoyed working for me. But he still talks to me, so I guess it wasn't too bad.'

In June 1971, four months after the filming of *200 Motels* and some 1,200 miles away at Cinecittà Studios in Rome, Ringo was playing out his childhood cowboy fantasies. Cast in Italian director Ferdinando Baldi's new spaghetti western *Blindman* (not uncoincidentally produced by Allen Klein's ABKCO), he was there to film his part as a Mexican bandit, with additional outdoor scenes to be shot in Almería in Spain.

Starr had, of course, already played a Mexican gardener in *Candy*. By sheer coincidence, his character in this new cowboy flick was 'Candy', not an obvious name for a vicious outlaw. In the intervening three years, however, Ringo's Hispanic accent had audibly improved, even if it still floated somewhere between Tijuana and Toxteth.

The super-slow, hazily plotted tale of *Blindman* involved the titular individual, a visually impaired cowboy badass (US actor Tony Anthony wearing pupil-dilated contact lenses) being hired to escort fifty mail-order brides to their future gold miner husbands. Starr is in love with one of the women, the flaxen-haired Pilar (Agneta Eckemyr) and seeks to thwart the mission.

He first appears twenty minutes into the film, riding into town at the head of his posse. Bearded and dirty-looking after a long ride, he throws water from a barrel over his head and demands 'Where is Pilar?'. From the off, he's pretty good: his big blue eyes peering out over his suntanned nose, his delivery that of a generic growling outlaw.

As the plot lazily unfolds, the fifty women are, of course – this being 1971 – treated horrendously. This rattles Ringo/Candy. At one point, he glowers and shoots a snake. Lifting the decked Blindman's head from the dust, Candy's face fills the screen as he intensely stares and offers the warning, 'If you don't tell me where she is, I'll break every bone in your *boday*.'

Considering he's playing against Anthony and Lloyd Battista (as Candy's brother Domingo), Starr carries his role with no little confidence. Later, he tracks Blindman and Pilar down to a cave and starts wildly firing his gun, yelling, 'Come out, you blind bastard! I kill you!' Then – spoiler alert – Blindman shoots him and he's dead after forty minutes on screen (although he later appears as a corpse in an open casket at his funeral).

It was a respectable effort and one that earned him – likely due to his pop stardom – a co-star billing on the poster alongside Anthony. Additionally, Ringo came up with a proposed theme song for the film, similarly titled 'Blindman', an atmospheric, trippy, almost *Revolver*-styled track replete with modern synth parts made in cahoots with Klaus Voormann (although it ultimately went unused by the director and ended up on the B-side of Starr's 1972 single, 'Back Off Boogaloo').

But while *Blindman* was released in both the US and Italy, it fell afoul of the British censors due to its misogynistic violence. Still, it was a youthful ambition realised, and another worthwhile addition to Starr's filmography.

'We're talking about me being an actor now, not being used for the name, like I have been,' he boasted, even if it was only half-true. 'In this film, I really feel as if I'm acting.'

In reality, he still wasn't an absolutely convincing screen presence. But he soon would be.

36

BACK ON THE BOARDS

The Concert for Bangladesh,
1971–1973

The Indian musicians on the stage at Madison Square Garden had just finished tuning up when the audience burst into applause.

'Thank you,' politely responded their leader, Ravi Shankar, with the hint of a smile. 'If you appreciate the tuning so much, I hope you'll enjoy the playing more.'

The moment was certainly a comical one, but it highlighted just how little a Western rock audience understood at the time of more exotic musical practices. In any event, most of the 20,000-strong crowd gathered at the New York arena, on the first day of August 1971 for the George Harrison-organised benefit for Bangladesh, were just counting down time until his all-star band arrived onstage.

When their set kicked off with 'Wah-Wah', the front line of this vast group was revealed to comprise Harrison alongside Eric Clapton, Billy Preston, Klaus Voormann, long-silver-haired piano player Leon Russell, Russell's guitarist pal Jesse Ed Davis, three members of Badfinger, brass sextet the Hollywood Horns and seven-piece backing singer troupe the Soul Choir.

Behind them, side-by-side at their twin drum kits, sat Ringo and Jim Keltner. It was the first time the latter had worked with the former, and he was almost paralysed by fear being in such close proximity to a Beatle. 'Ringo was beyond an idol for me,' Keltner confessed. 'So I was really, really doing everything I knew to do to keep myself from just falling apart with the nerves.'

Five numbers in, after a spirited rendition of 'My Sweet Lord' and a tight, funky 'Awaiting on You All', the spotlight found Starr and he launched into 'It Don't Come Easy'. The recent hit was greeted with recognition by the assembled and cheers rose up into the air when he sang the opening line, befitting the partial Beatles reunion that the moment represented. Ringo's pitch was unreliable and he forgot the words near the end, but it didn't seem to matter much.

It was the first time Starr had played a scheduled live show in half a decade. The Beatles' Apple rooftop performance in '69 had, of course, not been preannounced and so the momentous gig at San Francisco's Candlestick Park that had ended their touring days in August '66 was now five years in the past.

'It was a bit weird,' he later said of the experience of being back on an actual stage. 'I was crazy with nerves beforehand.'

The Concert for Bangladesh was originally Ravi Shankar's idea. The Bangladesh Liberation War, sparked by Bengali nationalists, had broken out in East Pakistan in March '71, forcing millions of refugees to pour over the border into India and resulting in a humanitarian crisis. 'I was very disturbed ... I was getting a lot of sad news,' said Shankar, himself a Bengali. 'I told George that I wanted to do something in a big way so that we could raise a lot of money.'

At the offices of Apple in London on 12 July, Harrison held a meeting announcing his intention to stage a benefit concert for the UNICEF children's charity. The next day, he was in New York, trying to drum up support from his fellow musicians. His notion, inspired by Lennon's peacenik campaigning, was to use his Beatles star power for the good by drawing massive media attention to the cause.

Inevitably, rumours of an impending Beatles reunion began to circulate. Harrison asked Lennon to get involved in the show and the precise reason why the latter failed to appear was forever lost in obfuscation: Klein, or Harrison, or both, seemingly didn't want Yoko to perform at the benefit and either she and John had a massive row about this, or John simply refused to turn up if his wife wasn't invited too. 'I told George a week before the show that I wouldn't be doing it,' Lennon said later. 'I just didn't feel like it.'

McCartney was approached to play but declined, citing Klein's involvement in the project. 'It would mean that all the world's press would scream that the Beatles had got back together again,' he reasoned, 'and Klein would have taken the credit. I didn't really fancy it anyway. If it wasn't for Klein, I might have had second thoughts.'

For his part, Ringo was in straight away. 'I just called him and said, "I'm coming",' he laughed. 'And that's how I got on the show.'

Speculation about an appearance by the Beatles continued to swirl and fans queued for hours outside Madison Square Garden. The combined 40,000 tickets for the two shows to be staged on the same day – one matinee, one evening performance – sold out within minutes. Even afterwards, the blocks around the venue remained buzzy, as touts succeeded in charging anything between $50 and $600 for a ticket with a face value of $7.50.

Rehearsals for the gigs were held a week before at Nola Studios on Manhattan's West 57th Street, near Carnegie Hall. One notable no-show was Eric Clapton, then in the depths of his alcohol and heroin addictions. The guitarist was, in his own frank estimation, 'in another world, not really there … I was in such bad shape.'

All the same, Clapton turned up at Madison Square Garden, where he and Harrison soulfully overlapped guitar solos on 'While My Guitar Gently Weeps', in the first live performance of the 1968 *White Album* track, to a thunderous audience response. Similarly ecstatic reactions met the debut airings of *Abbey Road*'s 'Here Comes the Sun' and 'Something'.

But Harrison's real coup was to tempt his friend Bob Dylan out of concert retirement, two years after the increasingly reclusive star had performed a comeback show at the Isle of Wight Festival in the summer of 1969. The night before the Bangladesh shows, however, on a recce to the Garden, Dylan tried to back out. 'He saw all these cameras and microphones in this huge place,' Harrison related, 'and he was saying, "Hey, man, this isn't my scene. I can't make this."'

During the matinee, Harrison had a setlist taped to his guitar. In the running order, after 'Here Comes the Sun', he'd simply written, 'Bob?'. 'It got to that point,' he said, 'and I looked around to see if there was any indication if Bob was going to come on or not.'

The stage was dark and, from his vantage point, Jim Keltner glimpsed a figure wearing a denim jacket walk out from the side of the stage. 'I knew it was him,' the drummer marvelled.

'He was so nervous,' Harrison noted of Dylan's demeanour, 'and he had his harmonica on, his guitar in his hand and he was walking right on the stage. It was like... now or never. And so I just said, "I'd like to bring on a friend of us all... Mr Bob Dylan."'

Harrison and Russell (having strapped on Klaus Voormann's psychedelically painted bass) fell in behind Dylan and they launched into 'A Hard Rain's A-Gonna Fall'. Ringo stood stage right, playing a tambourine: a seemingly simple task. But that was without factoring in Dylan's mercurial bandleading. In the first show, he played 'Just Like a Woman' in straight 4/4 time. For the second, without first announcing it to the musicians, he changed it back to its original 3/4 signature, as featured on his 1966 album *Blonde on Blonde*.

'It was very weird,' Starr noted. 'So I looked over at Leon. "Oh, it's a waltz this time, boys... Let's go!"'

~

In the end, the event broke new ground in terms of being the first ego-less gathering of star musicians united to perform in the name of an urgent cause. It was to later inspire everything from Live Aid to Farm Aid to Live 8. 'Bangladesh was important,' Starr stressed. 'It was the first huge show for charity with a mass ensemble.'

Released in the wake of a Harrison/Spector-produced triple live album, *The Concert for Bangladesh* film was issued in a 70mm, six-track stereo print to cinemas, forever preserving the events of 1 August. The money side of the operation was, however, a complete mess. As it transpired, Allen Klein hadn't registered the shows as charity events for UNICEF and so tax exemption was denied by both the US and UK authorities. The result was an estimated $10 million being frozen for a decade.

Worse, an article in *New York* magazine in early '72 claimed that Klein was syphoning off money from the project. He belligerently threatened to sue the publication for a staggering $150 million, before withdrawing the libel suit.

Klein held a press conference to protest his innocence and wrote an article for *Rolling Stone* breaking down the costs and profits of the enterprise. It didn't, however, deter activists from the anti-capitalist Rock Liberation Front from standing in the street outside the ABKCO offices chanting the slogan, 'You'll wonder where the money went, when Klein organises a charity event.'

Ultimately, these aftershocks didn't destroy the goodwill that surrounded the Concert for Bangladesh. At the 1973 Grammy Awards, held at the Tennessee Theatre in Nashville, Dusty Springfield and Johnny Mathis presented Starr (as Harrison's chosen representative) with the Album of the Year award for the live album. From behind a podium, wearing a tuxedo and glittery blue bow tie, he read aloud a prepared list of names to thank – including, strangely, his own, suggesting someone else had written it for him.

Nonetheless, his acceptance of this prestigious gong underlined the success of an endeavour that – perhaps most importantly in terms of his own career – had got Ringo back on stage playing his drums in public again.

37

RICHIE SNARE

Ringo and Harry Nilsson, 1968–1972

It was almost as if Harry Nilsson didn't want another hit record. In the spring of '72, his tender-to-explosive reading of Badfinger's 'Without You' was a transatlantic number one, thanks to his compellingly dynamic vocal that he claimed had caused him to 'bust a haemorrhoid on that big top note'. The playful, wayward American singer was in London, at Trident Studios, making his next album, the follow-up to '71's *Nilsson Schmilsson*, on the cover of which he'd appeared looking bleary-eyed, probably hungover, and wearing his dressing gown.

If big-selling songs of heartbreak were now to become his thing, he had a funny way of showing it. At the time going through the break-up of his second marriage, to Diane, mother of one-year-old Zak, his response was to write the '50s-styled rocker, 'You're Breakin' My Heart'. It had all the makings of a single, except for the fact that its repeated hookline contained the radio-unfriendly message 'Fuck you!'

Another song – on which Harry's new pal Ringo played drums under the Apple contract-dodging pseudonym of 'Richie Snare' – sounded like it might appeal to FM programmers. The confusingly named 'The Most Beautiful World in the World' was a slinky groover that transformed partway through into an old-fashioned, Hollywood-styled orchestral number. But, for the first half of the track, Nilsson insisted on singing in a ropey Jamaican accent, breaking off to loudly gargle and spit. His producer, Richard Perry, who also worked with the highly professional Barbra Streisand, quietly despaired. Harry seemed intent on torpedoing his career.

With all of its brilliant quirks, *Nilsson Schmilsson* had been what Perry termed a 'Beatles-quality album' and made number three in the US. But, in the wake of its success, Nilsson was derailed by his impending divorce and deep insecurity. He reacted by turning up at the studio already drunk, continuing to knock back cognac while blocking out his producer's suggestions and refusing to compromise in any way.

Ringo was along for much of the mad ride that was *Son of Schmilsson*, although at the sessions he tended to sit and laugh along and say nothing much at all. Harry was great fun to be around. As Apple PA Chris O'Dell colourfully put it, the singer existed in a 'bouncy little world of his own'. He and Ringo quickly became tight and, as O'Dell saw it, 'like brothers'. They had much in common: lingering psychic damage after both their fathers had left them when they were young children, a love of music, a taste for spirits and a daft sense of humour. 'Ringo and I spent a thousand hours laughing,' said Harry.

But, in tandem with Nilsson's, Starr's drinking was intensifying. While at this stage he didn't need much help in that regard, Ringo was beginning to keep dangerous company. The pair's alcoholic circle soon expanded to include the UK's number-one pop star Marc Bolan, the Who's demented drummer Keith Moon and *Monty Python*'s Graham Chapman. Typically, they'd start drinking brandy at around three in the afternoon at the Apple offices. As one by one they arrived, they'd each utter their group catchphrase, 'I hope I'm not interrupting anything?' By nine or ten, they'd be wasted yet ready to head off and continue the party at the exclusive West End hangout Tramp.

If, from the outside, it all looked like happy-go-lucky fun, for Nilsson, there seemed to be some grim self-destructive impulse at work. As far as Richard Perry was concerned, from this point on, Harry seemed to harbour a 'death wish'.

~

How the Brooklyn-born, Los Angeles-settled Harry Nilsson became what Fabs' publicist Derek Taylor termed 'the Beatle across the water' was through a circuitous route. Taylor was sitting in his car one day in LA in early 1968 when '1941', from Nilsson's second album *Pandemonium Shadow Show*, came on the radio. A baldly confessional song, with a baroque oompah arrangement, it detailed how his father had deserted him and his mother when he was three.

Taylor was blown away by the track and bought twenty-five copies of the LP to hand out to his friends. He posted one to each of the Beatles back in England, not least because the record also featured an audacious cover of 'You Can't Do That' that sewed together references to no less than eighteen other Lennon/McCartney songs. The publicist was himself fond of an early cocktail hour and began drinking with the singer in the La Brea Inn above Sunset Boulevard. Nilsson subsequently met George Harrison at a party at the latter's rented house in the Hollywood Hills.

In April '68, Nilsson was at home when he received a middle-of-the-night phone call from Lennon telling him how much he loved his 'fucking fantastic' album. (Of course, Harry was up anyway.) The next week, around the same time, McCartney called and offered similar praise, declaring Nilsson 'great, man'. 'The third week I expected Ringo would call,' Harry joked. 'He never did.'

But Starr had also become an instant fan of Nilsson, particularly his gutsy, slightly unhinged version of Ike & Tina Turner's 'River Deep – Mountain High'. 'It was bordering on madness,' he marvelled, 'and we thought, *We gotta meet this guy*'. So infatuated by Nilsson were Lennon and McCartney that when they launched Apple Corps in New York in May 1968, they were asked by a reporter if they had a favourite new artist. 'Nilsson,' Lennon responded. And their favourite group? 'Nilsson,' said both.

If it was the moment that made his career, Nilsson had at first hated the Beatles during their 1964 US boom, mainly because he felt 'they were beating me to the punch'. Then, in a dramatic volte face, they became for him the one and only band in the world. That same year, he co-wrote and sang a cash-in novelty single, 'All for the Beatles', replete with teen screams and a Bo Diddley beat, under the name the Foto-Fi Four. Then, with his grandstanding 'You Can't Do That' and a faithful reading of 'She's Leaving Home' on *Pandemonium Shadow Show*, Harry had effectively beamed his Beatle signal out into the night sky, hoping for some kind of response.

For him, it had already been a long journey to this point. Having been kicked out of his crowded Brooklyn family apartment at the age of fifteen, the teenage Harry Nilsson had bravely travelled across the country to Los Angeles, where he found a job at the grand Paramount Theatre movie palace before working as a computer operator at a bank, writing songs by night. His break came when he managed to sell 'Cuddly Toy', a strange and contemptuously misogynistic ditty, to moptop knock-offs the Monkees, whose version translated the song into a vaudeville toe-tapper. Now, here he was being endorsed by the actual Beatles.

At their invitation, Nilsson first arrived in London in the summer of 1968, finding Apple's Chris O'Dell and Ringo's chauffeur-driven Daimler waiting for him at the airport. Starr was out of town at the time, but Nilsson was asked to stay with Lennon at Kenwood in Surrey. The two sat up all night, bonding over childhood trauma, repressed anger and drug-refracted curiosity. Before the trip was out, Harry had also met Paul and visited the hallowed ground of EMI Studios in Abbey Road.

Nilsson returned to the US transformed, although not, in his producer Rick Jarrard's view, in a positive way. 'He changed and became somebody else that I no longer knew,' he bemoaned, mainly due to the fact that Nilsson, clearly seeing his horizons expanding, fired him by telegram three months later.

In the spring of 1972, the Soho passageway of St Anne's Court – nicknamed 'Pee Pee Alley' by Harry – was an unlikely portal to space. But there, at Trident Studios over the past three years, more than one artist had sonically ventured into the firmament. First, in '69, David Bowie had used the studio as the launch platform for his 'Space Oddity', before returning to record 'Starman' in the month before Nilsson arrived. Meanwhile, at the start of '72, Elton John's 'Rocket Man' had been mixed at Trident, fast becoming the biggest interstellar hit of all.

Bad timing, then, for Nilsson to blast off on his own trip into the heavens. 'Spaceman', propelled by the funky drumming of Richie Snare, detailed the exploits of a disillusioned astronaut, but it struggled to number twenty-three in the US and flopped entirely in the UK. 'It so happens Elton John had "Rocket Man" at the same time,' Harry lamented. 'Didn't know about that.'

There wasn't much else in the way of hit-making material on *Son of*

Schmilsson. Certainly not 'I'd Rather Be Dead', a jaunty polka on which Nilsson invited a coachload of pensioners from old folks' homes in Stepney and Pinner to sing along with him on a morbidly cheerful tune about welcoming death as opposed to facing a dotage of incontinence. Harry being Harry got them loaded on sherry until they were, as Richard Perry noted, 'stone drunk and ready to do anything'. Recording was briefly interrupted when one of their number, Old Tom, eighty-five on the day of the session at Trident, owned up to having a squeaky wooden leg that was audible on the recording. In the age of glam and hard rock, this was very much going against the grain.

Meanwhile, the high jinks and carousing involved in the album's creation was captured by a film crew for a never-officially-released documentary obliquely titled *Did Somebody Drop His Mouse?*. In it, Harry could be heard in voiceover lauding 'the brilliant drumming of Ringo. When there was a hesitation, he just bust his way through ... he was like a fender. Strong and straight.'

The appreciation cut both ways. 'He was my best friend,' Starr said of Nilsson. 'I loved Harry.'

For the two, there would be further, and even hairier, adventures to come.

38

PUT ME IN THE MOVIES, PART FOUR

Directing *Born to Boogie*, 1972

Once again, the sound of screaming filled Ringo's ears – only this time it wasn't directed at him. Sitting in the photographers' pit at the front of the stage at the Wembley Empire Pool arena on Saturday 18 March 1972, he was there to direct a five-camera film crew training their lenses on Marc Bolan and T. Rex, the biggest pop act in the UK since the Beatles' abdication. Starr was one of the camera operators, even riding the rails of a curved track at the front of the stage for sweeping, panoramic shots. Behind the safety barrier, 8,000 kids squealed and madly grooved away, many of them wearing glitter stars glued to their overawed faces.

By '72, Beatlemania was long gone and been superseded by T. Rextasy. Ringo was a big fan. 'I think T. Rex are fantastic,' he declared in the summer of '71, just as Bolan hit number one for the second time with the stack heel-crushing stomp of 'Get It On'. 'I like the *showbiz* in showbiz,' he said of Marc's flashy, peacocking style.

Bolan accepted the ex-Beatle's endorsement in typically wry, vainglorious style. 'I can't think of any likely comparison to us except Ringo and the dudes,' he shrugged. Starr, meanwhile, admitted that before the emergence of T. Rex, he was 'pretty bored with what was going on' in music. He admiringly noted that Bolan had been the first pop star since the Beatles to 'get the kids back out of their seats, jumping and screaming'.

The Starr-directed T. Rex film *Born to Boogie* – part electrifying live or studio band footage, part surreal *Magical Mystery Tour*-styled skits – opened with a black-and-white shot of the nine-year-old Mark Feld sporting a greased-back quiff and posing with an acoustic guitar in imitation of his hero Eddie Cochran. The image then morphed into a contemporary shot of the corkscrew-haired, pouting pin-up holding his Les Paul.

For a diminutive lad from Stoke Newington in north London, the son of a lorry driver dad and market stall-running mum, Feld always had bags (and bags) of confidence. His imagination fired by Cochran and Elvis Presley as a kid, this cocky, snappy-dressing character had shapeshifted through the '60s from rocker to ace-face mod to beatnik to cross-legged hippie. Explaining his latest transformation, he spun a fantastical tale about meeting a levitating wizard in Paris who'd taught him all kinds of arcane magickal knowledge. The rock press lapped it up.

The truth was more mundane. As a struggling mid-'60s hopeful, he'd first changed his name to Marc Bolan after signing to Decca Records in 1965. He'd been guitarist in failed rock band John's Children, then turned folky acoustic in the Tyrannosaurus Rex duo with multi-instrumentalist Steve Took. Going electric on his fourth album, 1970's *A Beard of Stars* – and replacing the increasingly drugged-out Took with percussionist Mickey Finn – he achieved middling album chart success, yet still had zero major hits.

That was until later that year when he and his producer friend Tony Visconti experienced a eureka moment as they reconfigured 1950s rock 'n' roll for the 1970s with the quasi-mystical, insanely catchy 'Ride a White Swan', which reached UK number two under the cut-down band name of T. Rex. Suddenly, Marc was a star and the hits flowed: 'Hot Love', 'Get It On', 'Jeepster', 'Telegram Sam'.

Born to Boogie kicked off with Bolan and T. Rex slamming into 'Jeepster' to the sound of massed hysteria in the Empire Pool, as the singer/guitarist cavorted in a silver glitter jacket, green satin trousers and a T-shirt cheekily bearing his own drawn-and-painted image. Eyeballing his teen screamers, he professed to being a vampire for their love who was 'gonna suck ya!'. In the next song, the swaggering 'Baby Strange', he promised to call them and then 'ball' them. Unlike his Fab predecessors, Marc wasn't content with mere handholding. The film, he later explained, was meant to be 'a very sweaty sort of thing ... very erotic'.

As his rollicking performance of 'Baby Strange' drew to its climax, he screwed up his face and knowingly exclaimed, 'Aw, back off, boogaloo...'

~

It was the name of Ringo's latest single that had appeared in the shops the previous day. 'Back Off Boogaloo' was a phrase coined by Bolan and co-opted by Starr for what was to be his biggest hit to date.

More than any of the former Beatles, solo Ringo was plugged into the changing musical current of 1971–72. 'Ride a White Swan' was later cited as the first glam rock record and Starr was quick to throw himself into the latest style.

In Ringo's eyes, Marc was an 'energised guy' and a funny one too, with his camp 'Ooh you, boogaloo' and 'Back off, boogaloo' catchphrases. One night, after a visit from Bolan, Starr found himself in the 'twilight zone' between waking and sleeping with Marc's colourful utterances rattling around his head and coalescing into a chanting melody. He jumped out of bed to record the hook before he forgot it, but couldn't find a working tape recorder. Fearing the tune was fast fading in his mind – or, worse, as he remembered, mutating into '"Mack the Knife" and I'm panicking' – he pilfered the batteries from one of the kids' toys, picked up a guitar (even though he only knew three chords) and sang a sketch of it onto a cassette.

Later, a rumour circulated that Marc Bolan had ghostwritten 'Back Off Boogaloo' for his new friend. But beyond inspiring its title, Bolan had no further involvement. Instead, it was another pal, the ever-dependable George Harrison, who played a furtive role in the song's creation. Ringo played his sketch to George and asked him, 'Would you put in a few more chords?' As with 'It Don't Come Easy', his old bandmate did it purely as a favour and only took a producer's credit (likely with an eye to building his own side career in that area).

The creative breakthrough in the Apple studio came when the track's rhythm was sounding too light and Harrison suggested a heavier beat on the bass drum, which Starr accompanied with a military snare tattoo that had the required glammy weight to accompany the song's circular, terrace-chant hook. Ringo played drums and sang, Klaus Voormann supplied the pumping bassline and honked on a sax, Harrison played a gliding guitar solo and *All Things Must Pass* keyboard player Gary Wright pounded away at a staccato piano part. Miraculously, another hit was in the bag.

A promo clip was shot for the single at Tittenhurst Park, the twenty-one-acre country estate near Ascot that Lennon and Ono had vacated when they permanently relocated to New York in the August of '71. There, wearing a black peacoat, Ringo was filmed being stalked around the grounds by a comedy version of Frankenstein's monster as he, in turn, bewilderedly searched for the mutant creature. The two were happily united, sat down to enjoy a picnic together and then danced over the grass, the monster waving a bunch of daffodils.

As 'Back Off Boogaloo' began to climb the charts, some speculated that its lyric contained snipes at McCartney with its references to a dozy 'meat head' pretending he was 'dead'. The cold war between Ringo and Paul had not abated. In '71, while filming *Blindman* in Spain, Starr gave an interview to *Melody Maker* in which he casually dismissed McCartney's second post-Beatles album, *Ram*.

'I feel sad with Paul's albums,' he offered, 'because I believe he's a great artist, incredibly creative, incredibly clever, but he disappoints me on his albums. I don't think there's one tune on the last one, *Ram* ... I just feel he's wasted his time, it's just the way I feel ... he seems to be going strange.'

Starr, for his part, always rebuffed the rumours about 'Back Off Boogaloo' and its seemingly pointed lyrics. In reality, its words were about as deep as a teaspoon and that was entirely the point: it was a throwaway pop song.

Yet, that spring-into-summer of '72, it managed to outperform the efforts of the other solo Beatles. While Harrison abstained from releasing a single that year, in the same period, McCartney's gooey cover of the nursery rhyme 'Mary Had a Little Lamb' made it to UK number nine (and US twenty-eight), while Lennon's provocative 'Woman is the Nigger of the World' flopped everywhere apart from a handful of European countries, largely due to the fact that no radio station would touch it.

By comparison, in May, 'Back Off Boogaloo' was sitting at number nine in the US and number two in the UK. Against all reasonable odds, Ringo was turning out to be the most commercially successful of them all.

~

To celebrate, Starr generally had a drink. Many happy daytime hours were spent getting slowly stewed in Savile Row where he was now running Apple's film division. The record company's new head of A&R, Tony King, vividly remembered that the building at this point 'had a warm vibe, a tone that was set by Ringo'.

It was in this setting that Starr first suggested the idea of a film to Bolan. Ringo initially called Marc with a different movie concept, saying, 'Come and see me. I've got this idea. See what you think. Yes or no.' While the details of the pitch were never disclosed, Bolan gave it the thumbs-down. 'But through that meeting,' Starr recalled, 'we got to know each other and became friendly.'

Bolan turned out to be a frequent visitor to Apple and was a reliably buzzy presence, constantly, if amiably, boasting about his latest chart positions. He would arrive with an acetate of his next single and theatrically declare to everyone that it would sell '300,000 in five days' and be 'number one in two weeks'. He was often proved right.

Ringo tended to regard Marc as if 'he was some crazy kid', even though Bolan at the time of making *Born to Boogie* was twenty-four, while Starr was thirty-one: a mere seven-year age difference. Still, beyond thirty, maintaining a career in music was a tricky endeavour, even for an ex-Beatle. Ringo was looking to move further into film, on both sides of the camera, and involving the biggest pop star in the land would be a great start in terms of his directing ambitions.

After hearing that Bolan planned to film his upcoming two shows at the Empire Pool, Starr suggested, 'Why don't you let me do it? I'm your pal.' Bolan said, 'OK, let's do it together.' Together, they cut a 50/50 deal and the shoot was on.

On the day, along with the five cameras filming the action, Tony Visconti was installed in the Rolling Stones Mobile Studio truck outside the venue, capturing the audio. The original plan had been to film and record both the matinee and evening performances, and then cut between them in the final edit. That notion was snuffed when, during the afternoon show, roadies pulled out the cables to the truck as they frantically tried to work out why bassist Steve Currie couldn't hear himself onstage. In any event, Bolan chose to wear different outfits for each performance, killing the continuity. Ultimately, only the second show was usable.

Reviewing the rushes afterwards, Starr decided that the concert footage alone felt insufficient and that additional scenes were needed to fully shape the movie. Thus developed what Bolan described as the 'surrealistic overtones' of *Born to Boogie*. The first of these wacky vignettes involved the image of a red convertible very, very slowly approaching the camera from the far distance over the runway at Denham Aerodrome in Buckinghamshire.

As the car moved closer, the figures in it were gradually revealed to be a stovepipe hat-wearing Bolan and a driver in a dormouse costume. Bolan took a phone call in the back as the faux rodent began making squeaking noises. Then, short-stature actor George Claydon magically appeared, wearing a black, purple-lined cloak, with a white lightning flash on the back. (Claydon had previously appeared as a photographer in *Magical Mystery Tour* and so was used to this kind of caper.)

Bolan slapped Claydon with a fly swatter, prompting the latter to angrily yank a wing mirror off the car and proceed to chew on it. This seemed to move Marc to recite some of his own poetry, in this case a piece entitled 'Electric Wind', involving 'rock and roll children born to dance to the beat of your heart and die to the rhythm of the universe'.

'What say you, friend?' Bolan asked the dormouse.

'Whaddya mean?' he responded in a suspiciously Scouse accent.

It was, of course, pure codswallop. Surely, the fans would much rather have had another T. Rex song instead of this self-indulgent screen-time filler. But while these interstitial passages continued to be baffling, they became funnier as the film progressed. One short scene involved Bolan and Starr attempting to trade the opening lines of 'Let's Have a Party', the 1957 Jessie Mae Robinson song made famous by Elvis Presley. Marc, looking heroically stoned, kept cracking up with laughter. Ringo, too, proceeded to corpse, dropping his fag before composing himself, turning pro and pointing out, 'We're running out of film… the light's going…'

A longer scene, shot at Tittenhurst, involved a Fellini-esque take on the Mad Hatter's Tea Party from *Alice's Adventures in Wonderland*, in which Bolan, Starr and Mickey Finn sat at one outdoor table, while Marc's wife June, his publicist Chelita Secunda and Ringo's business advisor Hilary Gerrard sat at another dressed as – what else? – nuns. Tony King remembered Gerrard as being in possession of a 'wonderful, long, beautifully manicured cocaine finger-nail, on which he would offer you coke. Ringo was very fond of him.' Presiding over the affair was actor Geoffrey Bayldon, playing a butler, but best known as the eleventh-century sorcerer transported to 1969 Britain in the popular ITV kids' series, *Catweazle*. Only Marc Bolan would have a wizard serving him hand and foot.

But the standout scenes in *Born to Boogie* were shot in the basement studio at Apple, the same room in which, three years earlier, the Beatles had been filmed seizing victory from the jaws of defeat for *Let It Be*. There had since been a glam makeover of the space, including a reflection-warping mirror, a stuffed zebra and a stuffed tiger. In the first of two numbers, Starr, tossing around his long, feathered mullet, sat in with T. Rex alongside drummer Bill Legend. A guesting Elton John thumped away on a grand piano, doing his best Little Richard as the ensemble rattled through 'Tutti Frutti'. Next, they kicked into a storming 'Children of the Revolution', later to be re-recorded solely by T. Rex for a September '72 single release, but here featuring a section where all of the other musicians dropped out for two bars to spotlight Starr's funky drumming.

Ringo was clearly having a ball, hanging out with his new cool '70s rock star pals, the '60s long forgotten.

~

Marc Bolan soon became a family friend of the Starkeys. Sometimes, he'd turn at up at their house at lunchtime and – while Ringo and Maureen were still in bed, sleeping off their hangovers, sometimes not rising until four in the afternoon – he'd spend time with seven-year-old Zak. Ringo owned several short-scale Fender Mustang electric guitars and Marc used them to patiently teach the kid some basic chords.

When the seventh T. Rex album, *The Slider*, came out that summer, Starr was credited as the photographer of its stark black-and-white cover shot of

Bolan. Despite the presence of tree branches in the background, Ringo remembered that he took the picture 'on the roof of Apple'. In fact, the picture had been casually snapped by Tony Visconti during downtime at Tittenhurst on the location shoot of *Born to Boogie*. He confronted Bolan, who simply said, 'Oops, I forgot'. But Visconti believed that Bolan had deliberately credited Starr, thinking it would stir up a bit of extra publicity. 'It was a typical Marc ploy,' he stated, knowingly.

All the while, the editing of *Born to Boogie* went on as Visconti struggled with the soundtrack, fixing various performance and tuning problems on the tapes with judicious overdubs. On 14 December, the film was premiered in London at the Oscar One Cinema in Soho, followed by a party at – where else? – Tramp, where Ringo, Marc, Elton, Bernie Taupin, Keith Moon and Donovan boozed the night away.

At a little more than an hour in length, it was barely a feature film. Yet *Born to Boogie* successfully toured the UK in place of the singer and his band, Starr having adeptly harnessed the thrills of a T. Rex gig in a cinema setting. Shrewdly, the final cut featured multiple shots of the crowd, making the fans feel part of the action, whether or not they'd been in the Empire Pool arena. 'We have a lot of close-ups of the kids,' Bolan stressed, 'and they are as much the stars as I am.'

Most critics hated the film, however. Nick Kent at the *NME* carped about Bolan's 'new heights of fey precociousness'. The *Daily Mirror* called it a 'nightmare of noise'. More than one reviewer singled out the Apple jams with Elton and Ringo as being the highpoints. Nonetheless, in later years, the consensus view of the movie was that director Richard Starkey had successfully immortalised Bolan at his absolute peak.

From there, Marc's star began to fall, confirming that he lacked the staying power of the Beatles. Through 1973, his chart positions slipped and, by '74, on the elaborate, mini-operatic single that was to lyrically chart his downward slide, he was wondering 'whatever happened to the teenage dream?'.

39

'YOUR FRIEND AND MINE, RINGO STARR'

Making the *Ringo Album*, 1973

'Just like that … no planning,' marvelled Richard Perry. 'The three ex-Beatles recorded one of John's songs. Everyone in the room was just gleaming.'

It was 13 March 1973 and, at Sunset Sound Recorders in the heart of Hollywood, Ringo, George and John were working together in the studio for the first time since the completion of *Abbey Road* almost four years before. For a session so loaded with significance, this three-quarters Beatles reunion had occurred entirely by chance – they all just happened to be in Los Angeles at the same time – and didn't last long. Tuning back into their Fab telepathy and relying on old muscle memories, the trio nailed Lennon's 'I'm the Greatest' within twenty minutes with trusted Beatle co-conspirators Billy Preston (electric piano, organ) and Klaus Voormann (bass) supporting them.

'We were like big girls again,' Ringo joked. 'We were just smiling while we were playing.'

Starr had embarked upon the sessions for what was to be his third solo album the week before, on 5 March, with Perry overseeing the proceedings. Harrison dropped by Sunset Sound five days in, listened to what was already on the tapes and enthusiastically told Ringo, 'I'm knocked out with what you've done.' Returning a couple of days later, he recorded some backing vocals. The next day, John and Yoko showed up.

Lennon had written 'I'm the Greatest' back in 1970, between Christmas and New Year, after he'd laid in bed at Tittenhurst and watched the UK TV

211

premiere of *A Hard Day's Night* being beamed into millions of British homes. 'A good projection of one façade of us' was how he now viewed the Beatles' first film. At the same time, seeing the movie again made him realise that he would probably never be able to escape that chirpy, cheeky image he'd created or live up to his past successes.

Oddly inspired, he started sketching a song, listing all the people down the years who'd encouraged some kind of greatness in him: his mother, his old friends. If it sounded as if he was inflating the balloon of his ego, it was only with the intention of puncturing it. He made a scratch recording of a few verses, vamping on the piano. In John's mind, he was comedy-bragging like Muhammad Ali. But he knew most people wouldn't get that he was being sarcastic.

Later, he demoed 'I'm the Greatest' another couple of times, but ended up giving the song to Ringo. Translated to Starr's everyman style, the song took on a breezier tone that revealed its inherent jokiness. The loping track grooved along nicely – Lennon's vocal unmistakably shadowing Starr's lead – without ever soaring to any great Beatles-y heights. Still, the thrashing, *Pepper*-ish coda, with Harrison's piercing slide guitar solo and Ringo's repeated 'alright!' chant surrounded by sound-effect crowd noise, came very close.

'Yeah, the three of us were there and Paul would most probably have joined in if he was around, but he wasn't,' John casually commented later. McCartney was indeed to feature on the album that was to be titled *Ringo*, a record that was to reunite the Beatles, if not altogether on any one track, then at least on the same piece of plastic.

It had become clear after the chart triumphs of 'It Don't Come Easy' and 'Back Off Boogaloo' that the commercial conditions were right for Ringo to make a mainstream pop-rock album. *Sentimental Journey* had served its purpose (and first introduced Starr to Richard Perry after he'd arranged the album's title track). Its successor, released only six months later in the autumn of 1970, involved an adventure into country music territory.

Beaucoups of Blues was a full-scale realisation of both Starr's early-years passion for country and an album-length exploration of the style he'd tapped into with everything from 'Act Naturally' to 'Octopus's Garden'. It came about, strangely enough, as the result of an airport pick-up Starr did as a favour to Harrison in the first week of June '70, sending his car and driver to collect US pedal steel-player Pete Drake to take him to play on the sessions for *All Things Must Pass*. On the drive, Drake noticed that Starr kept a collection of country cassettes in the car.

'When he got to the studio,' Ringo remembered, 'he said, "Hey, hoss, I see you like country music." The next day, he was talking to me about going to Nashville: "Let's make a record." And I was like, "Oh, I don't think so. How long have I got to be there?" Nothing against Nashville. Just like, "I don't think so".'

Drake told him he could enlist his various friends back home in Tennessee to write enough new material for a full LP in a week. He also mentioned that when he'd played on Bob Dylan's *Nashville Skyline* the previous year, the sessions had lasted only a matter of days. Starr still couldn't believe it could be done. Yet, before the month was out, he found himself on a plane to Nashville.

'I got there on Monday,' he said. 'We picked five songs on Tuesday in the morning, and in the afternoon and evening, we recorded them … and we did the same the next day, and it was over in two days.'

Made at Music City Recorders, a studio owned by Elvis Presley's original guitarist Scotty Moore, who also engineered the sessions, *Beaucoups of Blues* was a set of country songs that worked with Starr's limitations as a vocalist. Like *Sentimental Journey*, it cast him entirely as a singer, not a drummer, in this instance backed by Presley's one-time backing vocal quartet the Jordanaires. Moreover, it proved that Ringo Starr was country to his soul and somehow inherently hardwired to this often emotionally weighty music.

Accompanied by a cover image of Starr holding a cigarette, looking fed-up, perched on the stoop of a smokehouse shed, most of the tracks were sung by him in a gentle, lovelorn burr that turned rousing when required. It was a solid, respectable diversion into a different kind of genre album. 'It's a good record,' Lennon reckoned, before deflatingly adding, 'I wouldn't buy it, y'know.' Not many did. In the UK, it baffled the record-buying public, while scaling to number thirty-five on the US country chart.

Ringo, the album, was to be an entirely different proposition. For a start, it had a potential hit in the shape of 'Photograph', the yearning pop song written by Ringo and George onboard the *Marala* yacht in Cannes back in '71.

A preliminary version had been recorded by the pair in recent months during the making of Harrison's second solo album *Living in the Material World*, but in Los Angeles it was remade with a swirling orchestral and choral arrangement scored by Phil Spector associate Jack Nitzsche.

Starr's new-found glam stylisms were further investigated on his party-starting version of Randy Newman's 'Have You Seen My Baby?' and the shuffling, floor-filling 'Oh My My', co-written by Starr with Vini Poncia, ironically one of the authors, along with Spector, of the 1964 Cher-sung novelty single, 'Ringo, I Love You'. (Poncia was to play a significant role in Starr's future albums as the '70s progressed, becoming his key songwriting collaborator.) Elsewhere, there was more wistful country, in the shape of the pining, Harrison-penned 'Sunshine Life for Me (Sail Away Raymond)', rendered as a modern jug band hoedown wherein Starr's credibility was upped by being backed by four members of the Band.

Nostalgia for old-style rock 'n' roll was meanwhile raging in 1973, not least due to director George Lucas's '62-set *American Graffiti*, the soundtrack of which found Bill Haley, Del Shannon and Chuck Berry back blasting out of cinema speakers. Another of its song inclusions, Johnny Burnette's 1960 hit 'You're Sixteen', was coincidentally recorded by Starr during the *Ringo* sessions and rebuilt as a sturdy rocker.

Much like 'Boys', Starr clearly hadn't given much thought to the wider connotations of the lyric he was singing or that, in this instance, from the outside perspective, he was a thirty-two-year-old man openly lusting after a mid-teenage girl. To him, it was clearly just a cutesy song of puppy love from one youth to another. Nonetheless, he was to catch some flak for continuing to perform it in later years. ('This is for the girls who're young at heart,' he announced to his ageing female fans when introducing the song at the Greek Theatre in Los Angeles in September 2019, before quietly dropping it from his set at the age of seventy-nine.)

There was another problematic part of *Ringo* that spoke of a less enlightened time. In Starkey/Poncia's 'Devil Woman', the narrator expressed an urge to beat up the object of his confusing and infuriating lust (then, afterwards, to 'be kind'). It was obviously nasty, wrongheaded stuff, matching domestic violence to a groovy beat. But, then again, it was in an age where, eight years earlier, Lennon had gotten away with threatening to inflict violence upon – and possibly even murder – his paramour in 'Run for Your Life' on *Rubber Soul*.

For all of its creepy implications, 'You're Sixteen' was also clearly tongue-in-cheek, as illustrated by its 'mouth sax solo', a comedy root-tee-toot part performed on the track by none other than Paul McCartney. After the recording of 'I'm the Greatest', Starr had reached out to his estranged former bandmate, asking him to get involved with the album on some level. He told him, 'You can't be left out of this. I've got the other two on it. Have you got any tracks?'

In response, Paul, with some help from Linda, wrote the mid-paced piano ballad 'Six O'Clock' and Starr flew back to England to record it at Apple and Abbey Road. In truth, it was a sappy, regretful love song that sounded like a Wings B-side, but the significance of its creation was not lost on anyone. The initial session was fun and frivolous too, with McCartney's comedy brass parping on 'You're Sixteen' followed by Starr's sudden impulse to record himself tap dancing on the appropriately named 'Step Lightly' (his contribution credited to 'the dancing feet of: Richard Starkey, MBE').

Side Two closer 'You and Me (Babe)', written by Starr with ever-dependable Beatles gofer Mal Evans, offered a brilliantly bright George Harrison electric guitar part, in the style of 'Nowhere Man'. The track also featured some meta musing from Ringo, pointing out that he and the band were reaching the end (à la the reprise of 'Sgt. Pepper's Lonely Hearts Club Band'), but that he would forever be locked into the record's grooves for their listening pleasure.

Nicking a move from Harry Nilsson – who'd ended *Son of Schmilsson* by saying 'So long, folks!' and, to Perry, 'See you next album, Richard!' – at the close of 'You and Me (Babe)' our host listed the names of all involved, including the former Beatles notably all clumped together, and signed off as 'your friend and mine, Ringo Starr'.

It was a victory lap at the end of a record that found Starr squarely in the middle of the road. All in all, *Ringo* was a (mostly) light-hearted, catchy and house party-ready album that was his best yet.

~

The making of *Ringo*, involving close to thirty musicians in total, had also been quite the organisational feat, mostly supervised by Tony King at Apple.

Starr's ambitions for the artwork were equally elaborate and were to even delay the album's release. King remembered that Hilary Gerrard ended up buckling under the stress. One day, he walked into the business manager's office and found him hiding under his desk, pleading, 'I can't cope...'.

Tucked into the vinyl's gatefold sleeve was a twenty-two-page insert booklet featuring a Klaus Voormann lithograph for each of the ten tracks, the images ranging from a drive-in movie scene ('You're Sixteen') to a nightmarish hospital room ('Oh My My') and a cape-wearing, bare-breasted alien temptress ('Devil Woman').

But it was the cover of *Ringo* that was to prove most visually striking, as it translated the cast-of-dozens concept of *Sgt. Pepper* to the variety stage. In the foreground, caught by twin spotlight beams, an image of Starr stood amid his forename spelled out in lights, bizarrely accompanied by a pint-sized, curly-haired and moustachioed cherub. It was the painterly work of Tim Bruckner, who was at the time an apprentice jeweller working in Beverly Hills and touting his album artwork around, including, fortuitously, to Richard Perry. Bruckner understood exactly what Starr was looking for, noting 'how important humour was to him and his circle of friends. The cherub just seemed like a natural extension of that part of his character ... funny and a little mischievous.'

In the background of the image, multiple figures rendered in comic-book style crowded on a balcony at the rear of the stage; twenty-six of them real (Harrison, Lennon, McCartney, the members of the Band), the others fanciful (Humpty Dumpty, a newspaper-reading bear, the obligatory nun). At the top of the frame, between golden theatrical tragedy/comedy masks, sat a green apple on a pink flag, along with the curved legend 'Duit On Mon Dei' (an in-joke meaning 'do it on Monday' that Nilsson would pilfer for the name of his 1975 album).

Released on 2 November 1973, *Ringo* sailed to number two in the US (held off the top by Elton John's titanic *Goodbye Yellow Brick Road*) and number seven in the UK, with 'Photograph' reaching number one on the *Billboard* Hot 100 the same month. As to the album's virtual reformation of the Beatles, it did in fact prompt the four ex-members to privately discuss the possibility of it happening for real.

'We said, "No",' Ringo later revealed. 'We were taking our own roads now.'

Toasting Starr's success, Lennon sent him a telegram. It read: 'Congratulations. How dare you? And please write me a hit song.'

40

PUT ME IN THE MOVIES, PART FIVE

Starring in
That'll Be the Day, 1972–1973

The scene seemed to follow some kind of dream logic. In it, he found himself back in the smart dress jacket of a bar waiter, just as he'd been as a teenager on the *St Tudno* pleasure steamer sailing between Liverpool and north Wales. Here he was, once again weaving around tables of drinkers, balancing a tray and reproaching a moaning punter with the shirty response, 'Alright, mate, I've only got one pair of hands!'

At the same time, it appeared to be 1960 or '61, not 1956, and he wasn't on a ship, but instead in what looked like the Rock 'N Calypso Ballroom at Butlin's Pwllheli. On the stage, Rory Storm and the Hurricanes were in full flight. Except they were called Stormy Tempest and the Typhoons, and they had a different drummer who, even with his slicked-back hair, looked a lot like Keith Moon. Storm/Tempest meanwhile wore the face of Ron Wycherley, his old schoolmate at Dingle Vale Secondary, who'd subsequently transformed in the late '50s into teen scream idol Billy Fury.

On Ringo's jacket was embroidered the name 'Mike'. His barman pal's coat was meanwhile stitched with 'Jim', even though he appeared to be David Essex, the star of gospel-based hippie stage musical *Godspell*.

'They've been coming here for years, y'know,' Mike told Jim, gesturing towards the band. 'It's the birds,' he explained. 'You should see their chalets.

Like Roman bloody orgies. No future in it though, is there? In being a Typhoon. I mean, where will it get you?'

'No, not smart like us,' Jim sarcastically shot back, flashing his winning, dimpled smile.

Starr was reliving a jumbled-up version of his past in his role as Mike Menary, bar-working holiday camp greaser and incorrigible ladies' man, in *That'll Be the Day*, a late '50s-based coming-of-age movie set to a rollicking soundtrack of old rock 'n' roll hits.

Stranger still, the real Rory Storm had died, aged thirty-four, only three weeks before filming began. After Starr had decamped to the Beatles in the summer of 1962, the two acts had shared stages a few times, before the former band were propelled into the stratosphere and the Hurricanes were left earthbound on the club and dancehall circuit. Rory Storm/Alan Caldwell's infamous antics only intensified in the subsequent years. In 1964, he'd scaled a thirty-foot balcony column at the Majestic Ballroom, taken a tumble and broken his leg. At another show at the Pavilion on New Brighton Pier, he'd climbed on top of the roof during the gig and fallen through a skylight.

That same year of '64, Epstein arranged a deal with Parlophone Records for Storm and the Hurricanes, producing one single, a beat group take on Sondheim and Bernstein's *West Side Story* signature tune, 'America', that opportunistically namechecked the Beatles. When it flopped, Storm retreated back to his hometown. 'He was happy to be the King of Liverpool,' his sister Iris Caldwell stressed.

Still, Alan Caldwell went on to lead a peripatetic life, working as a DJ and water-ski instructor in Benidorm before moving to Jersey and then Amsterdam where, in 1972, he received word that his father had died. Returning to Liverpool while suffering from a debilitating chest infection that was causing insomnia, he one night took sleeping pills, chased them with alcohol, and died of an accidental overdose. Tragically, Caldwell's distraught mother, after discovering his body, is believed to have committed suicide, with a similarly fatal dose of tablets and booze. Their joint funeral was held at Oakvale Congregational Church on 19 October 1972. Starr didn't attend, likely fearing his presence would turn the ceremony into a media circus, although he was reported to have darkly pointed out, 'I wasn't there for his birth, either.'

Filming for *That'll Be the Day* began four days later. In it, Ringo really was acting naturally. Having lived through many of the experiences detailed in the script, now he was re-enacting them in some strange alternate reality.

~

The year 1973 turned out to be a golden one for Starr, with his hit singles and *Ringo* album, and now a successful film. In another serendipitous turn of events, *That'll Be the Day* had itself been inspired by Nilsson's '1941' and its tale of a paternally abandoned lad who runs off to join the circus. Former *Liverpool Daily Post* and then-*London Evening Standard* journalist Ray Connolly (who'd interviewed the Beatles a number of times) was visiting a movie producer friend, David Puttnam, when the latter floated the idea of a film loosely based on the story of the song.

'What if our boy runs off to join a fair?' Puttnam suggested to Connolly.

The journalist was immediately transported back to what he remembered as the 'dangerous glamour' of the visiting fairgrounds he'd spent time in as a youth, with their whirling Waltzers, high-volume rock 'n' roll records, alluring girls and dodgy characters. To his mind, it was a gritty, yet magical time 'just before the Beatles and the '60s changed everything'. In the months to follow, while maintaining his newspaper day job, Connolly wrote the script for *That'll Be the Day* late into the night.

Meanwhile, Puttnam tried to pull together the money to make the film. EMI Films agreed to invest £100,000, with Ronco Records matching that amount in a deal that required at least 40 rock 'n' roll hits to be featured in the soundtrack, with a various artists double album to be subsequently released by the label. An early enthusiast for the project was Keith Moon, at the time similarly imagining a future film career for himself and eyeing up the role of Mike Menary. 'Frankly, if it hadn't been for Keith,' Puttnam recalled, 'I'm not sure we would have got the film together.'

Around the same time, Connolly and Puttnam went to lunch with Starr and Neil Aspinall, juicing them for their memories of Butlin's holiday camps, and began to envisage the former in the role of Menary. Moon further persuaded Starr to take the part, having been promised a role as J.D. Clover, the Ringo-like star drummer in Stormy Tempest and the Typhoons.

On 23 October 1972, shooting began on the Isle of Wight, which at the time still looked pretty much as it had done in the late '50s. Brought in as director was Claude Whatham, who wasn't particularly partial to pop music, but who in 1971 had successfully translated Laurie Lee's 1959 boyhood memoir *Cider with Rosie* to TV. At its heart, *That'll Be the Day* wasn't a rock 'n' roll film anyway. It was about rites of passage, rebellion and the chain of generational hurt.

But in the screenplay for *That'll Be the Day*, the central figure of Jim MacLaine – deserted by his father and ultimately set to leave his own wife and child – was a feckless, disloyal and unfaithful character that Puttnam and Connolly worried might be irredeemably horrible. Enter the twinkly blue-eyed star of *Godspell*.

'It was probably my affection for him that made me able to portray him as a lovable rogue,' David Essex later reckoned, 'even when he became a cheating sex maniac. Claude Whatham was a skilled and helpful director, and any advance nerves I may have had about working with one of the Beatles vanished when Ringo proved easy-going, funny and warm.'

Given the relatively tight film budget, Connolly remembered that the principals involved were all each paid £5,000 (just north of £80,000 today). 'That was a fortune for me at the time,' he noted. 'But, I suspect, rather less of one for Ringo.' Still, it was immediately clear that Starr – who showed up on set in one of his own old Teddy Boy suits – could turn it on and light up the screen. In Connolly's estimation, Ringo was a 'revelation ... we'd no idea he could act so well.'

All of the cast and crew travelled to the Isle of Wight by ferry, except for the characteristically showboating Keith Moon, who arrived by helicopter, noisily landing on the roof of the Shanklin Hotel where everyone was staying and sending the makeshift landing pad of tablecloths flying over onto the beach. 'It's the only way to travel, dear boy,' Moon declared to Essex when he emerged from the chopper. 'I was in my front room in Chertsey twenty minutes ago and now I'm here. Where's the bar?'

With Moon, Starr and a visiting Nilsson in attendance, the partying kicked off, leading to a succession of dusk-to-dawn band jams in the hotel lounge. 'Once or twice,' Essex admitted, 'I found myself creeping onto the set at 5 a.m. after a riotous all-nighter.'

By day, when he wasn't required on set, the relentless prankster that was the Who's drummer often interrupted filming by shouting through a megaphone while hidden in a PA stack.

~

From the minute he first appeared on screen half an hour into the film, wearing a big quiff and sideburns and wandering through a holiday camp alongside David Essex, Ringo was comfortably great in *That'll Be the Day*. Once again, though, his lines were often painfully indicative of the sexist '70s, with their references to 'big knockers' and 'right slags'. To be fair, Mike Menary was supposed to be a lecherous misogynist, but Starr delivered his lines with gusto.

There was elsewhere further poetic licensing of Ringo's past. In one scene where Menary is washing his hair in the sink of his and MacLaine's shared chalet, he drops his white Y-fronts to reveal a love heart tattooed on his arse, inscribed with the word 'Dad'. MacLaine cackles with laughter and Menary explains, 'Ah, it was when I was at sea, wasn't it? Got pissed. Well, I wasn't *actually* at sea. I used to work on the ferries between New Brighton and Liverpool. One night I was out of me skull and me mates talked me into it. Bastards.'

Another scene ran counter to Starr's youthful reputation as a nifty holiday camp groover. Due to his clumsy moves, he and a girl are voted off early in a ballroom dance competition as Stormy Tempest and the Typhoons batter through the Pete Townshend-written 'Long Live Rock'. In terms of character development, meanwhile, as the plot developed, Ringo/Mike Menary proved to have a stronger moral compass than his onscreen sidekick. In one unsettling vignette, MacLaine is seen raping a young teenage girl. 'Pick on someone yer own size,' Menary castigates him.

As its writer, Connolly later apologised for the scene, blaming Whatham's direction. 'My thought when writing it [was] that the girl had been enjoying some heavy petting which had gone too far,' he reasoned, 'and she'd immediately regretted it. Claude had directed it differently.'

From this point on, it's made clear that MacLaine is a horrible individual. Menary find the pair of them work as dodgems operators at a fairground and sneakily teaches his friend a petty scam: waiting to hand hapless punters their change only once the bumper cars are in motion and before they can discover that they've been ripped off for a few shillings.

'For Chrissake, don't pick on anyone in a gang or you've had it,' he tells him, before failing to take his own advice. When Menary is beaten up by a group of thugs seeking retribution, MacLaine watches from the shadows before legging it. Menary is hospitalised, MacLaine steals a better-paid job on the waltzers that had been earmarked for his pal, and at this point Ringo's role is over.

All told, Starr was only onscreen for twenty-five minutes out of the total of ninety. But he nonetheless made a serious actorly impact that more than justified his equal star billing with Essex.

~

On 31 March 1973, while promoting *That'll Be the Day*, Ringo appeared on ITV chat show *Russell Harty Plus*. He was dressed like a Teddy Boy in a black, turquoise-lapelled suit, but looked more like an inelegantly wasted '70s rock star wearing mirrored shades and smoking a cigarette, with the whiff of cocaine and brandy about him.

'Before we start, am I going to be allowed to see your eyeballs?' Harty enquired.

'I just thought you'd like to see how you were looking, y'know,' Ringo responded. 'Don't look at that tie, man.'

'Do you like it?' Harty campily wondered, gesturing to his cream-coloured, black-zigzagged necktie.

'No,' Starr laughed, though not entirely warmly.

The influence of Moon and Nilsson was evident in his conspicuously cocky demeanour, and the ego-inflating effects of his successful solo endeavours were beginning to show.

Twelve days later, the film was released to UK cinemas and quickly proved an enormous, era-defining success. That summer, David Essex had his first hit single, written in his dressing-room downtime at Pinewood Studios during the shoot and inspired by a line that Keith Moon's character J.D. Clover said in the film: 'You've got to be American to write rock 'n' roll songs.' Released in August, the eerie avant-pop 'Rock On' became a key component of the hits soundtrack of 1973 and transformed Essex into a major pop star.

The final scene in the movie – Jim MacLaine quits his wife and child and buys a shiny red semi-acoustic guitar – inevitably led to talk of a sequel, even before the original was released. In it, Starr/Menary was to become the manager of Essex/MacLaine's band, the Stray Cats, guiding their Beatles-like ascension to international phenomenon. Surprising everyone involved, Ringo turned down the role, with singer-turned-actor Adam Faith stepping in as his replacement in 1974's *Stardust*.

'I just don't think it's right for me,' Starr said when the news broke. 'The follow-up is David Essex making it as a star. I've done that in reality and I don't want to go through all that torment again.'

He also pointed out that he believed cinemagoers had managed to suspend their disbelief when he was onscreen in *That'll Be the Day*. 'People tended to forget about Ringo and the Beatles,' he stressed. 'I don't think that would happen with the follow-up because it is a musical. People will keep relating to the musical situation.'

In addition, perhaps too close to the bone was the *Stardust* scene in which Menary sacks a key member of the band just before they go supernova, echoing the sad tale of Pete Best. But Ringo ultimately boiled his reluctance down to one simple explanation. 'I couldn't face Beatlemania again,' he said, revealing that he was in some ways still reeling from the trauma of that intense and life-changing experience.

At the time going through his own brief phase of 'Essexmania', his co-star could relate. Although contractually obliged to make the film, he had his own reservations about portraying the doomed MacLaine's rock 'n' roll burnout on the screen in *Stardust*. 'I could see why Ringo couldn't face making this movie,' Essex empathically pointed out.

'It was his loss, I think,' concluded Ray Connolly of Starr's decision. 'He could certainly act.'

41

PUT ME IN THE MOVIES, PART SIX

Son of Dracula, 1972–1974

Having made the best film of his career, Ringo immediately followed it with possibly his worst, ominously billed on its poster as 'The First Rock-and-Roll Dracula Movie!'.

Two long years in its tangled development, filming for the movie that started life with the working title of *Count Downe* had actually begun only three months after the end of the recording of *Son of Schmilsson*, in the August of '72. Following his directing debut with *Born to Boogie*, Starr, in his position as head honcho of Apple Films, wanted to try his hand as a producer, while at the same time starring in a light-hearted rock/horror caper. For his co-star, he imagined Harry Nilsson taking on a lead vampiric role.

Starr called Nilsson to tell him about his idea and Harry immediately said, 'Did you see the picture?'

Ringo said, 'What picture?'

Weirdly, he wasn't aware that Harry had already posed as Dracula, atop a stone staircase at George Harrison's neo-Gothic Henley-on-Thames mansion, Friar Park, for the sleeve image of *Son of Schmilsson*, released that July. Starr saw it as a 'freaky' sign of serendipity. 'You just couldn't argue with that coincidence,' he said.

Yet, the retitled *Son of Dracula* was to wait until 1974 for its almost comically limited cinematic release. Years later, Ringo would jokily point out, 'in

America, the movie only played in towns that had one cinema. Because if it had two, no matter what was on down the road, they'd all go there...'

Starr's main motivation for sinking a reported $800,000 of his own money into *Son of Dracula* was his desire to get his hands dirty with the day-to-day business of filmmaking. He involved himself in the casting sessions, held meetings with the technicians and generally tried to oversee every aspect of the production. 'I wanted to make the film in England,' he pointed out, 'because it's easier to learn at home.'

Ringo explained its simple, if shaky premise as involving his belief that if Dracula 'were around today, he'd be into rock'. The blood-sucking count was to be supported by a cast of random horror archetypes, and a significant mythical magician not previously known to have frequented Transylvania in the late nineteenth century. Ringo said, 'we've got the whole family in this one – Frankenstein, the Mummy, the Wolf Man, and me as Merlin'.

Essentially, *Son of Dracula* was to be a continuation of his and Harry's drinking and drugging and messing around, but this time at not inconsiderable expense and with wobbly cinematic ambition. Perhaps inevitably, its production was to fall foul of poor organisation and general intoxicated chaos.

By the end, it was hard to work out who exactly was in charge of the making of *Son of Dracula*. Ringo and Harry's buddy, ex-Monkee Micky Dolenz, likened it to a 'situation where there was really nobody driving the train. Everybody was in the cars, partying.'

～

To start off with, during the production planning, Starr made a seemingly wise choice in employing as the film's director Freddie Francis, the British-born, Oscar-winning cinematographer and director of various horror flicks for Hammer Productions. The screenwriter was to be the less likely figure of bit-part English actress Jennifer Jayne (most notably the co-star, alongside gurning comedian Norman Wisdom, in the 1962 British comedy film *On the Beat*). Jayne was at the time only just branching out into writing horror scripts, under the pseudonym of Jay Fairbank, and so brought with her almost zero experience.

In his deal with Apple Films, Nilsson was to be given no upfront monetary fee. Instead, the company agreed to have his rickety teeth fixed at their expense. Harry was self-conscious about his mouth and there were inevitably to be various fangs-focused close-ups. Starr was to later quip that Nilsson's mother 'was always thankful' for his footing the bill for her son's high-end dentistry.

When Jayne/Fairbank's script was ready, it involved a hazy, half-realised plot. In it, following the murder of Count Dracula in Transylvania, Nilsson, as his heir Count Downe, is called to London by family counsel Merlin (Ringo in black cloak over a flowing magical purple gown, with long, grey hair and matching beard). There, Downe is set to be coronated as the new King of the Netherworld. But, as it transpires, Downe doesn't possess a full vampiric DNA, his mother being a human. He proceeds to indulge in a spot of the old neck-biting in night-time London, but is clearly going through the motions. Later, he will choose to undergo an operation to remove his fangs and render him forever de-vampirised, having fallen in love with the alluring Amber (horror cult star Suzanna Leigh).

Filming began in London in the summer of '72, with band scenes for various musical numbers shot at Tramp nightclub (a rollicking 'At My Front Door' featuring Led Zeppelin's John Bonham on drums) and at Surrey Docks in south-east London. For the latter takes on 'Jump into the Fire' and 'Daybreak', Keith Moon was behind the kit as part of a motley troupe (the Count Downes) involving Klaus Voormann, Peter Frampton and Rolling Stones brass players Bobby Keys and Jim Price. Inevitably, the shoots involved hefty bar bills. 'It was costing £1,000 for booze,' Starr recalled. 'They were all gone.'

But the party atmosphere was quickly deflated by strict film union rules. 'Such a headache,' Ringo the producer moaned. 'Everyone shouts at you. I didn't know that if you didn't get the crew home and in their beds by midnight, you couldn't work them the next day. I'm a musician. If we start working and it starts to cook, we'll keep it rolling for three days if necessary.'

To be fair, the crew likely weren't fuelled by the same intoxicants as the musicians-turned-actors. One evening, after a day's filming, former Apple PA Chris O'Dell (now working for the Rolling Stones) found Starr and Nilsson at the Savile Row office typically overindulging. 'Music was playing, the lamps were lit,' she remembered, 'and the coke was laid out in lines on the desk.'

There was certainly a wired, nocturnal energy to parts of *Son of Dracula*. Not least when Harry, in his spooky cloak, heads out on late-night manoeuvres through London's West End to the soundtrack accompaniment of a mad, echoing drum solo, comically stopping short when he sees a copy of *Son of Schmilsson* in a record shop window. It was only when Nilsson had to deliver his lines that he came unstuck, his acting style a weird mix of laid-back and wooden. Starr was better in his role as the sagacious Merlin, given that he had pages and pages of lines to deliver, even if they mostly involved faux-mystical guff.

Voormann, in his other role as a visual artist, was tasked with creating a brief animated sequence involving Nilsson's transformation into a blue cartoon bat. Later, he would cringe at the memory. 'They wanted a bat that flies into the graveyard and sits on a gravestone,' he recalled. 'I mean, it was ridiculous in the first place. Bats can't sit. They can only hang.'

'So, I did this animated piece. I said, "You have to do it really slow." And in the film, it just *pyyooooo*, flew through. I mean, the whole film was a joke, just a joke. But it was big fun, I must admit.'

Perhaps this was the crux of the problem: *Son of Dracula* looked like far more fun to be involved with than to actually sit through. As it progressed, its plot grew ever thicker and more impenetrable. No one watching had to be as stoned as the film's participants to feel entirely lost.

~

One of the reasons why *Son of Dracula* ended up being such a mess was because its exasperated director quit before the movie was completed. 'I said, "Ringo, look, I'm ill at the moment. You better cut the film yourself",' Freddie Francis recalled. 'He had made it with a lot of his friends and of that, the least said the better.'

On the face of it, *Son of Dracula* was really no worse than some of the horror movies of the era. Shonky, slow and disjointed, for sure, but with the added bonuses of its rocking interludes. Illustrative of its mad ambition was the film's premiere, staged in Atlanta, Georgia on 19 April 1974: the first movie to be formally unveiled in the city since *Gone with the Wind* thirty-five years before. The evening involved a hoopla of hot-air balloons and hearses and even a horror-themed make-up competition. Reviewers, however, remained distinctly unimpressed, with one stating that the film 'had about as much appeal as a dubbed Mexican monster movie'.

'It's like a non-musical, non-horror, non-comedy comedy,' Ringo tried to explain. 'Or it's a horror-horror, musical-musical, comedy-comedy.'

In the end, the only lasting thing about *Son of Dracula* was its music, which proved to be worth the price of admission alone. An accompanying soundtrack album was to be the only release on Rapple Records (a one-time contractual melding of Harry's label RCA and Apple), and in the shape of the grooving 'Daybreak', it produced a US top-forty hit for Nilsson.

Much like *200 Motels*, *Son of Dracula* was destined for late-night and typically drugged viewers, albeit far fewer of them than for Ringo's previous movie for the 'heads'. Undeterred, Starr and Nilsson immediately began plotting another film: a mixture of live action and animation tellingly to be titled *Harry and Ringo's Night Out*. Its *Yellow Submarine*-ish plot was to involve the pair being transported to Rockland, a parallel realm where music was dying and where our dynamic duo arrive to save it. Along the way, they would be joined by cartoon sidekicks, the Tim Bruckner-sketched, moustachioed cherub who'd appeared on the cover of the *Ringo* LP and a wiseass crow.

Animators moonlighting from Hanna-Barbera were duly employed, live-action scenes were shot on a sound stage at Paramount in Los Angeles and a three-minute-long taster was cut together. There were, however, to be no takers at the studios willing to gamble on the enterprise and the project was shelved.

Meanwhile, Ringo didn't seem to be able to let go of *Son of Dracula*. In an attempt to salvage it from the skip of cinematic history, he employed Monty Python's Graham Chapman, along with his sometime co-writers Bernard McKenna and Douglas Adams (later to find enduring fame as the creator of *The Hitchhiker's Guide to the Galaxy*), to redraft the script.

'We went into a studio and revoiced a lot of it,' Starr noted. 'So it makes even less sense now.'

Ultimately, Ringo was to offer a characteristically no-nonsense appraisal of *Son of Dracula*. 'It's not the best film ever made,' he reasoned. 'But I've seen worse.'

42

UFOS OVER NEW YORK AND LA

Pussy Cats and
Goodnight Vienna, 1974

'**W**here's Ono?'

'She's sucking Ringo's cock!'

The drunken heckler was asking for it. But all that anyone would ever remember was John Lennon's jaw-dropping, X-rated response. In full sight and earshot of everyone packed tight around the tables in the 500-capacity Troubadour club in West Hollywood – including supercool movie idol Paul Newman, porn star Linda Lovelace, comedian Lily Tomlin and blaxploitation heroine Pam Grier – a Beatle was having a meltdown.

It was the evening of Tuesday 12 March 1974 and onstage were the Smothers Brothers, the struggling sibling musical comedy duo, hoping tonight to revive something of their '60s TV career with this comeback Hollywood show. Lennon, drunkenly aided and egged on by Harry Nilsson, really wasn't helping. On the table in front of the pair sat umpteen Brandy Alexanders – fast-curdling cocktails of milk and alcohol. Both were necking them like lemonade, while Lennon's girlfriend, the teetotal May Pang, sat there squirming.

'Hey, Smothers Brothers … fuck a cow!' Lennon barked at the stage.

Tommy and Dick Smothers' act depended on timing and it was being wrecked. The pair's manager, Ken Fritz, wandered over to Lennon's table, put his hand on his shoulder in gentle reproach and *boom*. The Beatle was up on his feet, glasses flying from his face, throwing half-blind punches in every direction.

Even after Lennon's party were thrown out onto the street, he carried on ranting and flailing, clearly hammered and demented.

'Don't you know who I am?' he slurrily snapped at a car-parking attendant. 'I'm Ed Sullivan!'

Lennon had been in Los Angeles since the autumn of '73, his marriage to Ono on the rocks after his similarly loud and drunken sex act with a random girl at a party the previous year on the night that Richard Nixon was depressingly re-elected for a second term. In a rash attempt to control his extra-marital urges, Yoko had pushed John in the direction of May, at the time the couple's personal assistant.

'We were together for *twenty-six* hours a day,' Ono later reasoned. 'I thought that he needed some kind of freedom which he didn't get because ... we were always together. Maybe that would lead to a situation where we might totally separate, y'know ... This might be the end of John and Yoko. I had that in my mind. I thought that could happen.

'He's gonna go to LA, he's gonna have fun ... why come back to me, y'know?' she added with a slightly nervous laugh. 'I thought, *If we're only together because we're scared of losing each other, that's not what we want.*'

While Ono was dangerously stress-testing the couple's marriage, her husband effectively reverted to his teenage Teddy Boy days: drinking way too much, starting fights and throwing himself back into the arms of his beloved rock 'n' roll. To that end, he'd half-made a sozzled covers album with Phil Spector at the tail end of the previous year, which remained uncompleted after the unhinged producer, wildly snorting ampules of amyl nitrate, had shot a bullet into the ceiling of a control room at the Record Plant West. The sessions finally collapsed when Spector stole the tapes, telling everyone they'd been destroyed in a fire.

And now here was John with Harry, being chucked out of the Troubadour. The next day, blurry shots of an out-of-it Beatle being ejected onto the Santa Monica Boulevard sidewalk made the papers. 'That ruined my reputation,' Nilsson later lamented. 'Get one Beatle drunk and look what happens.'

In truth, it was more than one Beatle that Harry was encouraging to become a hopeless pisshead. Ringo, too, was soon to descend into this messy Californian madness.

Ten days after the uproar at the Troubadour, Nilsson, Lennon and Pang moved into a Santa Monica beach house rented for Harry by his label, RCA. Then, Ringo, Keith Moon and Klaus Voormann moved in too. Lennon, nothing if not pragmatic and driven, even in this period when he was regularly wasted, wanted to corral his friends into making an album together.

'Seeing as we're stuck in this bottle of vodka together, we might as well try and do something,' he reasoned.

In the six months since he'd arrived in Los Angeles, Lennon had been living off favours. With his royalties tied up in the tangled affairs of Apple, and his $3,000 monthly stipend from the company (received by each Beatle) going to Ono, he'd embarked upon his Californian adventure with a $10,000 loan from Capitol Records organised for him by lawyer Harold Seider. Effectively he and Pang had been forced into an elevated level of sofa surfing, initially borrowing Seider's duplex in West Hollywood before relocating to producer Lou Adler's house in Bel Air and then the upstairs bedroom of Starr's rented duplex at the Beverly Wilshire.

When John told Ringo he was planning to produce an album for Harry and invited him to get involved, Starr told him, 'I wouldn't miss this for the world.' Moon agreed, and so did Jim Keltner. For the album that was to be the notorious, if innocuously titled *Pussy Cats*, they had three drummers.

Lennon thought it would be a great idea for them all (apart from the already LA resident Keltner) to share the beach house. 'There should be an asylum somewhere for aged rock 'n' rollers,' he told Pang. 'Then we can all be put in padded cells where we belong. Let's open an asylum. We should all rent a house and live together. Then we can watch Harry, save money and make sure all the musicians get to the studio on time when we start to work on Harry's album.'

It was a fine plan, in theory. The five-bedroomed house was set over two levels and so there was plenty space for them all. Downstairs was a large kitchen, and a dining room walled with mirrors. The bedrooms were upstairs: Lennon and Pang took the master, with Moon settling in next door. Down the corridor, and around the bend, appropriately enough, was Harry's room, with Klaus Voormann and Ringo's mercurial business manager Hilary Gerrard squeezed into smaller spaces elsewhere.

Starr had asked for an en-suite room, so he was installed in what was originally a library, converted into a bedroom. On the wall above his mattress sat a framed photograph of John F. Kennedy in the Oval Office in 1962, with his toddler son JFK Jr under his feet, peeking through the kneehole hatch in the Resolute desk.

Ringo's day-to-day – but mostly night-to-night – existence during his time in Santa Monica was virtually vampiric. He kept the blinds in his room permanently closed, which prompted Pang to nickname it the 'den of darkness'. Harry and Ringo, when they eventually rose in the late morning, or early afternoon, typically arrived at breakfast in bathrobes and shades. 'Daylight hurts,' Starr was heard to groan more than once.

The JFK photograph in his room was in fact a reference to another, albeit furtive previous resident of the beach house. The house had been built originally by MGM movie head Louis B. Mayer and was now owned by actor Peter Lawford, best known for his role in the original *Oceans 11* alongside Frank Sinatra and Dean Martin. Lawford had been brother-in-law to the Kennedy brothers and reputedly arranged for JFK's secret trysts with Marilyn Monroe to take place at the beach house.

'So, this was where they did it … Kennedy and Marilyn,' Nilsson told Lennon and Pang when he first showed them their deluxe bedroom.

Tuning into the vibes, Lennon was to develop a genuine belief that Monroe's ghost still haunted the rooms and that her spirit woke him up every morning. In true 'wow, man' fashion, all of them eventually agreed that it could only be Marilyn's spectre that was responsible.

Often in the evenings, many of the household's musicians – Lennon, Starr, Nilsson, Moon – joined Alice Cooper, and his pals Micky Dolenz and Elton John's songwriting collaborator Bernie Taupin, at the Rainbow Bar and Grill on Sunset Strip, collectively giving themselves the gang name the Hollywood Vampires. Their general aim was to outdrink one another until the last man was standing.

'Who was the most dangerous?' Taupin later wondered. 'Well, I suppose everybody would gravitate to Keith Moon. Harry Nilsson could be a bit overbearing when he was under the influence. But the playing field was levelled by our connection with each other. They were all people that were incredibly popular at the time, but also possibly on a slump. Y'know, their huge amount of fame … there was a slight downslope. But the interesting thing is that they were all really intelligent people who acted like ten-year-olds for a period of time.'

Lennon put it even better, likening this generally legless rabble to 'a teenage gang … even though we were thirty'.

~

At the end of the first session for *Pussy Cats* at Burbank Studios on 28 March 1974, Ringo left at around midnight to paint Tinseltown red. When he returned to the studio the next day, he noticed someone had moved his kit around. 'Who's been fiddling with my drums?' he wondered aloud.

It had been none other than Paul McCartney, who'd dropped by the sessions with Linda, unannounced, after Ringo had gone. Lennon and McCartney hadn't shared a recording space since *Abbey Road*, almost four years before, and this drunken, coked-out scene was to be setting for their inauspicious reunion, as part of a woozy jam with the other musicians and their associates who happened to be hanging out.

Lennon got behind an electric piano while McCartney settled down behind Ringo's kit, and they were joined by Harry (providing ragged backing vocals), Mal Evans and May (shaking tambourines) and Linda (playing hesitant organ), along with guitarist Jesse Ed Davis, Bobby Keys on sax and even Stevie Wonder, who'd been working in a neighbouring studio.

Sadly, the sound they collectively produced was a near-cacophonic mess, given the state of the participants. Together, they bashed through a selection of random cover songs – 'Lucille', 'Stand by Me', 'Cupid' – sounding like a band locked up in the drunk tank for the night. Almost two decades later, the shocking results were bootlegged under the all-too-fitting title of *A Toot and a Snore in '74*.

'I'm afraid it was a rather heady session, shall we say,' McCartney confessed. 'I don't think it was very good. I mean, that is kinda proof really that [a Beatles reunion] wouldn't necessarily have been great.'

'Paul chose to play drums,' reckoned Jimmy Iovine, the future Interscope Records and Beats Electronics boss who was the assistant engineer on the sessions, 'because he was alert enough to say, "This is not how the Beatles are getting back together". He was the one in the room who you could see got it.'

This monumentally significant yet decrepit jam session set the tone for the days that followed, as the *Pussy Cats* sessions quickly ran into trouble. Nilsson, chain-smoking and going even heavier than usual on the liquor and cocaine, was secretly trying to hide the extent of the damage he'd done to his throat. His previously flute-like singing tone had been reduced to a croak. In between takes, he was escaping to the bathroom to spit blood. There were even fresh red spots of it on the microphone.

Nilsson confided in Micky Dolenz who drove him to the hospital, where Harry was diagnosed with a ruptured vocal cord. He was advised not to sing, or even speak, for two weeks, but instead called Dolenz to come pick him up, insisting, 'Get me out of here. Bring me a bottle of brandy and cigarettes.' Micky agreed to the brandy, but not the smokes. 'And he walked out in a green robe,' Dolenz disbelievingly recalled. 'Just "Fuck it, give me a cigarette."'

Lennon had realised that Nilsson's voice was shot but initially blamed his throat problems on anxiety, caused by the unspoken pressure of the fact that 'I was producing him ... Harry didn't tell me 'til the end of the album that he was coughing up blood.'

Back at Burbank Studios, the party continued. But, on the deceptively jaunty 'All My Life', with Starr and Keltner cooking up gentle Caribbean rhythms behind him, and Moon clip-clopping on wood blocks, Nilsson seemed to renounce his hard-living ways and determine to change. But it was a different track that was to bottle the potent spirit of *Pussy Cats*: a turbo-charged zoom through Bill Haley's 'Rock Around the Clock' featuring all three drummers battering away at the same time, before they stopped and then clattered back in for an insanely paced finale.

'We were so crazy, man,' Keltner admits now. 'That was a really insane period in our lives. All of us, y'know, the producers, the engineers, the players ... all of us. It was a crazy time.'

Messily illustrating this was the photo montage that featured in the gatefold sleeve artwork of the *Pussy Cats* LP: multiple shots of the stoned musicians pulling daft faces in the studio, but also one frame of Nilsson having his throat examined by 'Dr. Eddie Kantor' and another of him lying on a hospital bed, his hand supportively held by a grinning Starr wearing shades. Another Burbank Studios picture blatantly showed Ringo sniffing – or snorting from – the back of Harry's hand. On the front cover of the album, meanwhile, John and Harry's faces appeared on the bodies of puppet cats in a miniature playhouse. Under a table in front of them lay one building block featuring the letter 'D', then a rug, then a block with the letter 'S': a daft, subversive code for 'drugs'.

With good reason, Lennon nicknamed the Los Angeles of 1974 'Lost Arseholes'. As if to underline the point, when Starr guested on the KROQ radio show hosted by former Mothers of Invention singers Flo & Eddie (who had been his co-stars in Zappa's *200 Motels*), he turned up plastered, with Moon in tow, and proceeded to say 'fuck' fourteen times in the first minute-and-a-half of airtime. The hosts, and their producer, were duly fired and complaints from listeners led to an investigation by the Federal Communications Commission regulator that ultimately led nowhere.

Everyone was spaced out, in more ways than one. In 'The Flying Saucer Song', an outtake from *Pussy Cats*, Nilsson played the parts of two drunks sitting at a bar, one of them reading the other an unnamed poem involving a mysterious ball of fire shooting across the night sky. He then proceeded to garble on about another guy he'd met who'd told him a tale about his experience with what he believed to be a UFO that had landed in a field. The multi-harmony choruses of the song had our befuddled narrator confessing that he identified with both phenomena: he's 'alive with a fire' and his life 'streaks across the span of time'. It was the closest that Nilsson came to confessing his apparent death wish and mission to burn brightly, but perhaps not for long; his aim to help others 'through the long, dark night'.

The mock conversation then dissolved into a sweary argument, before Harry again, as a narked bartender, entered the dialogue and warned the pair to quit their cussing.

'I wish I could think of a joke to tell you,' said the chief drunk, attempting to pacify his drinking partner. 'What are some of Ringo's jokes?'

'You mean Ringo Starr?' said the bartender, his interest suddenly piqued. 'Hey, you guys aren't who I think you are, are you? Uh… you ever gonna get back together?'

~

From the summer of '74 and into the autumn, UFOs seemed to be on everyone's gently warped minds, as their preoccupations turned towards the extra-terrestrial.

By the time *Pussy Cats* was released in August, and before it made its swift, hits-free journey to record shop bargain bins, Lennon and Pang had escaped Los Angeles and returned to New York. Since July, they'd been renting an apartment on the twelfth floor of the Southgate building on East 52nd St in Manhattan, living opposite diplomat Henry Kissinger and a minute's walk down the street from sequestered movie star Greta Garbo.

On the night of Friday 23 August, after returning from the Record Plant East, the studio where he was making his slick comeback album *Walls and Bridges*, Lennon stood on his rooftop balcony, naked in the dark, smoking. What happened next, he could never quite explain.

He was looking over towards the East River when he saw flashing lights. Then a huge object sailed over his head. 'It was oval-shaped,' he later attested, 'flying left to right with red lights on top.'

Lennon yelled for Pang, who was in the apartment on the phone, ordering a pizza. 'You're seeing what I'm seeing?' he incredulously asked her.

'There was no two ways about it,' Pang insisted years later when recalling the experience. 'This thing was floating above us. I was screaming.' The couple watched the UFO move slowly down the path of the East River and hover above one of the four towers of the newly built Waterside Plaza almost thirty blocks to the south. It then headed in the direction of the Williamsburg Bridge and shot up into the darkness. 'This thing is flying at different angles for a good solid fifteen minutes,' Pang said, 'and then I watched it go right up into the clouds.'

'I hadn't been drinking,' Lennon swore. 'This is the God's honest truth.'

Before the flying object disappeared, Pang managed to snap a few frames of it on her camera. The next day, the pair handed the film to their photographer friend Bob Gruen, who discovered 'there was not a single picture on the entire roll'. Gruen asked Lennon if he'd called anyone else to tell them about the unexplained phenomenon.

'I can't call the newspapers, say "I'm John Lennon, and I just saw a flying saucer",' he rightly pointed out. Gruen offered to phone the *Daily News* and was told that 'one or two people' on the east side of Manhattan had reported strange sightings. With no further explanation forthcoming, Lennon did the only thing he could. He left a cryptic message about his strange experience in the lyric insert of *Walls and Bridges*: 'On the 23rd Aug. 1974 at 9 o'clock I saw a UFO.'

On a different rooftop three months later and almost 3,000 miles away, Ringo, dressed in a purple/blue spacesuit adorned with a silver-mirrored star motif on his chest, stood on the lip of a grey flying saucer, waving, as if he'd just returned from being abducted. An oblique homage to the alien character Klaatu from the 1951 sci-fi film *The Day the Earth Stood Still*, it was the final scene in a minute-long TV spot for his new solo album, *Goodnight Vienna*, the follow-up to *Ringo*.

The advertisement's action began with Ringo playing a military snare drum amid a marching band, in the street at the intersection of Hollywood and Vine, before the sizeable if clearly theatrical prop UFO landed on the road, wobbling on a visible wire. Starr sauntered inside, some comedy smoke engulfed the spaceship and, in the next shot, it was shown being hoisted high into the air via a hidden crane, before landing on the top of Capitol Records' circular thirteen-storey headquarters.

In a voiceover later added – and as a favour returned to Starr after he'd voiced the TV ad for *Walls and Bridges* upon its release in September – Lennon touted Ringo's latest long-player.

'Is that Ringo Starr advertising his new album *Goodnight Vienna* on Apple Records and Tapes?' he began.

'It certainly is, John,' Starr chipped in.

'Why, you look so wonderful,' Lennon responded.

Lennon had a vested interest in the album since he'd written its title track, a thumping pop-rocker the name of which could be interpreted as meaning 'it's all over' or, even, 'that's all, folks'. The song's lyric, involving some edgy, surreal party, sounded like a kiss-off to Los Angeles and that whole blurry and dangerous phrase. Mirroring Nilsson's abstention-vowing 'All My Life' from *Pussy Cats*, elsewhere on the record Starr sang – and as a single took to US number three – Hoyt Axton and David Jackson's 'No No Song', in which our narrator, in a treacherously ropey Jamaican accent, renounces weed, cocaine and whisky. Like Harry's 'going clean' song, it was a groovy tune, but deliberately tongue-in-cheek – and barely credible in terms of the pair's actual lifestyles.

On the same day the TV ad shoot wrapped, a second film crew led by BBC director Stanley Dorfman arrived to film a promo for Ringo's gently bewitching version of the Platters' 'Only You (And You Alone)', a cover originally suggested by Lennon and softly haunted in this new recorded version by Nilsson's cooing, multi-layered harmonies. In the clip, the pair were depicted on the roof at Capitol: Ringo in his space get-up, singing into a microphone (and at one point with a joke-shop arrow shot through his head), while Nilsson played to type, sporting a bathrobe, in shades and baseball cap, smoking a cigarette while reading an issue of music biz trade rag *Radio & Records* featuring Ringo on the cover.

As night fell over Hollywood, and with the film in the can, the assembled inevitably ended up arsing around up on the roof. To entertain the people who'd gathered below, Starr agreed to have high-intensity spotlight beams trained on the mirrored star on his costume, and he lit up the sky for miles around.

Ringo's starlight was surprisingly far-reaching and there were reports of strange rays in the heavens for hundreds of miles outside the Los Angeles area. He'd ended up becoming an unexplained phenomenon all of his own.

43

THE LOVE YOU MAKE

Tangled Affairs, 1973–1994

hree days after the cash-strapped John Lennon had first landed in Los Angeles with May Pang in the September of 1973, back in England, the sale of his and Ono's Tittenhurst Park estate in Berkshire had gone through, after the property had been on the market for only a week. The buyer was none other than Ringo. The Starkeys were on the move again.

For Lennon, money worries were always rumbling away in the background. Until April of that year, like Starr and Harrison, he'd remained contracted to manager Allen Klein, until a slow drip of bad reality had made the three slowly come to accept that, as John reluctantly put it, 'possibly Paul's suspicions were right' about the shifty businessman who was continuing to look after their affairs. Klein's activities were opaque at best and murky at worst, and the trio's independent accountants were warning them that their finances remained in worryingly messy shape.

Klein had been good for Starr in some ways – in particular, by bagging him an above-average $150,000 (close to two million dollars in 2025) for his role in *Blindman*. Yet he'd grown increasingly elusive, even on one occasion pointedly avoiding a call from Ringo. Klein had only seconds before been on the phone to someone else in the same room as Starr. It was unthinkable to blank a Beatle, especially if you were supposed to be his chief representative.

In the end, all three refused to renew their management agreement with Klein and their contract was terminated on 2 April, the same day that the *Red* and *Blue* double LP Beatles compilations were released. Lennon remained in hock to the manager, however, due to unpaid loans, and the sale of Tittenhurst was believed to have been necessary to finally pay him off.

John, though, liked the idea of keeping Tittenhurst within the Beatle family. 'I've talked to Ringo a lot recently,' he told one reporter in September, 'because he's just moved into my house at Ascot, which is nice because I've always got a bedroom there.'

~

Two days before Christmas 1973, the Starkeys threw a little night-time soiree at Tittenhurst. George and Pattie Harrison were invited, as was Chris O'Dell, visiting from the States. Almost everyone was sat around the long, twelve-foot table in the kitchen: George and Ringo on one bench, Pattie and Chris opposite them. Maureen flitted around, serving food and topping up their drinks. The Starkeys' three children – Zak, now eight, his younger brother, Jason, six, and their three-year-old sister, Lee – were asleep upstairs.

It was nearing midnight when George picked up a guitar, began strumming away, then turned to Ringo and bluntly told him, 'I'm in love with your wife.'

There followed absolute silence.

'I think all five hearts in that kitchen stopped beating for a few seconds,' O'Dell recalled.

Starr stared down at the table and flicked the ash from his cigarette. O'Dell noticed that his jaw was clenched and that a muscle at the side of his mouth began twitching. No one said anything for a further few seconds, then Ringo looked at George and, in a steady tone, said, 'Better you than someone we don't know.'

Everyone was thrown into shock, but Pattie was humiliated by her husband's impulsive confession, even if her marriage to George was already in trouble, not least due to both Eric Clapton and Ronnie Wood determinedly wooing her during the period. She later remembered that, having maintained a calm exterior, Ringo quickly grew agitated, working himself up into a 'terrible state' and repeatedly muttering, 'Nothing is real … nothing is real', unwittingly echoing the words of 'Strawberry Fields Forever' in his distress.

Seven years later in 1980, Maureen cagily spoke of the incident in a rare interview. 'I was totally stunned,' she offered. 'He just … said it. It was a very difficult time. And even inasmuch as ... because I believe, whatever, but up until that point, I didn't know that it was...' She didn't need to say 'love'.

In truth, George and Maureen's fling had been going on for some time. Pattie's suspicions were first aroused when she returned from a weekend break in Devon with her sister Jenny to discover Maureen had stayed over at the Harrisons' Friar Park home and was now unabashedly wearing a necklace that George had given to her as a gift. On another occasion, she discovered the pair had locked themselves inside one of the many bedrooms at the mansion. She thumped on the door, shouting, 'What are you doing? Maureen's in there, isn't she?' Harrison opened the door and laughed, saying, 'Oh yeah, she's just a bit tired, so she's lying down.'

Pattie said that this discovery didn't seem to deter Maureen and she'd brazenly turn up at midnight at Friar Park 'to listen to George in the studio'. In her anger and frustration, Pattie called Ringo, pointedly asking him, 'Have you ever thought about why your wife doesn't come home at night? It's because she's here!' Starr apparently exploded with rage.

At the same time, having been together with her Richy for eleven years and married to him for more than eight, Maureen wasn't daft. Ringo had been a Beatle, with legions of girls throwing themselves at him. She, like the other Beatle wives, had been forced to silently accept some infidelity on the part of their worshipped husbands. But nothing had been overt, or close to home.

When she'd arrived in England for the Christmas holidays that year, Chris O'Dell had been surprised by the virtually open canoodling going on at Friar Park. Pattie and Ronnie Wood paired off, being 'childlike and playful', while George and Maureen were 'private and intense, sitting close together, obviously having an intimate conversation'. Harrison was clearly besotted with Starr's wife and, over those weeks, he also declared his love for her more discreetly by writing a song (destined for his 1975 album *Extra Texture*) plainly titled 'Can't Stop Thinking About You'.

Confirmation of George and Maureen's affair was, for Pattie, 'the final straw' that broke the back of their marriage. The news of this intra-Beatle bed-hopping was to stun others within their friendship group, too. Lennon, in his jagged analysis, deemed it to be 'virtual incest'.

Somehow, Ringo and Maureen's marriage – and Starr and Harrison's friendship – survived, and they all tried to move on.

Still, one of the main drivers behind Ringo's decision to split for Los Angeles early in 1974 was to escape the awkwardness and tensions of his domestic life back in Britain. Maureen had called Chris O'Dell in advance of his arrival, warning her that 'Richy's freaking out ... he's still really upset about everything ... says he just can't cope.' She asked her to look after him in LA.

In the weeks that followed, the pair hung out together: going to see Bob Dylan at the Forum on Valentine's Day, and visiting Lennon at the Record Plant West where he was producing a funky solo version of Holland/Dozier/Holland's 'Too Many Cooks (Spoil the Soup)' for Mick Jagger. At the studio, with the music pumping and the whisky flowing, O'Dell and Starr felt a growing attraction.

In her 2009 memoir, *Miss O'Dell*, she remembered thinking to herself that night, 'Sorry, Mo, I just can't help the feelings.' At one point, twinkle-toed Richy Starkey, his moves shaped and sharpened long ago on the faraway dancefloors of Butlin's, asked her to dance.

'That's when it happened,' O'Dell recalled. 'I saw into his eyes for the first time. It was as if two wires suddenly connected, sending an electrical jolt of attraction right through me.'

Later that night, after a detour to a weirdly flat party at Roman Polanski's house where the host lay in bed draped in girls and had not even bothered to get up when Starr arrived, they sat together on a sofa, gazed out over a view of the LA skyline and, as O'Dell put it, 'talked for three hours, or was it four or five?'. Back at the Beverly Wilshire, they watched the sun rise from Ringo's balcony before he disappeared into the bedroom and swiftly fell asleep. O'Dell, a touch confused, left and drove home.

Starr called her three hours later, saying, 'What happened to you?' and invited her for lunch at, of all places, Roger Moore's house, where the pair arrived hellishly hungover and struggled through the stiffly polite proceedings. That afternoon, they returned together to the Beverly Wilshire, fell into bed and, according to O'Dell, 'immediately conked out'. But that was that. They were together.

～

When Starr temporarily moved with the rest of the *Pussy Cats* mob into the beach house in Santa Monica, O'Dell followed, taking up residence in the Kennedy portrait den with her new, semi-secret beau. Quickly, though, the accompanying guilt that came with their affair began to eat into their thoughts and affect their day-to-day relationship – especially when Maureen called the house one day to speak to O'Dell. Ringo was busy at the time in another room playing poker with his booze and drug buddies.

'I think Richy is seeing someone there,' Maureen told Chris, without revealing the details of her suspicions.

'Gosh, Maureen... I don't know of anything going on out here,' O'Dell fibbed.

The next thing, Maureen was on a plane over to California. O'Dell initially tried to avoid her calls, before finally picking up and agreeing to visit the couple at the Beverly Wilshire duplex that Starr had kept on in the interim. She arrived wracked with guilt and anxiety. Maureen poured her a drink and, as Ringo got up from the sofa and stood nervously looking out of the window, she asked her, 'Are you sleeping with my husband?'

'I told the truth,' O'Dell revealed. 'How could I not tell the truth?'

Two days later, their friendship surprisingly undamaged by the revelation, Maureen called Chris in the middle of the night, speaking in a whisper and asking if she could come over to see her. 'Things have gone all awful here,' she said. Upon her arrival at O'Dell's apartment, she explained that the couple had just had an almighty row to end all rows. Their marriage was over. Maureen was devastated and flew home to England later that day to be with their kids.

'I truly believe she considered her relationship with George a fling without any lasting significance,' O'Dell reflected, even if one of the consequences had been her own affair with Starr. 'Ringo was the love of her life.'

～

Just as she'd fretted and compulsively rocked on the edge of her bed for the four days in 1964 when she and Richy had briefly broken up (and she believed he was off smooching with one of the Ronettes), Maureen was overwhelmed by her emotions in the wake of their final split.

Her friend Cynthia Lennon later revealed that Maureen had been 'so heart-broken that she got on a motorbike and drove it straight into a brick wall, badly injuring herself'. But Lennon also strangely noted that there had been an odd upside to this self-harming, possibly suicidal incident: 'Because of the injuries she'd received in the motorbike accident, she had plastic surgery on her face and was delighted with the result, which she felt made her look better than before.'

Maureen later told Chris O'Dell that she ultimately blamed cocaine for the death of her marriage, claiming it had changed her husband's personality. 'I always thought Richy was strong enough to deal with any drug,' she told her. 'All those years he never let any drug ever get hold of him and when he thought it was, he'd stop immediately. I always admired that about him. But cocaine changes your brain.'

On Thursday 17 July 1975, in a London court, a decree nisi was granted to Maureen Starkey for the divorce from her husband on the grounds of adultery. Ringo didn't contest the action.

In the summer of '74, following the end of his brief dalliance with O'Dell, Starr got together with Nancy Lee Andrews, a willowy American model and photographer who was at the time working as a publicist for David Bowie's management company, MainMan. As a friend of O'Dell's, Andrews was at the Santa Monica beach house one day when guitarist Jesse Ed Davis called her over to join his and the others' game of poker. She ended up sitting knee-to-knee with Ringo and helped him play his hand.

'He was so charming, playful, witty and cute as hell,' she remembered. Nonetheless, she was aware that Starr was suffering problems in his marriage and was currently seeing O'Dell. 'So I put him out of my mind as off limits,' she added.

At the start of August, Andrews, who'd been housing Lennon and Pang's rust-coloured Plymouth Barracuda in her garage while they were back over in New York, agreed to drive the car to the Beverly Wilshire for the visiting couple. Ringo surprised her by answering the door to the duplex. 'I remember you,' he said. 'You're my poker partner.' Lennon kept flashing sly winks at her and gesturing towards Starr. Pang told her that Ringo had 'been driving us crazy to meet you'.

The four travelled together to the studio for a *Goodnight Vienna* session, then repaired to a bar, The Fiddler, where Starr proceeded to get drunk and grow increasingly maudlin, repeatedly playing Charlie Rich's heartbroken country song 'The Most Beautiful Girl' on the jukebox, his head defeatedly resting on the speaker.

Watching on, Andrews said to Lennon and Pang: 'That poor guy. He's still in love with his wife. Look at him, his heart is broken.' Lennon told her, 'Nancy, he's a good lad ... give him a chance.'

'I was set up,' she later acknowledged, 'and pleasantly surprised that I really liked him. Even though he was short ... it didn't matter.'

It was to be the beginning of a six-year, on-and-off relationship for Starr and Andrews. Still, Ringo had clearly been burned by his divorce and so his quivering, tear-in-the-beer reading of Roger Miller's mournful country ballad 'Husbands and Wives' on *Goodnight Vienna*, detailing the slow break-up of a marriage, bore an audible ring of authenticity.

As part of the divorce agreement, Starr signed Tittenhurst over to the couple's children (which lessened the blow that his family were also required to move out of the property) and bought Maureen a house in the pricey west London area of Little Venice. For a time, though, she and the kids mainly settled locally, in Winkfield, five miles away from Tittenhurst, where she regularly threw parties attended by her rock star pals, including Keith Moon and Faces drummer Kenney Jones.

'I had a fine marriage for eight-and-a-half years,' Ringo reflected in 1976 in an American radio interview. 'And it just started slipping away. It wasn't being married, it was *trying* to be married. I just found it was doing my brain in, as well as hers. And so I just wanted it ended.' Asked about the current state of his relationship with his ex, Starr colourfully noted, 'We're friendly, like, Tuesdays and Thursdays. Some days it's fine and then some days we just are at each other's throats.'

As the years passed, the latter was increasingly the case and, in 1986, the pair's disagreements spilled over into the High Court in London, when Maureen attempted to have her annual alimony payments from Ringo increased from £44,000 to £70,000 and backdated seven years. His lawyer appealed and they were back in court five months later. Maureen received her increase, but

Ringo won the no-backdating ruling. He had also coolly pointed out in his statement that his former wife's current boyfriend, Isaac Tigrett, owner of the Hard Rock Café in London's Mayfair, was a millionaire.

The following year, a still-disgruntled Maureen decided to sue the law firm who'd handled her side of the divorce and sat through the entire three weeks of the resulting court case. Her own testimony turned nasty at one point when she accused Ringo, if a touch comically, of being a 'sodding great Andy Capp', likening him to the working-class *Daily Mirror* cartoon strip character known for his drunkenness and lechery.

In 1989, Maureen married Isaac Tigrett, before relocating in the early '90s to Los Angeles. On 30 December 1994, she died in a hospital in Seattle, aged forty-eight, having been diagnosed with leukaemia and following unsuccessful treatment involving bone marrow donated by Zak, by then twenty-nine. He – along with his brother and sister, Jason and Lee, their seven-year-old half-sister Augusta, and both Isaac and Ringo – were together in the room when she passed away.

'We had always been friendly because of our children,' Ringo said in the aftermath, 'but we had started to be friends again when she was struck down. We were right at her bedside when she died. I feel blessed that I was there.'

Paul McCartney may not have been there, but he was moved to write the tender and heartfelt acoustic ballad 'Little Willow' in tribute to the girl he'd known since Liverpool and the Cavern days. It was also hopefully intended as a letter of strength and consolation to her children and, ultimately, painted an impressionistic portrait of someone who had suffered from being blown around in the mad cyclone of a life she never could have expected.

44

PUT ME IN THE MOVIES, PART SEVEN

Lisztomania, 1975

Roger Daltrey wasn't ready for the enormous wave of fame that hit him when he became a film star. Up until 1975, as the singer in the Who he'd experienced international rock-star acclaim, but nothing quite on this level. Following his top-billing role as the deaf-blind protagonist in director Ken Russell's surreal cinematic rendering of the band's 1969 concept album, *Tommy*, the intensity of the sudden mainstream exposure threatened to overwhelm him.

'Oh, it was terrifying,' he admitted more than four decades later. 'Terrifying. I was a yob rock singer. I just wasn't ready for that at all.

'It was just horrible. I couldn't go anywhere. I liked to go down the pub and have a laugh with my mates. It's really weird when something like that happens ... the whole world around you changes their attitude to you. And people think *you've* changed. No, you haven't changed at all. You're the same, but you just don't know how to deal with it 'cos you're now on a different planet.'

If it was any consolation, Daltrey's new and unnerving state of movie stardom didn't last very long. By the time *Tommy* was released to screens in the March of 1975, swiftly becoming an international box-office hit, Russell had already cast Daltrey in its successor: an unhinged study of a figure the quixotic director considered to be 'the first rock star' – the nineteenth-century Hungarian composer, Franz Liszt. This equally mind-bending and head-scratching film entitled *Lisztomania* (after the term used to describe the rabid fan reactions that greeted Liszt's public recitals from the 1840s on) was set to be a colossal dud.

Initially, there was great excitement surrounding the project, with Russell noting that Daltrey 'was keen to play the randy Hungarian'. One of Russell's producers for the film was David Puttnam who, having successfully cast Ringo in *That'll Be the Day*, put Starr forward for a key role in *Lisztomania*. 'He suggested him as the pope,' said the unruffled director.

It wasn't exactly typecasting and, besides, the notion of a Beatle playing the supreme pontiff was an attention grabber. But, for the most part, Russell's mind was obsessively focused on portraying Liszt as 'the greatest stud in musical history'.

~

In the opening scene of *Lisztomania*, the director started out very much as he meant to go on, with Liszt/Daltrey having enthusiastic sex with French countess Marie d'Agoult to the speeding-up tempo of a ticking metronome, before her cuckolded husband arrives and – to the strains of an oompah-turned-country hoedown soundtrack – engages the bare-arsed composer in an acrobatic sword fight that suffers from a heavy whack of slapstick.

To be fair, from this point on and throughout the film, Daltrey's acting skills are decent. Considering the fact that he didn't have any dialogue to deliver in *Tommy*, and so was altogether more enigmatic, here he dispatches his lines in a slack-jawed west London rock-star accent with just the hint of the elocution lesson about it.

As the story freewheels on, Liszt's subsequent lover, the Polish peeress Princess Carolyne zu Sayn-Wittgenstein, plans to marry him, after seeking the pope's blessing for her divorce. A very long hour into the film, we find ourselves in a chapel at the Vatican. As Liszt mournfully plays the chapel's organ, a monk-like figure enters from the left of the screen, an altogether familiar proboscis poking out of his hood.

It's Ringo. Or the pope, in disguise, wearing a black eyepatch adorned with a silver cross. 'Your music is very beautiful, my son,' he tells Daltrey/Liszt in a fruity Scouse accent, 'but more suited to a funeral service than a wedding ceremony'. He ultimately fails, however, to grant a dispensation, following the intervention of the Russian tsar and Princess Carolyne's husband. She is incensed and Liszt for some reason decides to become an abbot.

Naturally, though, not a celibate one. He's next seen in a monastery, in bed with a girl. Ringo/the pope bursts though the door atop his ceremonial throne. He's there to deliver bad news: Liszt's daughter, Cosima, has married his musical rival, the (somehow) demonically possessed Richard Wagner.

'Poor Franz,' Ringo/the pope sympathises, expressing admiration for Liszt's latest pontiff-hailing cantata, before pointing out an even bigger problem for him. 'How can holy mother church give her blessing to music written by the father-in-law of the Devil?' There's only one thing for it, he instructs him: the composer must exorcise Wagner.

Exit Starr, after less than ten minutes in total of screen time, but before the movie entirely lost the plot in its third reel. Overall, *Lisztomania* was sadly representative of Ringo's film career during the period, in the sense that it was absolutely bananas.

~

Lisztomania was a big financial flop, too, failing to recoup its budget, which by the end had bloated to $1.2 million. In this instance, at least, Starr escaped being a major component of a terrible film, instead being a respectable bit player in a disaster.

'I don't need star billing,' he insisted in 1977. 'Before, I wanted to be a film star, and now I'd like to be an actor. I want good parts. I don't mind whatever the part is as long as it's got some meat.' Asked by the interviewer which films he believed he'd been 'quite good in', he responded, 'one... *That'll Be the Day*'. Two years after the release of *Lisztomania*, it turned out he'd yet to even see the film and so had no clue as to the quality of his performance. 'I still don't know to this day,' he shrugged.

For his part, Roger Daltrey, forty-three years on, managed to disguise his mild embarrassment about the movie, laughing and stating, with some pride, '*Lisztomania* is apparently a very "in" cult film now'.

45

YOU DON'T KNOW ME AT ALL

Jetsetter Blues, 1974–1976

Most nights, when the clubs and bars of Tinseltown emptied out at 2 a.m., Ringo could hear the hum of the engines of the cars as they came creeping up Sunset Plaza Drive, rising towards his house in the Hollywood Hills.

Starr and Nancy Andrews had moved into 1651 Haslam Terrace, a typically LA-styled four-bedroom celebrity rental (vast kitchen, fancy sky lights, obligatory outdoor pool) at the end of 1974. Being less than a ten-minute drive from the Rainbow Bar & Grill on the Strip where his rock-star cronies hung out, it soon became the go-to location for their after-parties.

'Once the bars close, they'll all drive up here,' Ringo wryly commented. 'All the old faces. "Hi, man." "Yeah, hi, come on in." I have to get away from this house, because it never stops.'

Often, of course, it was Starr making the woozy journey back up the hill from Sunset Boulevard to his house. 'Sometimes it was hard to find,' he only half-joked.

As one night bled into another and time oozed on, and if he ended up 'really wrecked', he opted to go to bed before his guests, telling them, 'You know where everything is. I'm off.' 'They don't mind if you're there or not,' he pointed out. 'That's LA for you. It's a great town because of the passing strangers.'

Whenever Led Zeppelin's frequently unhinged drummer John Bonham turned up, he usually replayed his party trick of chucking Starr into his own pool. 'Day or night, he wouldn't care,' said Ringo. 'I'd be ready to go out and… "No, John, no!" "No, I'm going to throw you in the pool!"'

Being the 24/7 party host-with-the-most was clearly exhausting, and Starr's thoughts occasionally drifted 300 miles or so north up the Californian coast, as he imagined a more laid-back and idyllic existence somewhere like Carmel or Pebble Beach. Realistically, though, for the sake of his ongoing career, he knew he couldn't afford to quit the film and music business epicentre of Hollywood.

'I guess I could go jam with the seals on the rocks,' he jested, picturing an alternative, if impossible, life as a beach bum in Big Sur.

~

Starr really only had one condition when it came to choosing a place to live. 'Anywhere with a palm tree,' he explained, 'and there aren't too many of them in Liverpool.' Before long, he was upping sticks once again, as he adopted a world-travelling nomadic lifestyle designed to stay one step ahead of the taxman.

As 1974 turned to '75, Ringo and his old bandmates suddenly had massive funds at their disposal, following the legal dissolving of the Beatles & Co. partnership that had bound them together since 1967. Unfreezing and splitting years' worth of royalties, both for the band's and their own individual solo records – meaning that they now took equal backdated shares in the profits to October '74 from *All Things Must Pass* and *Imagine* and *Ringo* and *Band on the Run* – made them all enormously rich. Starr's business manager Hilary Gerrard immediately began to cook up schemes to avoid punitive taxes, particularly in the UK, where they ran at 83 per cent for high earners.

As a 'non-resident' in California, Ringo was allowed to stay in Los Angeles for a maximum of six months a year without having to pay tax on his international earnings. A similar arrangement held in the UK, but only for up to ninety days per annum. This meant that Starr was forced to become a fiscally motivated globetrotter.

There was perhaps no greater financial haven than Monaco, where zero personal income tax was taken from residents by the government. Starr duly bought a three-bedroom, thirteenth-floor apartment in the exclusive Le Roccabella block in the principality's most famous district of Monte Carlo, only steps from the beach and the warm waves of the Mediterranean Sea.

Installed in the apartment was an upright piano, in case Ringo was suddenly struck with a song idea (which happened increasingly rarely these days). For the most part, with or without Nancy, he threw himself into the municipality's nightlife: drinking and gambling at Loews Casino (a ritzy establishment recommended to him by Peter Sellers) or dancing the wee small hours away at Régine's nightclub.

On one grimly notable occasion at Loews, Starr's drinking got him into trouble when he ended up in a fracas with a casino employee. The specific cause of their argument was never recorded – although the manager of Loews, Barry Sinkow, recalled that Ringo 'did not like to be accosted, or people coming up to him'. But the result was that the two men ended up pushing one another aggressively, as onlookers were left anxiously wondering which of them would throw the first punch.

Starr was duly ejected by security and banned from the casino. The next day, hungover and remorseful, he met Sinkow and told him, 'I'm so sorry. I would never do anything like that. I was out of hand.' When he then apologised to the employee he'd ended up scuffling with, the ban was immediately lifted. Ringo was, of course, both a big name and a big spender.

At the end of 1975, his peripatetic millionaire lifestyle took him back to England where he had a fling with the petite, Bambi-eyed singer-songwriter Lynsey de Paul. Jokingly, during their time together, Starr gave de Paul a gift of a fishing rod.

'But I don't fish,' she told him.

'You do,' he said, 'all the time. Fishing for compliments.'

Publicly proving that his and Nancy Andrews' relationship was on shaky ground, on 14 December he turned up for the Princess Anne-attended royal premiere of Michael Caine and Sean Connery's *The Man Who Would Be King* with de Paul on his arm. But it was to be a short-lived affair.

'Ringo and I were terribly fond of each other,' de Paul later commented. 'He had a wonderful sense of humour. We used to tell people, "We've fallen in *like* with each other."'

～

In March 1976, and finally free of his contractual obligations to Apple, EMI and Capitol, Ringo signed a new long-term record deal with Atlantic in the

States and Polydor for the rest of the world. The agreement tied him to delivering seven new albums over five years, setting him up with a heavy, perhaps unmanageable workload for the next half decade.

In Starr's mind, a change of record company merited a change of producer. Out went Richard Perry and in came Arif Mardin, the forty-four-year-old Turkish-born and jazz-schooled veteran of sessions with Aretha Franklin, Dusty Springfield and Donny Hathaway, who'd only the year before struck discotheque gold with the Bee Gees and 'Jive Talkin'.

'He had the voice and the looks of Dracula,' comically recalled Klaus Voormann, brought in to play bass on the album. 'Ringo loved that.'

Starr also fed off Mardin's physical enthusiasm in the studio. 'I tend to close my eyes when I'm playing,' he said. 'If looked up and Arif was dancing, I knew, *We'll keep going 'cos we're getting somewhere.*'

Jim Keltner, back on double drumming duties, noted there was a changed atmosphere in other ways with Mardin in charge. 'Arif was a serious, classy producer guy. He was different from Richard, in that Richard would join us. We would all be almost like a band. Arif was more the grown-up.'

Not that the producer's comparative seniority deterred the musicians from continuing their uproarious alcoholic activities in the studio. 'Ringo was drinking way too much all the time,' Keltner said, 'and so was I, and so was everybody else. It might have been a better record if there hadn't been such debauchery.' One work-in-progress track, 'Las Brisas' (named after an Acapulco hotel where Starr and Andrews had stayed), featured a mariachi band that Ringo had found after searching around various Mexican restaurants in LA, doubtless stopping for a drink or three along the way.

In August, continuing the trend, Harry Nilsson got married in Los Angeles, to his third wife, Una. Ringo was best man and was even tasked with choosing the bride's wedding ring. He turned up at Tiffany's in Beverly Hills to pick one out, before realising he had no clue as to Una's ring size. Leaving with a handful of different options, he promised the store manager he'd return in a couple of days with the leftover jewellery (which he duly did).

On the day of the wedding, as Nilsson richly remembered, 'the limousine arrived. Ringo gave me a toot for luck and the limo driver gave me a gram for luck. I was obliged to do some more with him, and even the priest. By now

I was shaking so much I could barely stand. Ringo reached in his pocket and displayed eight or 10 rings…'

Nilsson was to reprise his backing vocal role on his pal's new Atlantic/ Polydor album, which Starr was to cryptically title *Ringo's Rotogravure*, obscurely naming it after a cylindrical printing process. The word had jumped out at him from the lyric of Irving Berlin's 'Easter Parade' when he was watching a TV re-run of the Judy Garland/Fred Astaire-starring 1948 film of the same name. Still, even he couldn't quite explain the term to journalists who inevitably ended up quizzing him about it.

Starr pushed *Ringo's Rotogravure* hard, giving dozens of interviews in Europe and the US, hosting writers at his LA home or back at the George V in Paris where – only twelve years before but what must have seemed like a lifetime ago – the Beatles had leapt on Mal Evans's back with the news that 'I Want to Hold Your Hand' had hit number one in the US charts. Now, Ringo cut a less avuncular and more jaded figure, greeting journalists while looking for all the world like a weary Romany king: grey-flecked hair, clusters of rings on his fingers, jangling bracelets, three heavy gold chains hung around his neck, a diamond earring, and a drink always to hand (anything from white wine to brandy and apple cider to Mumm Cordon Rouge premium bubbly). Bart Mills of the *Daily Mail* sniffily observed: 'He struggles with champagne corks and repeats himself interminably.'

In the interviews, Ringo poked fun at the limitations of his singing voice, telling the *Sunday Times*, 'I've got the range of the common housewife'. He downsized his assessment when talking to *Creem*, reckoning he had 'the range of a fly' before quickly adding, 'a *large* fly'.

The cracks in his confidence that he'd masked since the early days of the Beatles were once again beginning to show. He was particularly paranoid, he confessed, about recording his vocals and admitted that he'd sometimes tape them while wholly intoxicated. 'You try it drunk, you go back sober, and you do it for real,' he reasoned. 'Some takes you use when you're drunk.'

In terms of his future plans, he completely dismissed a return to touring. 'I've been adamant that I don't want to go out there,' he stressed. 'I've done enough. I'm not living out of a suitcase on hamburgers ever again.'

Of course, he appeared to be so incredibly wealthy that he didn't have to return to the road or even need to work. And, yet, there quickly followed rumours that Starr was in dire financial straits. While that proved to be an exaggeration, he was clearly spending money like an overzealous lottery winner.

'I'm no billionaire,' he told *People* magazine. 'Rockefeller, he's *really* loaded. But if you think the Beatles didn't save any money, you're insane. Broke is relative. I'm just the biggest spender.

'I'm thirty companies, y'know, multinational,' he went on to quietly boast. 'We're in everything from dentist chairs to vending machines, but I don't talk about it.' Still, he let slip that he'd had his credit cards confiscated by his business manager. 'I use them like water,' he said. 'I used to spend them on jewellery, cars and my toys.'

In the greater scheme of things, it didn't help that *Ringo's Rotogravure* ended up stiffing, limping to number 28 in the States and failing to make any impression whatsoever on the British charts.

All the while, Starr remained, almost aimlessly, on the intensely whirling carousel of celebrity.

'Well, I'm a jet-setter,' he said. 'Whatever anyone may think and whoever puts it down, I am on planes half the year going different places. And in people's eyes, Monte Carlo is a jet-set scene. Los Angeles is a jet-set scene. It's a crazy kind of world.'

~

As if to illustrate the point, in one of the weirder incidents in a life filled with them, one day in the summer of '76, Ringo felt 'so hot' in Monte Carlo that he wandered into a barber's shop and asked to have all of his hair, and even his eyebrows, shaved off. 'The only hair I had left on my face when he was finished was my eyelashes,' he said.

Later, he offered a flippant, if revealing, further explanation: 'I went mad.' What had looked like a bit of impulsive fun suddenly took on a darker, almost self-harming edge. He confessed that he was 'feeling vaguely insane. It was a time when you either cut your wrists or your hair, and I'm a coward.'

Then, in another twist, a different story emerged, involving John Bonham being the one who'd sheared Starr clean in the middle of one of the pair's drinking and drugging benders. (Years later, this version of events was backed up by Bonham's son, Jason, who posted a photograph on social media of his father comically tapping Starr on the head with a mallet along with the words 'This was after Dad shaved Ringo's head!'.)

Whatever the truth, rather than hiding his extreme new look from the public, Starr chose to unveil it in a music video that offered the shock value of seeing a bald Beatle. Filmed in the streets of Hamburg and around Monte Carlo, the clip accompanied Starr's rendition of New Zealand songwriter Dave Jordan's jaunty if bruised-hearted 'You Don't Know Me at All' (a European-only single set to flop everywhere apart from the Netherlands). It opened with Ringo walking towards the camera in a palm-tree garden setting, before he sat down and delivered the opening lines while first removing his sun hat to reveal his depilated pate and then his sunglasses to show off his hair-free brows.

If he was deliberately trying to upend his public image, he was doing so in the strangest of ways. When the video was in motion, he came across as the usual song and dance man, capering around and, at one point, riding a horse and cart. But, in freeze-frame, some of the images were strangely haunting: particularly those where he appeared gaunt and brutally shaved, wearing a shirt patterned with thick vertical white and navy-blue stripes that unsettlingly resembled those worn by the inmates of Second World War concentration camps.

In them, there was also an echo of some of the photographs taken around the same time of Syd Barrett, Pink Floyd's acid-damaged, missing-in-action former leader: bald and somehow lost behind the eyes.

Instead of appearing to be enjoying a happy-go-lucky pop star makeover, Starr looked like someone suffering an identity crisis, at the very least. And from this point on, his jet-set lifestyle – zooming around from here to there but somehow getting nowhere – was only to grow ever blurrier.

46

ANOTHER BITE OF THE APPLE

Ring O'Records, 1975–1978

Now that the Inland Revenue only allowed Ringo to spend up to ninety days a year in the UK, Tittenhurst Park and its in-house recording studio, which John Lennon had named Ascot Sound and used to cut the basic tracks for *Imagine*, were left to gather dust. Never one to miss a business opportunity, Starr decided to use the facility as a commercial enterprise, renaming it Startling Studio, and – as if Apple hadn't been a bitter enough experience – set up his own record label.

The first news story about Ring O'Records (a clever-clever trading name suggested by Lennon) appeared in *Music Week* in the autumn of 1974, reporting that Starr had made an agreement with Polydor Records to market and distribute the company's product. It launched officially in April 1975, with Ringo giving a round of interviews to talk up his new venture. Echoing Paul McCartney's naively idealistic explanation for the founding of Apple seven years before – artists would no longer be forced 'to go on their knees in somebody's office' – Starr claimed his motivation for setting up Ring O'Records was so that 'no one will have to beg'.

There were likely business tax perks, too. Also, Starr was notably following the example of George Harrison, who'd formed his own Dark Horse Records only eleven months before, signing both his friend Ravi Shankar and south Tyneside pop duo Splinter. In a more eccentric move, the first album release on Ring O'Records was a synthesiser-based, entirely instrumental reworking of

'73's *Ringo*. It wasn't without precedent: McCartney had, in 1971, overseen a slightly bizarre easy-listening orchestral version of his *Ram* solo album, which he semi-anonymously released in 1977 as *Thrillington*.

Startling Music – starrily stylised on the cover as *Sta*rtling Music* – was made by and credited solely to David Hentschel, the former Trident recording engineer-turned-keyboard player for Elton John. Two years before, Hentschel's reputation had been further enhanced by his creation of the symphonic synth overture of 'Funeral for a Friend', from John's 1973's blockbuster LP *Goodbye Yellow Brick Road*.

Ringo had always had an interest in synthesisers, going back to his days in Highgate, where in 1970 he'd noodled around with a Moog in his shed with Maurice Gibb. After hearing a tape of Hentschel's most recent recordings, utilising his telephone exchange-proportioned ARP 2500 synth, Starr coaxed him into realising his conceptual reworking of *Ringo*. 'I mean, he really wanted to do a symphony,' he shruggingly told the *NME*. 'But I forced him into it.'

If it was an attempt to capitalise on the then-vogue for prog-adjacent, hi-fi-polished electronic sounds, Hentschel and *Startling Music* lacked the necessary cool of West Berlin's Tangerine Dream or Tokyo's Tomita. It wasn't all bad. Hentschel reimagined 'You're Sixteen' as squelchy reggae (with a guesting Phil Collins thumping away at a Wailers-styled beat), while 'Oh My My', also released as the first Ring O'Records single, attempted synthesised disco a year ahead of Giorgio Moroder's pioneering production of Donna Summer's 'I Feel Love'. Overall, though, the album had the slightly cheesy aroma of elevator muzak. Upon its release, it went almost directly to the discount crates in record shops (although hip-hop producer J Dilla would lend it some obscure kudos in 2002 by sampling Hentschel's fanfare motif for 'Photograph').

Later in 1975, Ring O'Records released another three singles: the funky, chanting 'Gimme the Key' by Starr's sax-player pal Bobby Keys, 'I've Had It' by plaintive-voiced Australian singer-songwriter Carl Groszmann, and a novelty update of the 'Hokey Pokey' fronted by the mysterious Colonel – in reality, early-days Queen bassist Doug Bogie – and renamed 'Cokey Cokey', which of course held some subversive appeal in the mid-'70s. Bogie explained his label boss's reaction to the record. 'I think he only liked it because when I went in to pitch it, he was with Harry Nilsson who took a liking to it.'

After that, Ring O'Records appeared to shut up shop. In the autumn of '76, one Polydor insider carped to *Rolling Stone* that 'Ringo was using it like a toy'.

'I wound up going to all these meetings,' Starr moaned, as if he didn't already have some knowledge of the drudgery of running such an operation. 'It was exactly the same as Apple, but it only took me a year to realise I was getting nutsy and there was nothing happening.

'Artists always try to run a record company or a career like it isn't a business,' he added. 'I am a business. So we're trying to get a new structure of the record company. It will probably start again next year, not in my fantasy.'

~

True to his word, Ring O'Records relaunched in the spring of 1977, with Polydor A&R man Terry Condon installed as managing director. His boss Mike Hales revealingly told the trade press that 'we are delighted to renew our association with Ringo's label, which after a slightly false start now has a manager in whom we have the greatest confidence'.

New signings included Skegness-born rocker Graham Bonnet (starting a run of singles from his self-titled album with a gutsy cover of Bob Dylan's 'It's All Over Now, Baby Blue') and New Zealand session singer Suzanne Lynch (launching herself with a version of Russ Ballard's rock belter 'Born on Halloween'). Later, Slade-styled US rock band Stormer and east London's punky mod Johnny Warman were added to the roster.

One of the last artists contracted to Ring O'Records was the Gerry Rafferty-affiliated Scottish folk-rock singer Rab Noakes, who remembered recording his 1978, Terry Melcher-produced *Restless* album at Tittenhurst, 'where John Lennon recorded "Imagine", in that big front room'. Noakes added that Starr remained distinctly hands-off during his entire time with the label. 'I only met Ringo once,' he said, 'but he did send me a thank-you telegram.'

This was perhaps the root of the problem with the company: Starr's lack of involvement. In the end, by the time Ring O'Records discreetly wound down in the summer of '78, it had yielded zero big hits – apart from the Graham Bonnet album, which went gold in Australia, albeit licensed through another label, Mercury Records.

As a strange postscript, one further single was due to be released on Ring O'Records in the form of another novelty 45 that took a reggae stab at the Scouts' and Girl Guides' anthem, 'Ging Gang Goolie'. Produced by Eric Idle and Ricky Fataar, it was credited to Dirk & Stig, their character names when portraying McCartney and Harrison in the Rutles' mockumentary *All You Need Is Cash*.

While the former Beatles had reportedly all had differing reactions to the sometimes-cruel spoof – Lennon found it hilarious, McCartney apparently not, while Harrison even appeared in it as a grey-wigged TV interviewer – this seemed to be tacit approval from Starr, who had apparently found most of the film funny, apart from the scenes lampooning the sad demise of the band.

The Dirk & Stig single subsequently appeared on EMI in August 1978, accompanied by a Pythonesque promo video featuring Idle, Fataar and their pals (including the bushy- bearded Hilary Gerrard) frolicking around as grown-up Scouts in the grounds of Tittenhurst. Ringo had lent them his extensive backyard for one last madcap Ring O'Records party. All in all, it was a frivolous ending to what had been a pretty much fruitless endeavour.

47

SIMPLE LIFE

Japanese TV Commercials, 1976–1977

A decade after he'd last visited Japan, Starr – accompanied by Nancy Andrews and Hilary Gerrard – landed back in the country in the October of 1976. The party were driven directly to the Tokyo Hilton where, ten years before, Ringo and the other Beatles had been effectively incarcerated by the authorities, mainly for their own safety.

Now, minus the moptop and a cavalcade of craziness following him everywhere, Ringo was virtually incognito, which afforded him almost total freedom to explore the island nation. The three travelled from Tokyo to Kyoto and then to Sapporo, with stop-offs in smaller cities en route. Only once was Ringo spotted by a group of camera-wielding teenage girls, who politely snapped away and kept their distance.

The visit was also something of a trade mission for Starr, since he had signed on to be the face of Japanese clothing company Renown's Simple Life leisurewear brand. The deal involved his appearances in a series of TV commercials shot between Kyoto and Los Angeles and soundtracked by either one of two jingles – the '69 Beatles-sounding thumping mantra of 'Simple Life' (basically the chorus groove of 'Come Together' threaded with electric sitar and Harry Nilsson aiding the harmonies) or 'I Love My Suit' (loping vaudeville, with both Nilsson and ex-Monkee Davy Jones on backing vocals). Throughout the campaign, Ringo happily acted the goat for an undisclosed amount of yen.

One of the commercials reprised his *Goodnight Vienna* video themes by featuring a UFO landing on a playing field, sending football-playing kids scurrying in wonder, before Starr popped out of its hatch, sniffed Earth air, mugged at the camera and announced, 'Hello to all Japanese people. I came here to talk about… the Simple Life.' Another seemed to borrow the strange concept of the Beatles' promo clip for 'Strawberry Fields Forever', in which they were seen playing with an odd piano-based contraption tethered to a tree. Here, in a beach scene, Starr (and his fake, bit-acting family) constructed a Heath Robinson-styled device from apparent junk and then watched delightedly as he switched it on, and it erupted with a galaxy of stars.

In the third ad, Ringo cheesy-grinned while playing a space-age silver piano in a field, before spreading his hands wide to magically create a rainbow. In the fourth, he danced down a dusty track alongside a donkey, then disappeared over a hill from where his spaceship rose back into the sky. All in all, they were harmless and doubtless lucrative fun, and unlikely to dent what remained of his credibility, since they weren't destined (at least until the eras of home VCRs and YouTube) for Western eyes.

It set a trend for Starr. From here, through the 1980s and '90s, he was more than happy to pop back over to Japan to flog Schweppes tonic water or Takara apple juice –'ringo', of course, fortuitously meaning 'apple' in Japanese – for a bit of extra pocket money.

48

STARKEY & SON

A Tale of Two Drummers, 1975–2024

Zak Starkey will never forget the night when Keith Moon managed to apparently kill, then magically resurrect his pet rodent. 'He fed my hamster meringues until it died,' he remembered with a deep laugh, many years later, seemingly unscarred by this potentially traumatising formative event. 'He put it in a shoebox full of straw and it came out about four or five hours later and it was alive.'

Of all the strange mates of his dad's, Moon was absolutely the strangest. Yet, to a child, he was also the most childlike: a ludicrous and unpredictable man-boy. When parties were regularly roaring downstairs at the Starkeys', the Who's drummer would slope off and happily become part of the kids' club happening upstairs. 'Keith would come up to our bedroom,' Zak recalled. 'Me and my brother and my sister would still be awake, 'cos of all the noise downstairs, and we'd be drawing and painting and playing Monopoly and wrestling.'

At first, the Starkeys' eldest son wasn't even aware that their wild-eyed 'Uncle Keith' – in fact his godfather – was a drummer. Zak still had plans to become a guitarist, after being encouraged when he was younger by Marc Bolan. Then, at the age of nine, he was flipping through his parent's record collection and pulled out *Meaty Beaty Big and Bouncy*, the Who's explosive 1971 singles compilation covering the period from 'I Can't Explain' to 'The Seeker'.

'It was the most exciting music I'd ever heard,' he enthused. 'By miles. By miles and miles and miles... So, basically, I switched to drums then.'

On his tenth birthday, 13 September 1975, the Starkeys gifted Zak a small-scale four-piece Ludwig drum kit (the same configuration that Ringo played

263

for most of the Beatles years). He later remembered that his father gave him only one drum lesson, teaching him a basic beat: *boom, chak, boom, chak*. The following day, Starr came back with a slightly more advanced beat for his son. 'Try this,' he said. *Boom, chak, boom-boom, chak.*

Zak told his dad, 'I can already do that.'

Ringo said, 'You're on your own, then.'

Headphones clamped to his head, Zak played along with the Who, the Small Faces, the Faces and T. Rex. But, notably, not the Beatles. In 1976, his nanny gave him a copy of Essex proto-punks Dr Feelgood's thrilling 1975 debut *Down by the Jetty*, which to his ears sounded 'as raw as the Who ... it changed my fucking life.'

Meanwhile, Kenney Jones of the Faces, another pal of the Starkeys, was the first to sit young Zak down and try to help him further his drumming. 'He taught me to play triplets. Every time he came over, he'd show me something to practise.' Moon, meanwhile, remained an influential figure for Zak, as well as a corrupting force.

Often when the Starkeys were in California, as Zak remembered, 'my dad used to send me to stay with Keith in Malibu for the weekend, which, in retrospect...' he acknowledged with a huge snigger, '... not the greatest babysitter ever, right? Y'know, it's sort of like, Who do I know is responsible? Oh, yeah, I'll send the kids over to stay with Keith.'

Moon, however, remained the number-one inspirational figure in Starkey Jr's development as a drummer, even if it was never in the form of one-to-one drum tuition.

'Me and Keith never sat down and played drums together,' he said. 'We sat down and drank beer together, even though I was ten or eleven. He got me into the Beach Boys, and he talked about surfing and girls. It turns out he'd only ever been surfing once, and he nearly drowned, and he never did it again.

'So, we were sitting up talking, and I was saying, "I've got a little kit, y'know, but I want to play like you." And he goes, "You can have my kit."'

Moon was referring to the eleven-piece monster drum kit he'd used on the Who's recent '75–'76 tours, with its twin, floor-shaking bass drums and double racks of thunderous tom toms, all finished in an elegant creamy shade of white with bright copper fittings. Kenney Jones recalled in 2024 that, following

Moon's sudden death in 1978, and after he'd become his drumming replacement in the still emotionally reeling band, he arranged to have the kit delivered to the Starkeys' home.

Jones remembered Zak telling him, '"Keith kept saying he was gonna give me his drum kit, the white one." He idolised Keith so he *should* have that drum kit. And if Keith said it, I believed him. It should go to him 'cos that's what Keith wanted.

'So when I was rehearsing one day at Shepperton Studios, I said, "Where did Keith keep his drums? Where's the white kit? Put it in the van." So we drove it over to Zak and I set it up in his front room just like Moony would set it up. It took up all the fucking room. So when he came home from school, I said, "Zak, I've got a surprise for you". He went in the front room and he couldn't believe it… all these drums.'

For his part, Zak Starkey recounted an entirely different version of events when it came to the appearance of this dream gift, insisting that it arrived sometime in the first half of 1977, the year before Moon's death.

'So, I didn't get the kit for ages,' he recalled. 'And obviously, I'm eleven, and I'm *desperate* for this kit, y'know. I think the kit must have been owned by the Who, maybe, or because Keith was in America, they weren't releasing it. They thought he was on some mad trip or something. I think Kenney got involved and helped to organise it being delivered.'

After he'd arrived home from school one day, Zak's mum Maureen handed him the house phone. On the line was Moon, who began to mysteriously chant, 'Where there's smoke, there's fire… where there's smoke, there's fire. Go and have a look around in your driveway.'

Zak found the humongous drum kit set up in the garage, with buckets positioned all around it emitting clouds of atmospheric dry ice.

'Much better than the go-kart I got the year before,' he wryly pointed out.

Still, he was clearly tickled by the fact that his father seemed bamboozled whenever he sat down at Moon's elaborate kit, which was entirely the opposite of his own, more minimalist set-ups.

'By the time I've decided which ones to hit,' Ringo told him, 'the fill's over.'

From this point on, Zak Starkey became an absolute nuisance to his family's neighbours, who even threatened Maureen with legal action if he didn't stop playing along to *Quadrophenia* twice in succession on a Sunday afternoon. All the while, Kenney Jones helped him maintain a link to his favourite band, inviting the lad to rehearsals where Zak noted that the group tended to play one song, then open up John Entwistle's flight case-cum-bar and proceed to spend the rest of the day drinking and telling stories.

By the age of twelve, Zak was playing pub gigs with a band called the Next, before he proceeded, through the 1980s and into the early '90s, to drum with the Spencer Davis Group, the Icicle Works and even his dad's All-Starr Band. In 1991, being chased by the taxman, he was forced to consider selling the kit that Moon had given him, first going to Entwistle to ask for his advice.

'I said, "Look, I'm skint, John,"' he grimly recollected. '"And the only thing I've got that's worth anything is Keith's kit." He said, "Look, if Keith was alive, he'd give you the money… except he never had any money, so I don't think he'd mind if you sell it."' The white kit duly went under the hammer at Sotheby's, fetching $12,000 (or $29,000 in 2025).

Then, in 1996, Zak's fortunes took an upswing, to previously unimaginable heights, when he was asked to join the Who. Kenney Jones had split with the group in 1988 due to money-related intra-group tensions (being replaced by Simon Phillips), but Starkey had impressed Roger Daltrey and John Entwistle after he'd briefly toured with the pair of them in 1995. His debut with the band was hardly low-key: a full performance of his previously neighbour-bothering *Quadrophenia* for the Prince's Trust in Hyde Park on 29 June 1996 in front of a crowd of 150,000, with his father proudly watching on.

Starr's younger son, Jason, also became a drummer, sitting behind the kit in the '80s with rock 'n' roll revivalists Buddy Curtis and the Grasshoppers, before moving into road managing and photography. But it was his sibling who was to prove the in-demand musician, playing down the years with the Lightning Seeds, Johnny Marr's Healers and Oasis. In addition to all of this – his style not obviously indebted to either Keith Moon or Kenney Jones, but solid and pyrotechnic in his own right – he fitted into the weird band dynamic of the Who for nigh on thirty years, mainly by following Pete Townshend's mercurial guitar parts onstage.

'The way the Who works is Pete is a conductor,' he expounded. 'The drummer follows the conductor. The bass player looks down the line at the drummer to the conductor. It's a guitar/drum thing, not a drum/bass thing, like most normal bands.

'My approach is, watch that bloke over there to my left or he'll gun me down with his guitar, at the knees. If I play the same fill twice, two nights running, I get a dirty look. He wants to be surprised, not bored. And that's my job – to make sure he's not bored. And it's the best job in the world.'

It was one that Starkey temporarily lost in a very public fashion in April 2025 after a Who show for the Teenage Cancer Trust on 30 March at the Royal Albert Hall in London. Onstage, a disgruntled Roger Daltrey stopped the last number, 'The Song is Over', and cracked up, blaming the drummer (performing, most excellently, in a bright-yellow hooded onesie) by saying, 'All I've got is the drums. "Boom, boom, boom". I can't sing to that. I'm sorry, guys.'

While the incident turned out to be the result of a sound level problem – the electronic kit was too loud in the singer's in-ear monitors – in the aftermath, Starkey was thrown out of the group, a representative for the Who stating, 'the band made a collective decision to part ways with Zak'. The drummer stood up for himself in a typically comical way, posting on social media, 'Toger Daktrey [sic] [is] bringing formal charges of overplaying and is literally going to Zak the drummer and bring on a reserve from the Burwash Carwash Skiffle 'n' Tickle Glee Club Harmony Without Empathy All Stars'. At the very least, it was firm proof that the Starkey humour gene hadn't skipped a generation.

Within days, in a dramatic volte-face from the Who, Zak was reinstated in the line-up. Pete Townshend made the public announcement, revealing that there had 'been some communication issues, personal and private, on all sides that needed to be dealt with'.

A month later, the drummer was sacked again, Daltrey apparently having prevailed. 'After many years of great work on drums from Zak, the time has come for a change,' Townshend affirmed. 'Zak has lots of new projects in hand.'

On the morning of 27 May 2025, Starkey was interviewed live on BBC One's *Breakfast* show. 'I wasn't fired, I was retired, because I was "too busy" … and I've got nothing on!' he laughed, clearly bruised yet breezy.

Throughout the entire drama, Ringo had maintained a public silence. His son, however, revealed that 'he's not too happy about it, either'.

Then, in the middle of June 2025, Zak revealed to *Rolling Stone* the true extent of his dad's disgruntlement, and feelings about Daltrey in particular – Ringo telling his son, 'I've never liked the way that little man runs that band.'

Back in 1996, when Zak Starkey first bagged his old job with the Who, Kenney Jones thought to himself, *Great, good on you*. At the same time, it reinforced his decision to help to transport Keith Moon's kit to the pre-teenager all those years before, in what now seemed to have been a fitting gesture.

'I think I did the right thing,' Jones said, while accepting that it had created a key staging point in Zak's stylistic independence from his drumming dad. 'I mean, I love Ringo's playing. It's not for me to interfere with father and son.' But, at the same time, Jones recognised in Starkey Jr a strong desire to move out from under the long shadow of being the son of the most famous drummer in the world.

'"I want to do things my way",' is how he described it. 'Zak's a bit like that.'

49

PUT ME IN THE MOVIES, PART EIGHT

Sextette, 1978

On one of the more memorable evenings during the non-stop party season at Ringo Starr's house in the Hollywood Hills, there was a significant guest of honour. Mae West, the bawdy, wisecracking screen star, now eighty-four-years-old and still resplendent in a tight-fitting dress and long, curly blonde wig, sat at the centre of the proceedings as a parade of wasted rock stars wandered by paying half-garbled homage to her.

There that night was T Bone Burnett, the producer and guitarist who'd first met Starr early in '76 when they shared a stage at the Houston Astrodome in Texas on Bob Dylan's Rolling Thunder Revue tour. 'Ringo had a *lot* of parties and I would always end up just being dragged over there,' Burnett said of that time, while remembering that West 'spent the whole evening almost on a throne, and received people, and was completely charming'.

West's image had almost a decade before been featured in the back row of faces (in between Aleister Crowley and Lenny Bruce) on the cover of *Sgt. Pepper*, after she'd initially turned down the Beatles' request to include her, archly declaring, 'What would I be doing in a Lonely Hearts Club?'. Now, in the '70s, old Hollywood was mixing with the new jet-set music millionaires. Mae was more than happy to hang out with the rockers.

'There were about 100 people at this party,' Ringo recalled. 'We had the Band, and a lot of musicians were there. Mae just sat in the corner in a big chair and all these rockers were on their knees to her because she was just so great. She had a huge personality and she could mix with the best of them.'

Mae West already had a significant rock-star buddy, in the shape of Elton John, who'd been friends with her since '72. He was also pals with the octogenarian but still piercingly sharp Groucho Marx.

'These people had been forgotten for a long time,' Elton later pointed out, 'so when they went out, they got the adulation that they'd been missing for years because they'd been sitting at home. You'd take them out and people would just be so incredibly awestruck and would just shower them with compliments. It was very touching.

'They were old people realising how valuable their careers had been and how much people loved them. I just sat there while Groucho told tales ... I sat there when Mae West was talking. You don't interrupt them. You're talking about people who've *lived*. And you're sitting with them and you're thinking, *Fuck, I can't believe where I am.*'

In many ways, Mae West was a woman born out of time, who'd perhaps found her era in the 1970s, just as her advancing years were catching up with her. Following decades of aggravating the censors with her trademark one-line double entendres, she was entirely at home in this freer and easier time. 'If a picture of mine didn't get an X rating,' she boasted, 'I'd be insulted.'

West was to make one last film, *Sextette* – based on a theatre production she'd written and staged in 1961 – in which Starr played a key cameo role. At the time, after his run of odd role choices, his own fortunes in the film industry were beginning to wane. 'I can't get an acting job,' he moaned. 'I've turned a lot down because I was getting offered such small parts.' Even if this was set to be another fleeting appearance on screen, the offer to play opposite Mae West – a superstar before Richy Starkey was even born – was impossible to resist.

Sextette was a fruity romp in which West played a version of herself as Marlo Manners, a six times-married movie star of an unspecified vintage. The movie opened with exterior shots of London (although the interiors were shot at Paramount Studios in Hollywood), with Manners having just married Sir Michael Barrington, played by the early thirtysomething Welsh actor

Timothy Dalton. The five-decade age gap between the two went unmentioned. Celebrations continued at the fictional 'Sussex Park Hotel' where, as chance would have it, Manners was forced to entertain a procession of her visiting exes to her suite.

The vibe was very much '30s Hollywood shoehorned into the '70s. West trotted out her old schtick. 'How do you like it in London?' one reporter asked her. 'Oh, I like it anywhere,' she saucily retorted. Inexplicably meeting a team of American athletes in the hotel's gym, one of whom told her, 'I'm a pole vaulter', she rolled her eyes and declared, 'Aren't we all?'. Elsewhere, very much giving a one-fingered salute to the censors, she announced, 'I'm the girl that works at Paramount all day and Fox [i.e. fucks] all night.'

Starr was cast as ex-husband number four – shouty European film director Laslo Karolny – and barrelled into the action wearing a grey beret and brown jodhpurs, and brandishing a riding crop. His scene, totalling fewer than five minutes, involved the shooting of a screen test in Manners/West's suite. Cue much in the way of 'Cut! Cut! Cut!' scenery-chewing action. Before he exited, he turned to Barrington/Dalton to say, 'D'you know, when your wife was my wife, your wife was *some* wife. I only hope my wife is *your* wife like *your* wife was my wife…

'Y'know what I mean?' he added as he departed, knowingly widening his big blue eyes, just as Peter Sellers taught him.

'I thought it would be fantastic to play with Mae, just to see what the legend was really like,' he reflected. 'But on the very first day of shooting, I got uptight. I felt completely left out of things. By the end of the second day, I would have stayed on as long as she wanted me.

'She's old enough to be my grandmother,' he added, 'so it's sort of embarrassing to say, but she's bloody attractive. And Mae's no Garbo. Mae doesn't want to be left alone!'

On set, the seasoned film star tended to sit patiently in her costume as make-up artists powdered her and hairdressers primped her wig. It turned out to be a tough shoot for West, for various reasons, one of them being that she and director Ken Hughes felt that much of the dialogue was weak, so the script was constantly being rewritten on the day. Ringo heard her complain, in her still-thick Brooklyn – or, more accurately, 'Bushwick Avenyah' – accent: 'They're flushing my play down the *terlet*.'

Tony Curtis – playing another of her exes, 'Sexy Alexei' Andreyev Karansky, who just happened to be the Russian delegate to a world peace conference bafflingly taking place in the hotel at the same time – felt that West was carefully trying to preserve her resources on set. 'She'd sit very composed, waiting,' he said, 'and then when they were going to shoot her, she had all this energy stored up.'

There were other problems, though. West's hearing was deteriorating and so she had to be fed her lines by the director via an earpiece hidden under her wig. After one scene inside an elevator, she failed to hear Hughes call, 'That's a wrap!', and was left there for half an hour before anyone noticed.

⁓

Once the edit of *Sextette* was complete, there was a private screening of the movie held on the Paramount lot. All of the film's stars, plus Mae and Ringo's mutual pal Elton John, were in attendance. An insider noted that 'Miss West was pleased by her performance, but the movie hadn't turned out as she had imagined it would'.

The film was an absolute bomb, grossing only around $50,000 against a budget estimated to have been between four and eight million dollars. Two years later, West tripped and fell at home when getting out of bed, and was subsequently diagnosed in hospital as having suffered a stroke. She died three months later on 22 November 1980.

In the years that followed, many of those involved in *Sextette* seemed keen to distance themselves from the film. 'I only agreed to the thing in *Sextette* because I thought it would be interesting not just to meet Mae West, but to work with her,' said Ringo. 'I can't claim it as a career highlight, but I can say Mae West was not a disappointment.'

'I don't think too many people saw it,' Tony Curtis noted. 'Just as well.'

Timothy Dalton, later cast in the '80s as James Bond for two films in the 007 franchise, seemed slightly embarrassed by *Sextette*. 'It's more of a museum piece,' he squirmed. 'She was wonderful. I mean, she was very old. She was vain enough to lie about her age. She said she was eighty-four. They *knew* she was eighty-seven and people that *really* knew said she was ninety-one.'

50

OGNIR RRATS

Ringo Starr Backwards, 1978

Decked out in a dark-blue suit and sporting a fashionable shoulder-length curly perm, George Harrison stood behind a nest of microphones and faced a group of reporters. He'd called this press conference, he announced, 'to clear up some of the rumours surrounding Ringo and his concert, which will be broadcast via satellite later this evening'. The assembled journalists proceeded to quickly fire questions at him. Was it true that Starr could no longer play the drums? Or that he was 'singing stranger than usual'?

Harrison stiffly reassured them that he'd spoken to Starr the previous night, but that he'd been unable to talk to his friend and former bandmate for long 'because he was being chased by the police'. This provoked an immediate hub-bub amongst the reporters. One asked, 'What *has* happened to him?'

'Let me start Ringo's story at the beginning,' said Harrison, revealing this not to be some weird and troubling newsflash, but the opening scene of Starr's NBC-broadcast 1978 American TV special, which riffed on Mark Twain's 1881 novel, *The Prince and the Pauper*.

'It seems two babies were born, at the very same moment, the very same second in the very same country... England,' Harrison went on. 'Remarkably, both children, though born of different parents, looked exactly alike. One of the infants was taken to America. The other became quite well known in certain circles. But fame and fortune did little to make him happy...'

Cut to Ringo sitting in the back of a limousine, being comedy-fondled by four foxy ladies, while looking utterly miserable. Within seconds, he's recog-nised by fans, who chase alongside his car and then mob him when he emerges from it. Retreating to the safety of a recording studio reception area, he has his photograph taken with his entourage, holding his latest gold disc, before he ungratefully chucks it on top of a pile of others.

The scene really was a fantasy, in the respect that gold records were becoming an increasingly distant memory for Starr. Having followed up *Ringo's Rotogravure* with a coked-up-sounding, yet strangely underpowered yacht rock-cum-disco LP in 1977's *Ringo the 4th*, he'd been dropped by Atlantic Records only two albums into his seven-record deal.

As a result, there was a lot riding on his next effort, '78's *Bad Boy*, due to be released in the US by Columbia Records offshoot, Portrait. The label-transfer process involved Arif Mardin vacating the producer's chair, to be replaced by Vini Poncia, Starr's sometime co-writer since '73, who brought with him a tighter focus and a new band, featuring both Dr John and Elton John bassist Dee Murray.

In an attempt to ensure its success, Starr played one of the best cards left in his hand: reviving his cuddly Beatle Ringo onscreen persona, deployed once again in this comedy/musical special simply titled – as if to hammer the point home – *Ringo*.

⁓

Back in the narrative, the viewer encountered one Ognir Rrats, Starr's long-lost, reverse-named brother/doppelgänger, an anorak-wearing nerd in specs with greasy, side-parted hair, standing in the street in Los Angeles selling maps of the homes of the stars. We then followed him to the Hollywood Walk of Fame, where he daydreamed about having his own name imprinted in the sidewalk, as he sang a '70s remake of 'Act Naturally'.

From here, the plot faithfully followed Twain's original story: Ringo and Ognir had a chance meeting; the gilded-caged former convinced the lowly latter to swap roles, and much mistaken identity hilarity was set to follow. Except, it didn't quite. The lumpy dialogue didn't help. At one point, after Starr had mock-completed taping a drum part in a recording studio scene, the engineer commented, 'Beautiful take, Ringo. What do you think?'

'Yeah, I think that's real fine,' Starr responded, suddenly coming over all Scarlett O'Hara. 'We'll lift up the bass layder.'

The arrival of Carrie Fisher onscreen brightened up the proceedings, her appearance being something of a coup since she was at the time one of the most famous faces on the planet thanks to her icon-making role as Princess Leia in *Star Wars*, released only the previous year. As Ognir's unlikely girlfriend Marquine, she mistakenly hopped into a car with Ringo, who proceeded to lead her – via a pop-art animation sequence – in a slushy (and once again slightly unnerving) duet version of 'You're Sixteen'.

Later, none other than Vincent Price popped up as a hypnotist, Dr Nancy, brought in by Starr's manager Marty Flesh (*Three's Company* sitcom star John Ritter) to bring Ringo (really Ognir) back to his senses before pushing him out onto the stage. Of course, the real Ringo duly appeared at the concert venue, with only seconds to spare before showtime and the old switcheroo inevitably took place, leaving Starr to get on with the real business of selling *Bad Boy* to the viewing public.

For the big finale, he referenced Elvis Presley's *'68 Comeback Special* with a showstopper featuring him alone in a white suit, on a star-shaped stage, performing the country ballad 'A Man Like Me'. As the camera slowly moved closer, he gazed intently down the lens at the record-buying folks sitting at home, unseen backing singers swooping in and an orchestra swirling skywards. The emotional impact of the song was only lessened in the minds of those who knew it from the previous year's *Scouse the Mouse* children's album, written by actor Donald Pleasance and voiced by Starr, where it had been called 'A Mouse Like Me'.

In outtakes and blooper reels that later leaked out, on set during the filming, Starr was spectacularly sweary and grumpy one minute, grinning and laughing and doing an Elvis impersonation the next. But, whenever the cameras rolled for real, he never failed to turn on the old charm and resume his act.

All in all, *Ringo* the TV special – screened much later in January 1983 on ITV in the UK – was enjoyable froth, but ultimately not career-saving material. Airing midweek on NBC on Wednesday 26 April 1978, five days after *Bad Boy* appeared in stores, it tanked in the US ratings and only managed to arrest Starr's commercial decline through slightly less disastrous sales. Where *Ringo the 4th* had reached an abysmal number 168 on the *Billboard* chart, *Bad Boy* scraped up to number 129. In Britain, neither album sold enough to even register on the charts.

When the campaign for *Bad Boy* fizzled out in the summer of '78 and Polydor (in the UK and Europe) followed Atlantic in ditching Starr from their roster, the road that stretched out ahead of him only seemed to be filled with obstacles.

51

BLOTTO

Bellyaches and Bummers, 1979

The days drifted by and there were fewer and fewer reasons for him to get out of bed in the morning. When he did eventually rouse himself, his own real purpose, as he emptily put it, was to 'fill the day' and cope with his general sense of aimlessness.

If he was staying at the apartment in Monte Carlo, he'd spend the afternoons lazing around in the sun, hiding his bloodshot eyes behind his virtually glued-on sunglasses. Then he'd hit the casinos at night, and drink and fritter away his money at the blackjack and roulette tables.

All the while, the booze was slowly corroding Ringo's already delicate constitution. Then the peritonitis he'd suffered as a boy returned to bite him again.

On 28 April 1979, and without much warning, as he grimly recalled, 'part of my intestines closed down, and I was in a lot of pain'. Starr was rushed to the Princess Grace Hospital and examined by chief surgeon Professor Jean Chatelain, who first of all administered a shot of heavy pain medicine. Feeling some relief, Ringo blithely announced, 'Oh, I can go now.'

'Yes, you can do,' the doctor told him. 'And you can die.'

Starr was diagnosed with chronic internal inflammation, but also an intestinal blockage that required urgent surgery. Under the knife, during the long and potentially life-threatening operation, approximately five feet of his intestines were removed. He spent five days in intensive care and a week in recovery, before his deep-seated hatred and fear of hospitals – still rooted in him after the prolonged stays of his youth – kicked back in and made him want to immediately escape.

Ringo managed to get himself discharged by 'conning my way out' and no doubt deploying his star power. Yet he didn't return home, instead taking up residence at the ritzy, five-star Hôtel de Paris. There he could normally be found convalescing in the bar, although not drinking or smoking. At least, initially. Instead, he used his characteristic sociability to buoy him and help him get over what he described as 'that low passage' following the shock and surgery.

He even took pleasure in lighting other people's cigarettes for them, likening it to a replacement 'buzz'. One day, he smoked one himself. 'Within a week, I'd bought a carton,' he later marvelled at the swift return of his heavy nicotine habit, 'and I was back on sixty a day.'

In all the recent years he'd spent focusing on his parallel careers as a solo singer and film actor, Starr's passion for drumming never left him, even if his capability sometimes did, due to his extracurricular habits. Still, there was always respite from his frontline stardom to be found by returning to behind the kit.

In the summer of '75, he'd been in Amsterdam at the same time that Elton John and his band were entering their notorious booze-and-coke phase while rehearsing to debut the *Captain Fantastic and the Brown Dirt Cowboy* album in full (and with audience-repelling consequences) at Wembley Stadium on 21 June. One day, at a film soundstage just outside the Dutch capital, Ringo sat in with Elton and the band, thrilling them by validating their cover version of 'Lucy in the Sky with Diamonds' with his Beatle-tastic signature swing and characterful fills.

Starr then voiced a desire to actually join the band for the upcoming date – and possibly beyond. There was much umming and ahing within the ranks, but it was ultimately felt that it would be unfair to ditch new drummer Roger Pope, and Ringo's offer had to be reluctantly declined.

In September of the following year, he happened to be in Copenhagen when he bumped into Cat Stevens in a hotel. Stevens was still riding high as the multi-platinum-selling figurehead of the post-hippy singer-songwriter era, and at the time was recording his tenth album, *Izitso*, in the city. He invited Ringo along to the sessions at Sweet Silence Studios and an inevitable party-time jam ensued, involving Stevens singing and playing guitar and Starr playing drums. Songs included Fats Domino's 'Blue Monday', Etta James's 'I Just Want to Make Love to You', possibly Lee Dorsey's 'Working in the Coal Mine'. No one could quite remember. The details were fuzzy. The tapes rolled, but no music from the session was ever officially released.

'He wiped me off,' Ringo later complained, before reviewing the situation more pragmatically. 'I mean, I can't blame him because… I was losing control. It's funny, because you cop such a resentment at the time: "What? He wiped me off?!" God knows what I played for him.'

Starr performed better during his appearance at the Last Waltz, the Band's great farewell to the road, held at the Winterland Ballroom in San Francisco on Thanksgiving Day 1976. Ringo doubled up on drums sitting behind the group's Levon Helm, backing a starry front line – which included Bob Dylan, Neil Young, Joni Mitchell, Van Morrison and Eric Clapton – for a ragged if rousing 'I Shall Be Released'. Next, a gaggle of the musicians stayed on stage for a couple of long improvised jams where Ringo swung back and forth in a half-trance and looked like he was in his absolute element. What's more, his appearance in the Martin Scorsese-shot film released to cinemas in the spring of the following year underlined his ongoing relevance as a drummer, as opposed to a mere personality.

In 1977, Starr guested on two tracks on T Bone Burnett's country power-pop outfit the Alpha Band's *Spark in the Dark* album. 'We asked him to come in and play on it,' Burnett remembered, 'and he did brilliantly.' Later, tellingly, Starr claimed to have no memory of this session whatsoever.

As far as his own record career was concerned, after the flopping of *Bad Boy* in 1978, he lacked any real impetus or sense of direction. In 1979, John Lennon, always keeping one eye on Ringo's career – and like the other former Beatles, growing concerned about his general state of health – sent him a postcard suggesting that the cool new wave disco of Blondie's 'Heart of Glass' was 'the type of stuff y'all should do. Great and simple.'

'In '79, my career was heading for hell anyway,' Ringo reckoned. 'I was taking less and less interest. I was more interested in being out of my head.'

As his boozing and drugging worsened, he began to drive his friends away. Even Klaus Voormann – who'd known Ringo since he was a virtual no one drumming for the Hurricanes at the Kaiserkeller – felt the burn of his friend's perma-intoxicated personality change.

'He was in a very bad state,' Voormann sadly remembered. 'He was drinking a lot. He was sniffing coke to an extent where he was unbearable. I didn't like him [during] that period at all.'

Voormann recalled the 1976–77 New Year's Eve party at Starr's house in Los Angeles as being a breaking point in their friendship, even if it proved to be a temporary one. The dress code for male guests on the night requested that they wear a smoking jacket and dickie bow tie. Klaus had neither.

'I had the best suit I could have,' he said, 'and a nice shirt and everything. Ringo said [slurring obnoxiously], "For crying out loud…". I turned my heels back to the car and went home. He could've said, "Come on, Klaus, here's a shirt and a dickie bow. Come on. Everybody's wearing them, so you should too."

'That's just to explain to you what state Ringo was in at that time. He was always the most reliable person, really. He was always caring for you. And then, when he was in that particular state, he was really terrible. And I didn't go to his house anymore.'

'Everyone was backing off,' Ringo admitted. 'Because of my alcohol problem, I was totally rejected, and I had huge resentments. I got in that drunk-and-insulting mode. I would come to your house just to insult you.'

7708 Woodrow Wilson Drive in Laurel Canyon had once been the home of Cass Elliot of the Mamas & the Papas and, in the '60s, had become a famed hangout spot for the likes of Joni Mitchell, Eric Clapton and Crosby, Stills & Nash. 'Cass's house was very much like she was Gertude Stein in Paris,' said Nash, comparing the scene to the American poet and novelist's legendary gatherings of artists such as Picasso, Matisse and Hemingway at her Paris home in the early decades of the twentieth century. 'She would use her house as a gathering space for interesting people to talk and to play music.'

Sometime after Elliot's 1974 death in his London flat, Harry Nilsson bought the Laurel Canyon property and then, in 1978, leased it to Ringo. While only a fifteen-minute drive from West Hollywood, the rustic location seemed half a world away from the city and the constant hum of traffic. At night, often the only sound to be heard was the cry of a coyote.

Entering this period of what appeared to be relative domestic stability, Starr and Nancy Andrews got engaged. However, this seemed to do little to change Ringo's self-destructive ways, particularly since he was frequently off gallivanting around Europe or living it up in London. Increasingly, though, he cut a sad figure: 'just some fucking celebrity', as he put it, turning up at film premieres with a bottle of cognac mixed with Coca-Cola in his pocket, so that no one – or so he believed – would realise he was drinking.

One night at his old nightclub haunt, Tramp, he met nineteen-year-old Stephanie LaMotta, daughter of *Raging Bull* boxer Jake LaMotta. The two flirted, LaMotta telling Starr (perhaps mindful of their twenty-year age gap) that he reminded her of Humphrey Bogart. Ringo then pulled the smooth movie-star trick of lighting two cigarettes at once, before passing one to LaMotta. Moving to a disco in Mayfair that had just closed its doors for the night, Starr bribed a doorman with £100 to open up for an extra hour to allow the two to dance alone.

Amping up their romance, Starr whisked LaMotta off to Vienna the next day, where the pair stayed at the plush Hotel Bristol. LaMotta was struck by how attentive and funny Ringo was. Leaving a restaurant one night, he self-deprecatingly asked her, 'Did I ever tell you about the time I got my nose stuck in a door?' As they slow danced in a nightclub another evening, Starr told LaMotta, 'Darlin', I'm falling in love with you.'

Their affair continued when they flew on to Greece but ended almost as soon as it made contact with reality after they'd landed back in London. In the end, it had been only a diverting fling.

～

In the last week of November '79 – on the 28th, a Wednesday – a local Los Angeles 'Action News' TV reporter hoisted a microphone under Starr's nose.

'Ah… the house went on fire,' Ringo chirpily stated with a grin, perhaps appropriately dressed in black and wearing his ever-present shades, as the words 'Ringo Starr Fire Victim' flashed up on the screen. 'That's all we have to say,' he added more impatiently, then shrugged. 'I mean, the house went on fire. Look at it.'

It could almost have been another TV special spoof. But this time the news footage was all too real.

'Ringo Starr was entertaining some friends in his rented Hollywood Hills home,' the anchor back in the studio explained, 'when sparks from a fireplace apparently started a fire on the second floor which quickly then jumped to an attic. No one was hurt, but it took six fire companies half an hour to put it out.'

The upper floors at the house on Woodrow Wilson Drive were almost completely destroyed. Worse, perhaps, Starr had been storing much of his Beatles memorabilia up in the attic. The news item showed images of firemen clambering on ladders over the burned-out roof as the last puffs of smoke rose into the air. Ringo's concerned neighbours milled around outside, including comedy actor Chevy Chase, who could be seen shaking his head sympathetically before wandering off. Meanwhile, some wag back in the music department had chosen 'It Don't Come Easy' to soundtrack the scenes.

All in all, the destructive blaze was the capper to what had been a terrible year for Starr.

Back in the studio, the oddly grinning newsreader concluded by telling his viewers, 'Well, the estimated damage in that fire... $135,000.' It almost seemed as if he was taking some pleasure in reporting this spot of celebrity misfortune.

52

PUT ME IN THE MOVIES, PART NINE

Caveman, 1980

Sunday, 17 February 1980, and in an interrogation room at Guadalajara airport, Ringo was being questioned and searched by the Federales.

Starr was travelling with Keith Allison, a former Monkees session guitarist who'd most recently been musical director for the *Ringo* TV special. On this trip, he was acting as Ringo's personal assistant-cum-drinking buddy. The two had landed in the west Mexican city with a two-hour layover until they caught a connecting flight to Durango. As the pair sat in a coffee shop, Ringo doing his best to stay incognito, they were approached by four policemen, who examined their passports and then marched them off to be interviewed.

Only the month before, Paul McCartney had been imprisoned in Tokyo for nine days after attempting to smuggle almost half a pound of marijuana into Japan at the start of a Wings tour. Starr had given his response to his pal's sorry predicament to reporters as he passed through Heathrow on his way to LA.

'It's the risk you take when you're involved with drugs,' he commented, sounding judgemental but, in reality, speaking from actual, live experience. 'He's just been unlucky.'

Now, the shadow of suspicion seemed to have followed Starr, too. As they sat there in the Guadalajara interview room, Allison began to feel that someone in the Mexican police force was seeking the kudos of busting a Beatle. While the pair weren't entirely strip-searched, the Federales took great care in examining the heels on their boots and even the buttons on their jackets, convinced that the two were trying to smuggle drugs into the country. The officers then took the banknotes out of Starr and Allison's wallets and tapped their edges onto a slab of black marble to see if any traces of cocaine could be found. Finally, the pair were told they were free to go.

In stark contrast to this heavy scene, Starr was actually in Mexico to make the biggest and – in the face of some strong competition – stupidest film of his career. In his first role as male lead, he was set to play a prehistoric runt-turned-tribal leader in the $6-million budget Hollywood comedy, *Caveman*: a rites-of-passage tale that was intended, in its knockabout humour, to be knowing enough for the heads, but silly enough for the kids.

For the film's top-billing star, first-time feature director Carl Gottlieb – who'd previously co-written the screenplays of *Jaws* and *The Jerk* – had been looking for an actor of diminutive stature and possessed of natural physical comedy skills. He'd initially fancied Dudley Moore (fresh from 1979 rom-com blockbuster *10*) for the role. When Moore wasn't available, Gottlieb turned his thoughts to Starr. The director felt that Ringo had 'been kind of exploited in *Candy* and a couple of other films and had made some odd choices' with his parts. Crucially, he assured Starr that his starring role in *Caveman* 'didn't depend on his being a Beatle'.

A decade after the band had split, Ringo, too, was looking back over those ten years gone. 'People forget that since the break-up, I've had a very good career on my own, and not only as a recording artist,' he was keen to stress. 'As an actor, people only really think about *Help!* and *A Hard Day's Night*.

'I've never really starred in a movie before,' he added. 'I've just done parts.' At the same time, he'd managed to maintain a steady screen career without having taken an acting lesson in his life, instead studying in front of the camera alongside the likes of Peter Sellers in *The Magic Christian* and Richard Burton in *Candy*. 'Practical experience is a thousand times better than any class,' he argued.

Ringo's co-stars in *Caveman* were to be up-and-coming US actors Dennis Quaid and Shelley Long and, with great significance for his future, Barbara Bach, fresh from her star-making role as a Bond girl playing opposite Roger Moore in 1977's *The Spy Who Loved Me*. In the summer of 1965, less than a fortnight before she'd turn nineteen, Queens-born Barbara Goldbach had gone with her younger sister Marjorie to what was for them a local gig: the Beatles' first, earth-shaking performance at Shea Stadium. Despite being witness to this moment of pop cultural history, she remained more into Bob Dylan and the Rolling Stones.

'I was never that much of a Beatles fan,' she said later, while pointing out that this had in fact helped her to avoid being starstruck when she was cast in *Caveman* alongside their drummer. 'I just treated him like anyone else,' she coolly emphasised.

At thirty-three, Bach already had a fairly long and successful career, starting out as a model in her late teens. In 1965, she'd cut down her surname and gone on to be a *Vogue* and *Elle* cover girl. From 1968 onwards, her striking and unusual features – a combination of her Jewish and Irish genes that made her look far more European than American – helped her to launch a film career in Italy, via a procession of slasher/horror and crime flicks. Then, in '77, she became a global face and name through her onscreen exploits as KGB agent Anya Amasova in *The Spy Who Loved Me*, rivalling Bond as they separately searched for a secret microfilm, before they joined forces and, inevitably, fell into bed.

From the first day of outdoor filming for *Caveman*, in the third week of February 1980, amid the dramatic vistas of the Sierra de Órganos National Park in the state of Zacatecas, security was provided by armed Federales who doubtless resembled those who'd tried to bust Ringo at the airport. A fortnight into the shoot, Nancy Andrews flew in to be with Starr and was surprised by the oppressive vibe on set. She was told by an assistant director that the police were a necessary presence to protect the cast and crew from rebel militia who had pillaged livestock and equipment from previous shoots and apparently even kidnapped women.

Despite this air of danger, on and off camera, Starr was buzzy and funny, buddying up and clowning around with Dennis Quaid in particular. If he had by now pretty much spent all of his Fabs currency as an actor and come to the realisation that he would have to push forwards on his own merits, this moment represented something like a fresh start to his film career.

'Maybe,' he reckoned on set, '*Caveman* is the dawn of an era for me.'

The dialogue in the script for *Caveman* was relatively easy to learn, and grunt, since it featured only a fifteen-word lexicon of mostly nonsensical words and phrases: 'macha' for monster, 'haraka' for fire, 'alunda' for love, 'zug zug' for sex. The rest of the action was pure japery and slapstick, which came easily to Starr.

Since Ringo appeared in almost every scene in the film, it's worth charting his absurd journey virtually step-by-step. So here are the selected 'highlights' of *Caveman*:

2 min: Wearing ragged furs, Ringo as the hapless Atouk wanders from his tribe out into the wild and mugs around as carnivorous plants try to eat him, before encountering an animated stegosaurus and scarpering, foolishly leading the creature into his camp.

5 min: Quaid as Lar tackles the intruding dinosaur as Ringo watches from behind a rock. The rest of the cave people climb to safety up a tree, which topples under their collective weight. One of the cavemen is dragged off by the stegosaurus and doubtless eaten.

8 min: Bach as Lana, the voluptuous wife of hulking tribe leader Tonda (former US football star John Matuszak), emerges from a cave wearing an animal-skin bikini.

9 min: Ringo spins a circular rock with a hole in it on a stick. He's on the verge of discovering something important. Then he lobs it away. He casts an admiring glance at Bach (as Lalo Schifrin's score kicks into stringy romantic mode), wanders over and hands her a guava, which she gives to Tonda. A dejected Ringo slopes off.

11 mins: The cavemen find a plant that looks suspiciously like marijuana. They get Ringo to test out one of its red 'berries'. He smiles dopily then keels over.

12 mins: Ringo hollows out another guava, pushes some of the druggy berries inside, then gives it to Lana, knowing she will share it with Tonda.

13 mins: Tonda and Lana both conk out. Ringo creeps towards the couple, cuddles up against the sleeping Bach, pulls her legs apart, then gets his head stuck between her knees. Tonda farts and Ringo is blown away (ending what is really a protracted attempted rape scene uncomfortably played for laughs. Very different times etc.).

16 mins: Morning. The three lie asleep together. Tonda rolls over and dozily tries to initiate sex with Ringo. When the brute comes to his senses, his eyes pop ('Atouk!!') and a rumpus quickly develops with Tonda threatening to kill Ringo with an enormous rock.

17–27 mins: Ringo runs away and a whole new plot develops involving himself and Quaid encountering the pretty, dippy Tala (Long) and her visually impaired father Gog (seasoned comedy actor Jack Gilford). Gog goes wandering and blindly bumps into a T-Rex, which proceeds to chase them all. By pure luck, Ringo spears it and is hailed a hero, especially by Tala, who throws her arms around his neck. 'Atouk, Tala zug zug?' she seductively enquires. 'Nah,' says Ringo. 'Atouk zug zug Lana.' He indicates that if he can kill the 'macha', he can kill Tonda.

35 mins: Night falls and it turns dark and stormy. They shelter in a cave and watch a tree being struck by lightning and catching fire. Cue a *2001*-styled orchestral fanfare in tribute to Richard Strauss. They all warm their hands and Ringo names it 'karaka'.

37–40 mins: He shows them all how to cook a dead bird by holding it over the fire. After a campfire feast, they all start banging rocks and making vocal noises, discovering music. Ringo, of course, has a pair of bone drumsticks. To be fair, they cook up quite the funky groove.

46 mins: Ringo's tribe discover a gigantic pterodactyl egg and jubilantly carry it away to the instrumental strains of the Second World War song 'The River Kwai March', more popularly known as 'Hitler Has Only Got One Ball'. Tonda and his gang find them and the two tribes chase around the giant egg for a bit.

49 mins: Mum pterodactyl flies over the heads of Tonda's tribe as they run away with the egg. They accidentally drop it off a cliff, it cracks and is handily poached in a boiling spring. Ringo's lot swoop in and eat the results while looning around.

57 mins: Ringo and gang are making their way along a dangerous cliff face when they realise that they are being followed by the returning T-Rex. Ringo spots a 'weed' bush and feeds it to the dinosaur, who gets so stoned it falls off a cliff. He is hailed a hero again.

59–61 mins: They find Tonda et al fishing, using the womenfolk as human 'rods'. Bach is swept away downstream and Ringo chases after her as she's lost in the rapids. He dives into the water and saves her life.

64–71 mins: The plot turns baggy as Ringo and crew are forced to rescue Quaid from some inexplicable ice-age scenario where he's been pursued by a horrible, fanged Neanderthal and they've both become encased in ice. They burn the ice block to free Quaid, but also release the savage in the process. Cue a slippery chase sequence.

75–82 mins: Ringo is determined to kill Tonda and win Bach. He plans an assault on his rival's cave and is inspired to create an array of weapons, including rock-flinging slings and sticks of fire. The raid is launched. Ringo spears Tonda in the chest and retreats. He returns riding the stop motion stegosaurus and batters everyone who gets in his way, including Tonda, whose chest he ends up jumping on, over and over, until he is dead. Bach and Long vie for Ringo's attentions and he wanders off with Bach. Long is miffed and on the verge of tears.

83–84 mins: Elgar's 'Land of Hope and Glory' plays as Ringo and Barbara stand atop a rock and are hailed as the king and queen of the clan. Then, he surprisingly dumps her in a pile of 'caca'. He approaches Long as Quaid whispers, 'Atouk alunda Tala'. The couple gaze into one another's eyes and then lead the triumphant tribe back into the cave.

85 mins: Fin.

~

As ludicrous as *Caveman* was, its tale was mirrored by Starr's real-life love rivalries. Bach later coyly admitted that during filming she'd been impressed that Ringo had leapt into the fast-moving Mexican river, without a stuntman, in spite of his poor swimming skills. 'By the time he reaches me, he's heading for the bottom,' she said of the scene in which Atouk rescued her. 'And when we get to the rock, I'm literally pushing him up.'

Despite Nancy Andrews' visit to the set, Starr's eye was clearly wandering. When the shoot moved on to Estudios Churubusco in Mexico City for interior scenes, Carl Gottlieb had Starr and Bach rehearse their 'cuddle' scene after hours in the latter's room at the Holiday Inn. Ringo presumably stayed, since the couple turned up holding hands on set the next morning.

When the shoot wrapped and Starr returned to LA, Andrews didn't hear anything from him for a fortnight. When the two did finally talk, Ringo told Nancy, 'I'm with Barbara now'. Andrews was furious: 'It was like being slapped in the face.' Still, one day she volunteered to drive over to the Beverly Wilshire and hand Ringo some photos she'd taken on the *Caveman* shoot. Bach was there, too.

'It was strange,' Andrews later recalled, 'visiting the man I had lived with just a month earlier, and was betrothed to marry, sitting with another woman, acting like a couple in love.'

Upon its release in spring 1981, *Caveman* was predictably panned by the critics. The *Guardian*'s reviewer hit the nail on the head: 'Worth about half an hour of anybody's time ... unfortunately it runs 97 minutes!' [*sic*]. It was, however, a modest success, making almost $10 million in profit at the box office.

But by far the most successful aspect of *Caveman* was the fact that Ringo Starr and Barbara Bach were glued together at the hip from now on. She called him Richy. He called her Doris.

53

CRASH...

A Brush with Mortality, 1980

It was the evening of Monday, 19 May 1980, and Starr, with Bach in the passenger seat, was driving his cream-coloured 1969 Mercedes-Benz 280SE to a party at Eric Clapton's house in Surrey. As they approached the notorious accident blackspot of the Robin Hood roundabout on the A3 near Richmond Park, the air foggy, the road slippery, Ringo lost control of the car.

Careering wildly at more than 60 miles an hour, it smashed into a lamp post, then another, then somehow rolled over onto its roof before crunching to a halt on the wrong side of the dual carriageway. Barbara remained in the car, while Ringo was ejected from the Mercedes by the impact of the crash, went flying and landed on a grass verge.

~

Two years and eight months earlier, and only two-and-a-half miles to the north east on Queen's Ride, bordering Barnes Common, Ringo's pal Marc Bolan had been killed instantly when the purple Mini 1275 GT being driven by his girlfriend Gloria Jones hit a steel post, then a sycamore tree. A subsequent investigation revealed that the recently serviced Mini had underinflated tyres and two loose front wheel nuts. Jones survived, but a nation of glam fans mourned the (albeit fading) pop star's shock death just two weeks before his thirtieth birthday.

In the wake of the tragedy, *Born to Boogie* was widely reappraised and reshown. In particular, a monthly celebration screening was held by Bolan heads at the Essential! arthouse cinema in Wardour Street, in Marc's old stomping ground of Soho. As the film's director, Starr had, it turned out, played no small part in helping to immortalise his friend.

~

Back on the A3, Starr and Bach had a lucky escape. Ringo picked himself up off the grass verge and rushed to the crumpled and upended Mercedes, pulling Barbara free from the wreckage, then propping her up and lighting cigarettes for the both of them.

'Ringo was pretty cool about it,' an eyewitness said later. 'He got a hell of a shake-up.'

Police and ambulance crews arrived, followed by a reporter. Starr told him, 'We had a crash ... it's cool', when it could have quite obviously been anything but. The couple were taken to Queen Mary's Hospital in south-west London, but were quickly discharged after it became apparent that they'd only suffered minor injuries – Ringo to his leg and Barbara to her back. The police didn't take any further action, as there had been no other vehicle involved, although Ringo was told he may face a bill from the local council to repair the destroyed lampposts.

The pair spent the night at the Dorchester Hotel on Park Lane and, the next day, caught a plane to Los Angeles. Overcome by the emotion of it all, Ringo proposed to Barbara on the flight.

'He believes that if we could survive that together, we could survive anything,' Bach said shortly after. 'We then decided to make sure we were never apart again.'

Later, in a move perhaps more befitting of Lennon and Ono, the couple had the Mercedes crushed and cubed and kept it as an art piece-cum-coffee table. The following year, they also had glass splinters from the car's shattered windscreen set into their wedding rings, forging their marriage in the fire of a miraculous escape.

54

BEATLES REUNITE!

Snapshots of Rumours, Chances and Possibilities, 1970–1980

1970

Only eight months after Paul McCartney publicly announces that the Beatles are over, in December *Melody Maker* reports that Klaus Voormann is on a shortlist of three names to replace him as bassist in the reformed band. None of the other candidates are revealed.

1971

The *Daily Mirror* persists with the Voormann rumour angle, claiming that he'd been present at a secret meeting held at Apple with Lennon, Harrison and Starr. As a result, he is said to have disappeared from his home in Hampstead and taken refuge from the press at Harrison's Friar Park estate. 'I'll be in a group with John and George and Klaus and call it the Ladders or whatever you want to call it,' says Ringo, 'but I don't think it would be called the Beatles.'

(More than half a century later, Voormann will tell the author, 'Ringo made a joke to some journalists or something. Y'know, I would never want to replace Paul McCartney. I can't do that. I can't sing. I can't write songs. So, I can't be a replacement for Paul.')

1972

On tour in France with Wings, McCartney is forced to comment on why he didn't make an appearance onstage at Harrison's Concert for Bangladesh. 'If I'd gone there, I know for certain it would have been played up as, "Hey, the Beatles are back together again". But it's ended. The Beatles have definitely ended.'

1973

Word of Lennon, Harrison and Starr recording 'I'm the Greatest' in LA for the *Ringo* album inevitably leaks to the press. 'Beatles to Record Again!' screams a *Melody Maker* headline, above yet another report stating that Klaus Voormann (who played bass on the track) is to be a permanent replacement for McCartney in the reformed band.

Paul responds to the piecemeal reunion of the group on *Ringo* by saying, 'I'm happy to play with the other three and I'm sure they are too if it's physically possible.'

'There's always a chance,' says Lennon later in the year. 'As far as I can gather from talking to them all, nobody would mind doing some work together again. I think we're closer now than we have been for a long time.'

1974

On Radio 1 in February, buttoned-up BBC presenter Brian Matthew begins a long and chewy question by asking Starr about 'these awful sort of chit-chat whispers that you see in the back pages. The most recent one I saw suggested something along the lines that Paul admitted that he missed John's verses, and John had admitted he missed Paul's choruses, and you look keen to do things with them all again, and George hadn't made up his mind yet.'

'Well, I think it's more that Paul and John would like to get together,' Ringo says. 'George possibly, and I don't care. The four of us haven't sat down and talked together, y'know, and said, "Shall we, or shan't we? Or what?"

'My attitude is to say no to the rumour, because it will cancel the rumour ... If there are any definite maybes, the rumour carries on.'

'Alright then, there you are from Ringo,' Matthew concludes. 'It ain't gonna happen.'

The same month, *Melody Maker* very confidently reports that peace meetings have been held in New York between the four Beatles and that a new album is definitely in the works. The chief motivation for the reformation is apparently the fact that all of the band's money has been tied up in the Apple dispute and they need the cash.

A week later, Ringo is spotted with Harry Nilsson in Macon, Georgia, at Capricorn Studios, the recording facility made famous by hirsute southern rockers the Allman Brothers. Rumours begin to swirl that McCartney, Lennon and Harrison are soon to secretly join them in this outlying location for the making of the Beatles reunion album. A tour is set to follow its summer release, with the first date to be 'in Monticello, near New York, in June or July'.

'Christ, we can't even get the four of us together for a meeting,' Lennon protests, 'let alone play.' Still, a few weeks later, he further assesses the prospect of a full reunion and even puts a likely date on it: 1976, when the band's EMI contract runs out. By November, he seemed to have made up his mind, coolly announcing to a journalist, after a big lug on his fag, 'I would like the Beatles to make a record together.'

Soon after, despite Ringo recently stating his belief that the band can't get back together because of the gulf remaining between Harrison and McCartney, George tells Alan Freeman on Radio 1: 'I just met Paul and I just know that whatever we've been through, there's always been something there that's tied us together. It's like we've come through a big dark tunnel and we've come back out the other end. I'm really ready, with John Lennon in particular, to kick down a few doors. Let's get going again.'

1975

Before splitting with May Pang and returning to Yoko Ono, Lennon surprisingly reveals, 'I'd be as happy as Larry to do "Help!". I've just changed completely in two years. I'd do "Hey Jude" and the whole damn show.'

1976

Bill Sargent, American music impresario and pioneer of pay-per-view TV events, boldly makes an offer to the Beatles to reunite for a single show, in any location of their choosing. His proposal guarantees $50 million for the band, with most of the receipts coming from $50 ticket fees for closed-circuit broadcasts in cinemas.

A month later, with no response forthcoming, Sargent doubles his offer, promises to get the group the money 'within 24 hours' and suggests a date: 4 July, the culmination of the US Bicentennial celebrations. The very next day, Mike Matthews of the Electro-Harmonix guitar effects pedals firm puts in his own, albeit lesser counter bid: £3 million with £30 million in CCTV broadcast receipts.

'Well, that's a big offer,' McCartney says of the Sargent proposal. 'The thing is, nobody, as yet, has spoken about it. We might do it, but then again, we might not do it. But then again, we might. It's a positive "maybe".' Two days later, his maybe is less positive. 'I'd read John Lennon was hottest on this. I spoke to the bugger and he didn't even mention it. Where do you go from there?'

On 24 April, Lorne Michaels, producer/sometime host of *Saturday Night Live* fronts a skit offering the Beatles a cheque for $3,000 to get back together. 'You divide it up anyway you want,' he says. 'If you want to give Ringo less, that's up to you.' Incredibly, Lennon and McCartney are hanging out together at the Dakota watching the broadcast and, for the briefest of moments, entertain the notion of heading down to NBC Studios while the show is still on air. 'We nearly got in the cab, but we were actually too tired,' Lennon later admits. A week later, Michaels increases the offer to $3,200, plus 'hotel accommodation'.

Meanwhile, creating what EMI are calling a new 'Beatles boom', all of the band's twenty-two singles are re-released in the UK (plus a new seven-inch of 'Yesterday', never before released on an A-side in Britain). For one week in April, the group occupies twenty-three positions in the Top 100. Ringo proudly assesses the catalogue as 'the finest pieces of plastic around that no one has done anything beyond yet'.

In May, in Detroit, on the Wings Over the World tour, Paul gets narked at a journalist who won't drop the Beatles reunion topic. 'Look, mate, it's 1976 and I don't think most people care what happened ten years ago,' he fumes. 'The past is gone and it won't come back.' Fuelling further speculation, however, two nights later, Ringo and George are spotted in the audience at the Wings show at Toronto's Maple Leaf Gardens arena.

In September, concert promoter Sid Bernstein, who'd booked early US shows for the Beatles, including both Shea Stadium appearances, takes out a full-page newspaper ad suggesting the Beatles reform for a 'one-off charity concert'. 'I didn't get a response from anyone,' he later admits. Ringo reckons that 'Sid Bernstein is trying to get his name in the papers. Next week someone's gonna come in with $500 million.'

At the same time, Starr is the first to mythologise the Beatles in his solo work (as opposed to Lennon lambasting them in 'God' and his Macca-knifing 'How Do You Sleep?'). The back cover of *Ringo's Rotogravure* features a photograph of the white front door of the Apple HQ at 3 Savile Row, now covered in graffiti ('Come together!', 'I need you George', 'Give John a green card ok'). Initial copies of the LP come with a magnifying glass so that the record buyer can properly inspect the fan messages.

Still, one track on *Ringo's Rotogravure* is to be the subject of a bitter division between Harrison and Starr that almost ends up in court (and that remains partly fogged in mystery). Ahead of making the album, Ringo reaches out to his ex-bandmates for any spare material and George offers him 'When Every Song is Sung', a track he had still to find a home for after writing it in 1970 (with Shirley Bassey in mind), trying it out for *All Things Must Pass* and then recording unreleased versions with, among others, Cilla Black and Ronnie Spector.

Retitled 'I'll Still Love You' on Ringo's album, it's very much unmistakably a Harrison love ballad, with its slowly descending chord sequence and gently tortured air, rendered in Starr's wracked but equally cracked delivery. Harrison hates Starr's version and, bizarrely, threatens to sue his pal. In the end, the matter is privately resolved by the two.

(Appearing together on the *Aspel* talk show in Britain in 1988, they address the bad blood between them at the time. 'He wrote this song,' says Ringo, 'and I had it mixed by somebody else and he didn't like the mix.' George snorts with laughter by his side. 'So he was gonna sue me,' Starr adds. 'In the end, I said, "Sue me if you want. I'll always love you."')

1977

'It's a joke,' George says in February of the continuing cyclone of rumours about an impending Beatles reformation. 'It's just crazy, y'know. It's trying to put the responsibility of making the world a wonderful world again onto the Beatles. I think that's unfair.'

'We did talk about it, but there's no interest now,' says Ringo around the same time. 'If anything, we'd do an album first, then prepare for a tour for six months, and we don't have that kind of time. And we wouldn't do it for the money. We were never into that.'

1978

No significant Beatles reunion rumour activity recorded.

1979

In May, at the Surrey-held shindig celebrating the wedding of George's ex Pattie and Eric Clapton, many of the invited musicians pile onto the stage, including Starr, McCartney and Harrison. The three play together for the first time in nine years (albeit amid an ever-changing rabble reportedly including Mick Jagger, Ronnie Wood, Donovan, Robert Plant, Jeff Beck and Charlie Watts). Tunes drunkenly part-murdered include 'Get Back' and 'Sgt. Pepper's Lonely Hearts Club Band'. Wings' Denny Laine later reports, 'It's lucky nobody made a tape. The music was terrible. Absolute rubbish.'

In September, Kurt Waldheim, secretary-general of the United Nations, calls upon the Beatles to perform a charity concert in aid of the Vietnamese boat people whose post-war migration from the country has resulted in a humanitarian crisis. No less august a publication than the *Washington Post* reports that 'Paul McCartney, George Harrison and Ringo Starr have agreed [to perform] and John Lennon is considering the idea.'

1980

In summer, at Super Bear Studios near Nice, Ringo and Paul record two McCartney originals ('Private Property' and 'Attention') for Starr's next album, tentatively titled *Can't Fight Lightning*.

On 9 September, the ever-persistent Sid Bernstein places an ad in the *New York Times* under the banner headline, 'An Appeal to John, Paul, George and Ringo'. His latest concert scheme is far grander and involves shows in Cairo, Jerusalem and New York, the last before an invited audience of UN members and their families and '100 children of the boat people'. He projects that revenues from the venture will total $500 million.

In November, Ringo records with George at the latter's Friar Park Studio, laying the backing track down for what will later become Harrison's 1981-released Beatles-nostalgic hit 'All Those Years Ago'.

Through the year, Starr makes periodic visits to the Dakota, where Lennon hands him cassette demos of possible songs for Ringo's solo record, including the jaunty country of 'Life Begins at 40' (both having respectively passed that significant age milestone in July and October) and the driving, hooky 'Nobody Told Me'. On 15 November, the two meet at the Plaza Hotel. 'He was really up,' Ringo later says.

On 28 November 1980, Lennon offers an eyebrow-raising statement in a legal deposition against the producers of the cheesy *Beatlemania* Broadway musical. The theatre production has been running for two years, using their licensed songs, but irks the band by, as their lawyers claim, 'appropriating' their likenesses and trademarks.

'I and the three other former Beatles,' Lennon states – if not physically there in court, but swearing to tell the truth, the whole truth, and nothing but the truth – 'have plans to stage a reunion concert.'

55

MERCY DASH

Rushing to the Dakota, 1980

They were led in via a side entrance; Ringo in a black leather bomber jacket, looking drawn and pulling hard on a cigarette, Barbara in jeans and Fair Isle shawl, her hair scraped back into a ponytail.

When they arrived on the seventh floor, they could still hear the mass of people in the streets below singing John Lennon songs.

'Ringo was the first to call and to physically show up,' remembered the Lennons' friend, Elliot Mintz. 'John loved Ringo ... spoke about him all the time, glowingly.'

Starr and Bach had been in the Bahamas when they received the call from England, from the latter's twelve-year-old daughter Francesca, telling them that Lennon had been hurt in a shooting. She called back to say he'd in fact been killed. The couple immediately chartered a flight to New York.

George Harrison was at Friar Park when he'd been woken by a call from his sister Louise in the States. Initially believing, too, that Lennon had only been injured, he went back to sleep. Later, when Harrison found out the awful truth, he issued a dazed-sounding statement. 'After all we went through together, I had and still have great love and respect for him. I am shocked and stunned. To rob life is the ultimate robbery in life.'

That day, he went to his home studio and attempted to work on a song, called 'Dream Away', which spoke of escaping real life through the subconscious mind, before stopping and giving in to his grief.

Paul McCartney, too, after being told the gut-punching news by someone from his MPL office, went to work, at AIR Studios in central London. He later said, 'I just didn't want to sit at home'. Passing reporters waiting at the gate of his Blossom Wood Farm in East Sussex, he told them, 'I just can't take it in at the moment'. At the studio, with George Martin behind the mixing desk, he tried to develop a song called 'Rainclouds', the lyric of which depicted someone moving through heavy weather.

When he later stepped out onto Oxford Street at the end of the day, McCartney made vague statements to the waiting media, telling them that he'd been 'just listening to stuff' in the recording studio. Before he left, he made a parting comment about Lennon's murder that would haunt him for years: 'It's a drag, isn't it?'

'That came out very flippant,' he sadly reflected decades later. 'It wasn't flippant. And anyone who saw me on that day knows it wasn't.'

After returning to Blossom Wood Farm, McCartney privately went to pieces.

'I wept like a baby,' he said. 'It was a heavy personal blow.'

~

Starr had called Ono from a New York payphone to tell her that he and Bach were on their way. But at the door of the apartment, Yoko gestured for Ringo alone to enter. 'Where I go, Barbara goes,' he insisted.

'I said to Yoko, "I know how you feel",' he remembered. 'And the woman, straight as a die, she said, "No, you don't". Because no matter how close I was to him, I was not half as close as she was to him.'

All the while, as they tried to talk, there were cries rising up from the street, calling for Yoko, and even the five-year-old Sean, to come to the window. Starr later admitted that he'd felt 'disgusted' by the fans' behaviour.

'It would have been better if they'd all left her alone,' he reasoned, 'because they were not going to bring him back. And they didn't help her by having this whole crowd outside playing his music. And then when we came out, I didn't need to hear people telling me how much they loved the Beatles, or any of that, when we'd just lost John.'

Leaving the Dakota from the front entrance on West 72nd Street, Starr and Bach faced a terrible crush of mourners and rubberneckers and had to push their way through them on the very sidewalk where Lennon had been murdered fewer than twenty-four hours before. TV news footage showed the couple stuck in the middle of the mob, their faces etched with uneasiness edging into very real fear.

'I was given two bodyguards,' Ringo said, 'and there were two of Yoko's supposed to be looking after me. But… we lost all the bodyguards.'

The scene was almost a horrible negative image of Beatlemania. When after much shoving, the pair managed to free themselves from the crowd, Ringo gently pushed Barbara into the waiting car, then got in himself and they pulled away.

~

'Afterwards, I did have several threats on my life,' Starr told Beatles biographer Hunter Davies five years later. 'I had to have guards living with me. I hated it. I always felt safe in America until John was shot. But you can't go on living in fear.'

56

DOUBLE VISION

Two Boozy TV Appearances
and a Wedding, 1980–1981

Ringo had appeared to be drunk on TV before, but this time was different. This time, he was definitely drunk.

On 28 July 1980, he and Barbara turned up on *The John Davidson Show* in the States. Davidson, with his blow-dried, side-flicked hair, was an imperturbable chat show host, and also a modern-day Renaissance man who'd recorded albums as a singer for Columbia, appeared as a drag cabaret entertainer/serial killer on *The Streets of San Francisco* and been a regular celebrity contestant on game show *Hollywood Squares*. Yet, he wasn't quite equipped to deal with a wasted one-time Beatle.

In what was to be a spot of pre-publicity for *Caveman*, Starr, sans Bach, first walked out onto the set, to a wave of applause, wearing a black suit, bushy salt-and-pepper beard, almost impenetrably dark shades and bright white shoes, while snapping Polaroid pictures of his co-guests – Bee Gee little brother Andy Gibb, and *Little House on the Prairie* actress Karen Grassle. Only when he sat down, the camera closed in and he began to speak was it obvious that he was slurring.

'Do I say Ringo or Richard?' Davidson wondered.

'You can say "Ringo"', said Ringo.

'Do your close friends call you Richard?'

'Yes,' he beamed, and said no more.

Davidson gamely pressed on, trying to engage Starr in some chat about his pre-Beatles childhood. It produced not much more than single words or short sentences delivered in a semi-smug fashion, and ripples of nervous laughter from the TV studio audience.

Was he a 'nice kid'? 'Fabulous.'

Was it true that for a while in his childhood, he'd spent some time in hospital? 'Yeah, most of my life.'

For what reason? 'I was sick.'

How had that affected his life? 'Well, it made me thin.'

'Ringo, obviously, this is not going to be your regular interview,' Davidson pointed out with a grin that was lost somewhere between cheesy and uneasy. Starr then grabbed Davidson's questions card from him and held onto it. 'Let me ask you this,' said Davidson, without his notes and regaining some of his composure. 'Do you enjoy doing this? Talk shows?'

'Only with you,' Starr smiled, like a cat toying with a mouse, before handing Davidson his questions back.

After the commercial break, Ringo played the game a bit more, chatting about his fourteen-year-old son Zak being in a heavy metal band and wanting to leave school to pursue music.

'I have to be a father and say, "No, you'll go to school, or Daddy will go to jail".'

'Did somebody say that to you?' Davidson wondered.

'The police,' Ringo boom-tished, producing a gale of laughter in the audience. It was almost turning into a Beatles press conference fuelled by hard liquor.

Davidson, with some relief, then introduced 'the lovely Barbara Bach'. As she and Starr hugged and settled together on the sofa, the host said, 'Let me ask you, right off the bat. You two are having a love affair?'

'It's easy for you to say,' garbled Starr.

Had Bach, Davidson ventured, had a crush on her James Bond co-star, Roger Moore?

'I did,' Ringo flashed back.

'Oh, I liked Roger very much,' Bach politely responded. 'I also liked his wife. I must say, Roger was not my type actually. Richy is my type.'

'What is it about Richard that you love?' Davidson asked.

'I'm in love with him, so it's very hard to explain,' Bach offered with a coy smile. 'He's one of the kindest, sweetest, most human persons I've ever met in this business.'

'Is this Ringo Starr we're here with today?' Davidson leadingly enquired, presumably meaning the smartarse booze-hound sitting before him.

'This is Ringo Starr,' Bach confirmed. 'There are many faces to Ringo Starr.'

Nine months later, and only three after Lennon's murder, it was a very different, far more emotionally raw Ringo Starr who faced the cameras of ABC TV and the more developed interrogation tactics of host Barbara Walters. At first, Ringo kept up his chirpy-chappy act, though his mushed words still sounded as if they'd been dipped in 40 per cent-proof cognac.

At the start of the short item, broadcast on 31 March 1981, he was seen in the studio in LA, pretending to teach Bach to play guitar, with a cigarette dangling from his mouth ('That's right, then we do the counting like this. Ah–1–2–3...'). The couple then sat side-by-side to be interviewed.

'Barbara, is it difficult to be with a man who is part-legend as well as part-man?' Walters began, immediately throwing a curveball.

'All legend,' Ringo boomed. 'All man.'

'I don't live with the legend,' Bach tried to explain. 'I live with my Richy. Every once in a while, Ringo comes popping out at me.'

Asked to further define the difference between 'Richy' and 'Ringo', Bach confessed, 'Ringo's the loudmouth sometimes. Ringo's the shades and the drink and the cigarettes when you would prefer him not to. Ringo is the...' – her voice dropped a couple of octaves – '... deep voice.' Both laughed. 'And Richy is my Richy, y'know.'

'Do you drink too much?' Walters bluntly asked Starr.

'No, she just thinks I do,' he insisted. 'It's just our little joke, y'see, and when it goes over on TV, it'll be in all the national papers. "Oh, he's a drunk. Did you see him on the Barbara Walters show? And he had his shades on? It must mean he was on drugs."'

The action cut to Starr back in the recording studio, without his sunglasses on, talking about the surviving Beatles. He began to grow emotional as he referred to 'the other two'.

'Isn't it funny when you say that now?' he waveringly noted. 'Y'know, it's so new to me that I always sort of…' – he briefly clutched at his throat – 'it clogs you up a bit when you say it.

'But I'm sure he's OK,' he mysteriously added.

There followed a heavy pause.

'I'm really sad,' he said. 'I still miss John a great deal. I'll always miss him, but it's still brand-new.'

Walters wondered how Starr had first heard about Lennon's death.

'Barbara's daughter called us up saying, "John's been shot",' he began to explain. 'And so that drove me crazy. But you think, *He's shot in the arm, shot in the leg.* And then they came back, and they said, he's, uh, he's dead.

'Do you want to stop that now?' he said, meaning the filming.

'No,' Walters whispered.

'Because,' he sighed, his eyes red and filling up, 'it doesn't help, y'know. It always gets me upset.'

'Do you feel that you're in touch with John at times?' Walters asked, picking up the metaphysical thread that Starr had earlier touched upon.

'No, not right now,' he responded, attempting to drop it.

But Walters kept prodding, wondering if 'every now and then, you look up and you say, "You OK up there, fella?"'

'Oh, well, I believe he's OK,' Ringo concluded, enigmatically.

～

Four weeks later, on Monday, 27 April 1981, Richard Starkey and Barbara Goldbach were married in London, at the Marylebone Town Hall register office, the same venue used by Paul and Linda McCartney for their wedding a dozen years before.

The McCartneys were in attendance, along with George Harrison and his wife of two years, Olivia. 'Over thirty police officers were assigned to control the crowd that gathered to watch the celebrities arrive,' reported a correspondent for the BBC. 'With the John Lennon shooting still fresh in their minds, they were taking no chances.'

Harry Nilsson was inevitably there, along with Beatles-era pals Neil Aspinall and Derek Taylor. Richy's mum and stepdad, Elsie and Harry, both now in their late sixties, were also there to watch him get married for a second time. The bride wore an expensively elegant dress designed by husband-and-wife team David and Elizabeth Emanuel, who were around the same time busy stitching together their world-famous bridal gown for Lady Diana Spencer, in preparation for her July wedding to Prince Charles.

The Starkeys' reception knees-up was held at Rags, a club in Mayfair, where the celebrations of course spilled onto the stage. George grabbed a guitar and Harry and Paul took turns playing piano, while Ringo added a percussive accompaniment by clattering a pair of spoons on his knee, just like at one of the old parties back in the Dingle.

Sadly, it seemed to be the only music that anyone had been interested in hearing him play in a long time. Six months later, to the day, on 31 October, the solo album he'd been making with the working title of *Can't Fight Lightning* was finally released under the blessings-counting, life-appreciating new name of *Stop and Smell the Roses*. But neither these positive vibes, nor indeed sympathy from the public, could save his musical career from continuing its steep nosedive.

57

PUT ME IN THE MOVIES, PART TEN

Give My Regards to Broad Street, 1982–1984

Paul McCartney was stuck in the back of a car driving to London writing the script for a film that began with him stuck in the back of a car driving to London, writing a song. This then became the opening scene of his grand cinematic folly, *Give My Regards to Broad Street*, the title of which riffed on songwriter George M Cohan's 1904 showtune, 'Give My Regards to Broadway'.

In its own way, the 1984 movie was an attempt to revive the long-lost tradition of the Beatles Film. Since the mid-'70s, McCartney had been gradually incorporating more and more of his Fabs-era songs into his live setlists. *Broad Street* meanwhile was to be the first step in the shoring up of his legacy in the wake of Lennon's murder (and subsequent near canonisation), bringing to the big screen Beatles originals and remakes, at a time when the band's stock was super-low in the era of synth-pop troupes and indie guitar bands.

A crime caper-cum-elongated music video, *Broad Street's* Beatle-y credentials were slightly hobbled by the absence of George Harrison, with whom McCartney still had something of a prickly relationship. 'The truth is, he's not a ham,' Paul told one reporter. 'I don't think he's got any ambitions in front of the camera. He was the least keen to be acting in *A Hard Day's Night* and *Help!*'

Whereas Ringo, most of the time, had been the keenest. Naturally, then, Paul asked his old pal to get involved in this new, big-budget adventure. After

John's death, the two had seemed to pull closer together. Only two months after the horrific event, as both were still reeling from the shock, Starr flew to the Caribbean to record with McCartney at George Martin's recording studio outpost of AIR Montserrat, which had opened for business two years before.

Ringo's standout contribution to what was to be McCartney's 1982 solo album *Tug of War* was his syncopated twin drumming performance on 'Take It Away' with celebrated Steely Dan/Paul Simon collaborator Steve Gadd (who'd previously appeared on *Ringo the 4th* and approvingly noted that Starr 'played so different from [how] other drummers do').

Starr subsequently appeared in the video for its single release, visually emphasising the reconnection of his bond with McCartney via a series of time-period vignettes. At the beginning of the four-minute clip, the pair were seen sporting Teddy Boy quiffs, playing in a '50s front room that looked like an approximation of the one in Paul's childhood home at 20 Forthlin Road. Surrounding them were Gadd, Linda on tambourine, George Martin on piano and Eric Stewart, ex of 10cc, on guitar. By the end of the video, in the contemporary '80s, Ringo performed maniacally on the drums while wearing a bubble perm before acting entirely naturally by swigging champagne in a posh party scene.

In fact, Starr and McCartney had also appeared onscreen together earlier in '82, when the latter's MPL production company had overseen a ten-minute mini movie, *The Cooler*, featuring the three songs from *Stop and Smell the Roses* produced by Paul: the cringey pop of 'Private Property', Carl Perkins' country song 'Sure to Fall' (an old Beatles fave) and brassy bopper 'Attention'. The plot, or concept, really, was that Ringo was an inmate in a prison camp run entirely by women, the commandant being the foxy, red-visored authoritarian figure of Barbara Bach. Linda McCartney fleetingly appeared as another guard and Paul popped up as first a fellow prisoner and then the grey-haired double bassist in a country and western band.

The short film, directed by in-vogue video team (and also former members of 10cc) Kevin Godley and Lol Creme, was confidently premiered at the Cannes Film Festival in the spring of '82, yet overall this semi-Beatles reunion went largely unnoticed. Only those who arrived early at UK cinemas to see dud high-school musical sequel *Grease 2*, with which *The Cooler* was paired as a B-movie, ever really caught a glimpse of it.

The premise of *Give My Regards to Broad Street* was inspired by a story that Abbey Road engineer-turned-Sex Pistols producer Chris Thomas had told McCartney about the master tapes for the punk band's 1977 album *Never Mind the Bollocks, Here's the Sex Pistols* being temporarily lost, having been left by a lackey on a rainy train station platform. McCartney spun this into a far-fetched tale of the tapes for his next album being apparently stolen by a former criminal (but now a trusted employee of his) named Harry. Paul's team of stern business associates fear that Harry plans to bootleg the recordings and a mad search begins.

In his car journeys up and down to London, McCartney sketched out the plot of the film on page after page of foolscap. At first envisaging it as an hour-long TV special à la *Magical Mystery Tour*, he made what he called the 'fatal mistake' of thinking it could easily be expanded into a full-length feature film. Worse, he overrode director Peter Webb with his ideas; 'I started telling people how to write,' he admitted. Still, even after the film went into production in November 1982, McCartney began to have his doubts about the project. 'Halfway through I started to think, *Oh God*,' he later confessed. 'But we were stuck with it. *We'll have to see it out.*'

Worse, perhaps, the famously frugal McCartney had started out financing the project himself to the tune of $3 million. 'In the first week alone,' he bemoaned, 'we'd spent nearly all that and I was writing a new cheque.' A deal was subsequently cut with 20th Century Fox and the budget ballooned to $9 million, along with the expectation of handsome profits.

Starr was clearly happy to work with McCartney on a new film, though wasn't so keen on revisiting his past via Paul's notion to remake some of the old Beatles classics. In the end, he left Fairport Convention drummer Dave Mattacks to provide the rhythm track for the reworked 'The Long and Winding Road'. 'He didn't want to attempt a new version,' said Paul of Ringo. 'He didn't even want a comparison.'

Ten minutes into the movie, Starr first appeared, in a recording studio scene, uncharacteristically banging a huge gong, then tinkering with an enormous, Keith Moon-proportioned drum kit, the likes of which he never played. After a stiff conversation between Paul and Ringo, in which the former told the latter about the stolen tapes, there followed a series of gags in which the two made fun of their former rivalries.

'So what are we doing?' Ringo asked, meaning which song.

'The medley,' said Paul.

'What medley?' Starr wondered, then held aloft a pair of sticks, before being instructed by McCartney to use brushes. A grumpy Ringo stomped off to find a pair, rummaging through a flight case as Paul and a brass section launched into 'Yesterday', then 'Here, There and Everywhere'. The hapless drummer finally found a pair of brushes, but, hilariously, by then the song was over.

Later, in a Thameside rehearsal warehouse, Paul asked the band, 'Shall we try "Not Such a Bad Boy"?'

'Do we have to?' Ringo huffed.

'Yeah,' Paul responded, firmly and bossily.

At the end of the toothless rocker, McCartney turned to Starr, saying, 'That's great, that', meaning his drum part.

'Yeah, I know,' Starr humphed. 'It's about time you noticed.'

In truth, Starr had pushed for 'Not Such a Bad Boy' to be included in the film after McCartney grew unsure about the song. 'Linda and Ringo really loved it,' Paul said, 'and requested its reinstatement.'

Elsewhere, in a '50s ballroom rehearsal scene, Starr – his hair swept back up into his quiff, his grey streak undyed – and Barbara Bach, playing a bespectacled journalist, enjoyed a flirty encounter. The rest was all guest celebrities and delving into the dress-up box. Tracey Ullman turned up as a punk rocker called Sandra. British wrestler Giant Haystacks appeared as a heavy named Big Bob. Starr was meanwhile spared appearing alongside Paul and Linda et al, in white make-up and coiffured black-and-platinum hair, as a New Romantic band performing 'Silly Love Songs'. Toto drummer Jeff Porcaro gamely stepped behind the kit looking like an extra from *Doctor Who*.

Ultimately, the problem with *Give My Regards to Broad Street* was that, aside from a few decent musical performances (Ringo and Paul playing 'Wanderlust' with the brass ensemble, and the full band – including guitarists Chris Spedding and Dave Edmunds – running through the new wave-y 'No Values'), even an hour in, there wasn't much in the way of thrills and spills.

When the action did finally get going, Macca's psychic rumblings about his pal Harry's innocence led to a preposterous Victorian fantasy sequence freighted with incomprehensible significance. Back in the real world, Paul suddenly remembered that the last thing Harry had told him was that he was heading to Broad Street station. Rushing there, he found the tapes sitting on a platform bench and his accused pal innocently locked inside a guard's shed he'd mistaken for a public toilet. Paul phoned Linda, who was sitting at home with Ringo and Barbara, and hearing the news, they uncorked a bottle of bubbly in celebration.

Then, every last molecule of credibility evaporated when McCartney awoke in the back of his car and the whole thing turned out to have been a dream.

⁓

Visually, at least, *Give My Regards to Broad Street* looked crisp and colourful, throwing every last cent of its $9 million budget up onto the screen. Sadly, with its theatrical release, it lost more than $7.5 million. Reviewing the film on BBC1's *Film 84*, critic Barry Norman reserved a particular barb for one of the key players, stating, 'Ringo Starr drifts in and out in a performance which suggests he should run, not walk, to the nearest acting school'.

'There's a couple of redeeming features about it,' McCartney later reflected to writer Paul Du Noyer, 'but it's just not very good. What can you say?

'I mean, George did *Shanghai Surprise*,' he added, digging at his former bandmate, who'd taken a multi-million-dollar bath by producing the notorious Madonna- and Sean Penn-starring 1986 flop. 'You've just got to own up when it's a bit of a bummer.'

That same year, though not apparently through its association with the cinematic turkey that had borrowed its name, the actual Broad Street station in the City of London was demolished.

58

BEATLE FOR SALE

Hosting *Saturday Night Live*, 1984

The English auctioneer faced the seated rows of prospective bidders and buyers and opened his mouth to reveal his noticeably gappy and discoloured British teeth. A sign behind his head read: 'International Beatle Memorabilia Auction'.

'Do I hear $50,000 for this guitar pick used by John Lennon in the recording of "Eight Days a Week?"' he asked the assembled. 'No? Sold for $45,000 to the gentleman sitting in the front row.' He hammered his gavel and moved onto the next item in the catalogue, Lot 35. 'This is a very exciting little piece,' he said. 'A toothbrush used by the fabulous Paul McCartney in the recording of the album *Rubber Soul*.' The bidding opened at $60,000 and, after only a few seconds of eager activity, ended at $110,000.

If the dentally challenged trader looked familiar, and suspiciously like comedian Martin Short, it was because this was the 'cold open' of NBC's *Saturday Night Live* show of 8 December 1984.

'And now, ladies and gentlemen, please turn to page 22 in your catalogue,' Short instructed. 'Take a look at Lot 36. Ringo... Starr.'

At this point, Ringo was wheeled in, on a stand-up gurney, wearing a collarless Beatle jacket in the style of '63, to screams and roars of surprise from the studio audience. He and Short soaked it up for a full twenty seconds.

'He was, for nine years, the drummer with the Beatles,' Short went on, as Starr silently grinned, 'and performed with them on all their albums and tours. Now, as you can see, he's in very good condition.'

The bidding, after opening at $75,000, was non-existent. An elderly couple got up and left. Short quickly dropped the opening price to $65,000 and hopefully pointed out that Starr was also 'the owner of a large ring condition'. One man in the front row, *Airplane!* actor Robert Hays, enquired about Ringo's jacket: 'Was it by any chance ever worn by Paul?'

'No, it wasn't, I'm sorry,' Short gurned as Starr remained mute. 'Now, do I hear $15,000 for Ringo Starr? Good lord, we're dealing with a human being here.'

New *SNL* cast member Pamela Stephenson in the second row put up her hand.

'Does he actually do anything?' she anxiously wondered.

Short brought in his colleague 'Ann' (Mary Gross) who knew more.

'Well, he plays the drums,' she said, 'and he has a very interesting ring collection.'

'Can he talk?' asked Stephenson.

'Oh, yes, I think so,' said Gross, handing him a card. 'Ringo, would you read this?'

Starr scanned the words, then looked into the camera and delivered the famous catchphrase, 'Live, from New York... it's Saturday night!'

~

Four years to the day since John Lennon's murder, and only twenty-one blocks south-east of the Dakota, Starr was in Studio 8H at 30 Rockefeller Plaza, giving fresh life to the old cliché that laughter is the best medicine by sending up his and his former group's legacy. To be fair, Lennon, a fan of the show, likely would have loved the Beatle-belittling ridiculousness of the skit.

Starr's acceptance of the offer to host an episode in the tenth season of the NBC comedy sketch show, watched by more than ten million viewers, was proof of the lasting power of his celebrity as he moved into the mid-'80s. His fellow hosts during that season ranged from *Jaws* actor Roy Scheider to *Beverly Hills Cop* star Eddie Murphy and *Superman* Christopher Reeve.

In truth, behind the scenes, the *SNL* team were shattered by the time they got around to the Ringo-starring episode. Due to the high demands of rewriting their scripts right up until the camera lights turned red in a bid to keep the show ultra-current, the writers were operating on fumes. Executive producer

Dick Ebersol remembered that a Wednesday evening cast read-through of that week's proposed sketches was 'a travesty'. Afterwards, Ebersol walked Starr and Bach to their hotel. 'Don't worry,' he assured them.

Returning to the writers, the producer told them, 'We have nothing. I know everybody is exhausted. But let's take all our best characters and write a show around them.' Most of the team went without sleep for the next forty-eight hours, resulting in what Ebersol later tepidly reckoned to be 'a pretty good show'.

Bagging Ringo Starr as *SNL*'s host was a seemingly big deal. Martin Short's wife Nancy Dolman turned up on set, caught sight of Ringo, became over-whelmingly starstruck and began physically shaking. 'That is a *Beatle*,' she disbelievingly pointed out to her husband.

In the episode's running order, following the opening memorabilia gag and as was the tradition, Starr turned up solo (wearing an oversized grey overcoat, stripey shirt and bow tie) for an introductory to-camera monologue. 'Well, I might have changed my name, but I didn't change my nose,' he quipped. 'Michael Jackson changed his nose,' he added, nodding knowingly.

He was then joined by Billy Crystal, lampooning Sammy Davis Jr in toe-curling blackface (and this in the supposedly enlightened 1980s). Together they sang an overlong swinging medley of songs cut-and-shutting 'Photograph', 'Act Naturally', 'Octopus's Garden' and 'Yellow Submarine'. During Ringo's *Sgt. Pepper* signature tune, and producing the segment's best gag, Crystal turned to the camera and sang, 'I got high with a little help from his friends'.

As the show progressed, Starr appeared in various sketches. Opposite Short's pointy-haired and overactive man-boy character Ed Grimley, he played it deadpan as 'a very unlucky man' repeatedly struck by lightning. Then, he and Bach sat either side of Billy Crystal as they were interviewed by him in the guise of his debonair, if lecherous playboy character Fernando. He largely ignored Ringo to pay greasy compliments to Barbara: 'You look marvellous.' At one point, he mentioned to Starr, 'That Beatle thing really took off, didn't it?'

Then, in a follow-up to the auction sketch, Ringo was seen sitting on the sofa at the home of his eventual buyer, Pamela Stephenson, and her disgruntled husband, played by Jim Belushi. 'Can I have my bubble wrap, please?' asked the human purchase, before annoyingly bopping away to the theme song of sitcom *The Jeffersons* blasting out of the television. By this point, there may have been some buyer's remorse going on. Julia Louis-Dreyfus then appeared and offered to buy Ringo from the couple for $1,700, or 'the price of two deluxe La-Z-Boy lounge chairs'.

By the end – as mirrored in real life by '84 when his days of being a working musician were fading, and he was fast becoming best known as a media personality – it was hard to tell if Starr's value was going up or down.

59

ACROSS THE UNIVERSE

Ringo in Space, 1984–2023

High in the flat upland of Coconino County, Arizona, at the Anderson Mesa Station observatory on the evening of 31 August 1984, US astronomer Brian Skiff was scanning deep space. Tracking an asteroid, roughly seven kilometres wide, spinning silently amid the detritus of the solar system, he chose a name for it: 4150 Starr.

Ringo – at least in a symbolic sense – had made his first move into space.

Still, in keeping with the John, Paul, George and Ringo pecking order of the Beatles, he was the last of the four to be immortalised in space rock. Lennon, as ever, was the first, the previous January 1983, with a bright vestoid that Skiff called 4147 Lennon. McCartney's surname was given to another minor planet, 4148 McCartney, in July of the same year, before 4149 Harrison was discovered and designated by the Beatle-headed night sky-watcher the following March.

In fact, Ringo's asteroid had been spotted long before, in the spring of 1957, by a member of staff at the Goethe Link Observatory, 1,600 miles across the US in Martinsville, Indiana. But this was back when Richy Starkey, sixteen-year-old part-time drummer with the Eddie Clayton Skiffle Group, was carting his kit around the streets of Liverpool while trying to avoid marauding Teddy Boys.

No one was interested in naming anything, and particularly not a far-distant asteroid, after him.

⌒

On 7 July 2020, an astronaut, Chris Cassidy, commander of the International Space Station, was floating 260 miles above Earth.

'Hi Ringo,' he said into a wobbly camera. 'Happy birthday. My crew mates and I would like to extend our sincere and best birthday wishes to you. As an icon of music, your message of peace and love has echoed around the world for decades. Our crew and the entire NASA family would like to extend this message to the world and across the universe from our orbiting laboratory.'

The occasion was Ringo's eightieth. He quickly responded via his official Twitter account:

'Wow, this is a first ... peace and love from outer space ... I sent you right back peace and love ... thank you.'

Even the Curiosity rover, which had landed on Mars eight years before, sent its cosmic congratulations through the medium of social media ventriloquism, while acknowledging that its home planet was at the time paralysed by COVID-19.

'Happy 80th, Ringo!' 'said' Curiosity in a break from roaming around studying Martian geology. 'Here's my view of Earth (and Venus) from the surface of Mars where I'm thinking about your message of #PeaceAndLove, and how in good times and in tough ones, we all get by with a little help from our friends.'

In an unlikely twist, both of these events were to spark a mutual love affair between Ringo Starr and NASA.

Seven months later, when the Perseverance rover successfully touched down on the surface of the red planet on 18 February 2021, Ringo immediately tweeted his blessings: 'Congratulations NASA ... we landed on Mars ... well done peace and love peace and love.'

He excitedly followed this message with a series of his favourite emojis – a yellow smiley face wearing shades, a two-fingered peace salute, a golden star, a red heart, three musical notes, a partial rainbow, a piece of broccoli, two clapping hands and a white CND/peace symbol within a purple square.

~

Six months later, on 16 October 2021, NASA launched the *Lucy* space probe on its planned twelve-year journey – way beyond 4150 Starr – to the Trojan asteroids sharing Jupiter's orbit around the sun.

Lucy was named after the fossilised female hominin bones discovered by Donald Johanson and his paleoanthropological team in Ethiopia on 24 November 1974. On the first night of the excavation trip, Johanson and crew had played one song loudly and on repeat, 'Lucy in the Sky with Diamonds' – hence the adoptive name given to the 40 per cent-reassembled skeleton of this 3.2 million-year-old woman. Starr later poetically noted that she was essentially 'the mother of all of us'.

It was also a name deemed altogether fitting for *Lucy* the spacecraft's mission to the outer regions of the solar system forty-seven years later. The probe was being sent on its long voyage to study what are believed to be remnants of the primordial material of the outer planets – Jupiter, Saturn, Uranus and Neptune. Scientists hoped these might prove to be the 'fossils of planet formation'.

In the tradition of *Voyager 1* and *2*, both launched in 1977 and still star-sailing through interstellar space, *Lucy* contained an equivalent of the 'Golden Records' onboard those twin craft, which had offered music from the human race – everyone from Bach to Chuck Berry – to extra-terrestrial lifeforms (along with instructions on how to actually play a vinyl record). Fitted to *Lucy* was a golden plaque, inscribed with quotes, past and present, from significant global 'thought leaders', including Carl Sagan, Martin Luther King Jr and John Lennon.

Ringo, when asked to contribute, seized his chance, not unexpectedly offering the words 'peace and love'.

Sometime after 2033, once her mission is complete, *Lucy* will remain in the solar system, moving between the Trojan asteroids and the orbit of Earth for what NASA reckons to be 'at least hundreds of thousands, if not millions of years'. And so there is the possibility, however remote and head-spinning, that some future civilisation or intelligence might discover her and find the plaque.

In his online video message to commemorate the probe's launch, Ringo could scarcely contain himself with big-kid glee. Sat behind his Ludwig drum kit in his home studio in LA – backdropped by an array of cartoonishly thin woodcut pop-art figures of himself (for instance, beatific '67 Ringo with a red spray-painted face; moody and hungover '70s Ringo in sunglasses), he performed a loud, fat roll and looked up towards the camera.

'A little noisy but I'm so excited,' he announced. '*Lucy* is going back in the sky with diamonds.' He opened his jacket to reveal a T-shirt bearing Lennon's scribbly self-portrait. 'Johnny'll love that.'

'Anyway, if you meet anyone up there, *Lucy*, give them peace and love from me,' he concluded, flashing his trademark four-digit salute.

⁓

Thirteen years earlier, in the summer of 2008, an interviewer had asked Starr what he would like from his fans for his upcoming sixty-eighth birthday.

'I don't know where it came from,' he later reflected. 'But I just thought, *You know what would be great? If they could all break off at noon, wherever they are in the world and spend a moment thinking of peace and love.* Then I had this great idea to have a get together.

'I was on tour in Chicago ... we stood in the street giving out little cakes,' he added, before wryly pointing out, 'some of which were on the internet four hours later for $300.'

By the summer of 2023, Ringo's birthday had become something of a big international deal. On the occasion of his eighty-third, 'peace and love' video blessings came in from twenty-seven locations around the world, everywhere from Tokyo to Ticino, Barcelona to Buenos Aires.

NASA – who, on his eighty-first in 2021, had posted a message on their website declaring 'almost boundless' birthday wishes to him, 'extending all the way beyond Mars to our solar system's asteroid belt, home to the asteroid that bears his name, 4150 Starr' – decided to make a grand gesture for his eighty-third. They took a pre-recorded 'peace and love' message from Starr and hatched a plan to send it – as he put it, in a most Ringoishly fashion – 'out there way out there there'.

At midday on 7 July 2023, the message was beamed skywards from one of the dish antennas at the Goldstone Deep Space Communications Complex in the Mojave Desert and relayed via a chain of interplanetary craft in the direction of the Stephan's Quintet galaxies, 290 million light-years away – destined, perhaps, to echo through space for ever more.

'Peace and luv…'

'Peace and luv…'

'Peace and luv…'

'Peace and luv…'

'Peace and luv…'

'Peace and luv…'

'Peace and luv…'

'Peace and luv…'

'Peace and luv…'

'Peace and luv…'

60

THE LITTLE MAN IN THE MURAL

Thomas the Tank Engine & Friends and *Shining Time Station*, 1984–1989

For a generation of kids born in the late 1970s and early '80s, David Bowie was not a shapeshifting genius of pop, but the elaborately wigged goblin king Jareth in Jim Henson's daft 1986 musical fantasy film, *Labyrinth*. For that same generation, Ringo Starr wasn't the drummer in the Beatles, but the warm-voiced Scouse narrator of UK children's TV series *Thomas the Tank Engine & Friends* and, in vastly reduced physical form, the 18-inch tall Mr Conductor in its American offshoot, *Shining Time Station*.

Starr always had a voice that was suited to kids' stories. It was a talent he'd chanced upon and one that could be traced back to his (unused) spoken-word introductions to Beatles songs: the mad walk from Land's End to John O'Groats that preceded 'Yellow Submarine' and the toys-tidying instructions at the start of 'Good Night'. Both sections had ultimately been snipped but showcased his comfortable and friendly tones.

In some ways, from there, it was a career strand that he seemed almost destined to pursue. In 1977, he'd released the children's album *Scouse the Mouse*, involving the tale of a Liverpudlian rodent emigrating to the US. More recently, he'd revoiced – replacing Dustin Hoffman's original narration for contractual reasons – Harry Nilsson's 1971 animation *The Point!* for its 1985 release on video tape.

'Well, I've always sort of felt I've got on with kids,' Ringo reckoned. 'I like kids. I used to be one.'

In 1983, UK TV producer Britt Allcroft visited Starr at his Tittenhurst mansion with an offer for him to narrate a televised adaptation of *The Railway Series* books authored by the then-septuagenarian Reverend Wilbert Awdry. Allcroft had already funnelled a lot of her own money into the project, even remortgaging her house in the belief that the series could be a big hit. Still, she was struggling to find a voice actor to fit the show and had gone through dozens of unsuitable candidates, including Sir John Gielgud. Then, one night at home in 1982, she was passing her living room where her family happened to be watching a BBC One screening of Starr's appearance on *Parkinson in Australia*.

'I said, "That's it!",' Allcroft later recalled of the eureka moment when she realised that Starr's ripe Liverpudlian delivery was perfect for the series. '"It's Ringo!"'

At Tittenhurst, Starr listened to Allcroft's pitch, looked for reassurance that the animation wouldn't be 'cheap looking', but in the end turned down her proposal, believing that kids in the '80s were more into 'dinosaurs with guns on their backs, and spaceships'. However, the producer persevered, subsequently convincing Ringo to record five of Awdry's stories as a de facto demo tape. Everyone was so pleased with the results that he was contracted to narrate a full twenty-six-episode series. Crucially, Starr was also given an 8 per cent stake in Allcroft's company. It was to prove to be a highly lucrative deal.

Employing a combination of moving model trains and clay animation, the series related the tales of the titular blue steam engine with the human face, zipping around the fictional Island of Sodor and getting into mishaps and adventures with his pals Gordon, Edward and Henry, as overseen by their boss Sir Topham Hatt aka the Fat Controller. These were gentle stories of friendship, collective effort and mild peril aimed at two-to-six-year-olds. Starr complemented the format perfectly, sounding smooth and unflustered, knowing and droll, yet at the same time capable of rising in pitch and urgency in moments of high excitement.

If he had the perfect voice for children's TV, his rumpled demeanour at the time was less appropriate, as was proven when he appeared on live ITV breakfast show *Good Morning Britain* to promote the show on the Tuesday morning of 9 October 1984 at the – for him – ungodly hour of 8.14 a.m. Bearded and sounding husky, wearing dark aviator sunglasses and looking like he'd been up half the night (which he quite possibly had), he sat side-by-side on the sofa with the grey-haired, dog collar-wearing Reverend Awdry.

During their chat with presenters Nick Owen and Jayne Irving, Starr explained that he'd recorded his contributions to the series over eight days, before having to return to redo four episodes that had been taped one morning when he'd sounded particularly rough. His voice dropped an octave to demonstrate. 'Hello kiddies,' he growled. 'It's Uncle Richy 'ere.'

The reverend didn't add much to the conversation, except to confirm that Starr had done 'an excellent job'.

Owen, of course, tried to gently swerve the conversation onto the Beatles. 'Do you find it actually difficult, Ringo ... to find new boundaries to cross over?' he gently probed. 'Because you've achieved so much.'

'Yes, I know it's difficult,' Starr responded, adopting a mock-luvvie tone. 'Getting out of bed's the problem these days,' he added, hinting at the truth.

Undaunted, Owen pushed on. 'But seriously,' he said, 'I would genuinely think that you've got nothing else to achieve.'

'That's ridiculous,' Ringo snapped back. 'There's lots to achieve. Um, there's records to make ... there's still acting I'd like to do.'

'You don't lack self-confidence when you're doing something new?' Owen wondered.

'I don't lack self-confidence *ever*,' Starr firmly stated.

Later, Irving announced that 'one of our guests on the show today is a duck that can't swim'. Turning to Ringo, she wondered if that might be of interest to him 'because you're a bit into animals, aren't you?'

'Well, not *that* way,' he smirked.

It was enough to make parents across the land spit out their toast as they were getting ready to take their kids to school. Still, they all tuned in, in their millions, when the show debuted that day at noon.

～

Starr signed on to do a second series of *Thomas the Tank Engine & Friends*, broadcast in 1986, and put his name to commercial spin-off after spin-off in the form of audio books and VHS compilations. But one thing he'd said about the show in the *Good Morning Britain* interview was telling: 'I wish I was in it more than just the voice.'

In 1988, Allcroft sold the format to PBS in the US and expanded it into the series *Shining Time Station*. It mixed the tales of Thomas et al with live action scenes involving a cast including *Grease* star Didi Conn as the benevolent, nanny-like station master Stacy Jones and *Sesame Street*'s Leonard Jackson as big, friendly engineer Henry 'Harry' Cupper.

But Ringo was the true star of *Shining Time Station* in his role as Mr Conductor, a tiny rail official who lived in a mural painted on a wall in the station house and who could magically teleport himself via a toot of his whistle and a puff of gold dust.

Following its debut in January 1989, the show quickly became a success, regularly pulling in audiences of more than seven million. For a while, the nature of Starr's fame, particularly in the US, completely changed. 'I know if a kid comes over to me now and says "Ringo!", his mother sent him,' he laughed. ''Cos the kid's … "Ah, it's Mr Conductor!"'

Still, he only committed to one series (and a Christmas special) of *Shining Time Station*. Mr Conductor went to live at the North Pole with Santa Claus, so his cousin, stand-up comedian George Carlin, picked up the pint-sized role for the next two seasons, although Starr continued to pick up the cheques through his shares in the production company. (In a slightly strange twist, in the UK in 1991, Michael Angelis, brother of Paul Angelis who'd voiced Ringo in *Yellow Submarine*, took over his *Thomas* narrating job.)

But Starr's role as Mr Conductor was all the more fitting given that he had just emerged from a long, dark tunnel of his own.

61

ROCK BOTTOM

A Trip to Arizona, 1988

Ringo couldn't remember being onstage with the Beach Boys, even though there was visual evidence to prove that he had been.

Three days before he turned forty-four, Starr guested with the Californian band at a 1984 Independence Day concert in the parkland of the National Mall in Washington, DC, for a vast audience of more than half a million people.

'Somebody showed me a photo,' he said later, 'so I know it must have happened.'

Seven songs into the band's daytime set, he arrived onstage, wandered up to the microphone and sang a snatch of the Crystals' 'Da Doo Ron Ron' while performing a funny little dance, then clambered behind the drum kit. He and the group then kicked into a cover of the Beatles' homage to the Beach Boys, 'Back in the USSR'. No one seemed to mind that Ringo hadn't ever really played the song, after quitting the sessions for *The White Album* following his studio rehearsal argument with McCartney, who'd quickly picked up his sticks. Now he was attempting to perform it to an enormous crowd while squiffy.

He wasn't staggering drunk, but he'd obviously imbibed enough to blot out any recollections of the day. Still, his musicianly muscle memory didn't fail him and any sloppiness in his playing was covered up by the Beach Boys' rotating drummer and percussionist, Mike Kowalski and Bobby Figueroa, supportively driving the song along on either side of him. Starr then helped the band close out their set with a selection of their best-known '60s hits – 'Good Vibrations', 'Help Me, Rhonda' and 'Fun, Fun, Fun'.

At the end, he walked back to the front of the stage. 'Quiet!' he shouted, in a failed effort to kill the applause. 'I've just got to say it's been a pleasure to play with these boys.' Clearly, he was aware of where he was and what he was doing, even if his mental snapshots of the event were to quickly disintegrate.

Next, everyone flew down to Florida to play a second massive show on the same day, on Miami's South Beach, for an estimated audience of quarter of a million. Photographs taken backstage caught Starr looking sweaty and bemused, as his ever-radiant wife took his hand and led him in the right direction.

It had been less than four years since Barbara Bach, in the first bloom of their relationship, told *People* magazine that 'Ringo is part of my stability now. He has given me even more than I already had and that's what I want for our future. We have no intention of losing each other.'

But only eleven months after their April '81 wedding, newspaper stories in the US and UK appeared suggesting that their marriage was on the rocks. In March 1982, New York tabloid the *Daily News* reported the couple had been seen fighting in public in Antigua: 'Bottles flew through the air and slaps were administered.' Incensed, Starr called the offices of the *Daily Mirror* in the UK in a bid to kill what he described as the 'nonsense' rumours. 'Barbara is here with me now,' he said, 'and I'm telling you in front of her that I'm deeply in love with her, and we are very much married … Now and forever!'

Six years later, in 1988, the *People* newspaper in Britain similarly published a story claiming that Starr and Bach had been involved in another 'typical public punch-up' in a hotel in Jamaica. Gobsmacked fellow guests had apparently watched on 'in amazement as the angry pair stood 20 ft. apart lobbing bottles at each other, then swooped and started slapping each other'. One onlooker was quoted as saying, 'It was like a Laurel and Hardy slapstick, only they weren't acting.'

These messy scenes also continued behind closed doors. Later, the couple would admit that during this time 'we used to go on long plane journeys, rent huge villas, stock up the bars, hide and get deranged'. Trying to make light of their dark predicament, Ringo joked, 'Barbara and I would have parties every night, and we were the only two people there.'

For Starr, cocktail hour typically began around 9 a.m. He subsequently confessed that where he'd previously appeared to be a happy-go-lucky rock 'n' roll boozer, he'd been quite the opposite, even prior to Lennon's killing. 'I wasn't well when he got murdered,' he said, 'and I wasn't well after it.

'I was in such great pain that I hardly noticed,' he claimed, even if he'd obviously had the presence of mind to immediately fly to New York to see Yoko and Sean.

'I was just trapped as an alcoholic,' he said. 'A drunk.'

~

It certainly didn't help that, on New Year's Day 1987, Ringo's mother Elsie died, at the age of seventy-two. (She was survived by Harry Graves, who would succumb to pneumonia seven years later.) After the funeral, her son collected some of her personal boxes from her attic and was touched to discover that she'd kept mementos, cuttings and ticket stubs from every period of his life and career.

'She was such a hoarder,' he said astonishedly. 'Who knew? The woman loved every second of my life, and remembered every second of my life. She was the best.'

In the midst of his grief and incessant drinking, Starr misguidedly endeavoured to make another album, his first since 1983's *Old Wave*. In 1986, when the extent of his alcoholism had yet to be revealed, he'd been hired as the face of Sun Country Classic, a sweet and fizzy 6 per cent blend of – as he sold it in the ad campaign – 'premium wine and fruit juice'. While shooting a commercial in the Bahamas, Starr one day bumped into Chips Moman, the Memphis-based producer responsible for the late-'60s Elvis Presley hits 'Suspicious Minds' and 'In the Ghetto'.

The two bonded in the Caribbean as drinking pals and together hatched a plan to make a record in Tennessee at both Moman's 3 Alarm Studio and the legendary Sun Studio. Between February and April 1987, close to twenty tracks were recorded, all of which were duly scrapped.

The modus operandi was an old one for Starr, going back to *Sentimental Journey* and *Beaucoups of Blues*: he was to sing over arrangements put together entirely by the producer. Quickly, though, the sessions turned boozy and druggy, being lubricated by wine, cognac, tequila and what Starr vividly referred to as 'several unrecognisable substances'. In the studio, Moman's wife, the perhaps appropriately named Toni Wine (co-writer, with Carole Bayer Sager, of the Mindbenders' 1965 hit, 'A Groovy Kind of Love'), was on hand to help Ringo work out his vocal parts. Her task, in his mind, was to stop him from slipping into the role of an easy-listening crooner.

On the evidence of the various tracks subsequently bootlegged, a few of which tried to drag him fully into the '80s with gated drums and slap bass, Starr didn't sound so much intoxicated as noncommittal. Only with the arrival of none other than Bob Dylan did Ringo rouse himself into action. In the reflective, middle-aged rock ballad, 'Wish I Knew Now (What I Knew Then)', he turned in a tremulous, if heartfelt-sounding performance, as Dylan traded lines with him in the second verse, harmonised along in the choruses and added a wheezing harmonica solo.

In a leaked rehearsal take of the moody, funky 'Hard Times' (not to be confused with the song of the same name on *Bad Boy*), Starr was audibly sloshed. 'Woo, I love freeform!' he exclaimed at one point, before bizarrely declaring, 'Excuse me, we're off to India.' With no little irony, during the same sessions, he recorded a version of Johnny Nash's international 1972 hit, 'I Can See Clearly Now'.

Midway through the recording of the album, a media storm blew up in Memphis after it was discovered that Starr was currently in the city. In a provocative rant printed in local paper the *Commercial Appeal*, columnist Rheta Grimsley Johnson sniffily opined that 'the other three Beatles were not just better looking; they were accomplished musicians. Ringo's songs were comic relief. An aging Beatle is yesterday's news.'

Moman was furious, particularly because he was at the time trying to attract other acts to the town, and felt that such negative publicity might deter them from booking his 3 Alarm Studio in the future. He even arranged a protest outside the newspaper's offices, rallying somewhere in the region of 100 demonstrators whose placards variously stated, 'Up With Memphis Music', 'We Love You Ringo' and, in reference to Starr's recent ad campaign, 'I'd Rather Buy A Wine Cooler Then [*sic*] Your Paper'.

'I mean, that's the thing that this paper's done,' Moman fumed to a news reporter from the city's WREG TV, 'is to stop people coming here, with this kind of trash.'

Starr, for his part, didn't seem too fussed by the furore. When the album sessions ended in April, he generously threw a big party for more than 250 guests on a riverboat, the *Island Queen*, cruising down the Mississippi River. Onboard, typically unruffled, he told a journalist, 'I've been in the game too long now to worry about what anyone's saying.'

Still, he later disowned the Memphis recordings, taking Moman to court when the producer made a move to release them as an album on his own CRS Records label. Starr successfully argued that he and Moman had been under the influence of alcohol and marijuana in the studio and, as a result, his performances were sub-par. In the end, Ringo bought the master tapes back for $75,000, almost half of what Moman claimed he had spent funding the album.

'We put an injunction on it,' said Starr. 'It just never came out.'

At the beginning of 1988, cutting ties with the past and once again restlessly moving on, Ringo sold Tittenhurst Park for £5 million (more than £17 million adjusted for inflation) to Sheikh Zayed bin Sultan Al Nahyan, the then-ruler of Abu Dhabi (who had, six years before, employed Starr and Robin Cruikshank's ROR to refit his guest palace in the United Arab Emirates' capital).

One day, a workman helping Starr to remove the contents of the house was shocked when, out in its grounds, Ringo burned a pile of John Lennon's left-behind letters, clothes, tapes and drawings.

'I don't want anybody else to have them,' Starr reportedly told him. 'They'll only make money out of them.'

There was no firm plan about where Ringo and Barbara were to settle next and so they continued to move around the world, becoming increasingly aimless. It was a heightened extension of the jet-setting, globe-trotting nothingness that taken over his life in 1976, except that now he didn't have work to distract him or (even marginally) temper his drinking. By this point, as he would later admit, booze had entirely wrecked his drive, particularly as a musician.

'I just got caught up in that strange belief that if you're creative, you have to be brain-damaged,' he reflected, three years on. 'I was too busy taking stuff to do *anything*.' Most days, whether he was in England or California, even the thought of going into a recording studio disturbed him because, in his mind, it would involve being 'in the car for forty minutes without a drink'. By this advanced stage in his addiction, he was able to 'sink a bottle of brandy in five hefty shots, then pick up another'.

Even worse, he and Bach were now locked in a dangerous co-dependency. 'Barbara fell into the trap because of me,' he guiltily acknowledged. 'Then her career went the same way as mine. Working two days a year is not having a career.'

All the while, the benders grew longer, sometimes going on for days, and the arguments and fights and subsequent blackouts worsened. That was until one significant day in early October 1988.

'Out of a blackout, I came to and I had done a lot of damage,' he confessed thirty years later, without colouring in the details, in a fundraiser speech for the US non-profit organisation Facing Addiction and the NCADD (National Council on Alcoholism and Drug Dependence).

'I was about to lose the love of my life, Barbara, and everything else,' he went on. 'It was my moment. I said to Barbara, "You've got to get us into one of those places." We thought she was a professional because she'd gone to one the year before... for one day.'

At first, no rehabilitation centre would accept them as a couple. Only the Sierra Tucson treatment facility, set amid 160 isolated acres in the Arizona desert, agreed to take them in.

Like a man condemned, but with access to as much booze as he wanted, Starr got hammered on the flight over. 'I drank all the way,' he bleakly recalled, 'and got off the plane completely demented. I thought I was going to a lunatic asylum.'

⁓

It wasn't Ringo Starr and Barbara Bach who entered the facility in the second week of October '88. It was 'Rich' and 'Barb', as the staff called them. There, the pair were given individual rooms, with no access to telephones or television, and were treated the same as any of the other in-patients. 'To begin with,' said

Starr, 'I didn't know if I could handle it. They had us doing the laundry and cleaning the ashtrays.'

Meanwhile, in the outside world, as the story broke, TV news helicopters circled over the Sierra Tucson, their cameramen hoping to capture a glimpse of the celebrities in their delicate state of recovery.

For their friends, it was a moment of some relief, as they could now publicly confess how worried they'd been for Starr and Bach. 'I'm really glad he's sorting out his problems,' George Harrison commented. 'Ringo's a lovely bloke and a great mate.'

Linda McCartney candidly stated that 'Paul and I knew about Ringo's addiction to the bottle for years, but were afraid to say anything. We were only too aware that Ringo and Barbara were wrecking their lives, but we dreaded what would happen to the friendship if [we] tried to intervene. There was nothing we could do about it. It was up to Ringo and Barbara to sort it out. If we had said anything, they would not have stopped drinking, and we would have lost our friends.'

During their first week in the clinic, Starr remained resistant to the rehabilitation process. 'Eight days in, I decided, *I am here to get help because I know I'm sick.* Then I did whatever they asked me to.'

Digging into the dirt of his emotional past during psychotherapy sessions, he began to trace the roots of his problems back to his father, Richard Sr, abandoning him as a child.

'I felt really angry,' he said, 'going through therapy in rehab, when I came to look at myself and get to know my feelings, instead of blocking them all out. For me, I felt I'd dealt with it when I was little. I didn't understand that really I had been blocking my anger out. You get on with it. That's how we were brought up.'

After completing the six-week treatment plan, the couple flew back to England in the last week of November. 'Thank God, it pulled me through,' Starr said of the life-changing experience. 'I can never thank that clinic enough.'

~

Four years on, Ringo and Barbara co-authored the foreword to former Beatles publicist Derek Taylor's 1992 book, *Getting Sober... and Loving It!*, an anthology of first-hand recovery accounts from the likes of Eric Clapton, Anthony Hopkins, Ian McShane, and, unfortunately, Gary Glitter.

'All the pain and wreckage of our past is now serving us well,' wrote the pair. 'You find that you don't have to live with fear and denial any longer. You can face up to your problems and learn acceptance. Accept yourself and other people.

'It isn't all doom and gloom and ginger ale,' they also pointed out, on a brighter note. 'You are in a fog which starts to lift after you put down the last drink or drug. At first you are on a pink cloud. Sober at last! Then you have to start work on yourself.'

62

SONGS YOU KNOW AND LOVE

Ringo Starr and
His All-Starr Band, 1989–2025

Standing front and centre on the stage at no less likely a venue than the Lake Compounce Amusement Park in Bristol, Connecticut, Ringo introduced 'No No Song', his 1974-recorded ditty jokingly rejecting offers of marijuana, cocaine and moonshine. 'It means a lot more to me now than it did then,' he told the audience, a mixture of middle-aged Beatles fans and their kids.

It was 2 August 1989, the eighth show on the inaugural tour by Ringo Starr and His All-Starr Band, sponsored by Diet Pepsi and billed on the posters as 'A Concert for All Generations'. Against perhaps all reasonable odds, only nine months after completing his rehab programme, Starr was back on the road in the US for the first time since the Beatles took their final bows at Candlestick Park in San Francisco in the late summer of 1966, twenty-three long and eventful years before.

After he'd been sober for a couple of months, a light switched on in Ringo's head and he remembered he was actually a musician. 'I'd become so derelict, for all those years, that I'd forgotten that.'

The catalyst for Starr's return to touring was a business pitch from US promoter David Fishof who, three years previously in 1986, had arranged a successful (and lucrative) twentieth anniversary reunion tour for the Monkees. Fishof offered Starr a million dollars and a sponsorship deal with Pepsi, expecting him to turn it down. Instead, he was invited to fly to London for a meeting where Ringo confessed he'd already been thinking about getting back out on the road. Somehow, in March 1989, the *Daily News* in New York got wind of the meeting and teased their readers with the rumour that 'an epidemic of Beatlemania may hit the US this year'.

For Starr, the notion of performing as a solo artist was a daunting one. 'I was so insecure because I'd never toured on my own before,' he confessed. Worse, he was now to be without his emboldening potions and powders, even if they had in recent years only served to snuff out his talent. 'That's where I ended up,' he lamented. 'I couldn't play sober, but I also couldn't play as a drunk.'

The company he was keeping in the All-Starr Band were not all similarly clean: Joe Walsh wouldn't crash and go into recovery until 1993; Rick Danko and Levon Helm privately struggled with heroin addiction; and Dr John later confessed that his time in the group inspired him to tackle his own addictions. At the outset, Starr had explained to everyone that he'd 'just come out of a clinic', but that he wasn't banning booze from the tour. 'A lot of people in that band weren't sober,' he said. 'They were all sort of on something. But we pulled it together.'

Facing a crowd without a drink turned out to be manageable for Starr. It was after the shows that he struggled. For years, his system had grown to expect the rewards of intoxicants when he came offstage. Now, in the post-gig comedown period, his body was screaming for alcohol. He would force himself to sit in a chair and remain entirely still, refusing to talk to anyone, even his wife.

'All my sinews and veins and brains,' he recalled, with a typical semi-comic flourish, 'were like "Let's get fucked up".'

~

By sheer coincidence, in September 1989, Paul McCartney launched his first tour as solo artist, following Starr by only two months. These were also the first tours that either of them had embarked upon since Lennon's murder. But where Paul was a natural frontman, Ringo shrank from the spotlight when it came to the prospect of carrying a whole show on his own.

Particularly during this highly fragile period, he also recognised the value in building a band of friends around him, as opposed to hired-hand employees. He remembered the weird loneliness he'd sensed in Elvis Presley when the

Beatles met him in California in 1965, surrounded by his bought-off yes-men buddies. 'Being a solo artist,' Starr recognised, 'it's got to be really hard.'

Aside from Walsh, Helm, Danko and Dr John, Ringo pulled together a top-flight band that also included his drumming compadre Jim Keltner, his old *Get Back/Let It Be* pal Billy Preston, and Clarence Clemons and Nils Lofgren of the E Street Band. Initially, Starr hadn't been filled with confidence when he picked up the phone to ask them all to get involved. At one point, he'd half-doubtfully mentioned one name to Keltner, who had to tell him: 'Are you kidding? You're going to have to try to slap him away, man. Everybody's going to be wanting to jump in on this.'

'I mean, it was just a concept in his head,' Joe Walsh pointed out. 'And, y'know, turning a concept into something real takes some work, and you just hope that it's going to work out. He just wanted to put together something special. He didn't quite know what.

'I was the first one he asked, and I said, "Sure, I'll help. This is a great idea." I tried to encourage him, and then we picked the people, and he called them, and they all said yes.

'Then he said, "Oh God, what we do *now*?" He never thought everybody would say yes. It was pretty funny.'

Walsh also had to update Starr on the ways that tours had changed since the '60s: they were no longer the unrelenting slogs of old. Fishof wanted to book more than thirty shows and Ringo believed that the band could easily complete those within a month. Walsh had to explain to him that 'three shows a week is great, four is OK and five is stretching it'. In the end, partly due to high demand, the tour proved a touch more intensive, involving five or even six gigs a week and running for seven weeks between late July and early September.

During pre-tour rehearsals in Los Angeles and, later, in Las Colinas, Texas, Starr realised that he was performance-rusty and asked his fellow musicians to be patient with him. 'I had to learn all my songs again,' he said. 'I'd sung a tune like "Yellow Submarine" on the record, but I'd never played it live.' Starr wasn't exactly short of big numbers to pull out of the bag, and 'Photograph', 'It Don't Come Easy', 'Act Naturally', 'Boys' and, inevitably, 'With a Little Help from My Friends' all made it into the set. Crucially, though, this was to be a hits tour involving vocal performances/jukebox contributions from most of the others: Walsh's 'Rocky Mountain Way', the Band's 'The Weight', Preston's 'Will It Go Round in Circles'.

Pepsi launched a widespread and highly visible ad campaign for the tour. But in the end, it wasn't really needed, as the tickets for the dates sold out within minutes thanks to a preceding pile-up of newspaper reports about what New Jersey's *Courier-Post* – a touch sardonically – called 'the year's most outrageous old-timers tour'.

'I've never known anything like it,' said the manager of the 17,500-capacity Garden State Arts Center in Holmdel, New Jersey, pointing out that Starr's show there on 5 August had sold out 'faster than Michael Jackson or Bruce Springsteen', requiring a second date to be booked for six days later. 'The word of mouth was crazy,' Walsh remembered.

Opening night, at the Park Central Amphitheater in Dallas on Sunday 23 July, saw the birth of a new Ringo, a consummate showman with his hair scraped back in an '80s top-knot ponytail and unveiling a new tour wardrobe that involved shirts festooned with stars – and even a pink Chinese silk jacket patterned with dragons and accessorised with tassels. 'Yes, I did get it from Elton's sale,' he camply jested.

In a way, it was a production that both returned him to the loud sartorial stage colours of his Hurricanes days and the Beatles-shaped safety of a multi-vocalist band. The arrangement afforded him the space to sing a song or two of his own, then get behind the drums for a couple, as others took the microphone – whether it be Dr John cavorting around in his feathered and horned Mardi Gras head-dress as he performed 'Iko Iko', or Rick Danko nightly having them weeping in the aisles with his aching version of Buddy Holly's 'Raining in My Heart'.

'At that point in his career,' observed Keltner, 'Ringo didn't necessarily relish the idea that he had to be knowing the arrangements and doing the drummer thing *all* the time. He wanted to have fun and be able to sing and play too. It was perfectly ideal for him.'

The only downer came with the fact that, even though the band were playing mainly mid-sized outdoor arenas in the middle of the summer, heavy rain seemed to follow the tour around. Ringo darkly joked that 'they should have sent us to Ethiopia'.

Still, the wet conditions couldn't compete with the fervent fan reactions that greeted An Actual Beatle. Up onstage, still raw from his recent experiences, Ringo was sometimes overcome with the emotion of it all. 'It was just really, really moving. The love that was coming from the audience ... it was just sensational.'

At the second New Jersey show, the state's native son Bruce Springsteen sang and played guitar on the last five songs, including 'Get Back' and 'Long Tall Sally', before comedy actors Chevy Chase and John Candy got up to holler along or shake a tambourine. The same gig saw the twenty-three-year-old Zak Starkey drumming on 'With a Little Help from My Friends', a role that slowly expanded through the dates to his taking over the drum stool whenever his dad walked to the front of the stage to sing. The tour ended with two lap-of-honour shows at the Greek Theater in Los Angeles on the 3rd and 4th of September, filmed for posterity and then released on VHS and LaserDisc.

Whenever Starr was behind the drum kit, he found that he was rediscovering a key part of himself: 'The love of my life, the dream I'd had when I was thirteen, which, in a haze of alcohol, I'd gradually forgotten.'

It may have been the era when rock stars were being criticised for accepting the corporate shilling, but even the Pepsi sponsorship seemed oddly fitting for someone in recovery (and the Diet variety even more so for the still-whippet-thin singer). 'We're very pleased that Ringo's endorsing our product,' commented the company's Lisa Kolvitz. 'Our logo is everywhere. We're also delighted that Ringo's tour [was] such a success. It's worked out well on both sides.'

Seven dates in Japan followed in October and November, and there were plans afoot to take the All-Starr Band to the UK, Europe and perhaps even Russia.

'Now I'm back in the limelight,' Starr noted with some pride, 'we're getting invitations from everywhere.'

~

Three years later, on 4 September 1992, Ringo and the All-Starr Band were soundchecking at Caesar's Palace in Las Vegas when Harry Nilsson wandered in. No one had been expecting him. At the age of fifty-one, Harry hadn't curbed his hard living ways and was now heavy-set and looked older than his years. He'd spent the early '80s trying to break into movie soundtracks, initially via his critically slated songs for Robert Altman's 1980 movie *Popeye*.

When his friend Graham Chapman asked Nilsson to write the score for his 1983 film *Yellowbeard*, its producers remembered the thumbs-down reactions to *Popeye* and also doubted Harry's reliability as a songwriter working to schedule. His career was slowly vanishing. Lennon's murder had also hit Nilsson hard; for much of the decade, he'd become a campaigner for US gun control.

Some of the musicians grew nervous with his arrival at the Vegas venue. 'Harry was something of an enabler and had previously gotten Ringo into a lot of trouble,' recalled Todd Rundgren, one of the new faces in the line-up, along with Dave Edmunds and Walsh's former Eagles bandmate Timothy B Schmit. 'Ringo had built a whole new lifestyle around getting into AA and cleaning up. Not that their friendship had been off limits, but hanging out with Harry was one of the things he *wasn't* supposed to do.'

Nilsson had always had a strong aversion to performing live after being laughed offstage by an African-American crowd in San Diego County when he was part of a folk duo back in 1964. In all of his years of subsequent recording industry success, he'd never played a gig.

That night, seventeen songs into a near-two-hour set, Starr announced: 'To be a member of this band, you have to have had a hit some time this century. And he had probably the biggest, most beautiful hit of the '70s… "Without You".' To a mixture of astonishment and Vegas supper-club indifference, Harry stepped onto the stage and launched into his operatic heartbreaker.

He started off the first verse sounding like a tired baritone. Then came the humongous chorus, where – aided by Rundgren on the tricky top notes – he growled with tenor-range passion as the audience helped him along. The song's key had been dropped four semi-tones by the band to accommodate the ravages of time and substances on Harry's voice, but there was no doubting his passion – or his capacity to wow a crowd.

Five months later, in February 1993, Nilsson suffered a heart attack. He was to die, from heart failure, aged only fifty-two, on 15 January 1994.

Harry's passing was such a sensitive topic for Ringo that he found it impossible to talk about him publicly. More than a decade later, he turned down an invite to appear in John Scheinfeld's 2006 documentary, *Who Is Harry Nilsson? (And Why Is Everybody Talkin' About Him?)*.

'It was just too emotional for him,' said Scheinfeld, who pointed out that Starr was otherwise happy to supply personal photographs and give permission for scenes from *Son of Dracula* to be included, which the director noted had 'been locked away in a London vault since 1974'.

Scheinfeld subsequently heard that Starr had seen the completed film and felt that some elements of the story were missing. 'I said to myself,' the director laughed, 'Yeah, Ringo, *you* were missing...'

~

After the launch of the All-Starr Band in '89, the group kept touring and evolving through the decades, taking on an amorphous form. Down the years, such disparate characters as John Entwistle, Peter Frampton, Jack Bruce, Ian Hunter, Howard Jones, Richard Marx and Sheila E all passed through its ranks. By 2024 and moving in 2025, the outfit featured Toto's Steve Lukather, who brought his band's yacht-rock classics 'Africa' and 'Rosanna' to the repertoire, Men At Work's Colin Hay (offering the antipodean knees-up 'Down Under') and the Average White Band's Hamish Stuart (the super-funky 'Pick Up the Pieces').

Klaus Voormann guested with the All-Starr Band onstage in Hamburg in 2018, adding his voice to the choruses of 'With a Little Help from My Friends'. He attested to the uplifting power of the show. 'The public gets not just Ringo,' he stressed. 'They get a variety of different hits. It's a great idea.'

'I still love to play,' said Ringo in 2024. 'And, y'know, I get a chance to play to all *their* songs, and I get a chance to play a couple of my songs and drum. Then I go down the front and I'm that guy in the front.'

He paused, before laughing and nailing what for him was the absolute appeal of the All-Starr Band: 'I just never wanted to be that guy in the front for the *whole* show.'

63

TIME TAKES TIME

A Creative Resurgence (and a Blue-Haired Fan), 1991–1992

Ringo's 1964 Beatles drum kit, in all of its black oyster pearl wonder, sat in the corner of Conway Recording Studios in Hollywood. To the eyes of Andy Sturmer, lead singer and drummer of San Francisco neo psychedelic band Jellyfish, it seemed to glow. He found himself becoming utterly entranced by the sight of it.

'Nothing else existed in the world,' Sturmer later remembered with lingering awe. 'I wanted to touch it – yet I *didn't* want to touch it.'

Then he heard a voice behind him saying, 'Got that for *The Ed Sullivan Show*.' Sturmer hadn't even realised that Ringo was in the room. The two immediately fell into an easy conversation about drums, with Starr showing the younger musician what Sturmer was surprised to note were the 'terribly dirty' cymbals he'd used on the same history-making TV show, still ingrained with the grime of legend.

At the beginning of the '90s, a wave of West Coast American bands such as Jellyfish, Hawthorne, California's Redd Kross and Bellingham, Washington's the Posies had arrived on the scene trading in power pop that was in thrall to the '60s and early '70s. The latter group had, in 1990, enjoyed a minor US hit with a sunny, strummy song with the *Abbey Road*-punning title of 'Golden Blunders'. Starr chose to record his own version of it for *Time Takes Time*, his first album in almost ten years and his most credible one in close to three decades.

Andy Sturmer and Roger Manning Jr of Jellyfish had been invited by producer Don Was to contribute some songs to the record, Starr being a fan of their 1990 debut, *Bellybutton*. Sturmer was never to forget the moment when the call came through from someone at his label, Charisma Records. 'After I picked the phone up off the floor – I had dropped it when I heard this – I said, "Sure".' The pair duly wrote five bespoke songs, with their perky early Beatles shuffler 'I Don't Believe You' – sketched 'in a couple of hours as an afterthought' – being the one chosen for inclusion. Cheekily, the lyric included a reference to nose-powdering in its second verse, which Starr gladly rubber-stamped, before allowing the pair to sing their call-and-responses on the track.

Sturmer and Manning also contributed harmonies to the album's opening track and first single, the breezy, empathetic 'Weight of the World', with its bright, chiming 'Nowhere Man' guitars. They even appeared in its video, looking like Furry Freak twins beamed in from Golden Gate Park in '67, adding improbable counterbalance to Starr, who stood on the opposite side of a pair of huge theatrical scales that swung up and down. In a visual echo of the past, he wore a jacket similar to the orange-striped ones that the Beatles had sported back in '66, but in darker hues.

All the while, Sturmer and Manning remained completely starstruck, the latter describing the entire experience as 'wonderful, exciting, but just *bizarre*'.

~

Ringo's profile in the pop culture of the early 1990s had also received something of an unexpected boost when Marge Simpson was revealed to have been a big-time Starr devotee back in the '60s. In an episode of *The Simpsons*, 'Brush with Greatness', first shown on 11 April 1991, Ringo's cartoon likeness appeared in the show, voiced by Starr himself.

In a story involving Homer (as ever) attempting to lose weight, he and Bart were rummaging around in the attic for his dumbbells when the pair found a portrait of Ringo, in what looked like '66, wearing a maroon velvet jacket and with the tip of his nose resting on his upper lip.

'Hey, who's the moptop with the big schnozz?' Bart wondered.

'Don't you know anything, boy?' grunted Homer. 'That's Ringo Starr. Your mother must have painted this. I guess she thought he was kinda cute.'

Marge then arrived on the scene and confessed to her teenage crush on Ringo. Lisa was more interested in finding out why her blue-haired mother's artistic dreams had been quashed.

In a flashback, the young Marjorie Bouvier was seen at school being casti-
gated by her art teacher, sneering about her having painted yet another portrait
of 'that bongo-beating Liverpudlian'. Upset, she'd posted the painting to Starr,
'the only man on Earth whose opinion I could trust'. Having received no
response, she had ultimately given up painting.

Meanwhile, somewhere in England (as the caption read) in the modern
day, the action cut to a palatial English home with a Union Jack flying from its
roof. Ringo – in regulation shades and beard, blue suit and bootlace tie – sat
in a wingback chair, clacking away at a manual typewriter, surrounded by piles
of fan letters and sacks of air mail.

Picking up a large flat parcel, he blew the dust from it and said, 'What's
this? From Springfield, USA.' He opened it and found the portrait of himself.
'Gear!' he declared.

Later, back in Springfield, Homer was rummaging through the post and
picked out a letter 'for you, Marge, from Merrie Old England.'

She ripped it open and discovered that it was 'from the desk of
Ringo Starr'.

'Dear Marge,' he began, 'thanks for the fab painting of yours truly. I hung
it on me wall. You're quite an artist. Love, Ringo. PS Forgive the lateness of
my reply.'

~

Meanwhile, back in reality, after the 1987 fiasco with Chips Moman in
Memphis, Ringo hadn't attempted to make another studio album. This was
partly due to the fact that, even after the live success of the All-Starr Band,
no record company seemed to want to take a chance on him. Until one did.

Private Music had been launched by Peter Baumann of German proto
electronic group Tangerine Dream as a label specialising in instrumental
albums, tapping into the vogue for ambient, new age-y sounds. Now, Private
was attempting to slip into a tributary of the mainstream, signing Canadian
folk sisters Kate & Anna McGarrigle, American blues artist Taj Mahal and a
drumming-and-singing onetime Beatle down on his recording luck.

Once the deal was done – and hedging his bets – Starr decided to work
with an array of producers on the new album: Jeff Lynne of Beatles-indebted

behemoth ELO (and George Harrison's mucker in supertroupe the Traveling Wilburys); '60s pop star-turned-LA producer Peter Asher (of Peter and Gordon fame); Phil Ramone, architect of hits for Paul Simon and Billy Joel; and Don Was of arty funkers Was (Not Was), who could corral the talents of anyone from Michael McDonald to Iggy Pop. The majority of the ten songs were bought in, with Starr co-writing three.

It might have been four, if the first McCartney/Starkey credit had come to pass. As was by now an old tradition, Ringo reached out to Paul to see if he had any new material. McCartney wrote a song specifically with his old pal in mind, opening with a message that came directly from 'Richy', requesting permission to look into your eyes and promising that he was – as the title made explicit – an 'Angel in Disguise'. Paul's demo was however half-baked loping funk with too-many-words-squeezed-into-each-line. And yet, when Ringo heard it, he knew it needed even more, in the form of a third stanza. McCartney suggested he write one himself.

'I understand he has written a third verse,' McCartney told a writer. 'If it's another "With a Little Help from My Friends", great. If it isn't, great!'

A version of the song was essayed in the studio with Peter Asher. But 'Angel in Disguise' was then – remarkably – deemed surplus to requirements and left on the cutting room floor.

'Because it's McCartney and Starr, anyone in their right mind would put that on,' Ringo rightly assessed, if not for the song's quality then at least for its newsworthy value. 'It just didn't fit. This is my best shot, in my opinion, of *my* album.'

He was right. 'Weight of the World' was Starr's most precisely aimed stab at a hit since the '70s, yet on its release in the spring of 1992, it missed the Top 40 everywhere apart from Sweden and Switzerland. Still, on 22 May, Ringo confidently released *Time Takes Time*, clearly his best and most cohesive long-player since *Goodnight Vienna*.

As was the way of things in the early 1990s, Starr bolstered its arrival with an EPK (electronic press kit): a mini-documentary issued to the media, featuring behind-the-scenes footage of the making of the 'Weight of the World' promo, along with a Ringo interview offering quotes to be freely pilfered by the press.

'I haven't been as happy with an album since my *Ringo* album, y'know, in 1974, '75,' he said, forgetting it had in fact been 1973. He singled out one co-written track (with Johnny Warman and Gary Grainger), the driving, Lynne-produced 'Don't Go Where the Road Don't Go', as being a very personal one. The song's message was less of a direction and more of a warning.

'Because you end up lost,' he sagely advised, obliquely referring to his darkest period. 'I still feel it's actually magic that I get up after the sun and I'm not terrified of it. I used to absolutely believe that I was an insomniac and frightened of the dark. And, guess what, I'm neither of those two things.'

If the title of *Time Takes Time* sounded like a Beatle-y Ringoism (or an aphorism from a seasoned drummer), for him it held a deeper meaning.

'I was and still am, in a way, impatient,' he said. 'Y'know, "I want it now!"'

'I was listening to somebody talk,' he went on, without specifying whether it was a friend, a therapist or a spiritual teacher, 'who said, y'know, "If you want to do anything, time takes time." And I'm really trying to live like that now. Instead of [looking for] instant gratification.'

His patience and focus were already beginning to pay creative dividends. Even his drumming on *Time Takes Time* was once again sharp and imaginative. 'He has that feel that's between a shuffle and straight eighths ... Ringo territory that nobody else can do,' Andy Sturmer enthused. 'He played some amazing stuff on that album.' Indeed, when Ringo let Zak hear the record, his son zoned in one of the drum fills on the long, swirling outro of closing track 'What Goes Around' and approvingly pointed out, 'Only you could get away with that, Dad.'

Critical appraisals of the album were mixed, though. Even an updated Beatle was a tough sell in the era of R.E.M. and Nirvana. But *Rolling Stone* accurately recognised *Time Takes Time* as 'a charming, unpretentious pop album doing what he did best as a Beatle', calling it 'the drummer's most consistent, wide-awake album since *Ringo*'.

The problem was that the record-buying public weren't listening anymore. The only charts that the album scored on were in Austria (number nineteen) and Sweden (number thirty-eight).

'I thought it was brilliant,' Starr proudly stated. 'But people didn't seem to want to go for it.'

64

MEET THE THREETLES

Paul, George and Ringo,
1994–2001

The story of *The Long and Winding Road*, the Beatles' official, decades-in-the-planning documentary, turned out to be far longer and way more winding than anyone had ever imagined.

The idea for an authorised retrospective film, to follow in the wake of *Let It Be*, was first set in motion in 1970. Neil Aspinall at Apple assembled a rough cut comprising what George Harrison described as 'all the footage we'd filmed of ourselves, or that we owned of ourselves, and whatever [newsreel] footage he could get hold of, and he put it in a chronological order'.

On 10 April of that same year, the day that the front page of the *Daily Mirror* blared the dramatic headline 'Paul Quits the Beatles', Harrison closed himself off from the outside commotion and, inside the walls of the Beatles' HQ at 3 Savile Row, viewed Aspinall's work-in-progress. The eighty-one-minute cut of the documentary ran from the black-and-white Granada footage of the Beatles rattling through 'Some Other Guy' in the Cavern basement in 1962 to the 1969 promo film for 'Something' featuring all four Beatles, filmed separately and remotely, with their respective wives.

If it seemed as if Harrison had decided to mark the public passing of the Beatles by privately wallowing in nostalgia, then work on the documentary immediately stalled. 'We'd had enough of all that,' he flatly divulged.

Down the years, there was talk of the project being revived. Lennon, in 1974, said that there was a Beatles movie 'in the offing … of all the films we've collected from the tours and all the interviews all over the world'. In 1976,

Harrison loaned a video copy to his friend Neil Innes, whose creative partner Eric Idle used its chronological outline as the template for the Rutles' 1978 *All You Need is Cash* spoof.

By 1981, yet another version of the Beatles film had been completed, but Aspinall found it impossible, for one undisclosed reason or another, to get all three surviving members to sign off on it. A year later, and following the home-video success of MGM/UA's two-hour 1982 doc *The Compleat Beatles*, the word from Apple was that *The Long and Winding Road* was in the can and on its way.

Then, nothing. Part of the problem appeared to be the worry that any official resumption of band endeavours would spark off the 'Beatles Reunite!' rumours that, incredibly, even Lennon's death hadn't snuffed – particularly after the twenty-one-year-old Julian Lennon launched a moderately successful music career in 1984. In the minds of some, it was merely a question of simply replacing John with Julian and, hey presto, the Beatles were back.

'All that dogshit about us getting together with Julian Lennon or Sean Lennon, it's never gonna happen,' Starr emphatically confirmed in 1991. 'The Beatles are finished.'

Harrison's position on the matter was Pythonesque, but pointedly clear. 'There will never be a Beatles reunion,' he stated, more than once, 'as long as John Lennon remains dead.'

But Ringo at the same time once again raised the spectre of the documentary. 'The Beatles have an unreleased movie called *The Long and Winding Road*,' he said, 'and Paul keeps saying the three of us should do some incidental music for it.' It was an intriguing concept and sounded like a very cool, low-key move for the three to make. But even McCartney himself went off the notion. 'It just never felt like a good idea.'

In 1991, however, talking to the *Toronto Sun*, Paul seemed to be buzzed overall about the idea of finishing the documentary. 'We could do voiceovers where we tell our side of the story, or put in home movies nobody has ever seen,' he said, revealing that he had cine footage of the Beatles in Rishikesh in 1968, 'looking like total wallies, wearing these little Indian things'.

Three years later, on 19 January 1994, at the Waldorf Astoria hotel in New York, McCartney posthumously inducted Lennon into the Rock & Roll Hall of Fame. In a very public display of détente, he and Yoko Ono were seen hugging. At a press conference afterwards, side-by-side with Yoko, Paul made the surprise announcement that the trio of remaining Beatles were to enter the studio the following month. 'Give the three of them a chance!' Ono exhorted.

During the same trip, McCartney visited Ono at the Dakota, where she handed him tapes of a number of Lennon's never-released, home-recorded song sketches. On his return to England, Paul got ready to let Ringo hear the recordings. Before he pressed play, he warned his former bandmate 'to have his hanky ready'.

In the weeks leading up to Friday 11 February 1994 and the first recording session for the group that would later be nicknamed 'the Threetles' by the press, Paul McCartney grew increasingly nervous. 'I got cold feet about it,' he admitted. 'I thought, *Does the world need a three-quarter Beatles record?*

Also hanging over the project was the fact that Paul had given the nineteen-year-old Sean Lennon the power to veto the release of any finished tracks, being sensitive to the fact that it might prove emotionally unsettling for him to hear his late dad singing on a new record. McCartney remembered that Starr and Harrison were alarmed when they heard about this part of the arrangement. 'What if we love it?' they argued.

Still, Harrison was the least enthused about the lost Lennon material, particularly the dreamy half-finished song, 'Free as a Bird'. A miffed Paul later claimed that George told him, 'I sort of felt that John was going off a little bit towards the end of his writing.'

Blanking out Harrison's negativity, McCartney sold a concept to his bandmates to help them all get over the unavoidably tragic fact that Lennon wasn't there. He suggested they should just pretend that John had gone on holiday to Spain and had left them with these recordings he'd entrusted them to complete. He remembered that Ringo's response was, 'Oh! This could even be joyous.'

The venue for the sessions was McCartney's private Hog Hill Mill studio in rural East Sussex, a suitably cut-off environment for such a secretive experiment. At first, he'd naturally asked George Martin to oversee the recordings. But Martin, recently turned sixty-eight and suffering from impaired hearing, was forced to decline the offer. Harrison wanted to bring in Jeff Lynne (who had, of course, worked with Ringo on *Time Takes Time* two years before). In spite of Paul's worries that Lynne might end up siding with his fellow Traveling Wilbury in the studio, George got his way. In the end, all five – Lynne, McCartney, Harrison, Starr and even Lennon – were credited as producers.

On day one at the studio, McCartney was heartened to witness Starr's now evidently healthy-living ways. 'Ringo's walking around with, like, a bag of seeds,' he later remembered. 'Ringo is fantastic for a guy who's been in intensive care, nearly dying for most of his life.

'His mother was told he'd be dead when he was three,' he added, when the young Richy Starkey had in fact first been hospitalised at the age of six. But then, revealing just how bad Ringo's 1979 intestinal health scare had been, McCartney let slip that 'when he got into really heavy drinking, in Monaco, he was put on a life support system with seven other very nearly dead people in the room'.

If it was indeed a marvel that all three – and not just two – Beatles were around to make these new recordings, there was no avoiding the heavy emotions stirred up by the fact that they were together in the studio working with the sound of Lennon's voice. 'It was very weird,' said Ringo. 'It was the closest we'll ever come to having him back in the room. So it was very emotional for me, and I know it was emotional for the other two.'

As soon as the trio began to play together along to Lennon's tidied-up vocal and piano for 'Free as a Bird', their constituent parts instantly clicked back into place almost a quarter of a century after the three had recorded 'I Me Mine', their final track altogether, at Abbey Road back in January 1970. 'From the very first downbeat,' the engineer Geoff Emerick recalled, 'you knew it was a Beatles record.' Later, Starr sat in the control room as Harrison and McCartney overdubbed harmonies, excitedly telling them that 'it sounds just like the Beatles'.

Adding to the strangeness of the experience was the fact that the quality of the original tape, even when cleaned up and processed, still gave the impression that Lennon was singing from behind some ethereal veil. Nonetheless, in whatever form it came, it was the miracle of John Lennon's sonic resurrection. 'Hearing him in the headphones,' said Paul, 'it was like he was in the next room. That was kind of thrilling, like, *Fuck, I'm singing harmony with John*. It's like an impossible dream.'

348

According to McCartney, the magical atmosphere of the sessions somewhat evaporated after Starr packed up and left, and he and Harrison were left to complete their parts. The long-dormant creative difficulties between the two began to reawaken. 'Me and George, we had a little bit more tension,' said Paul. 'But I don't think that's a bad thing. It was only like a normal Beatle session: you've got to reach a compromise.'

Work on the track continued through February and into March. The three then reconvened in the last week of June '94, this time at Harrison's home studio, FPSHOT (an awkward acronym for Friar Park Studio, Henley-on-Thames). A camera crew captured much of the action, including the trio sitting around a kitchen table, reminiscing about how Ringo would always leave the light on in hotel rooms when he and Paul shared them on tour. 'Because I was frightened of the dark!' Starr protested.

In the studio, with Harrison and McCartney perched on stools playing acoustic guitars and Ringo thwacking away at his kit with a pair of brushes, all of them appeared a tad self-conscious, knowing they were being filmed. Then George began strumming Paul's 1958 Buddy Holly-knock-off, 'Thinking of Linking', and they all began cracking up. 'There's no second verse!' McCartney pointed out. Busking through 'Blue Moon of Kentucky', they regained a bit of Beatle-y propulsion.

Later, sitting on a picnic blanket in the garden of Friar Park, McCartney and Harrison holding ukuleles, they plinked away at Jimmy Reed's 'Baby What You Want Me to Do', as Ringo slapped out a rhythm on his knees. George strummed through what he could remember of his Rishikesh-written 'Dehra Dun', as Paul irritatingly began to voice an exaggerated tanpura drone. Finally, they ended with a jokey take on the 1920s Tin Pan Alley standard 'Ain't She Sweet?'.

'Well, this has been a really nice day for me, chaps,' said Starr, as he got ready to leave. 'It's been really beautiful and moving. I like hanging out with you guys.'

Paul put a hand on Ringo's arm and – making a random reference to the song from *Chitty Chitty Bang Bang* – affectionately called him his 'Little Chu-Chi Face'.

It was to be another eight months before they regrouped, in February 1995 back at Hog Hill Mill, to tackle another Lennon demo, 'Real Love'. By now, they appeared to be falling back into an easy routine.

McCartney remembered there being 'one real nice moment when we were doing "Real Love" and I was trying to learn the piano bit, and Ringo sat down on the drums, jamming along. It was like none of us had ever been away. And the best thing was, it was hysterical, Ringo with his little plastic bag of grains.'

When 'Real Love' was in the bag, a third track, 'Now and Then' (also known as 'I Don't Want to Lose You'), was attempted, although it proved impossible to filter out Lennon's piano to achieve a clear and usable vocal. The track was duly ditched. 'We'd done two in that way,' said Ringo. '"Let's not get too crazy…"'

In-between these last two bursts of Beatle activity, a newly compiled, fifty-six-track radio sessions album, *Live at the BBC*, had been released on 30 November 1994, hitting UK number one and going on to sell more than eight million copies worldwide. Its success, particularly in the light of the previous decade when the band were generally viewed as passé, surprised everyone involved.

'I knew it would do OK, but it just took off,' Ringo said. 'It was great. I love it because it showed people that the Beatles weren't just fab and famous. We were really cool musicians.'

The dust of the Beatles' influence was meanwhile beginning to swirl once again in the early '90s, as young men in British bands grew moptops and, in the case of the sometimes chords-and-lyrics-xeroxing Oasis, performed a storming live cover version of 'I Am the Walrus' that they imbued with a fresh and edgy attitude.

Meanwhile, there was a tape trawl through the vaults going on at Abbey Road. George Martin, acting as sonic archaeologist, was installed in one studio, tasked with listening back through all of the Beatles' recorded outtakes, choosing bits, then sending them off to Geoff Emerick in another room, who'd pull out the original master tapes and remix them.

At the same time, Starr, Harrison and McCartney were regularly attending the edit sessions of *The Long and Winding Road*, now being co-directed by

Geoff Wonfor (an alumni of Channel 4's *The Tube*) and Bob Smeaton, and retitled *The Beatles Anthology* after George apparently protested that the story of the band shouldn't be named after a Paul song. Together in the edit room, tucked away on residential Wendell Road in Shepherd's Bush, their memories both flowed and conflicted.

'We wanted, to the best of our abilities,' said Ringo, 'to get rid of the myths and lies and stupidity.'

'We were fed up,' stressed Paul, 'with every milkman's son writing books about us when they hadn't even met or talked to us.'

'Paul remembers so many stories, and just to get together with him was interesting,' said George, revealing the remaining warmth in his and McCartney's friendship. 'We'd be talking about stuff and he would mention something we hadn't thought of for years and years.'

One day in March 1995, Wednesday the 29th, the three idly wandered round to a local café. But when they stepped inside, the owner was so shocked to see three Beatles that he dropped his tray of cups and saucers and everything clattered to the floor, causing them to erupt with laughter before parking themselves down at a table.

In the middle of November, the vast, multimedia project *The Beatles Anthology* was finally launched, following a bidding war for what had expanded into a three-part feature-length TV series aired by ABC in the US (and in six parts by ITV in the UK). It was supported by three double-CD outtakes compilations stagger-released across eleven months, an expanded eleven-hours-plus home video version in 1996, and a coffee-table oral history book in 2000.

In the US alone, 27 million people tuned into the first episode. Throughout the series, revisiting the major staging posts of their still-incredible story, new to-camera interviews illuminated each band member's personality, in turn showing the lasting effects that being a Beatle had had on them. McCartney often appeared cocky, when he was likely only being defensive of his reputation and key role in the band at a time when it was in danger of being eclipsed by that of the near-saintly Lennon. Harrison seemed strangely divorced from the phenomenon yet intangibly damaged by it. 'The Beatles gave their nervous systems,' he said, referring – like the others often did now – to the group in the third person.

Starr meanwhile came across as pragmatic, honest about his imposter syndrome crisis circa *The White Album* and entirely unchanged in many ways. He was clearly moved by the experience of revisiting his past.

'I do get emotional when I think back about those times,' he confessed. 'My make-up is emotional. I'm an emotional human being. I'm very sensitive and it took me 'til I was forty-eight to realise that!'

Sometimes, it seemed – likely because of his unique viewpoint in the set-up – he was able to see the bigger picture far better than the others. 'The music was positive,' he concluded. 'The basic Beatles message was "Love".'

Three months after 'Free as a Bird' was released, reaching number two on the UK chart (held off by Michael Jackson's ecological howl, 'Earth Song'), 'Real Love' was issued as a single in March 1996. But, somehow, and so soon, the novelty of new Beatles material had begun to wear off. Scandalously, Radio 1 even refused to playlist 'Real Love', deeming it not to be 'of sufficient merit'.

'It's not exactly going to ruin us overnight,' McCartney cattily pointed out. 'Is Radio 1 as important as it once was? As Ringo said to me, "Who needs Radio 1 when you've got all these independent stations?"'

Still, by November 1996, all three seemed determined to reseal the Beatles' time capsule and put an end to conjecture about their future plans. A short statement released by Apple read: 'The end has finally arrived... The Beatles are no more. The official word is that Paul McCartney, George Harrison and Ringo Starr will never play together again as a group, and that they have decided that there will be no more singles issued from their back catalogue.'

This time, once and for all, it really seemed to be over.

～

Ringo turned sixty on 7 July 2000 and wasn't too happy about the fact.

'I don't mind other birthdays,' he said, 'but this one really gets up my nose.'

Nonetheless, it was an occasion that deserved to be celebrated, for a number of reasons. The Starkeys threw a party at their new home in England (since 1999), Rydinghurst, a twelve-roomed seventeenth-century mansion near Cranleigh in Surrey, set within a 200-acre estate.

There, Pattie Boyd snapped what was to be the last photograph taken together of Paul, George and Ringo. In it, McCartney is sat on the left, with

Starr in the middle, being jokily force-fed a glass of wine by Harrison on the right. All three were grinning like the goofy youths they essentially remained.

'They form part of my life,' said Harrison later the same year. 'It's fun to go to a birthday celebration and see how we have matured' – although, at least on the pictorial evidence, it wasn't by much.

Harrison, reflective by nature, had turned even more so in the aftermath of an horrific attack he'd suffered at home seven months earlier. In the early hours of 30 December 1999, two days before the end of the old millennium, he'd been awoken at Friar Park by the sound of breaking glass and rushed downstairs. There he was tackled by an intruder (a thirty-four-year-old paranoid schizophrenic from Liverpool) who stabbed wildly at him with a knife, until Olivia Harrison managed to knock out the attacker with a table lamp.

George reportedly suffered two stab wounds to the chest: one that narrowly missed a major vein and punctured his lung, and another that was, according to a hospital spokesman, 'less serious'. Ringo, however, spoke to Rolling Stones drummer Charlie Watts a month after the event, and disclosed to him the true extent of Harrison's injuries following what had in reality been a serious murder attempt.

'George was stabbed about forty times,' said Watts. 'The papers did say that one wound punctured his lung, but a lot of the others were just as horrific.'

Harrison's public statement about the dreadful episode spot-lit his humour: 'The attacker wasn't a burglar, and he certainly wasn't auditioning for the Traveling Wilburys!'

In 2000, he was asked by one writer about whether the experience had changed his outlook on life.

'Yes and no,' he averred. 'Adi Shankara, an Indian historical spiritual groovy type person once said, "Life is fragile, like a raindrop on a lotus leaf", and you better believe it.'

However, the impact upon Harrison's health was compounded by the fact that, in 1997, he had received radiotherapy for throat cancer. In the eyes of Pattie Boyd, still friends with her ex, George 'wasn't noticeably changed, but I think the trauma weakened his body's ability to fight the cancer'.

In 2001, he underwent surgery to remove a growth from his lung and was soon after treated for a brain tumour. Starr last saw his friend when he visited him in Switzerland in the last weeks of his life. 'He was very ill,' he said, his eyes brimming. 'He could only lay down.' Harrison died on 29 November 2001, aged fifty-eight.

'Although I knew George had been ill for some time,' said Paul, in a statement to the media outside his home in St John's Wood, 'I had always hoped that some kind of miracle might happen.'

'George was a best friend of mine,' said Ringo in his own statement. 'I loved him very much and I will miss him greatly. Both Barbara and I send our love and light to Olivia and Dhani. We will miss George for his sense of love, his sense of music and his sense of laughter.'

Not long before, Ringo had called Paul and George 'the only two who don't look at me like I'm a Beatle. We knew what it was *like*.'

The world mourned the fact that there were now only two living Beatles. But Starr, really Starkey, had lost someone who'd known him for so long, *really* known him, no matter their ups and downs, and who could always see through Ringo to Richy.

65

SOME OTHER OTHER GUY

Being a Ringo Doppelgänger, 2016–2025

For Gordon Elsmore, performing as the drummer in the Bootleg Beatles comes with certain unexpected challenges. The onstage hazards involved in Being Ringo range from performing a summertime gig in Malta while boiling in a woollen Chesterfield '63 suit to having the movement of your hands hampered by the sleeves of a tomato-red '69 rooftop raincoat and getting your bass drum pedal caught up in the flared leg of your hot-pink satin *Sgt. Pepper* trousers.

But perhaps the trickiest part of Elsmore's nightly transformation into Starr is his careful glueing-on of a silicone rubber nose: a process that takes around ninety minutes and involves a two-part adhesive.

'I go through about fifteen noses every six months,' Elsmore wryly reports. 'I can get maybe three or four shows out of each one.' Sometimes, when perspiring heavily under the stage lights, he finds himself fretting that the fake proboscis will slip south. 'It would scare the children in the front row, I think, if it came off,' he says. '"What's happened to Ringo's face?!"'

Elsmore's only other real worry about mimicking Starr tends to surface whenever the Bootleg Beatles perform at a major festival, whether it be Glastonbury or the Isle of Wight, and a camera zooms in on his face and prominent faux feature for the side-stage screens and accompanying TV broadcast. 'You're thinking, *Oh, fuck, this is going to look enormous,*' he admits, while noting that his custom-made imposter beak 'is just maybe a shade too big'.

Aside from the complex nose-application procedure, channelling Ringo requires physical demands other than learning his trademark early Fabs mop-top shake. 'Beyond the head toss is the stooping,' says Elsmore. 'The stool is very high, you're stooping over, you're moving your body from side to side. It's a very uncomfortable position to be in.' But it's also a contributing factor to Starr's characterful playing style. 'If Ringo had been taught, all of that would have been taken out of him. They would have said, "Put your stool down, sit up straight." And of course, it wouldn't be Ringo, would it?'

Postural discomfort and costume comedy aside, performing as Starr in the Bootleg Beatles is a serious business. First established in 1980, by three ex-cast members of the British production of the *Beatlemania* musical (and with a slowly changing line-up through the intervening years), they are the world's foremost Fabs tribute group, touring globally and winning fans from David Gilmour to Liam Gallagher. Elsmore, a drummer since his teens, joined in 2016, by which time he was already a Ringo-copying veteran, having played in what he estimates to be between twenty to thirty other Beatles-aping acts, including the Paperback Beatles, the Instant Beatles, the Counterfeit Beatles, the Fab Beatles and the Cheatles. Prior to becoming part of the band, he'd caught various Bootleg Beatles shows down the years and always considered them to be the best.

'The thing with Beatle bands is you'll get a good Paul, and then everybody else is a bit rubbish,' he says. 'Or you'll get a good George and a good Ringo, but the Paul and John aren't very good. The Bootleg Beatles have always had four members that've been pretty good.'

By observing various other Ringos, good and bad, and through his own practical experience, Elsmore is in a choice position to understand what makes Starr special or, indeed, unique as a musician. Being a left-handed drummer playing a right-handed set-up kit is one key component, he reckons, as it resulted, particularly during Ringo's Beatles period, in 'fills that had an unequal number of hits in them', so that he could quickly move his hands into position for the first beat of the next bar.

But more important is the fact that, as Elsmore puts it, Starr is 'a thoughtful drummer. A lot of the big drummers of that era, like Ginger Baker in Cream and Mitch Mitchell with the Jimi Hendrix Experience, were jazz-infused drummers. They had that virtuosity. That wasn't where Ringo was at all. Ringo was the song drummer. He was the drummer that had to find a part that built into the song.

'But he's a deceptive virtuoso,' Elsmore emphasises. 'You think it's simple. But it's not simple. It's just not flashy.'

He also has his own theory as to why Starr got a bad rap as a drummer, citing Brian Epstein's poor scheduling as the reason Starr underperformed at his first Beatles session on 4 September 1962 at EMI and was replaced by Andy White the following week on 'Love Me Do'.

'I feel that Brian Epstein had packed too much into that week before they went down to London,' he says. 'They were travelling around a lot and I think when they got there, they were exhausted. You can hear that they're tired.

'So there was always this speculation going around: who was the drummer on these records? And especially as Ringo had been ditched on one record, maybe he had been ditched on others.'

Elsmore can testify to Starr's skills having studied them in great depth, whether it be closely watching Ringo's bass-drum foot on the Washington Coliseum footage from 1964, learning all of the originally improvised parts of 'A Day in the Life' in order, or finding a hitherto unrecognised link – namely a three-beat fill – in his playing on 'Do You Want to Know a Secret' in '63 and 'Don't Let Me Down' in '69.

It's a process that's been vastly aided in recent years by the ever-increasing volume of Beatles reissues outtakes and Giles Martin remixes, particularly the early years tracks that have been digitally reverse-engineered and then reassembled. 'I listened to "She Loves You",' Elsmore says of Martin's 2023 mix, 'and I noticed, *Oh, there's more toms going on there than I realised.*'

All of this really boils down to one simple argument: if you still think Ringo Starr was a crap drummer in the Beatles, try playing what he played.

'Anything from *Abbey Road* is fucking hard,' Elsmore states, offering just one example. 'Because it's a fill bonanza that album. Y'know, he's on the toms all the time and every single fill is pretty much different.'

In his devoted practice of what we might call 'Ringo-ology', Elsmore has sometimes found himself in online dispute with other tribute band Starrs and general Beatles know-alls. 'If you put anything on Instagram,' he says, 'there's always some comment there, going, "Ooh, he hasn't got that bit right." And you think, *Yeah, I have.*'

Meanwhile, recreating Ringo's drum parts accurately for live performance in the here and now proves to be a pursuit without end.

'You're updating your information all the time,' Elsmore says, 'and you're having to change things as you go along to get closer to the originals. It's an ongoing process. It never stops.'

66

PHOTOGRAPH

Fans Reunited, 1964–2013

O n 7 February 1964, the epoch-making day when the Beatles arrived in the US like visitors from some strange new world, a group of six New Jersey teenagers from Fair Lawn High School – four boys, two girls – decided to skip class and drive the thirty-odd miles south-east to John F Kennedy International to try to catch a glimpse of the band.

Seventeen-year-old Charlie Schwartz wandered into the school's student lounge that morning to be met by his classmate Gary Van Deursen who told him of his plan to drive to the airport in the Chevrolet Impala convertible (white with a snazzy red interior) that he'd borrowed from his father.

'You in or you out?' asked Deursen.

'I'm in,' said Schwartz.

The pair corralled together four other rule-breaking friends – Bob Toth, Suzanne Rayot, Arlene Norbe and Matt Blender – before sneaking out the building and setting off. An hour later, after joining the estimated 4,000-strong mob of kids on the airport's outside viewing balcony, they all waited together in high anticipation. Blender loudly affected an English accent and was asked by a radio reporter if he'd agree to be interviewed live on the air to lend his perspective as a British Beatles fan in the US. 'I was laughing so hard,' Deursen recalled, 'I had to move away.'

In the end, it was utter chaos and they gave up. 'It was such a mad scene at JFK that we left disappointed,' Toth remembered. 'We just thought there was no way we'd get close to the band.'

Driving home on Van Wyck Expressway through Queens, the six were passed by what they believed to be a funeral procession, before realising that it was in fact the Fabs' motorcade. In the adjacent lane, Deursen sped up ahead of the cars and then slowed back down so that they would have to pass them again.

In one of the limos, Starr wound down his window and gestured to the teenagers to do the same. Toth remembered that Rayot began 'screaming her lungs out'.

Ringo shouted over, 'Hello, love'. It wasn't clear which of the two girls he was addressing, 'but I hoped it was me,' said Rayot. She impulsively threw her pinkie ring at him as a gift. Starr asked them where they were from and Schwartz proudly hung his Fair Lawn school jacket out of the car to show him.

Before the cars parted, one of the youths cheekily asked Starr if he could get them tickets for either of the band's two sold-out shows at Carnegie Hall on 12 February. 'He said he was sorry he couldn't help,' Deursen recalled.

Then the Beatles' convoy sped off and Ringo was gone forever.

~

Or not quite.

In 2013, Starr published *Photograph*, a collection of his private family pictures and shots he'd himself taken through the years. Printed across a double-page spread near the middle of the book was a black-and-white picture he'd snapped of six teenagers in a car in the '60s in what he seemed to remember was somewhere in Florida, probably Miami.

It was annotated with his own words: 'They're looking at us, and I'm photographing them. The first couple of years, we saw a lot of places from the car because we couldn't go out anywhere. We were just too big time. Everybody wanted a piece of us.'

In the picture, Deursen is at the steering wheel pulling a toothy grin, with Toth beaming to his right. Behind them sit an entranced Rayot (her hand touching her face and still wearing her soon-to-be-flung pinkie ring), Norbe (looking more serenely posed) and Schwartz (scrunching up his eyes and, for some reason, holding his hands outside of the car in a karate-styled pose). Peering over his left shoulder, and mostly in darkness, there is the just-visible image of Blender.

On 21 October 2013, *USA Today* journalist Edna Gundersen launched an appeal in the paper to find the mystery teens, under a banner headline asking: 'Beatles fans, did Ringo Starr snap your photo in 1964?' It was a cute human-interest story that was soon picked up by many other media outlets.

'I mean, I just put it in the book because it's a great shot,' Starr commented. 'Then, suddenly in America, everyone was trying to find them.'

Arlene Norbe was watching the TV news when the photo flashed up onscreen and she thought to herself, *Wait a minute, that's me*. Her phone then rang and it was her sister shrieking, 'Did you see yourself?!'

Charlie Schwartz got a call from an old Fair Lawn High School pal who disbelievingly told him, 'Ringo Starr is looking for you!'

Gary Van Deursen meanwhile couldn't even remember Ringo taking the picture.

The teenage friends – now, of course, in their sixties – were reunited on NBC's *Today* morning show and recreated the photograph forty-nine years later. The only sad note was that they were now reduced to five, with Matt Blender having died of heart failure two years earlier in 2011. For a follow-up item, the TV producers offered to fly the group to Las Vegas in November to watch Ringo perform at the Pearl Concert Theater in the Palms Casino Resort in Las Vegas, where they also would meet the man himself.

'I never knew that you were such a gifted photographer,' Norbe told Starr with a laugh.

'That was a lucky shot,' Ringo joked in response. 'Don't tell anyone.'

67

9 MADRYN STREET SAVED

And Other Neglected Starkey Landmarks, 1992–2025

O n the rainy summer's morning of 6 July 1992, the day before he turned fifty-two, Ringo stood on the pavement outside the house where he was born.

'It looks exactly the same!' he cried.

But it really didn't. Number 9 Madryn Street was utterly derelict, its front windows smashed, their frames broken and partially covered by sheets of chipboard scribbled with fan messages including 'Ringo, My Love' and 'Back Off Boogaloo'. It was a pitiful sight, and yet Beatles bus tours still made regular stops outside it every day.

'It's like a home for pigeons now,' Ringo accurately observed. If he was saddened by the fact that the property he'd lived in until the age of five hadn't received much in the way of care or respect in recent years, he didn't let it show.

Starr was back in his home city to perform with the All-Starr Band at the Empire Theatre that night. It was his first gig in Liverpool since the Beatles' last, when on 5 December 1965, more than 40,000 fans had applied for the 5,000 tickets available for the two performances at the same theatre.

Ringo had decided to mark this occasion by filming a TV special in conjunction with the Disney Channel, titled *Going Home*. In it, he served as a tour guide for the camera crew and his twenty-five-year-old son Jason, looking heavy metal chic in his long ponytail and black leather jacket. The two were joined by the eighty-year-old Harry Graves (touchingly introduced by Starr as 'my dad') in his raincoat and fedora.

The three wandered down High Park Street, past the Empress pub featured on the cover of *Sentimental Journey*, where Elsie had worked as a barmaid and young Richy had got his teenage taste for booze. As they turned into Admiral Grove, Starr began telling his younger son about how as a kid his mother used to wash him in a bath made of 'aluminum', tellingly using the American phrasing. He then reminisced with Harry about when the Starkeys had first had a telephone installed in the early months of the Beatles' success. Ringo had been thrilled to get a call from a fan, until he realised she'd reversed the charges. 'I went, "Whoop!", and put the phone down,' he chuckled.

Number 10 Admiral Grove looked pretty much the same as it had done when he'd left it and moved to London in 1963, even if the rest of his old neighbourhood seemed entirely foreign to him. 'I suppose if you're just always living here, you don't see the change,' he contemplated. 'To me it's like another country.'

He then took Jason into town and to the original site of the Cavern, which was now a car park.

'One day you could play here,' he told him.

His son broke into a fit of giggles. 'I prefer London,' he said.

His dad turned to the camera and affectionately called him a 'cockney horror' before proudly adding, 'he's another drummer, y'know'.

Later, after the soundcheck at the Empire, there was a tea party thrown in Starr's pre-birthday honour at the Adelphi Hotel, where the 15-year-old Richy had seen '50s heartbreak crooner Johnnie Ray standing on a balcony throwing photos of himself down to screaming girls ('I thought, *Wow, this is fabulous*,' he remembered. '*This is the job for me*'). His wider family and old friends, including Roy Trafford, all turned up, and Ringo worked the room, hugging everyone.

The final cut of the TV special featured live footage from the Empire show, where Zak Starkey was now the resident drummer in the All-Starr Band, confidently motoring them along and joining his dad in the old Merseyside family trade with a double tub-thumping rendition of 'Boys'. 'That one lesson I gave him really paid off,' Ringo laughed.

But when *Going Home* was screened in the US in the April of 1993, as the credits rolled over car-shot footage of Madryn Street, passing along its terraced row of well-tended houses, number 9 stood out like a rotten and broken tooth.

~

Eight years later, in 2010, plans were in place to demolish Madryn Street and the surrounding 'Welsh Streets' of Toxteth (Powis, Rhiwlas, Gwydir...), comprising more than 400 Victorian-built houses designed by architect Richard Owens for migrant workers from Wales who'd relocated to Liverpool.

Incredibly, Liverpool City Council drew up a plan to have 9 Madryn Street, at an estimated cost of £200,000, taken apart brick-by-brick and reassembled at the Museum of Liverpool on the city's waterfront, which was due to open in 2011.

Starr commented on the proposal, stating that in his opinion it didn't make sense to move the house; he hoped it would remain in its original location. 'If you want to see where I come from,' he said, 'it only works, as far as I can see, if it's there.' It was clearly a madcap scheme, one that was quietly dropped.

Veering from one extreme to the other, the house was now set to be destroyed along with the rest. Number 9 was secured with a metal door and window shutters to prevent souvenir hunters from seizing their final chance to find random items inside to keep for themselves or to sell on eBay. Meanwhile an online petition calling for the house to be preserved by the National Trust collected almost 4,000 signatures.

But then the demolition project was pulled after the coalition Conservative/ Liberal Democrat government came into power in 2010. In 2012, housing minister Grant Shapps announced that 9 Madryn Street was to be spared the wrecking ball, along with thirty-one other houses in the area. Shapps posed outside number 9, alongside Liverpool mayor Joe Anderson, for the assembled media. 'Ringo Starr's home is a significant beacon of Beatlemania,' he told them.

In spite of this, the following year, his Tory colleague, communities secretary Eric Pickles, scrapped the plan for the area's redevelopment, which was deemed to be too expensive. In 2013, 9 Madryn Street was valued at £60,000. The following year, its worth had dropped to a derisory £525.

Jonathan Brown from UK charity SAVE Britain's Heritage maintained pressure on the government to prevent the property from falling into a further state of disrepair. 'To paraphrase John Lennon talking about Ringo,' he said, mistakenly quoting the joke that Lennon had never made, 'this isn't the best house in the world. It's not even the best house in Liverpool, but it does draw thousands of tourists from all over the world and you've got to wonder how little they must think Liverpool values the Beatles to let these houses be run down in this way.' The sustained campaigning worked and, in 2016, the regeneration was approved and put into the hands of Manchester-based developers Placefirst.

That same year, 10 Admiral Grove was valued at £55,000 (a tad less than similar properties in the area) and, put up for auction, was bought by a Beatles fan, Jackie Holmes, for £70,000. Restrictions imposed upon the sale by its owners, Plus Dane housing association, prohibited it from being used as a Ringo/Beatles-themed museum or any kind of tourist attraction. Holmes said she planned to rent the house to an occupant who would 'cherish' it.

By 2018, the renovation of Madryn Street was underway, but number 9 still remained very much uncherished. In 2019, the National Trust turned down an offer from Placefirst to acquire the house, as the organisation had done in 1995 with McCartney's childhood home at 20 Forthlin Road. (In 2002, Yoko Ono had purchased Mendips, Lennon's former home at 251 Menlove Avenue, which she'd then – echoing the words of 'Happiness is a Warm Gun' – donated to the National Trust.)

It was considered to be another snub to Starr and the Madryn Street house – even if the heritage charity hadn't shown any interest in either of George Harrison's one-time abodes at 12 Arnold Grove or 25 Upton Green. Steve Barnes, the founder of the campaign Save Madryn Street, stated that the organisation had missed a 'golden opportunity' not to buy the property and allow fans 'carefully controlled access' to it, in the same way the National Trust had done with Lennon's and McCartney's homes.

'It's crazy to mothball it,' Barnes added. 'I can't understand why they wouldn't want to add Ringo's house to the list of destinations, now that it's been saved for posterity.'

By 2020, the Madryn Street renovation was completed, although number 9 was left vacant and used as a showroom for the rest of the development. 'We are a housing company, not a tourist operator,' said a spokesman from Placefirst. 'We recognised that it cannot be tenanted because of the interest from tourists. We cannot stop visitors from arriving, but the house will not be open.'

~

Stand outside 9 Madryn Street in the summer of 2024 and the impression is that not much has changed since. The house remains unoccupied, although someone has thought to open the windows. Plants wilt on the inside sill. Tourists who've paid the extra for a private Beatles taxi tour – as opposed to jumping on a coach filled with rubberneckers – stand in the middle of the quiet residential road. A guide, clutching a folder turned to a page featuring an old, '40s-era black and white photograph of Richy and Elsie, talks them through the building's history. It's a quiet reminder that the novelty of being a modern-day neighbour of a house where a Beatle once lived would quickly wear off.

Two minutes' walk away, 10 Admiral Grove appears to still be privately owned, although apparently empty. A nosey peek through the front window reveals a pot of paint and the fact that someone has been doing a spot of decorating. The white brickwork and pink windowsills outside could similarly use a touch-up, but otherwise it's in a decent state.

In the mind of the fan, it's easy to conjure up the vision of Ringo rushing out of his front door, being mobbed by kids, jumping into George's sports car and zooming off, as seen in the '63 documentary *The Mersey Sound*. But if you weren't already in the know, there is no indication that Starr ever lived here.

Turn to the right, however, and it becomes blindingly obvious. On the wall of the three-storey Empress pub, there is a huge mural tribute to him, painted by Liverpool artist John Culshaw in 2022, who used a cherry picker to access the upper reaches. In its design, a greyscale close-up of mid-'60s Ringo is set inside the fantastical, multi-coloured world of Pepperland, replete with *Yellow Submarine* Beatle figures and a humungous Blue Meanie. More than anything, it serves to emphasise the almost cartoony elements of Starr's life.

Left of the pub's doorway entrance on High Park Street, above images of the *Pepper* Beatles staring out from the window, there are now the words: 'This building appeared on the sleeve of Ringo Starr's first solo album, *Sentimental*

Journey.' Elsewhere, all of its brick sills and rooftop cornices are painted in swirling psychedelic patterns, like a flashback to the fated Apple boutique.

If Starr now artfully dominated the area he grew up in, the Empress remained closed, following reports that it had been put up for auction with a starting price of £275,000 in January 2024. It was unclear whether it had sold and, as of summer 2025, it had yet to reopen, with its future remaining uncertain.

Meanwhile, SAVE Britain's Heritage continued to push to have the former pigeon loft that was 9 Madryn Street preserved as a Grade II-listed building and be given the status that was afforded both Lennon and McCartney's homes in February 2012.

The lingering feeling was that, even by 2024 in Liverpool, Ringo Starr seemed to be everywhere and, at the same time, nowhere. The city's multi-million-pound Beatles industry had in some ways overlooked the landmarks of his life.

But maybe that was also because, following the events of 2008, many in Liverpool had a complicated attitude towards Ringo.

68

THE HEADLESS HEDGE

A Northern Uproar,
2008–2025

On the evening of Friday 11 January 2008, the blocked-off roads around St George's Hall and Lime Street Station were overflowing with somewhere in the region of 50,000 revellers. The occasion was the People's Opening, an event marking the beginning of Liverpool's year as European Capital of Culture. For this grand celebration with its firework finale, one of the city's most famous sons had returned as the show-closing star attraction.

High atop the first-floor balcony above the striking neoclassical columns of St George's, his image beamed onto two massive screens, Ringo and his latest musical mucker, onetime Eurythmic-turned-record producer Dave Stewart, were performing 'Liverpool 8'. Or, at least, they were miming to its pre-recorded track on a set fashioned from a shipping container, befitting a jamboree in one of the world's most famous ports.

The song was also an appropriate one, being a chugging, string-soaked anthemic rocker sketching Starr's story, from ferry bar worker to drummer with Rory Storm and the Hurricanes to the stage at Shea Stadium, along the way namechecking his fellow Beatles and the Liverpool streets where he'd lived. If his lyric was oversimple or clunky in its rhymes – 'sea' with 'Roar-ee', 'cool' with 'Liverpool' – its sentiment sounded genuine. His central message was that he may have left Liverpool but, as one of its most illustrious ambassadors, he'd never let the city down by tarnishing its reputation. In this majestic setting, it represented an enormous public declaration of his love for, and ongoing connection with, the city.

To emphasise the point, the song built to a big football chant ending, quickly adopted by the masses in the packed streets below: 'Liverpool!! Liverpool!!'

'The city is dynamic now,' Ringo enthused to *GMTV* presenters Ben Shephard and Fiona Phillips when he was interviewed live on their studio sofa the following Monday morning. Describing the vast crowd's reaction to his Friday performance, he added, 'You could feel the vibe and everyone was really, "It's Liverpool!" It was great.'

Four days later, in the opening minutes of his appearance on *Friday Night with Jonathan Ross* on BBC One, Starr was altogether less charitable about his hometown.

'What do you miss about Liverpool when you're not there?' the host enquired.

Ringo let out an involuntary chuckle.

'I didn't know that would get a laugh,' said Ross. The studio audience chortled in response. 'Obviously this is going to be a great answer. *Are* there any things that you miss about not being in Liverpool anymore?'

'Uh... no,' Starr smiled.

Ross immediately cracked up, along with everyone else.

'Surely the people... the sense of humour?' he gently suggested.

'No, I love Liverpool,' Ringo maintained, although dispassionately. 'I was a child ... I grew up in Liverpool... y'know, family members are in Liverpool. But...' he shrugged. 'Y'know...'

'I *love* your honesty,' Ross beamed, acknowledging that this was a moment of TV gold happening in real time.

Getting further into his stride, Starr then admitted that he'd fibbed to the crowd during his and Stewart's second performance in the city, the previous Saturday night, at the 10,000-capacity Liverpool Echo Arena.

'I had to tell the audience,' he said, '"It was so exciting over the weekend, I was *that* close"' – he displayed a two-inch gap between thumb and forefinger – '"to coming back."'

They all had a good laugh at that one.

'But I had a great time,' he quickly added, perhaps sensing that he'd gone too far. 'I loved it up there over the weekend. It was exciting.'

Ross then enquired as to how people on the streets of Liverpool treated Starr these days: 'Do they go crazy still?'

'They love me,' Ringo joked, before turning a tad more serious. 'No, really, they love me.'

But, for many Liverpudlians, it was a love that instantly curdled to hate. Almost as soon as the show finished, the online forums of the *Liverpool Echo* erupted with Scouse fury and indignation. 'I'm disgusted by the way he mocked Liverpool after having the red carpet rolled out for him last week,' fumed one aggrieved poster. 'The irony is that his song suggests he's never let us down!' snorted another.

City councillor Mike Storey subsequently added his voice to the uproar. 'It's hugely disappointing and sad [that] someone who came to lead Capital of Culture year should go away and be so negative about it.'

'It's not helpful on national TV,' agreed council leader Warren Bradley. 'But that's Ringo's style ... to be flippant.'

~

Two months later, in March 2008, a new topiary sculpture was unveiled outside Liverpool's South Parkway rail station, in the district of Garston, south of the city centre. Funded by local transport executive Merseytravel and created at great, undisclosed expense by Italian artist Franco Covill in Tuscany – by fashioning a series of metal skeletons in which its hedges were grown and shaped – it depicted the four Beatles in the form of faceless foliage: three of them holding guitars and one sat at a bushy green drum kit.

Sometime on Sunday 6 April, it was discovered by a couple of station security employees that Ringo had lost his head. It had been sheared cleanly off by some mysterious and well-prepared vandal, whom they'd very nearly caught in the act. The other three Fabs were left untouched, leading to the suspicion that the action had been in response to Starr's snub. This supposition was lent further credence by another rail worker revealing to a reporter that 'last month someone squashed Ringo's head, but this time it's been completely cut off. Whoever did it must have come armed with cutting equipment.'

Throughout that week, the story was covered by an increasing number of news outlets.

'Following the TV appearance,' the *Liverpool Echo* dryly surmised, the offender 'took things into their own hands and gave the newly placed topiary sculpture of the famous moptop an extreme short back and sides.'

By Thursday 10 April, the story had even made it to the pages of the *New York Times*, under the intriguing headline, 'Ringo Loses Leafy Head'.

'Public art is important,' a Merseytravel spokesman told the paper. 'The topiary was put there to bring a bit of life and soul to the public transport network.'

The article also revealed that an enquiry was underway by British Transport Police, who were carefully analysing CCTV footage from around the station. But, a week after the hedge attack, the *Mail On Sunday* gravely reported, 'the head has not been found'.

For his part, Ringo didn't comment on this symbolic act of art destruction. But he did offer an apology for his flippant comments, while qualifying it by saying it was aimed squarely at Liverpudlians only and not any affronted non-residents.

'No real Scouser took offence,' he reckoned. 'Only people, I believe, from the outside.'

~

In all of the intervening years, the phantom decapitator has never come forward and spoken about their role in the incident. That is, until now. Following a series of introductions through Merseyside backchannels, contact was made by the author with the individual in question.

Starr was wrong in one respect: the saboteur was indeed a Scouser, and also a drummer himself. It transpires that the deed was done en route to a gig.

Here the mysterious perpetrator anonymously gives his side of the story, beginning with his own reaction to the inflammatory comments made by Starr to Jonathan Ross:

'It felt like a kick in the stonks, yet again, to our city. So, unfortunately for Ringo, or should I say the hedge, the following commenced...

'We happened to be playing a gig in [location redacted] on the Sunday. Armed with me arl fellah's (Dad RIP) Spear and Jackson clippers, myself

[nickname redacted] and our manager [nickname redacted] decided to descend on Liverpool South Parkway Station to administer the "beheading".

'It was a stealth-like situation.

'[Redacted] parked up under strict instruction to "not move" due to the level of security at the station (Hi Vizzy jobsworths).

'I read Ringo his rights… then one clip… off with his head…!!

'Followed by, "Oi, what you doing, lad?"

'I was by this time on me toes frantically looking for the car that wasn't in the place we agreed.

'With legs ribboned by brambles I spotted said car. [Redacted] flung the door open, I dived in the back, pursued by the Hi Vizzys. I was trying to close the still wide-open door.

'Subsequently I decided to celebrate my day in the sun by parading it all over social media, which went down a storm…

'Until… the Monday evening when I was alerted by a famous Liverpool musician (who shall remain nameless) to turn on the local news (Granada Reports). The reporter was live at the scene of the beheading, suggesting it was a disgrace. I immediately removed all my social media posts, clearing myself from any involvement in the ghastly deed.

'The rest is history.

'Though as a drummer meself I would like to distance meself from the "Ringo as a [crap] drummer" hate brigade. Ringo's style and what he brought to the table was groundbreaking.

'Oh… and Ringo never moved back and… I've hung up me clippers!'

69

'PEACE AND LOVE... BASTARDS!'

A Farewell to Autographs, 2008–2010

B ack in the Apple boardroom in London in the April of 2010, Ringo was considering another highly newsworthy event that he'd found himself at the centre of in 2008. On 13 October of that year, in a video posted to his official website, he'd made a brief, if cranky announcement. Almost five decades after he'd first perfected his autograph with a star-shaped flourish for Butlin's holidaymakers back in his Hurricanes days, his relationship with the fan-wielded biro or marker pen had come to a firm and decisive end.

The forty-three-second clip began with a close-up on his sunglasses and nose before the shot pulled out to his head and shoulders. Then, in a tetchy tone, he stated: 'This is a serious message to everybody watching my update right now, peace and love, peace and love.' He offered only a one-handed peace sign, rather than his regular two.

'I want to tell you, please, after the 20th of October, do not send fan mail to *any* address that you have. Nothing will be signed after the 20th of October. If [it] has [that] date on the envelope, it's going to be tossed.'

'I'm warning you with peace and love,' he went on, with passive-aggressive determination, 'but I have too much to do. So no more fan mail. Thank you, thank you... and no objects to be signed... *nothing*! Anyway, peace and love, peace and love.'

A year-and-a-half on, I asked him why exactly he'd felt moved to make such a public declaration. Was it just 'the eBay effect' (autograph hunters selling on inscribed albums or memorabilia) or was he genuinely pissed off signing stuff?

'Well, it was the eBay effect,' he sighed. 'Because I found in New York that people were screaming at me to sign scratch boards of guitars and then I'd see it on eBay for $3,000. A shitty guitar with a scratch board that I'd signed. And I also felt, I have signed *enough*. And so I decided that day, I'm gonna end it on my website.

'I never thought it was gonna go on CNN,' he added, still mildly incredulous. 'It was on every fucking news channel.'

Now, having had time to reflect, he'd realised that he 'could've done it nicer. I could've done it in a more loving way. But it was the mood I was in.'

It was quite funny, though, I pointed out. Your message was sort of 'peace and love … don't fucking send me anything to sign … peace and love.'

'I know!' he laughed. '"Peace and love … bastards!"'

Later, when I spoke to Klaus Voormann, he said he could sympathise with Ringo, having himself, through the years, signed thousands of copies of *Revolver* featuring his iconic cover art.

'I mean, sometimes it gets on your nerves,' Voormann confessed. 'I, in a very small way, have similar things, like when people come with twenty album covers.' He mimicked an impatient fan. '"Come on, sign these!" I get pissed off, y'know. So he did get pissed off, too, and to such a bigger extent. He was just fed up with doing all these signatures. I can understand it.'

So, the obvious follow-up question to Starr was… did the fan mail stop coming in, then?

'Oh, yeah, great! Oh! Incredible…'

Your postman must have been chuffed?

'Oh, three postmen in three countries are *really* chuffed. And I was really chuffed. I was spending my days… I mean, it was a lot coming in, a *lot* coming in. I'm not talking about two or three. I'm talking about *mounds* taller than me. And I thought, *No, I'm not doing it no more.*'

I said I could appreciate why it had become such a hassle.

'What?' he responded, with a sly smirk. 'Have you signed a lot in your day?'

Signed on the dole, I told him.

'Yeah, I signed on meself,' he said, before the subject was quietly dropped.

70

'SOME STRANGE FAIRY TALE'

Here and Now and Then,
1940–2025

Sometime in the early 2010s, Ringo Starr and Paul McCartney were having dinner in Los Angeles with their mutual buddy, Foo Fighter Dave Grohl, and their respective wives. At one point in the evening, there was a flashback to the moment captured in the last photograph taken of the three surviving Beatles together at Ringo's sixtieth in 2000, when George Harrison was snapped attempting to tilt a glass of wine into the drummer's mouth.

Likely tipsy himself, McCartney now decided to test Starr's sobriety by gently taking the mickey out of him about it.

'C'mon, Ringo, have a whisky,' he urged him.

'What?' Starr shot back. 'And end up looking like you?'

'I deserved it,' McCartney accepted, talking to *Rolling Stone* magazine in 2015. Still, it was a revealing moment. For all of the unimaginable distance they'd travelled together, and the experiences that really only the two of them could ever understand, they remained a pair of sarky northerners, quick of wit and sharp of tongue.

All jibing aside, and even more tellingly, in 2015 McCartney pushed for Starr to be inducted as a solo artist into the Rock & Roll Hall of Fame. It was a process that began with Robbie Robertson (formerly of the Band) casually pointing out to Paul in conversation that he felt it was a glaring oversight. The Beatles had been honoured in 1988, Lennon posthumously in 1994, McCartney in '99, and Harrison three years after his death, in 2004. There remained a conspicuous Ringo-shaped hole.

'Let me see what I can do,' McCartney told Robertson, before rallying further support for the idea from Bruce Springsteen and Dave Grohl. Then he made an offer to the Hall of Fame's committee to deliver the induction speech himself. 'That took care of it,' he assuredly stated, acknowledging the lasting power of the forces-combined extant Beatles to make things happen.

Ahead of the ceremony, held on 18 April 2015 at the Public Auditorium in Cleveland, Ohio, which was to culminate in a Starr-fronted celebrity band performance, he and Paul were caught in behind-the-scenes footage joking around with Stevie Wonder. 'We're re-forming the group, man,' Ringo told him. 'You wanna join?'

On the night, McCartney's speech sounded like it came from the heart, as Starr sat at a table in the audience alongside Bach, appearing visibly moved. After Paul briefly stated that Pete Best 'was great', he vibrantly recalled the moment when Ringo first sat in with the Beatles, exhilarating them as they played a cover of Ray Charles's pacey and tricksy 'What'd I Say' (the rhythm of which they'd subsequently pilfer for 'I Feel Fine').

'Most drummers couldn't nail the drum part,' he said. 'But Ringo nailed it.'

Some guy in the crowd yelled, 'Woo!'

'Yeah... Ringo nailed it!' McCartney continued as a huge cheer from the audience rose into the air. 'And I remember standing there and looking at John and then looking at George, and the look on our faces was like, *Fuck! What is this?* And that was the beginning, really, of the Beatles.' McCartney then further testified to Starr's rock-solid reliability as a musician. 'You see these other bands, they're looking around at the drummer, like, *Is he going to speed up? Is he going to slow down?* You don't have to look with Ringo.'

When it came time to hand over the gong, Starr walked onstage to the strains of 'Photograph'. 'My name is Ringo,' he dryly reminded everyone, 'and I play drums. I want to thank Paul for all those great things he told us. Some of them were true.'

Three minutes into what felt like it was going to be a long speech, as Ringo was recalling his days as a part-time musician and factory worker, McCartney wandered back towards the podium and amiably showed Starr his watch, as if to chivvy him along.

'Yeah, yeah ... after the things I've sat through tonight ... blah, blah, blah...' Ringo only half-joked in response, as the crowd hooted in amused disbelief at both his honesty and his audacity. Yoko Ono and Olivia Harrison laughed along from their tables. 'I got some stories!' he warned.

He appeared to be relishing the moment and, seven minutes later, as McCartney approvingly smiled away on the side of the stage, Starr was still going strong, reminiscing about his early tours with the Beatles, before offering a parting tip for any aspiring bands.

'When you're in the van, if you fart, own up,' he sagely advised. 'We made a pact and that's why we got on so well.'

Introducing his live performance, he began with 'a number I've done since 1960'. He and Californian punks Green Day (inducted at the same event) then bashed through the deathless 'Boys', before Joe Walsh arrived to add strumming support to 'It Don't Come Easy', a song that had accumulated life-experienced resonances for Starr, as made even more apparent during this victory lap.

'The stage seems a little empty to me,' Ringo then announced, like some old-time vaudeville MC, signalling the arrival of another friend 'who plays bass occasionally'. He and McCartney were reunited for the inevitable 'With a Little Help from My Friends', with everyone from Beck and Miley Cyrus to Patti Smith and Dave Grohl running on stage to chip in on the choruses, followed by a turbo-charged 'I Wanna Be Your Man' in which all of the guests played out their Fabs fantasies.

At its close, Paul whispered 'the bow!' to Ringo and they lowered their heads in the old, slickly coordinated Beatles move well-practised back in the days when there were four of them.

~

Almost ten years later, with both of them in their eighties, Starr jumped up on stage with McCartney for an encore appearance on the final date of the latter's *Got Back* tour. At the O2 in London on the night of 19 December 2024, they kicked off with the perennially thumping reprise version of 'Sgt. Pepper's Lonely Hearts Club Band', before slamming into, of all things, the demandingly rocky (and now age-defiant) 'Helter Skelter'.

'There's a connection between the bass player and the drummer,' Ringo had emphasised to the *LA Times* three months earlier. 'You're both the deep end of it all. Paul's still the most magical bass player I know.'

If there was a lingering expectation that, as the last two survivors of a still-bewildering phenomenon, they somehow had an obligation to keep the Beatles flame alive, they didn't seem to pay much attention to it. At the same time, they both enjoyed the opportunity to re-evaluate their past in new and novel ways, whether it be through Giles Martin's twenty-first-century-polished Beatles catalogue remixes, or their creation, in 2023, of the track dubbed 'the last Beatles song', 'Now and Then'.

The idea to finally complete the third John Lennon demo abandoned during the *Anthology* sessions in the mid-'90s was first floated by McCartney in one of his regular FaceTime chats with Starr. 'He wanted to know if I'd be interested in joining him to put "Now and Then" together,' Ringo casually stated. 'And I said, "Yeah".'

Giles Martin, brought in to co-produce the 2023 version of the lost track with McCartney, recognised that the original attempt may have been triggering for Paul, George and Ringo, starkly reminding them both of their friend's murder and the necessity to creatively preserve his memory with a high level of quality control. 'That's a hard thing to deal with,' he stressed. 'Not only dealing with your mate who's dead, but you're playing on a record where it's like, "What does it sound like?"'

'It hung around for a while,' said McCartney. 'Years. Every so often I'd kind of go to the cupboard and think, *There's a new song in there, y'know. We should do it, we've got to do it.* But it would go back in the cupboard. A couple of years ago, I said, "No, we've *really* got to do something."'

The key to unlocking the new version of the track was *Get Back* director Peter Jackson's use of WingNut Films' MAL (or Machine Assisted Learning) de-mixing software. Previously used for Martin's 2022 *Revolver* stereo remix and the section of Paul's *Got Back* live show where he duetted with an onscreen John on 'I've Got a Feeling', it gave the team a miraculously cleaned-up version of Lennon's vocal. Finishing 'Now and Then' once again seemed possible.

Giles Martin was at Abbey Road doing a Dolby Atmos mix of Wings' 1973 album *Red Rose Speedway* when McCartney first told him that he'd been working on 'Now and Then' and had added a new bassline and piano part (echoing Lennon's), while retaining George Harrison's electric and acoustic guitars. He asked him if he'd be interested in mixing the song. After hearing the work-in-progress track featuring Starr's '90s-recorded beats, Martin told McCartney he felt the drummer's parts should sound way more natural and characterful.

Starr quickly laid down his new parts at his Roccabella West studio in Los Angeles. 'He sent the files from England, and I just played drums and sang on it,' said Starr, typically imperturbable, even when it came to this quietly momentous act. He also wryly noted that McCartney had then flown all the way to Los Angeles to add an orchestra to the track. 'There's no string sections in England,' he sardonically quipped.

Still, the spirit of the Beatles was truly invoked in 'Now and Then'. McCartney's Harrison-mimicking slide guitar solo in the song was so authentic-sounding that it even briefly managed to fool Starr. 'I'm sitting there thinking, *I don't remember George doing that solo*,' he admitted. 'Then Paul said, "No, it's me."'

When the track was complete, the emotional impact of 'Now and Then' finally hit Ringo. 'It's so far out,' he said. 'John is so clear now you know it's him. Because on the original one we were working to, I couldn't tell if it was John or Paul singing half the time. Now you know it's John.'

'It's hard not to be overwhelmed with emotion,' said Sean Lennon, 'when you hear Paul and my dad singing together, and you're hearing Ringo on drums. It's bittersweet and it's very beautiful. It's so sweet and touching and sad and happy at the same time.

'I can't look at it with any neutrality. Y'know, it's a golden thing to be gifted with at this time. When the world is so complex and difficult, it's really nice to have this gift of another Beatles song.'

The making of 'Now and Then' also left the door open to the possibility of remixing 'Free as a Bird' and 'Real Love' using the same Lennon-enhancing software. As time passes, it increasingly seems as if, as audio technologies advance, the restoration of the Beatles' recordings may go on forever.

Commenting on Starr in the here and now, at the beginning of 2025, Paul McCartney expanded upon his past appraisal of his friend and bandmate as 'a natural genius'.

'Y'know, he didn't have a sort of heavy education, like a lot of people,' he stressed. 'So anything he knows is self-taught... most of it. He's very clever that way. He picks things up and is very witty. And, above all else, he's an amazing drummer who just knows how to do it. Simple as that.'

Moving into his mid-eighties, Starr was also an impressive octogenarian specimen – skinny, and sprightly, and keen to prove it, often (and appropriately) performing star jumps on stage with the All-Starr Band. There have, however, been a couple of worrying moments along the way. On 20 September 2023, at the Rio Rancho Events Center in New Mexico, he tripped over onstage and went flying, before immediately recovering like a pro. Quickly getting to his feet and smoothly slipping into 'Give Peace a Chance', he explained 'I fell over to tell you that.'

In the autumn of 2024, Starr was forced to cancel a couple of US dates due to what the headlines called a 'mystery illness'; a 'mystery' mainly because Starr didn't reveal too many details about it, other than to say that it wasn't COVID-19 and that he'd been suffering a high white-blood cell count of 12,000 per microlitre (generally caused by underlying infection or inflammation). Ringo colourfully, if evasively, called it 'a mad thing eating my body ... and with pills and medication, I got over it in two weeks'.

Around the same time, Ringo's long-term friend Bernie Taupin attested to how vigorous Starr remained in his advanced years. 'He looks absolutely amazing,' he said. 'Extraordinary. But then again, I suppose that's because he lives on blueberries and broccoli, y'know. I'm not sure I could do that. But it works for him.'

Similarly, Joe Walsh was constantly amazed by the fact that his brother-in-law – whom he revealed usually 'smells of kale' – was quite such a picture of health. 'Yep, he's totally taken care of himself,' he said, before adding with a laugh, 'and he yells at me when I don't.'

T Bone Burnett meanwhile witnessed Starr's surprising athleticism first-hand when Ringo and the All-Starr Band played at the Ryman Auditorium in Nashville in September 2023. 'He took an intermission and he *ran* upstairs,' he said. 'He's completely fit. I don't think he has an ounce of fat on him. And he's with it, he's sharp. And, of course, he's smart.'

For Jim Keltner, Ringo has simply become a good and dependable pal. 'I love that he's one of the only friends of mine that will pick up on the first ring,' he offered with a deep chuckle. 'It's always kind of shocking, like you don't get a chance to adjust your seat or anything. There he is, y'know. And I always comment on it, and he says, "Well, of course, I pick up if it's you!". He's a bit of a cornball. He wears his heart on his sleeve and I just love that about Ringo.'

Having been friends with him for more than fifty years – and having seen him at his best and probably his worst – Keltner was also in a position to view how Starr had changed through the decades. 'I think the biggest change occurred when he got completely clean,' he said. 'He always had a good heart. He never was mean-spirited or egocentric. But he got more accessible. He got more real in his friendliness when he got sober.

'He has helped me tremendously. Y'know, substance abuse. I pretty much got away from it around the time that Ringo did. His story, how he got sober, is really dramatic – and very inspiring.'

~

Nowadays, at family gatherings, Joe Walsh can't quite stop himself from looking over at Ringo sometimes and thinking, '*Holy shit, one of the Beatles!* We're pretty much best friends and all, but still, I just can't help it, y'know. He's just bigger than life.' As to the source of Starr's continuing drive, when he could easily retire, Walsh made one insightful and important point.

'Well, he's not really interested in being *more* famous, y'know. But he's not done playing.'

At the same time, in spite of his true desire to simply play drums or sing a tune, Starr's life still regularly pinballs from the surreal to the bizarre. One year, 2018, he's at Buckingham Palace being knighted for his services to music by Prince William, in a long-overdue upgrade to his 1965 MBE. The next, 2019, he's being forced to threaten legal action against an 'adult product designer', contending that their 'Ring O' penis accessory – 'super stretchy' and a snip at $8.99 for a triple pack – was a violation of his trademarked name. The action was dropped in 2021 when Starr's lawyers successfully argued that their client wanted to avoid any possible confusion that his 'newest venture was sex toys'. An agreement was reached where the manufacturers promised to use a clear gap between 'Ring' and 'O' on the packaging in the future.

All the while, for Ringo (no space), there's work to do, shows to play, records to make. Closing the circle of his childhood love of country music, in two gigs in January 2025 celebrating the *Look Up* album, he performed at the Ryman in Nashville – formerly home of the storied Grand Ole Opry radio broadcasts – with a parade of guests including Billy Strings, Molly Tuttle, Emmylou Harris and Brenda Lee.

Jack White, invited to perform 'Matchbox' and 'Don't Pass Me By', lost his characteristic cool and turned into a gushing fanboy when he was interviewed backstage by Anthony Mason of CBS News. He remembered that *The White Album* had been the first vinyl record he'd ever bought, from the Harmony House record store in downtown Detroit, back in 1989 when he was fourteen.

'So to be able to sing the song from that record is pretty cool,' he enthused.

Mason asked him, 'Did you ever think you'd be playing the Ryman with Ringo?'

'No, not at all!' White exclaimed with a goofy laugh. 'Neither of those things…'

It was yet another moment that proved that contact with An Actual Beatle could be a disorientating experience. As I knew well.

~

Back on our Zoom call in November 2024, I'd tried to round up my interview with Ringo – even though I realised it was a near-impossible task – by asking him to attempt to sum up his intensely eventful life.

'I feel blessed,' he offered. 'I do feel blessed and lucky that my dream at thirteen, getting over tuberculosis, was to be a drummer. Because we were all laying in bed, and they came with maracas and tambourines and a little drum, and this woman teacher gave me a drum. She'd point at the red marks [on the board], and you'd hit the drum, and the yellow, you did the triangle, whatever. Just to keep us busy.

'Y'know, the second part of that story is, I did learn to knit,' he laughed. 'Because that keeps you busy too.

'But that's the point. From that moment, I only wanted to be a drummer. I did get out of hospital a year later. And I did go to the music stores in Liverpool, and I was always just looking at the drums. And the craziest thing was, I got behind a kit for the first time, sat down. "Oh, this is great." And it was a right-handed kit, but I'm left-handed.

'Really weird, strange things. Y'know, I'm looking at life now and a lot of it is just, y'know... I look that way and there's a path. There's something happening. You can't plan every moment of it.'

I reminded him that when he'd received his honorary doctorate from the Berklee College of Music in 2022, he'd given a speech in which he'd brilliantly described his story as 'some strange fairy tale'. Could he elaborate?

'Well, no,' he said, before attempting to, weaving back through parts of his past, his mind boggling at the serendipitous connections. 'I mean, you can sit there all day and think about, *Well, if I had've got the visa to go and live in Houston, then what would have gone down then?* And just by chance, y'know, a guy came over named [Bruno] Koschmider and he was booking Liverpool bands to go to Germany. Rory and I and the Hurricanes went. The Beatles were already there. And so we sort of got to know each other a bit, hanging out.

'Then, y'know, a knock on my front door in Liverpool... Because I was a musician, you didn't get up too early. But it was Brian Epstein saying, "The Beatles are playing the Cavern, a lunchtime session. Do you think you could play?" I said, "Oh, sure, y'know". I could play with any band, because we all did the same songs. The Beatles were a cover band, the Hurricanes were a cover band. It wasn't like everybody was writing their own songs, like it ended up. Because of John and Paul, really. They instigated that worldwide.'

It seemed that, as he looked back, he only saw all of the magical coincidences and the sliding-doors opportunities that could have been so easily missed. One of them was the fact that Ed Sullivan had booked the Beatles to appear on his CBS TV show in February '64, unveiling the band to more than 73 million viewers, through pure chance, after witnessing feral fan scenes at London Airport in October '63.

In many ways, it was the singular moment that had changed Ringo Starr's life forever.

'We got off a plane from Sweden, and Ed Sullivan got off another plane from New York. He was coming to England. He didn't know us. We'd never heard of him, and he booked us. And, y'know, by the time we got to America, we had a number one, which was so far out. That's how it unfolded.'

In the end, he was still marvelling at his and the Beatles' story as much as the rest of us were – although he confessed that he had a fail-safe method that helped him to preserve his sanity.

'I try,' he concluded, with a familiar, cheeky grin, 'not to overthink it.'

BIBLIOGRAPHY

Andrews, Nancy Lee, *A Dose of Rock 'n' Roll* (Dalton Watson, 2008)

Badman, Keith, *The Beatles Diary Volume 2: After the Break-Up* (Omnibus, 2009)

Badman, Keith, *The Beatles Off the Record 2* (Omnibus, 2009)

The Beatles, *Anthology* (Apple Corps/Cassell, 2000)

The Beatles (edited by John Harris), *The Beatles: Get Back* (Apple Corps/Callaway, 2021)

Boyd, Pattie (with Penny Junor), *Wonderful Today* (Headline Review, 2007)

Braun, Michael, *Love Me Do! The Beatles' Progress* (Penguin, 1995)

Brown, Mick, *Tearing Down the Wall of Sound: The Rise and Fall of Phil Spector* (Bloomsbury, 2007)

Brown, Peter & Gaines, Steven, *All You Need is Love: The End of the Beatles* (Monoray, 2024)

Brown, Peter & Gaines, Steven, *The Love You Make: An Insider's Story of the Beatles* (New American, 2002)

Cardinal, Scott, *Tittenhurst Park: A Pictorial History of a Beatles' Landmark* (Campfire, 2017)

Carr, Roy, *Beatles at the Movies: Scenes From a Career* (UFO, 1996)

Chandler, Charlotte, *She Always Knew How: Mae West, A Personal Biography* (Simon & Schuster, 2009)

Connolly, Ray, *The Ray Connolly Beatles Archive* (Plumray, 2011)

Cross, Charles R, *Room Full of Mirrors: A Biography of Jimi Hendrix* (Sceptre, 2005)

Davies, Hunter, *The Beatles* (Ebury, 2009)

Doggett, Peter, *You Never Give Me Your Money: The Battle for the Soul of the Beatles* (Bodley Head, 2009)

Emerick, Geoff (with Howard Massey), *Here, There and Everywhere: My Life Recording the Music of the Beatles* (Gotham, 2006)

Essex, David (with Ian Gittins), *Over the Moon: My Autobiography* (Virgin, 2012)

Fletcher, Tony, *Dear Boy: The Life of Keith Moon* (Omnibus, 1998)

Goodden, Joe, *Riding So High: The Beatles and Drugs* (Pepper & Pearl, 2017)

Gruen, Bob (with Dave Thompson), *Right Place, Right Time: The Life of a Rock & Roll Photographer* (Abrams, 2020)

Harry, Bill, *The Ringo Starr Encyclopedia* (Virgin, 2004)

Haskins, Mike, *The Beatles' Liverpool* (Pitkin, 2022)

Hibbert, Tom, *Phew, Eh Readers? The Life and Writing of Tom Hibbert* (Nine Eight, 2024)

Houghton, Richard, *The Beatles: 'I Was There'* (Red Planet, 2016)

James, Andrew, *Drumming is His Madness: The Ringo Starr Discography* (independently published, 2023)

Johns, Glyn, *Sound Man: A Life Recording Hits with the Rolling Stones, the Who, Led Zeppelin, the Eagles, Eric Clapton, the Faces...* (Plume, 2015)

Kane, Larry, *When They Were Boys: The True Story of the Beatles' Rise to the Top* (Running, 2013)

Kelly, Deirdre, *Fashioning the Beatles: The Looks That Shook the World* (Sutherland House, 2023)

King, Tony, *The Tastemaker: My Life with the Legends and Geniuses of Rock Music* (Faber & Faber, 2023)

Kozinn, Allan and Sinclair, Adrian, *The McCartney Legacy Volume 2 1974–80* (Dey Street, 2024)

Kubernik, Harvey, *Canyon of Dreams: The Magic and Music of Laurel Canyon* (Sterling, 2009)

Lennon, Cynthia, *A Twist of Lennon* (Star, 1978)

Lennon, John, *Skywriting By Word of Mouth* (Vintage, 2012)

Lewisohn, Mark, *All These Years, Vol. 1: Tune In (Extended Special Edition)* (Little, Brown, 2013)

Lewisohn, Mark, *The Complete Beatles Chronicle* (Hamlyn, 1995)

Lewisohn, Mark, *The Complete Beatles Recording Sessions* (Hamlyn, 2004)

McCartney, Paul and Muldoon, Paul, *The Lyrics* (Allen Lane, 2021)

Martin, George (with Jeremy Hornsby), *All You Need is Ears* (St Martin's, 1979)

Matteo, Steve, *Act Naturally: The Beatles on Film* (Backbeat, 2023)

Miles, Barry, *Frank Zappa* (Atlantic, 2004)

Miller, Jason Andrew and Shales, Tom, *Live From New York: The Complete, Uncensored History of Saturday Night Live* (Little, Brown, 2014)

Norman, Philip, *George Harrison: The Reluctant Beatle* (Simon & Schuster, 2023)

Norman, Philip, *Shout! The True Story of the Beatles* (Pan, 2004)

O'Dell, Chris (with Katherine Ketcham), *Miss O'Dell: My Hard Days and Long Nights with the Beatles, the Stones, Bob Dylan, Eric Clapton and the Women They Loved* (Touchstone, 2009)

Pang, May (with Henry Edwards), *Loving John: The Untold Story* (Corgi, 1983)

Paytress, Mark, *Bolan: The Rise and Fall of a 20th Century Superstar* (Omnibus, 2009)

Rees, Dafydd, *The Beatles 1963: A Year in the Life* (Omnibus, 2024)

Shipton, Alyn, *Nilsson: The Life of a Singer-Songwriter* (Oxford, 2013)

Sikov, Ed, *Mr Strangelove: A Biography of Peter Sellers* (Hyperion, 2003)

Spector, Ronnie (with Vince Waldron), *Be My Baby* (Pan, 2023)

Spitz, Bob, *The Beatles: The Biography* (Little, Brown, 2012)

Stanley, Bob, *Bee Gees: Children of the World* (Nine Eight, 2023)

Starr, Michael Seth, *Ringo: With a Little Help* (Backbeat, 2015)

Starr, Ringo, *Another Day in the Life* (Genesis, 2019)

Starr, Ringo, *Photograph* (Genesis, 2013)

Starr, Ringo, *Postcards from the Boys* (Cassell, 2004)

Taylor, Alistair, *With the Beatles* (John Blake, 2011)

Taylor, Derek, *As Time Goes By* (Faber & Faber, 2018)

Taylor, Joan and Derek, *Getting Sober... and Loving It: Hope and Help From Recovering Alcoholics* (Vermilion, 1992)

Townshend, Pete, *Who I Am* (HarperCollins, 2012)

Turner, Steve, *Beatles '66: The Revolutionary Year* (Ecco, 2016)

Wenner, Jann S., *Lennon Remembers* (Arrow, 1971)

Willetts, Paul, *Members Only: The Life and Times of Paul Raymond* (Serpent's Tail, 2010)

Womack, Kenneth, *Living the Beatles Legend: The Mal Evans Story* (Mudlark, 2023)

ACKNOWLEDGEMENTS

For their generous interview time and for quotes (in conversation with the author) that made their way into this book, thanks to Ringo Starr, Paul McCartney, Yoko Ono, Sean Lennon, Zak Starkey, Klaus Voormann, John Leckie, Elton John, Bernie Taupin, Giles Martin, Jim Keltner, Joe Walsh, May Pang, Roger Daltrey, Kenney Jones, Gordon Elsmore, T Bone Burnett, Roger Manning Jr, Bob Gruen, Danny Thompson, Howie Casey, Jimmy Iovine, the late Alan White, Roy Cicala and George Martin, and the Phantom Hedge Decapitator.

Massive thanks to my agent Matthew Hamilton, for shepherding this one along a difficult path, and to Pete Selby at New Modern (whose idea this book was in the first place) for getting the band back together. Special thanks to Danny Eccleston and Ian Harrison for commissioning the original 2024 and 2010 Ringo interviews for *MOJO*. Big up too to the rest of the crew: John Mulvey, Jenny Bulley, Mark 'Wag' Wagstaff, Mark Blake, Keith Cameron, David 'Hutchie' Hutcheon, Victoria Segal, Stevie Chick and Chris Catchpole. For direct or indirect assistance: Sue Harris, Elizabeth Freund, Jonathan Clyde and Chris Hewitt.

Peace and love (both hands) to: Simon Goddard and Sylvia Patterson, my travelling companions on our Toxteth adventure, and to Paul Fitzgerald for being the Merseyside guide, driver and host with the most. Shout out to Heather and Brian and all my family in Dundee, and my other pals: the White Label/Ping Pong Disco/Hornsey Automatics massives (Anth Brown, Dave Tomlinson, Kieran Heneghan, Calina De La Mare, Pete Scott), Jon Bennett, James Hall, Matt Delargy (for his solo Beatle PTSD theory), Paul Weller, Mike Brown, Steve Aungle, Gareth Nicholls, John Aizlewood, Dave Black and Steve Wilkins.

Online resources: YouTube, The Beatles Bible, The Beatles Ultimate Experience, The Daily Beatle, The Beatles FAQ, The Paul McCartney Project,

ACKNOWLEDGEMENTS

The Beatles on Film, Simpsons Wiki, Goldmine, Ultimate Classic Rock, Gary Astridge's RingoBeatleKits.com, Surrey Live, Silvascreen.com, Pauldunoyer.com, Communita Queeniana, Rock & Roll Hall of Fame, Andrew Dixon's YouTube channel.

Print and online newspaper and magazine resources: *MOJO*, *Rolling Stone*, *USA Today*, *Mersey Beat*, *Q*, *NME*, *Melody Maker*, *Saturday Evening Post*, *Daily Mirror*, *Evening Standard*, *Datebook*, *Daily Mail*, *Mail on Sunday*, *Mirabelle*, *Variety*, *Esquire*, *People*, *Music Week*, *New York Times*, *Washington Post*, *Commercial Appeal*, *Modern Drummer*, *Toronto Sun*, *Liverpool Echo*.

TV and Radio: BBC, ITV, Disney+, Apple TV, NBC, CBS, ABC, PBS, WREG.

And, finally, love love love to Karen for her immaculate purple penning of this book and for putting up with me for nigh on forty years, and to Eddy for our crab conversations, keeping me topped up with my Anti-Moaning Tablets and for being the real Bounceback Kid.

The team at New Modern would like to thank the following individuals:

Nige Tassell for copy-editing
Peter Stoneman for editorial support
Jane Henshall for proofreading
Marie Doherty for typesetting
Paul Palmer-Edwards for final cover design
and **Alex Kirby** for his contribution to initial cover designs
Amanda Russell for image research
Dusty Miller for publicity
**Charlotte Rose, Andreina Brezzo and the team
at Simon & Schuster** UK for sales and distribution